MW00806675

A HISTORY OF
Davis County

A HISTORY OF

Davis County

Glen M. Leonard

1999
Utah State Historical Society
Davis County Commission

ISBN 0-913738-43-3
Library of Congress Catalog Card Number 98-61323
Map by Automated Geographic Reference Center—State of Utah
Printed in the United States of America

Utah State Historical Society
300 Rio Grande
Salt Lake City, Utah 84101-1182

Dedicated to
Burnham J. and Allene Green Leonard,
Gerald R. Purdy,
and the residents of Davis County,
past and present

Contents

Acknowledgments

Commissioner Gerald R. Purdy first approached me early in 1992 about writing a history of Davis County. His dream was for a history that was both informative and interesting to read. The book was to be part of the Centennial History Project administered by the Division of State History. The mandate of the Utah State Legislature was that each of the twenty-nine volumes in the series should take a broad, comprehensive approach. Each should span the full period from settlement to the present. Appropriate background information on the natural setting and early peoples was encouraged. The book was to include economic, political, religious, educational, and cultural history. Just how the story was to be told was left to individual authors. Commissioner Purdy's encouragement, and the memories of his enthusiasm for the project, kept me moving forward after his untimely death.

Davis County has had a most fascinating history. The Daughters of Utah Pioneers captured the first snapshots of that history with their dedicated efforts to write and publish the story of the first settlers and their times. Historians in every county community have followed with town histories. Many of those volumes bring the story forward into the twentieth century. Individual biographies and institutional histories offer additional insights into the county's past. All of these efforts provided the groundwork upon which this synthesis is based. The authors and compilers of these valuable studies are listed in the footnotes and bibliography. Their contributions are greatly appreciated.

Thanks also go to many residents of Davis County who have shared information and insights along the way. Only a few of them can be named, but each one of them made a valuable contribution to my understanding of the past. Janice P. Dawson and Leslie T. Foy were especially generous in sharing research materials from their files. Janice willingly went looking for other information that I needed, as did Laura Stratton, Harris Adams, Elaine Kammeyer, Clayton Holt, and others.

The current Davis County commissioners—Dannie R. McConkie, Carol R. Page, and Gayle A. Stevenson—have lent consistent support and encouragement to this project. County officers and courthouse employees shared insights into the operations of government. Allan Kent Powell and Craig Fuller provided encouragement, shared leads to useful information, and patiently waited for the completion of this labor of love.

My parents first awakened in me the notion that a sense of community exists in Davis County. Their families, extending back two and three generations, were residents of the county and lived through many of the years described in this history. As I learned about these early tillers of the soil, railroad builders, herdsmen, entrepreneurs, women and men of faith, teachers, parents, and civic leaders, I came to know this special county on a personal level. It seemed as though everyone in the county knew everyone else in those days before the rapid explosion of growth that now has made that common sharing of experience impossible. Yet, even now, I find threads of commonality existing here. It was in part because of a fascination with how Davis County has defined itself and its various communities within other communities that I agreed to accept Commissioner Purdy's challenge.

If this history is not what he expected, or what other readers want to know about Davis County, at least it is a beginning. Other retellings of the story will follow. I encourage those with an interest in sharing their perspectives to do so. My attempt to make sense of a fascinating history was accomplished in great part because my wife, Karen, allowed me to pursue this dream. I thank her for her sustaining love and encouragement, and acknowledge with appreciation her willingness to share in the adventure of discovery.

General Introduction

When Utah was granted statehood on 4 January 1896, twenty-seven counties comprised the nation's new forty-fifth state. Subsequently two counties, Duchesne in 1914 and Daggett in 1917, were created. These twenty-nine counties have been the stage on which much of the history of Utah has been played.

Recognizing the importance of Utah's counties, the Utah State Legislature established in 1991 a Centennial History Project to write and publish county histories as part of Utah's statehood centennial commemoration. The Division of State History was given the assignment to administer the project. The county commissioners, or their designees, were responsible for selecting the author or authors for their individual histories, and funds were provided by the state legislature to cover most research and writing costs as well as to provide each public school and library with a copy of each history. Writers worked under general guidelines provided by the Division of State History and in cooperation with county history committees. The counties also established a Utah Centennial County History Council to help develop policies for distribution of state-appropriated funds and plans for publication.

Each volume in the series reflects the scholarship and interpretation of the individual author. The general guidelines provided by the Utah State Legislature included coverage of five broad themes encompassing the economic, religious, educational, social, and political history of the county. Authors were encouraged to cover a vast period of time stretching from geologic and prehistoric times to the present. Since Utah's statehood centennial celebration falls just four years before the arrival of the twenty-first century, authors were encouraged to give particular attention to the history of their respective counties during the twentieth century.

Still, each history is at best a brief synopsis of what has transpired within the political boundaries of each county. No history can do justice to every theme or event or individual that is part of an area's past. Readers are asked to consider these volumes as an introduction to the history of the county, for it is expected that other researchers and writers will extend beyond the limits of time, space, and detail imposed on this volume to add to the wealth of knowledge about the county and its people. In understanding the history of our counties, we come to understand better the history of our state, our nation, our world, and ourselves.

In addition to the authors, local history committee members, and county commissioners, who deserve praise for their outstanding efforts and important contributions, special recognition is given to Joseph Francis, chairman of the Morgan County Historical Society, for his role in conceiving the idea of the centennial county history project and for his energetic efforts in working with the Utah State Legislature and State of Utah officials to make the project a reality. Mr. Francis is proof that one person does make a difference.

ALLAN KENT POWELL
CRAIG FULLER
GENERAL EDITORS

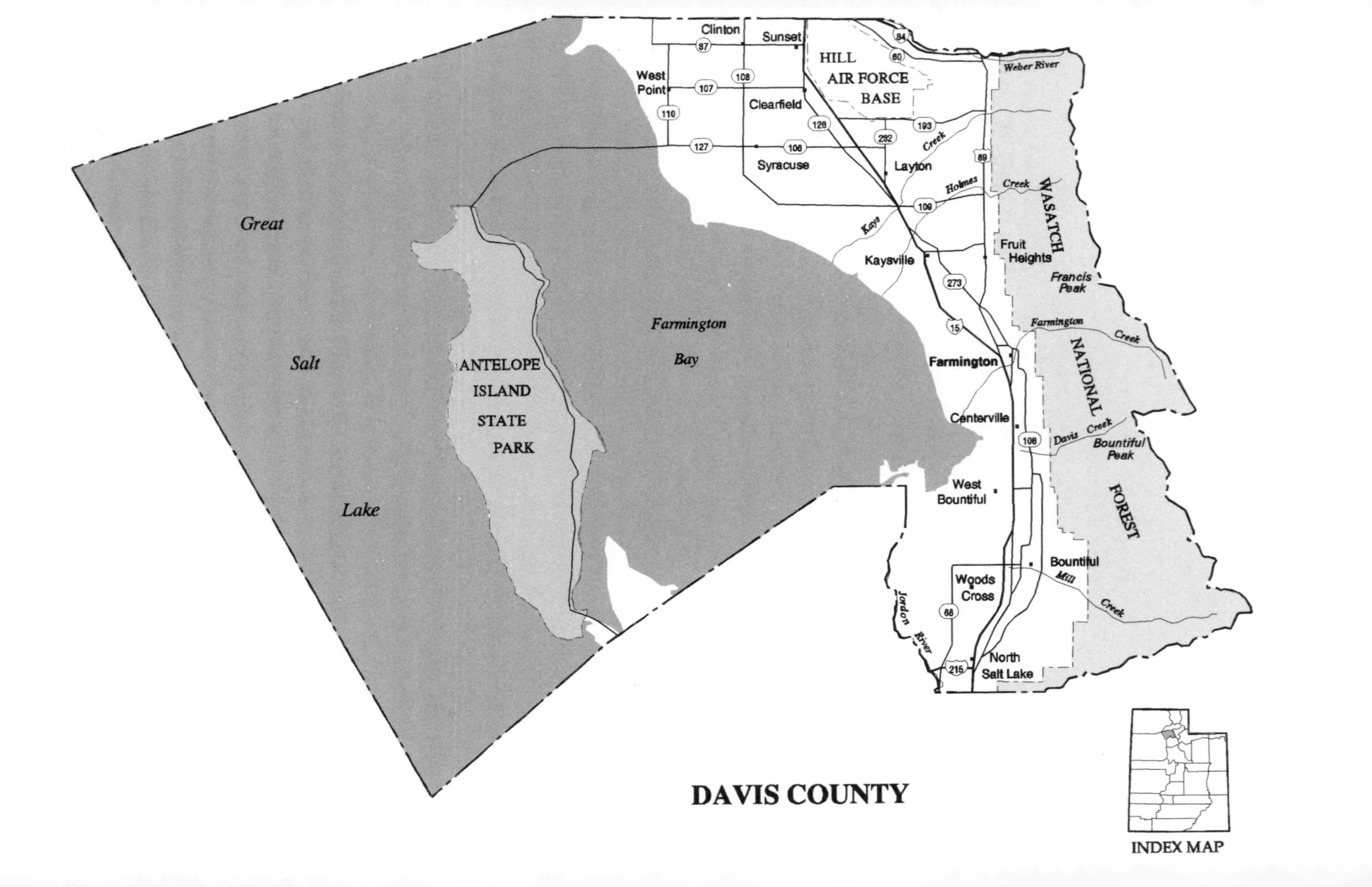

DAVIS COUNTY

CHAPTER 1

THE LAND IN BETWEEN

Passing Through

The lure of the West drew thousands of Americans toward the Pacific in the late 1840s. Expansion beyond the United States boundary at the Missouri River satisfied personal desires for prosperity and fulfilled political yearnings for conquering a continent. The spirit of Manifest Destiny blossomed earliest in the Mexican province of Texas, where a revolution led first to independence and then American statehood in 1845. On the Pacific Coast, migrating pioneers did not wait for the 1846 treaty with Great Britain before heading into the Willamette Valley at the mouth of the Columbia River. Oregon fever soon spilled over into coastal California, and American farmers and entrepreneurs saw opportunity awaiting. Then the gold rush of 1849 created an explosion in the westward movement. Overall, the 1840s redefined American boundaries and eventually added seventeen territories and states, among them Utah.

Most of the people heading west avoided the Great Basin. Oregon pioneers, starting from Independence, Missouri, hugged the

Platte River as they crossed the Great Plains, then glided through the Rockies at South Pass and headed northwest through the Snake and Columbia river basins to Oregon City. The California Trail diverged at Fort Hall in present-day Idaho and followed the Humboldt River toward Fort Sutter. It was an attempt to find alternate routes that brought California immigrants through what would a few years later become Utah's Davis County.

A wagon party of thirty-four California-bound settlers led by John Bidwell and John Bartleson stayed north of the Great Salt Lake in 1841 as they drove the first wagons through what would become Utah. Other migrating westerners deviated from the established route only after promoter Lansford W. Hastings proposed a permanent shortcut. Hastings and John C. Frémont wanted to encourage California settlement to further their political ambitions. In 1845 Hastings published an *Emigrants' Guide to Oregon and California.* The following spring he marked out a route around the southern edge of the Great Salt Lake. Five emigrant parties that year followed the new shortcut. Leading these groups were Edwin Bryant, George Harlan and Samuel C. Young, James Mather, Heinrich Lienhard, and Jacob Donner and James F. Reed. All but the last of the 1846 emigrant groups passing through Utah pushed down Weber Canyon and along the rocky foothills and fertile lowlands of Davis County to the south end of the Great Salt Lake. The difficulty of getting wagons through the Devils Gate narrows of Weber Canyon prompted the Donner-Reed party to blaze a new trail. Brigham Young's party of Mormons followed that shortcut through Emigration Canyon in 1847.[1]

With their hearts set on a home in California, the westering migrants of 1846 had only a casual interest in the Utah landscape. Several of them recorded their observations in diaries. On a sweltering 29 July, Edwin Bryant, whose party traveled on mules, rode southward from a campsite at the mouth of Weber Canyon. The party followed a route along the low hills lying close against the mountains. They traveled eighteen miles and struck camp "on a small spring branch" near what would later be the site of Farmington. Bryant descibed the sunset that evening as splendid. "The surface of the lake," he wrote, "appeared like a sheet of fire, varying in tint from crimson to a pale scarlet." This Kentucky newspaper editor was equally impressed by the sunrise the

The California emigrants of 1846 described Davis County much like this view looking from the foothills toward Antelope Island, but without the thin line of lowland farm sites barely visible in this 1916 photograph. (Utah State Historical Society)

following morning. Shaded by the Wasatch Mountains behind him, he watched as the morning light lit the distant Oquirrhs and Antelope Island in the Great Salt Lake and then swept eastward toward the creek-side campsite. As the emigrants continued their foothill route southward, they negotiated a number of ravines and mounds of rocky debris washed down from the mountains by ancient floods.[2]

A week later, the German emigrant Heinrich Lienhard halted his wagon party on Kays Creek for the night. Arising on 7 August, the loosely organized group pushed the full thirty-two miles to the Jordan River. Riding along the bottomlands near Farmington Bay, Lienhard noted "luxuriantly growing bulrushes." He described the scene and offered his personal reaction:

> The land extends from the mountains down to the lake in a splendid inclined plane broken only by the fresh water running down

from ever-flowing springs above. The soil is a rich, deep black sand composition [loam] doubtless capable of producing good crops. The clear, sky-blue surface of the lake, the warm sunny air, the nearby high mountains, with the beautiful country at their foot, through which we on a fine road were passing, made on my spirits an extraordinarily charming impression. The whole day long I felt like singing and whistling; had there been a single family of white men to be found living here, I believe that I would have remained. Oh, how unfortunate that this beautiful country was uninhabited!"[3]

Lienhard lacked knowledge that trapper Miles Goodyear and his Indian wife were gardening at the time on the lower Weber River. Had Lienhard's party arrived a year later, he would have found Latter-day Saint immigrants pasturing their livestock at several points between the Weber and Jordan rivers. Like Leinhard, the herders recognized the fertility of the land. Unlike the California emigrant, they stayed as farmers to establish Davis County's first settlements at Bountiful, Farmington, and Kaysville.

Others besides the California immigrants saw and recognized the potential of the land between the mountains and the lake from the mouth of the Weber to the outlet of the Jordan. Trappers collected and traded beaver pelts in the area, government explorers examined routes and collected information on the lake and the land, and Native Americans drew sustenance from the animals and plants of the region.

Deciphering the Lake and the Land

The fertile lowlands lying east of the Great Salt Lake formed gradually over many hundreds of years. An ancient Lake Bonneville, filled with water from rivers feeding into the eastern Great Basin about 70,000 years ago, moved soil from the mountainsides and canyons into the later valley. After the lake receded, some 20,000 years ago, vegetative matter that accumulated further enriched the loam. Natural sculpting continued as the streams flowing out of short, steep canyons created alluvial fans and deltas of soil, sand, gravel, and debris. The impact of Lake Bonneville covered the evidence of two earlier lakes in the same region.[4]

Lake Bonneville marked the mountainside with three major terraces, seen in this 1908 photo looking toward Farmington Canyon from the Lagoon softball field. (Utah State Historical Society)

Evidence of the lake can be seen as terraces on the mountainside and benchlands along the foothills of the mountains. Lake Bonneville created its highest major beachhead nearly 1,000 feet above the valley floor, at an elevation of 5,150 feet above sea level. The lake actually rose even higher before finding an outlet to the sea via the Snake River plain at Red Rock Pass in northern Cache Valley. As it dropped rapidly below the Bonneville level, the lake stabilized first at the Provo level, at an elevation of 4,800 feet, and formed a prominent bench. The Weber River delta, which extends into northern Davis County, was formed and merged with the Provo level at this time. The lake moved gradually downward in numerous small steps to the less-visible Stansbury level, at around 4,450 feet, and the Gilbert level, around 80 feet above the present lake level of about 4,200 feet. As evaporation continued, the ancient sea receded to form both Utah Lake and its landlocked remnant, the Great Salt Lake.[5]

Howard Stansbury first linked the evidence with the cause while mapping the Great Salt Lake in 1849–50. Forty years later, Grove Karl Gilbert's U.S. Geological Survey report named the most visible terraces and popularized knowledge of the ancient shorelines. Gilbert also named Lake Bonneville after Captain Benjamin L. E. Bonneville, an adventurer who knew nothing of the ancient lake but who had tried in 1837 to put his name on the Great Salt Lake, which he had never visited. Long after its waters receded, Lake Bonneville's physical impact influenced later human inhabitants of the area. The lake's deposits provided the foundation for rich soils and its deltas still furnish sand and gravel for construction. Davis County's earliest towns were established on the gently sloping and fertile Stansbury level, at an elevation of around 4,300 feet, a safe distance above the salty inland sea. Twentieth-century suburban expansion has crept upward toward the Provo shoreline, and, in some locations, even higher.[6]

Even though Davis County's earliest peoples—both ancient and historic Native Americans—knew of the Great Salt Lake, knowledge of its existence reached the outside world through Spanish, British, and American explorers. In 1776 two Franciscan priests from Santa Fe who were seeking a route to California visited Utah Lake. Indians there told the missionary explorers, Francisco Atanasio Domínguez and Silvestre Veléz de Escalante, of a large salty lake to the north. The friars and their mapmaker called it Lake Timpanogos after the Ute band who told them about it, and subsequent maps continued that designation for some time.[7]

The mountain men contributed a new name for Lake Timpanogos through their word-of-mouth communications. Known to some of them as the Grand Lake, to others as the Great Lake, it was first publicized in a Missouri newspaper by William H. Ashley in November 1826.[8] The first white man known to have visited the lake was James Bridger, one of Ashley's fur trappers. In 1824 he followed the Bear River south from Cache Valley to settle a question about the existence and nature of the legendary body. Discovering the lake's saltiness, he concluded that the Bear River dumped into an arm of the Pacific Ocean. His brief encounter with the lake likely did not take him south into Davis County.[9]

Trapper James Clyman and three associates paddled bull boats

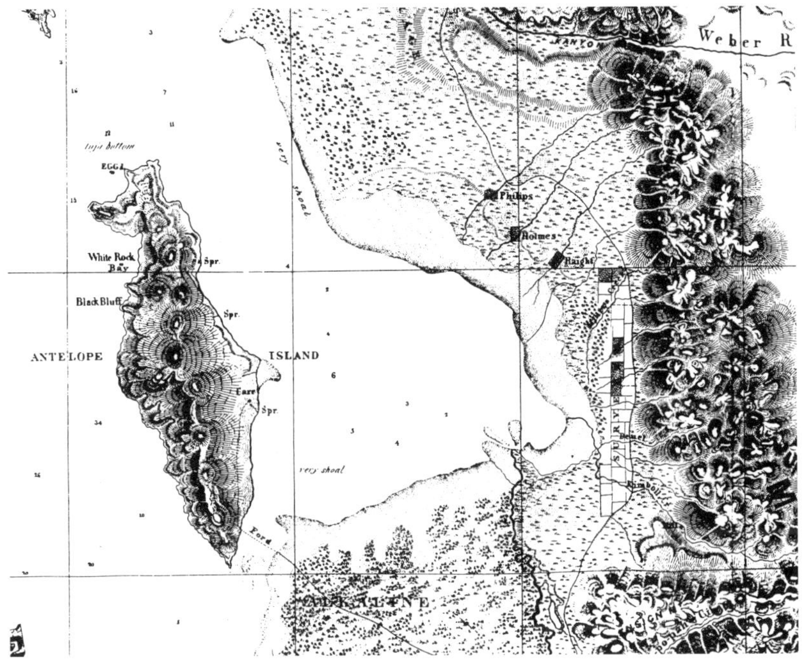

Howard Stansbury's 1850 map of the Great Salt Lake identified surveyed lands and the beginnings of settlement in Davis County.

around the lake two years later, correcting Bridger's oceanic assumption and discovering that the lake had no outlet. They passed along the east shore from south to north during the heat of summer. Another mountain man, Daniel Potts, hearing of their trip, wrote home to Philadelphia. His description contrasted the wild sagebrush and short grass on the barren western edge of the lake with the fertile lands along the eastern rim. This letter is the earliest known use of the name Great Salt Lake.[10]

Information gleaned casually by trappers did not satisfy the need for more precise descriptions of the lake and its environment. This need was met through a series of explorations sponsored by government agencies. Captain B. L. E. Bonneville's reports and maps included information gathered by a trapping expedition headed by his chief scout, Joseph R. Walker. Washington Irving published Bonneville's journal in 1837. A map in the volume included islands in the lake for the first time. With the captain's encouragement,

Irving named the lake after Bonneville, a reference that did not survive.[11]

A more accurate survey was accomplished by John C. Frémont. He visited the lake in 1843 and again in 1845, during his second and third western expeditions. During his September 1843 visit, Frémont explored the northeastern corner of the lake in an inflatable boat made of rubberized canvas. With Kit Carson and three other companions, Frémont scanned the lake with a spy glass from a peak on an island that was named in his honor by Howard Stansbury in 1850. Frémont determined the lake's elevation at 4,200 feet above sea level. During his October 1845 visit to the south shore of the Great Salt Lake, he hunted on the lake's largest island and named it Antelope Island after the game harvested there.[12] His descriptions of the lake and surrounding regions were published by Congress. Copies of the reports found their way to Nauvoo, Illinois, where Mormon leader Brigham Young and his associates studied them prior to the initial westward migration of members of the Church of Jesus Christ of Latter-day Saints in 1846–47.

When Captain Howard Stansbury arrived in 1849 to conduct a thorough examination of the lake, the first Latter-day Saint settlers were living along its eastern shore. Stansbury's party took lake depth soundings, accurately mapped the islands and shorelines, and studied the flora and fauna of the surrounding area. His 1850 map of the lake is the first to place in context the early Mormon settlements and land surveys of Davis County. It contains more detail than the sketch map made by T. H. Jefferson that traced the route of Heinrich Lienhard's immigrant party of 1846 (published in New York in 1849). Both maps reflect the influence of Frémont.[13]

In early April, Stansbury's party left Salt Lake City, explored Antelope Island and triangulated the highest peak, and then moved on to Bear River Bay and an examination of other islands. While Stansbury's main group continued their survey of the western and northern shores of the lake, Lt. John W. Gunnison returned to the city and headed up a crew assigned to the lake's southern and eastern edges.[14] Gunnison's party traveled through Davis County on 2 and 3 May. The group spent the first night in tents at Sessions Settlement, where a heavy east wind blew all night. After gathering specimens of wildflowers, the men traveled northward past the Porter home in what became Centerville and stopped at the farm of Samuel O. Holmes in Kaysville. While there, they took readings for the map that Gunnison and Charles Preuss would draw for Stansbury's report. Gunnison's reference points included five distant landmarks on Antelope Island, Castle Point on Fremont Island, and the chimney on Hector Haight's homestead two miles southeast of the Holmes cabin. Continuing along a road described by Gunnison as "heavy sand at various places," the party traveled up a gentle slope to a bridge across the Weber River west of Ogden.[15]

Stansbury's work described the Great Salt Lake in detail. He gave the islands of the lake the names they still bear and created a reliable map of the lake and its immediate environs. Later surveys by Clarence King in 1860–70 and by Thomas C. Adams in 1934–35 refined Stansbury's data but did little to challenge his conclusions. The 1850 Stansbury report remains an important landmark in historical geography.[16]

The Lay of the Land

The reports of the government explorers, together with later investigations, defined the geological and natural features of Davis County. The writeups described the plant and animal life and the natural resources available to those who lived on the narrow strip of fertile land along the east shore of the Great Salt Lake. Because of the way ancient lakes washed against the mountains, no other side of the present lake enjoys an inhabitable border quite like that in Davis County. The other shores, in fact, remain inhospitable.

The Wasatch mountain range along Davis County's eastern border was formed nearly 100 million years ago during the Cretaceous period of geologic time. The uplifting of ancient sediments at that time brought to the surface sedimentary and igneous rocks that had been formed more than 2 billion years earlier, including some in Farmington Canyon that at 2.6 billion years of age are the oldest visible in the state. The Wasatch Range took its current form during a period of renewed faulting and uplifting during the Tertiary period, 60–40 million years ago. Shallow oceans had covered the area for millions of years. The weight of sediment deposited on the ocean's floor helped to encourage the sinking of the region westward that is now known as the Great Basin. The resulting Wasatch Fault line extends along the mountains' western edge from Collinston, in Box Elder County, south to Nephi. It is still an active earthquake zone.[17]

The native wildlife and vegetation found in Davis County in prehistoric times included some species that have been eliminated over time and others that are still extant. The musk ox, mammoth, camel, and ancient horse disappeared into the sand pits of North Salt Lake before modern man appeared.[18] Buffalo had retreated from the Great Salt Lake Valley not long before the Mormons arrived. Davis County's first settlers found coyotes, bear, elk, moose, and a few mountain lions and bobcats, along with other animals, birds, fish, snakes, and insects familiar to residents today.[19]

Vegetation common in the valley in the 1840s varied according to the nature of the soil and the availability of water. Sagebrush and scrub oak survived on the bench lands, cottonwood trees grew along the seasonal streams in nearby gullies, and pasture grasses filled the moist lowlands. The wild plants commonly found in natural habitats along Utah's Wasatch Front also are found in Davis County.[20]

Weather patterns during the first half-century of white settlement followed cycles not unlike those tracked in meticulous detail since the 1890s. An unofficial record for the quarter-century beginning with the winter of 1866–67 noted seasonal snowfall ranging from four feet nine inches to six feet six inches. Rainfall averaged between sixteen and twenty inches annually. Old-timers believed that snowfall had been heavier before 1866 and rainfall lighter.[21]

Much of the water useful to settlers along Davis County's narrow strip of irrigable land originates in the rivers and streams that emerge from the mountains on the east. The Weber River was eventually tapped to supplement the scarce supply of water furnished by the streams of the short canyons along the Wasatch Front. Until then, the snowmelt which ran steadily from around early April until late August provided water for gardens, livestock, and farm crops. Nineteenth-century settlers lifted culinary water out of wells dug ten to thirty feet deep near their homes.

Early Peoples

For centuries before white men arrived to note their presence, Native Americans lived in Davis County, drawing from the natural environment to survive. They may have occupied the region as early as 12,000 years ago, in nomadic cultures called the Paleo-Indian and (later) the Archaic centered around the hunting of mammoths, camels, bison, and then smaller animals and the collection of wild plant foods. About 1,500 years ago the prehistoric peoples of Utah became farmers when they domesticated crops, including corn, beans, and squash.

These horticulturists have been called the Fremont culture, which inhabited much of the Great Basin area and has been divided by many modern researchers into five subgroups. Those in the northern portion of the Great Basin lived in shallow, earth-covered dwellings in settled villages near marshlands, where they supplemented their diet with waterfowl and other animals and plants of the area. They hunted bison with the bow and arrow, made baskets, plain and painted pottery, shell pendants, bone disc beads, and moccasins. The Fremont culture was replaced throughout the Great Basin region around A.D. 1300 when Numic-speaking groups from the southwestern Great Basin moved in. These were the ancestors of modern Southern Paiute, Ute, Goshute, and Shoshone Indians, all of whom spoke Numic languages.[22]

Archaeologists have paid little specific attention to the prehistoric peoples of Davis County and have focused their studies in areas less impacted by modern development. Though largely forgotten by today's residents, the ancient peoples who camped and hunted in Davis County left evidence of their presence. Pictographs painted on rocks in local canyons offer a fragile reminder of the Fremont people. Campsites, burial places, grinding tools, and projectile points have been identified in dozens of locations in Davis County.[23]

The culturally related Ute and Shoshone peoples established separate territories that overlapped in the Great Salt Lake Valley. This area was shared by the groups but not aggressively claimed or defended—a fact that greatly benefited the Mormons when they later arrived in the valley. Escalante reported the presence of the Utes

The Weber Utes hunted and farmed the lands of Davis County during historic times. This late-nineteenth-century photo was taken at an unidentified Utah location. (Utah State Historical Society)

south of this area in 1776, and the mountain men of the 1820s moved and lived among both groups. Bonneville's map of the Great Salt Lake area accurately placed Shoshone Indians (including the Goshute branch of the Western Shoshone) north and west of the lake and "Eutaw" Indians east and south of the lake. Davis County was home to Indians from both groups. Intermarriage created a group known to anthropologists as the Cumumba or Weber Utes. The nomadic lifestyle of Numic peoples centered around a hunting and gathering cycle that took them into the valleys for the winters and into the mountains during the summer months. They hunted large and small game—including buffalo, antelope, and jackrabbits—gathered insects, berries, nuts, and seeds, and fashioned clothing and shelters from furs, skins, bark, and textiles.[24]

For the first two decades or so, the Latter-day Saint settlers and the Weber Utes interacted as neighbors. The natives sometimes approached settlers for food, and occasionally an Indian would kill a sheep or steal property or crops. Generally, however, the new and old residents lived in relative isolation from one another. After the 1860s, resident Native Americans were seen less frequently in Davis County, as Native Americans generally had been displaced from the areas of white settlement. Burials continued as late as 1861, and an active winter camp existed near the Weber River well into the 1870s.[25]

In the mid-1980s, Indian graves near the mouth of Farmington Canyon that had been disturbed over the years were properly rededicated by Ute representatives. The event, co-sponsored by members of the Ute Tribe and local Boy Scouts, brought full-circle the process of remembering the heritage of a people who had occupied the land for many years prior to the arrival of its current residents. B. Grant Johnson, an Arizona-born Latter-day Saint who spent his adult life living near an abandoned Native American agricultural site along the Kaysville-Farmington border, once remarked to the author, "The Indians lived on this land before I came, and they'll probably live here long after I'm gone." The increasing diversity of Davis County's population in the late twentieth century may yet bring to pass his comment of the 1950s. At any rate, the transitory nature of cultures over time is a sobering thought for any temporary occupant of Davis County's verdant land.

ENDNOTES

1. S. George Ellsworth, *Utah's Heritage* (Salt Lake City: Peregrine Smith, 1972), 117, 123–27.

2. J. Roderic Korns and Dale L. Morgan, eds., *West from Fort Bridger: The Pioneering of Immigrant Trails across Utah, 1846–1850,* revised and updated by Will Bagley and Harold Schindler (Logan: Utah State University Press, 1994), 79.

3. Ibid., 144.

4. Don R. Murphy, "Lake Bonneville," in Deon C. Greer et al., *Atlas of Utah* (Provo: Weber State College/Brigham Young University Press, 1981), 44.

5. Ibid., 44–45; Frederick J. Pack, *Lake Bonneville,* Bulletin of the University of Utah, vol. 30, no. 4 (Salt Lake City: University of Utah, 1939), 26–33, 46.

6. David E. Miller, *Great Salt Lake, Past and Present,* 2nd ed., revised (Salt Lake City: Miller, 1977), 44; Dale L. Morgan, *The Great Salt Lake* (New York: Bobbs–Merrill, 1947), 99–100, 105–7; Murphy, "Lake Bonneville," in Greer et al., *Atlas of Utah,* 44–45.

7. Morgan, *Great Salt Lake,* 50, 60–64.

8. Ibid., 78–79, 82.

9. Miller, *Great Salt Lake,* 32–34.

10. Morgan, *Great Salt Lake,* 80–82.

11. Miller, *Great Salt Lake,* 34–35.

12. Ibid., 35–36.

13. Korns and Morgan, *West from Fort Bridger,* 192 and map; Brigham D. Madsen, ed., *Exploring the Great Salt Lake: The Stansbury Expedition of 1849–50* (Salt Lake City: University of Utah Press, 1989), map.

14. Madsen, *Exploring the Great Salt Lake,* 316, 319, 326, 361.

15. Ibid., 388–89, 392–94.

16. Miller, *Great Salt Lake,* 36–37.

17. Greer et al., *Atlas of Utah,* 17, 19, 22–27; Thomas G. Alexander, *Utah, the Right Place: The Official Centennial History* (Salt Lake City: Gibbs Smith, Publisher, 1995), 10–13.

18. Pack, *Lake Bonneville,* 103–10.

19. Lee D. Bell, *South Weber: The Autobiography of One Utah Community* (South Weber, Utah: Bell, 1990), 25–27.

20. Ibid., 27.

21. *Davis County Clipper,* 9 March, 26 October 1893, 11 January 1894.

22. David B. Madsen, "Utah's Prehistory," in Greer et al., *Atlas of Utah,* 74–76; L.S. Cressman, *Prehistory of the Far West: Homes of Vanished Peoples* (Salt Lake City: University of Utah Press, 1977), 98–100, 143–45, 152–56.

23. Various town histories mention the archaeological evidence. See, for example, Bell, *South Weber,* 33–35; George Q. Knowlton, *A Brief History of Farmington, Utah* (Farmington: Janetta K. Robinson, 1965), 13. Burials are noted in "Journal History of The Church of Jesus Christ of Latter–day Saints," 4 May 1861, Church Archives, The Church of Jesus Christ of Latter–day Saints, Salt Lake City; and Bell, *South Weber,* 33–36.

24. Kathryn L. MacKay, "Indian Cultures, c. 1840," in Greer et al., *Atlas of Utah,* 77; Alexander, *Utah, the Right Place,* 41–45.

25. *Deseret News,* April 18, 1860; Glen M. Leonard, "A History of Farmington, Utah, to 1890" (M.A. thesis, University of Utah, 1966), 9–11; Bell, *South Weber,* 33–35.

Chapter 2

Establishing Communities

It is well known that the Mormons, members of the Church of Jesus Christ of Latter-day Saints, came to Utah to find a refuge from the troubles that had plagued them in the Midwest. Those who first established permanent white settlements in the area that became Davis County arrived with that motive. But the immediate impetus for pushing north from Great Salt Lake City was the need to keep livestock from destroying the first crops planted in the Salt Lake Valley. During the winter of 1847–48, herdsmen grazed several hundred cattle on the lush grasses of southern Davis County. They brought their families into the area as soon as they gained church permission to do so the following spring. Between 1848 and 1850, settlers clustered along sixteen canyon streams, planted crops, and established farms. They came as families and friends, and their immediate need was to establish subsistence agriculture. Not until it became necessary to organize to manage the spiritual and practical aspects of their lives were new communities born.

The First Wave of Settlers, 1847–1850

Most of Utah's founding families came from towns along the upper Mississippi River. Over a period of just a few months in 1846, more than 10,000 Latter-day Saints left their homes in Nauvoo, Illinois, and the surrounding countryside and headed west to establish a new place of religious refuge. Church members established temporary towns and farms across Iowa and along the middle Missouri River. At those places, they prepared themselves for the arduous trek along the North Platte River to the Great Salt Lake Valley. Life's cycles went on, with births and deaths, courtships and marriages. Some settlers remained in their Iowa waystations as long as six to ten years. Church leader Brigham Young, however, headed out in April 1847 with a select group of about 150 to pioneer the way for those who would follow that year and later. Immediately upon arrival, these pioneers explored the Salt Lake Valley. Nearly 1,500 Mormons left the Missouri River in mid-June. They arrived during the last week of September. Young himself and designated explorers inspected the valley to locate winter camps and determine exactly where the arriving immigrants should establish permanent homes.

One of the exploring parties, led by Jesse C. Little, traveled north around the point of the mountain near the hot springs on 9 August 1847 and headed along the lowlands lying east of the Great Salt Lake. After visiting Miles Goodyear at his home on the Weber River, the horsemen continued on to the Bear River, then made a circuit of Cache Valley before returning to the main camp through what became Davis County. The men spoke favorably of the northern region's rich soil and plentiful water for farming, but for the first winter Brigham Young restricted settlers to Salt Lake City and directed the construction of a protective fort of sun-dried adobe brick. In a formal epistle on 9 September, he directed that the several thousand head of cattle arriving with the first year's migration be pastured in the southern and western parts of the Salt Lake Valley or other contiguous valleys to the south, west, and north. Before Young and other leaders left for Iowa to organize the 1848 migration, they appointed a twelve-member high council as a temporary civil and religious government. To this council fell the responsibility, among other things, of managing the use of local natural resources, including the grasslands, timberlands, and water.[1]

The Salt Lake high council, acting under its president, John Smith, authorized several of its own members to winter cattle on the grasslands between the hot springs and the Weber River. These councilors were Daniel Spencer, Ira Eldredge, Thomas Grover, and Shadrach Roundy. They had crossed the plains together, and by the time they arrived in the valley, on 24–25 September, the men had become well acquainted. Spencer had served as captain of their immigrant company, the First Hundred (four other hundreds arrived the same week), with Eldredge and Perrigrine Sessions as captains of two divisions. Roundy gave up the herding assignment when he joined Brigham Young's company heading back to the Midwest in mid-August. The other herdsmen recruited helpers. As directed in writing by Brigham Young, they made private arrangements with immigrants and charged according to the number of cattle taken to the common pasture. In keeping with Young's policy, the men left their wives and younger children in the main camp in Great Salt Lake City in log or adobe homes built inside the protective stockade. They planted winter wheat in designated Salt Lake farm plots and frequently visited their families during the winter months.[2]

Sessions, a thirty-four-year-old farmer from Maine, scouted out the land immediately beyond the hot springs on horseback on 27 September. He selected a grazing site about five miles north of the springs. With the help of Samuel Brown, John Perry, and Hector C. Haight, Sessions moved 300 head of cattle into the area. The men set up camp along what became known as Barton Creek (near 300 North and 200 West in present-day Bountiful). Brown left soon afterward to pursue other interests, and Haight and three colleagues established a herding ground farther north. This left Sessions at the camp, with at least one family member[3] and the fifty-year-old Perry, an English immigrant. The herders kept warm during a relatively mild winter by creating a sod-roofed dugout in the creek bank as an annex to their wagon. Local histories mention that Wallace Noble spent the winter in the area as well, farther west, near some springs.[4]

When Hector C. Haight left the Sessions camp, he moved north eight miles and set up camp near where North Cottonwood Creek emerges from Farmington Canyon. His partners included a brother, Isaac C. Haight, and two other men, probably fellow high council members Daniel Spencer and Ira Eldredge. After a few months, the men moved the cattle entrusted to them three miles to the northwest, within a mile of the marshy shores of the Great Salt Lake. There, beside a stream they called Herd Creek but that would later bear Haight's name, they built a dugout for the winter under a tall bluff.[5]

These herding grounds easily satisfied the livestock grazing needs. The herdsmen saw also a potential for farming, and that meant establishing homes and families in the area. In the spring of 1848 the herdsmen of Davis County moved their families to the two herding grounds. Two other herders and their families arrived early in that same year with more cattle. When a special Latter-day Saint church conference in the fall of 1848 created an option for living permanently in the area, other families quickly joined them to create the nucleus of what became two, and soon four, new communities.[6]

Because they grew out of herding camps, the towns of Davis County did not begin like many Utah settlements outside the Salt Lake Valley—that is, with a carefully organized immigrant company, its members handpicked for the skills they could offer the community they had been sent to create. Davis County's proximity to Salt Lake City made its settlement a natural extension of the initial gathering place. However, the settlers of Bountiful, Centerville, Farmington, and Kaysville did not arrive in an entirely haphazard fashion either. No doubt, as the immigrants considered settlement options, they weighed economic factors, including employment opportunities, the availability of land, and the presence of flowing mountain streams—useful for both irrigating crops and for culinary water. However, when choosing among a number of good places, many people chose Davis County because friends or relatives already lived there. Personal ties were a strong influence that was evident with the arrival of the first herd captains and their friends—and later their families—and continued with subsequent settlers. Friendship and kinship ties influenced the establishment of each of the first four communities. By the time a federal census taker made a belated visit to Davis County in January 1851 to gather data for the 1850 census, there were 1,134 residents living in 215 dwelling places—an average of more than five to a house. Population density ranged from a high of 5.3 per house in Bountiful to 4.7 in Farmington, with the other two communities near the average.[7]

The growth of Sessions's camp into the community that later became known as Bountiful began in the spring of 1848 when Sessions and John Perry gave up herding for farming. They moved their wives, Lucina Sessions and Ann Perry, and their children out of the Salt Lake fort and built simple log homes for them near their winter campsite on Barton Creek. The families of Jezreel Shoemaker and Orville S. Cox joined them in the new venture. These first families broke the sod and planted basic crops for summer eating and winter storage: wheat, corn, beans, peas, pumpkins, squash, and melons. Another two dozen families arrived that fall and took up farms watered by North Canyon Creek, Mill Creek, and Stone Creek. The January 1851 census reported 444 settlers living in eighty-four houses in Sessions Settlement, the largest of the four new Mormon villages.[8]

The settlement of Centerville began as an undifferentiated northern extension of Bountiful. Among the earliest to arrive were two members of the Salt Lake high council intent on herding cattle: Thomas Grover and Shadrach Roundy, who had been part of the Brigham Young pioneer company. They made a winter camp along what later became Deuel Creek near the future townsite. They were soon joined by three well-to-do families who had made the trek to Utah together in 1847 with the Charles C. Rich company and wintered at the Salt Lake fort. They settled together as neighbors along Deuel Creek. Aaron B. Cherry was a prosperous Illinois farmer who brought three wagons and a band of horses to Utah. He purchased Grover's log home and claim to make a home for his wife, Margaret, and their nine children. New Yorkers Osmyn M. and William H. Deuel and their families also came with ample goods. Osmyn, his wife, Mary, and an older single brother, Amos Deuel, established a farm and blacksmith shop on Deuel Creek. William and Eliza, with their three children, became farmers nearby.

Over the course of the summer and into fall another twenty-five to thirty families arrived, among them the families whose surnames became attached to the creeks north of the first cluster of settlers' homes—Samuel and Fanny Parrish, John P. and Eliza Barnard, and

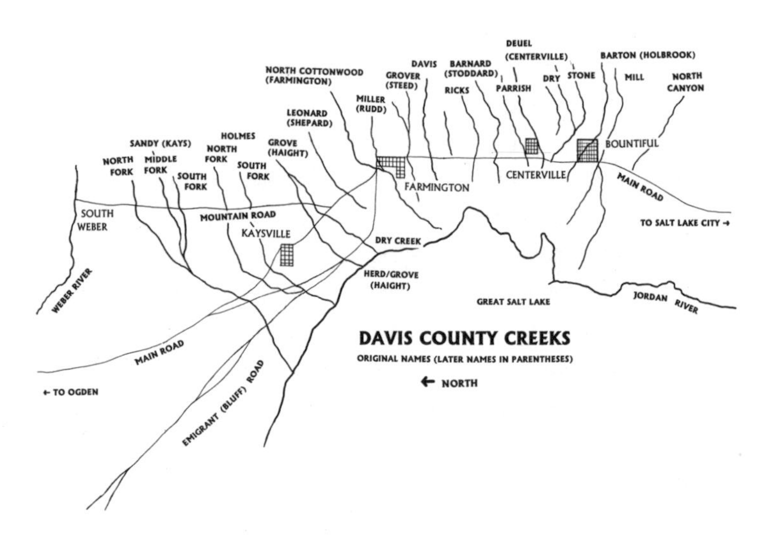

The first Mormon settlers established farms along the streams flowing out of the canyons. It was twenty years before dry farming techniques made the county's northern Sandridge area productive as farm land. (Glen M. Leonard)

Joel and Eleana Ricks. Family farming and its related activities rather than herding for others dominated the efforts of these settlers. Growth continued during 1849, and by early 1851 the population included 217 residents in forty-three houses.[9]

The pattern of seeking out land for irrigated agriculture was repeated farther north. For a few years after their arrival, Hector Haight and his sons, Horton and William, continued wintering cattle herds in the lakeshore meadows while establishing a farm that was bisected by Herd Creek. In addition, Hector and Julia Haight soon established an inn for travelers at what they called Blooming Grove. The autumn migration of 1848 brought five families to the region of the first Haight camp on North Cottonwood Creek and other nearby mountain streams in an area that later became Farmington. William O. and Rhoda H. Smith and their daughter and son-in-law, Emily and Allen Burke, claimed land watered by North Cottonwood Creek (later Big Creek or Farmington Creek). Daniel A. and Charlotte Miller camped on a tributary they called Miller's Creek (now Rudd Creek). Thomas Grover moved his family, including wives Caroline, Hannah, and Laduska, from their first campsite on Deuel Creek to homestead on Grover Creek (later Steed Creek). Daniel C. Davis, a Mormon Battalion veteran, settled on a stream that still carries his name. These and another twenty families who arrived the next year became known as the North Cottonwood settlement. By January 1851 they numbered 287 individuals in sixty-one houses.[10]

North of Haight Creek, settlers began to establish homes in what would become Kaysville and Layton. New Englander Samuel O. Holmes set up a herd cabin in 1848 between two forks of a stream that soon bore his surname. His wife, Eliza, and four children accompanied him.[11] Other settlers did not arrive in the area until the spring of 1850, when three English families—Edward and Hannah Phillips, John H. and Susannah Green, and William and Mary Kay—built log homes for their families close together along lower Sandy Creek (later Kays Creek) in west Kaysville. A few other families arrived that year before the census was taken. Most of them settled along the emigrant road that extended northwesterly from Haight's farm past Holmes's home and on to Kay's Creek. A few found homesites in three locations against the mountain, where the two forks of Holmes Creek and Haight Creek intersected the 1846 emigrants' route from Weber Canyon. Settlers avoided the region between Kay's Creek and the Weber River because of the sandy ridge that bordered the river and the lack of water for irrigating the lowlands. The 151 Kaysville/Layton area settlers identified by the first census occupied thirty houses. The poll included an additional fourteen people, guests at Hector Haight's inn at Blooming Grove.[12] The Haight properties were annexed to Farmington in 1859, so the family is claimed as the founding family for both Kaysville and Farmington.

Growing into Towns, 1850–1869

As might be expected for a people initially dependent on raising their own food, the first settlers located along the streams that were essential for irrigating their farmlands. The farmsteads clustered along sixteen principal watercourses, in a pattern that did not by itself suggest a way to define towns. By the end of 1848, however, an irregular geographical settlement pattern was emerging, as three separate although as yet undefined communities—Sessions Settlement (later Bountiful), Cherry Creek Settlement (later Centerville), and North

Cottonwood Settlement (later Farmington). It took a few more years before boundaries were in place recognizing these settlements. By the time Kays Ward (Kaysville) congealed as more than a scattering of settlers' homesteads, the four communities had acquired names that replaced the names attached to the streams as addresses.

Ecclesiastical jurisdictions first defined the clusterings of friends and relatives on Davis County's well-watered farms. The boundaries were externally imposed on the scattered farmers, but they were not without some logic. In February 1849 a committee headed by Presiding Bishop Newel K. Whitney organized Latter-day Saint settlers in the Salt Lake Valley into geographically defined districts known as tithing wards, each under the leadership of a bishop. The committee first created nineteen wards in Salt Lake City and suggested that each ward fence itself in to keep livestock out of gardens. Two days later, on 16 February, eight wards were created outside the city limits, including two units in what later became Davis County. The people of what were already being called the Sessions and Cherry Creek settlements were placed in the North Mill Creek Canyon Ward, soon shortened to North Canyon Ward. Settlers north of the Cherry Creek Settlement to the Weber River became members of the North Cottonwood Ward.[13]

Within a month, these same boundaries and names were used to create precincts and appoint magistrates under the Provisional State of Deseret, but this convergence of ecclesiastical and precinct lines ended with the creation of counties and new precinct lines in 1850.[14] Nor did the initial ward boundaries endure for long. In January 1851 the two Davis County wards became four. A new Kays Ward included everyone north of Haight Creek, while a new Centerville Ward served the Cherry Creek Settlement—people living along Deuel, Parrish, and Stoddard Creeks.[15]

The creation of inclusive geographical boundaries for religious and civic purposes gave residents a new way to identify the places where they lived. The names of the creeks, unless they had been adopted for other uses, gave way, and eventually a common town name emerged. Most confusing was the transition in Sessions Settlement. Residents adjusted to the name North Canyon for their ward and precinct but retained Sessions for the community name. A post office was then established and named in honor of Bishop John

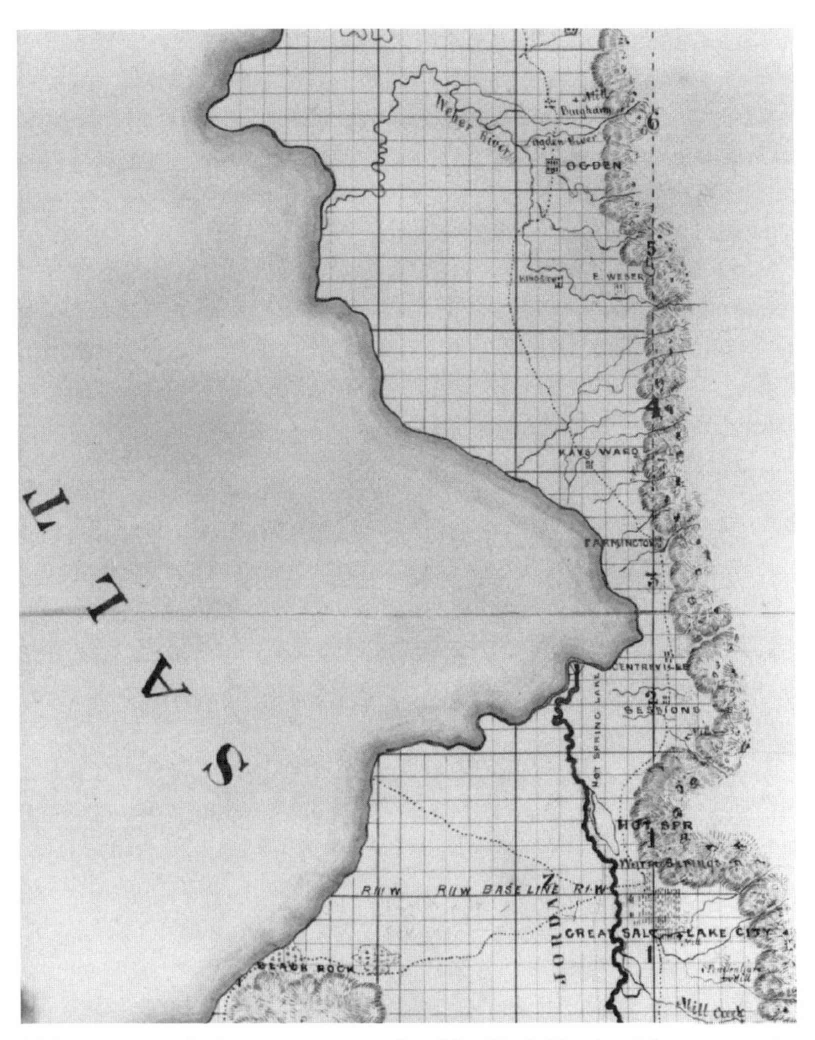

This segment of a larger map completed by Utah Territorial surveyors in 1856 identifies early settlements and mill sites in Davis County and the route of the territorial road. (Intellectual Reserve, Inc., courtesy LDS Church Archives)

Stoker. Some residents began using Stoker as a town name, while others used either the name Sessions or North Canyon. The bishop solved the problem by suggesting a Book of Mormon name, Bountiful. It was adopted in February 1855 as the city name. Eventually it was used to identify the ward, precinct, and post office.[16]

In the county's other towns, the transition was more straightforward, but it also took several years for old terms to fade and new ones to prevail. The people in the Deuel Creek area had adopted the name Cherry Creek Settlement as an early name for their community, which included residents along Deuel, Parrish, and Barnard Creeks. Cherry Creek Settlement persisted as a name for the place to at least 1855 even though an LDS ward organized in the spring of 1852 took the name Centreville.[17] The townsite surveyed in 1853 also was named Centreville. It was a decade before the ward name prevailed (with a later modification in spelling) to identify both the congregation and the community.[18]

Farther north, because the name of North Cottonwood Creek identified both the settlement and the ward, it easily prevailed over the post office designation, Miller's Creek. But after the territorial legislature picked North Cottonwood as the county seat in 1852 and called it Farmington, that became the precinct name. After a few years, the settlement and ward names followed suit. In contrast, the residents of Kays Ward experienced only one change, a gradual secularizing of the name to Kaysville.[19]

Walled Cities. Even though the creation of Latter-day Saint wards and secular precincts established geographical boundaries for the religious congregations and their corresponding secular communities, these administrative units did not require the establishment of cities or towns. The first settlers remained in a scattered rural settlement pattern—living in small log or adobe homes on farms convenient to the canyon streams. This random pattern did not please the master planners of Utah's settlement, however.[20] Latter-day Saints had always held as their ideal a cooperative urban life. As first described in 1831, the ideal City of Zion included homesites on lots large enough for a garden and outbuildings, with farms located beyond the city limits. Ideally, the farmers would live in the city along with tradesmen and commute to their farms as needed.

Salt Lake City set the pattern for other Utah towns in August 1847 when surveyors laid out a plat patterned after the four-square City of Zion. In Davis County, however, surveys of farmland in 1849 did not address the question of city plats. The first townsites resulted

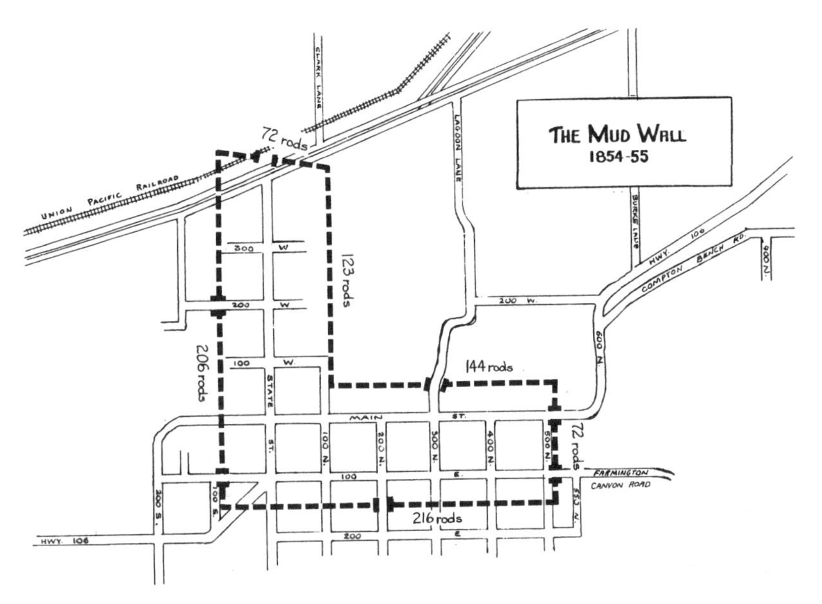

Surveyors platted other town walls in Davis County as compact squares or oblongs, but the natural terrain suggested this elongated pattern for Farmington's mud wall. (Glen M. Leonard)

from efforts to create walled cities as protection against potential Indian attacks.

Farmington led out in establishing a town survey during the fall of 1853. Surveyors defined a town plat on a foothill bench wide enough from east to west for only two or three full city blocks. At the time of the survey, seven homes had been built within the inhabitable part of the town's boundaries. Even though the streets were laid out at right angles after the City of Zion pattern, the geographical restrictions of the chosen site destined the village to a string-town growth pattern north and south of the surveyed plat.[21] The other cities in Davis County found more expansive sites on larger, gently sloping alluvial fans that permitted almost square plats. These were established in 1854 in Bountiful, Centerville, and Kaysville under the direction of Jesse Fox as part of the effort to create walled forts around a town site.[22]

The perceived threat from Indians actually stemmed from a situation outside Davis County. Because of clashes with Indians in central and southern Utah beginning in 1853, territorial leaders first encouraged residents of the threatened communities to build forts for protection. In late July, Governor Brigham Young and Lt. Gen. Daniel H. Wells of the Mormon militia, the Nauvoo Legion, expanded the request to all thirteen of Utah's military districts. They ordered district commandants to pick sites for forts, corrals for stock, and stack yards for grain. The officers were to cooperate with local leaders in overseeing construction of the community projects.[23]

In Davis County, the order brought immediate results only in Farmington and Centerville. By September 1853, in conjunction with its town plat survey, Farmington residents designated boundaries for a fort under the direction of Major Thomas S. Smith. Initially Smith proposed a rock wall to enclose a small defensive fort; but, after some opposed the site and the material, a town meeting altered the plan. In March the citizens were told to begin building a six-foot-high adobe wall on a four-foot-wide base. A visit from the First Presidency of the LDS church soon afterward ratified the decision.

The Farmington wall defined an L-shaped site with seven entrances, although no gates were ever hung. It enclosed 112 lots, the equivalent of fourteen full blocks and six half blocks. Able-bodied men were expected to build or hire others to build a seven-rod section of the wall for each lot located within the fort. By December, about two-thirds of the wall had been completed, with the remaining sections under construction. Joseph L. Robinson described it as "a dirt wall partly around us, to protect us, but whether it does or no, verily there is one thing more that is certain, it doth show."[24] Centerville residents began enclosing a nine-block parcel during the summer of 1853. They halted after erecting only part of the north wall, a mud barrier with a rock filler, narrowing from bottom to top.[25]

Residents of Bountiful and Kaysville were among those in Utah who apparently ignored the order to move into walled cities, because they saw no serious threat from local Native Americans. Brigham Young acknowledged the difficulty of convincing procrastinating Utah citizens of the need. He told the territorial legislature in December 1853 that some people were obeying the order by tearing down their scattered houses to build and occupy walled cities, while others remained unconvinced.[26]

The governor personally intervened in Bountiful. He visited the community in April 1854, picked a site, and set the dimensions of a city wall. Young's visit prompted the survey of a fifty-four-block city plat, about half the size of his recommendation. Each lot owner was assessed twenty-five dollars as a property tax to fund construction of a wall entirely enclosing the city. By the end of November 1854 the mud wall stood six feet tall, half the intended full height, but encircled the new city.[27]

In 1854 Young may have visited Centerville as well. Whatever the reason, residents resumed construction on the fort they had begun the previous year. Before snowfall that year, they completed the north and east walls of to a height of eight feet on a base six feet thick.[28] In north Centerville, Judson Stoddard began a private eight-foot wall, eighteen inches thick, around his property north of Chase Lane.[29]

Kaysville residents started a fort wall in June 1854, after Jesse Fox laid out the city plat. Initially, the survey enclosed nine blocks, but it was later extended westward to contain fourteen full blocks and six half blocks. The adobe fort was to be six feet high, tapering from five feet at the base to three at the top. When construction began, each landowner was assigned a section. The men dug a moat-like ditch outside the wall and shoveled the clay soil into lumber forms to create a mud wall. Only portions of the south and west sides were completed, however.[30]

The original Kaysville Fort District included people living some distance north of the fort in what later became Layton. Even though these distant settlers contributed funds and labor to the Kaysville project, several families built a smaller "Little Fort" (also known as Parish Fort). It was located about halfway up Kays Creek, near the present intersection of Fort Lane with Gordon Lane.[31]

Despite the progress made during 1854, Brigham Young remained unhappy with the efforts of Utah communities to build forts. In his message to the territorial legislature in December, Young reiterated his call to complete the forts. It was a time of peace, he acknowledged, but a time of need would yet come.[32] Lawmakers acted on his request with a bill replacing military oversight with civilian. As required by the new law, the Davis County Court created five fort districts and appointed three-member committees in each district to select and survey sites. A twelve-dollar poll tax, plus a tax on each lot and general property taxes were to pay for the work. The committees included men of influence within their communities to signal the importance of the task. Even with this encouragement, however, the lack of serious danger from attack and the press of daily work hindered progress.[33]

At the county seat in Farmington, the new committee included Thomas S. Smith (the militia officer who launched the project), Bishop Gideon Brownell, and Thomas E. Ricks. The citizens gathered at a public meeting and voted to accept this committee as construction managers. Those at the meeting also supported the committee's nominee for superintendent of construction and an assessor-collector. Despite an effort to complete the wall by seeding time in the spring, little more was accomplished before the onset of a grasshopper invasion and the press of summer's work. The following spring, the county court ordered the fort committee to "proceed with the Forting as fast as circumstances will admit." The wall enclosed the city, but it was at varying heights and without protective gates. Within a decade, ward teachers reported that residents were beginning to level out the dirt humps on their city lots and homes were being built outside the enclosure.[34]

Results were similar in neighboring towns. Bountiful's civilian fort committee included Bishop John Stoker, Joseph Holbrook of the county court, and Chester Loveland. The committee encouraged each able man to donate one ten-hour day to the work of topping off the wall; but little more was completed, gates were never installed, and without ongoing maintenance the mud wall around Bountiful soon began to deteriorate.[35] (Only the walls in Bountiful and Farmington entirely enclosed the towns, but they also remained without gates). Centerville's west wall remained unfinished, and Kaysville did little beyond its initial partial effort on two sides of the fort.[36]

For Davis County, it was an unnecessary effort to enclose the town plats as protection against local Indians. The no-man's land between the Utes to the south and the Shoshones to the north was, by longstanding native understanding, off-limits to warfare in order that those tribes and the western Paiutes could enjoy unhampered access to salt on the lake's shores. Though not needed for defense, the mud-wall projects and accompanying city surveys did prompt local farmers to respond to the Mormon colonizing plan for living in centralized settlements.

The response to the call to "fort up" varied from town to town. In 1855 about thirty houses, or fewer than one-quarter of Bountiful's families, were within the city fort. Brigham Young had given residents the option of remaining in their cabins on their farms but had promised greater prosperity if they built substantial homes in the city. Bishop Stoker encouraged further consolidation by abandoning his own log home outside the wall and moving into town. His example led some other settlers to purchase town lots at prices ranging from five to twenty-five dollars.[37] By 1860, the earlier southern Indian wars had ended, a federal army was camped in Utah, and citizens felt at liberty to remain on their farms surrounding the city plat. While specific information could not be found, it is likely that Centerville's partial enclosure did not encourage much centralization of the forty families already established on farmsteads by early 1855. Those living outside the walled townsite referred to it as "The Fort"—implying a place of protection rather than a friendly New England-style town.[38]

Farmington area citizens responded initially to church directives with notable obedience. A reporter from Salt Lake City wrote that the number of homes within city boundaries increased ninefold within one year. The wall appeared to be shaping the town into a prototypical Mormon farm-village pattern. However, the consolidation movement in Farmington continued for only a half-dozen years, a typical response throughout the county. Then, in the early 1860s, the line village formation returned, and the community stretched for more than six miles along the county road between Centerville and Kaysville.[39]

In Kaysville, an estimated eighteen families had located within the unfinished fort by 1862. The plat included another forty-two unoccupied lots. Layton's Little Fort east of Kays Creek protected the area's six families.[40]

Meanwhile, just beyond Davis County's north boundary, near the mouth of Weber Canyon, another community was being defined in the same ways that Bountiful, Centerville, Farmington, and Kaysville came to be. South Weber had its beginnings as part of a larger community existing on both sides of the Weber River in what was initially all part of Weber County. Boundary changes brought the community into Davis County in 1855. The small farming district near the canyon mouth began to attract settlers in 1851–52, when families claimed land on both sides of the river. Those nearest the canyon mouth were known collectively under the name of East Weber or Easton. Byram L. Bybee, who lived on the north side of the river, served as presiding officer of the Latter-day Saints and as the civil officer of Easton. Residents who identified themselves as part of this community extended as far south along the Mountain Road as Hobbs Hollow. When the East Weber Precinct was formed in 1854, Bybee became justice of the peace, and David B. Bybee became president of the Easton District, an ecclesiastical division under the supervision of Lorin Farr, president of the Weber LDS Stake and mayor of Ogden.[41]

A second cluster of Mormon farm families, about 2.5 miles downstream from the mouth of the canyon, established farms on the south side of the river and called their neighborhood South Weber. Politically they affiliated with the Easton Precinct, and ecclesiastically they belonged to the Easton District. In October 1853 Brigham Young visited the South Weber area to encourage creation of a fort. At the same time, he invited the Saints there to select a bishop and organize a ward, which they did. Thomas Kingston became the bishop. The fort was called by some Kingston Fort, after the bishop, but others referred to it as the South Weber Fort, after the ward name. Since a bishop had a higher ecclesiastical authority than did a district president, and since a ward was a larger and more complex organization that a district, Kingston assumed jurisdiction over Latter-day Saints on both sides of the river.[42]

Apparently Bishop Kingston and his ecclesiastical superior, Weber Stake President Lorin Farr, had serious disagreements over some unrecorded matter (possibly boundaries). Early in 1855 the territorial legislature redefined the county line. The new boundary followed the center channel of the Weber River as far as a point in the river aligned with the west side of Kingston Fort and then headed due west to the lake. Lawmakers created a new precinct in Davis County to serve this annexed section and called it the Weber Precinct. It extended from the mountains on the east to the lake on the west. The limits of the South Weber Ward were adjusted to extend over this same region. Thomas Kingston remained bishop in South Weber, which joined the other wards in Davis County in the Salt Lake Stake. The East Weber settlement on the north side of the river was given the name Uintah to define what was left of the original community. People living on the south side of the Weber River affiliated with the new precinct and ward in Davis County. The names East Weber and Easton fell out of use.[43]

Like other forts in Davis County, construction of the Kingston fort moved slowly after its beginning in 1853. Territorial surveyor Henry G. Sherwood plotted the site for the fort near the intersection of modern Fort Lane and 6650 South Street. At the same time, Sherwood established boundaries for the surrounding farmland. Residents had little incentive to build the wall, even though a relatively large number of Weber Utes lived along the river. The Indians accepted the Mormon settlers as neighbors and gave the new residents no reason for concern.

The project languished until John Firth arrived from Salt Lake City in 1855. He spearheaded the effort, carrying rock from the river bottom and encouraging others to help. The walls, like many others in the territory, were made mostly of mud, and the stones served as a reinforcement. Within a year, the fort was finished. Log homes lined both sides of the long, narrow enclosure, with a street down the middle and entrances at both ends. The extent to which South Weber residents abandoned farm homes for the fort is not known; but, like their neighbors to the south, the families along the Weber River did not let the call to fort up permanently discourage them from living on their farms.[44]

Even though only a portion of Davis County's old settlers responded to the invitation to move into the new platted cities, the surveying of towns forever changed the face of the land. The forts became community centers and, over time, the towns served their urban function. They became the commercial, cultural, and religious centers for city residents and for the families on surrounding farms who ignored the ideal City of Zion plan that called for a daily commute from a house in the city to the outlying fields.

Meetinghouses. The most prominent symbol identifying Davis County's new cities as spiritual gathering places was the meeting-

Completed in March 1863 under Brigham Young's general supervision, Bountiful's tabernacle measured 44 feet wide and 86 feet long, topped with a five-spired tower. (*The City Bountiful*)

house. In a pattern reminiscent of New England towns, each of the county's five Mormon communities built a meetinghouse in a central location in the town—three of them on the various Main Streets. All of them were completed as soon as local resources permitted, in the early 1860s. They replaced earlier but temporary log or adobe cabins that typically doubled as both meetinghouse and school. Thus, within twenty years of the founding of the settlements, the simple adobe or stone religious structures became the most important buildings in town. With its imposing tower, the Bountiful LDS Tabernacle dominated its urban landscape. Elsewhere in Davis County, simpler versions without steeples nevertheless reinforced the importance of religion in community life through their strategic locations and their uses.

Before an LDS ward could afford a full-fledged meetinghouse, members congregated in schools or large homes. The adobe school built in Bountiful in 1851—a building twenty by thirty feet—served its multiple purposes for thirty years. Neighborhood Sunday Schools continued to meet there even after the local congregation completed an impressive tabernacle on Main Street in 1863. Local craftsmen built it of sun-dried adobe bricks, a material favored by Brigham Young because of the scarcity of timber and his belief that the adobe would solidify in time and become as hard as rock. Workmen overlaid the three-foot-thick walls with a coat of stucco to give the building a finished look. Architect Augustus Farnham, a New Englander who moved from Salt Lake to Farmington while the building was under construction, used the Greek Revival style, with double front doors and a three-stage tower. Construction took six years, utilizing local materials for the rock foundation, adobe walls, and red pine framework. Additions and remodelings have kept it in continuous use longer than any other Latter-day Saint meetinghouse. Farmington's stone meetinghouse, completed in 1864, and a frame church built in 1868 at Pine Valley, Utah, rank just behind Bountiful's tabernacle in longevity of service.[45]

Centerville's Latter-day Saints built a combined school and church meetinghouse on the north bank of Deuel Creek in 1855 and a new adobe meetinghouse in 1862 that later served as a school. The town's last nineteenth-century meetinghouse, built in 1879 of stone, has remained in use since its completion. Like many other buildings from the period, it has undergone later additions and remodelings to maintain its usefulness. It also shares with the other pioneer Mormon meetinghouses of Davis County a simple design patterned after a typical New England meetinghouse, suitable for a religion that emphasizes the congregation rather than ritual. These congregational-style halls feature a single large assembly room, often with a small two-story vestry behind.[46]

Farmington's residents met for two seasons in a small log school and then for a short time in an adobe structure. In 1855 church meetings were moved to the upper room of the county courthouse, built in part with church money. Construction of a rock meetinghouse, designed by local builder Reuben Broadbent, began in 1861. A scarcity of funds soon delayed the project, with the walls only partially laid up. Then, early in 1863, county officials denied any further use of the courthouse for religious purposes, so the ward moved its

Local members hauled rocks, sand, and gravel from nearby foothills to build the Farmington Rock Church. They hewed framing timbers in Farmington Canyon and donated wood to buy additional lumber and lime in Weber and Salt Lake counties. (Utah State Historical Society)

meetings back to the schoolhouse. The eviction helped push the forty-by-sixty-foot meetinghouse to completion, the builders using local timber and rocks. The LDS church's First Presidency and eight apostles participated in dedicatory services on a wintry day in January 1864.[47]

A *Deseret News* reporter in 1862 reported from Kaysville that that town's meetinghouse foundation was bare—strong winds had toppled the unfinished adobe walls. Church architect Truman O. Angell had designed the 4,000-square-foot building with a basement level divided into four rooms, and construction had begun in 1855. Before the disruptions caused by the Utah War two years later, the basement had been enclosed with a temporary roof and was in use for at least some church meetings and community socials. Members had met previously in two log schoolhouses built in the early 1850s, and, when construction on the meetinghouse resumed in 1858, they congregated in private homes.

In April 1863 the 900-seat hall was dedicated for religious services and the basement was adapted for other uses. In two underground rooms the bishop kept his storehouse. Foodstuffs contributed as tithing, and used to feed the poor, stayed fresh in the cool spaces. Students in the adjacent schoolroom complained of the cold, however; their room was heated imperfectly by a woodburning stove. The fourth room served as a hall for theatrical performances and socials. The stuccoed adobe meetinghouse served the congregation well for a half century.[48]

At South Weber, the first Latter-day Saint meetings convened in the home of presiding elder Byrum Bybee. After the survey for the fort in 1853, residents built a cottonwood log building along the north line of Kingston Fort and used it for both a school and church. Six years later, a more commodious one-room adobe school and church was opened with a public dinner organized by the bishop. The Farmington Brass Band and accompanying singers provided entertainment. The adobe hall served the community as an educational, religious, and social center until it was replaced in 1884 by separate school and church buildings.[49]

Financial backing for building meetinghouses came through the generosity of prosperous local farmers and merchants and from the sacrifices of other members of the congregation. Those involved in all of these locally funded projects struggled to marshal the resources to hire skilled carpenters and brick- or stonemasons for the task. A growing population made necessary these halls when modest schoolrooms and private homes no longer allowed the Latter-day Saints of various areas to meet comfortably.

Growth and Mobility

Between the 1850 and 1860 censuses, Davis County's population more than doubled, rising from 1,134 to 2,904. Growth continued at a slower but steady pace over the next decade, reaching a total of 4,459 residents in 1870, at what is considered to be the end of the pioneer period. The growth during these two decades reflected the impact of natural increase through births, natural losses by deaths, and the movement of people into and out of the county. Many of the early settlers who stayed until death presently have fourth and fifth generation descendants as residents of the county. These modern

Davis County residents keep the names of their ancestors alive locally; but many of the pioneer generation did not stay on the homesteads they established—they left for opportunities elsewhere, some close by and others in farflung Mormon colonies. In many cases, their names and contributions have been forgotten.

People left for reasons as diverse as personal gain and selfless duty. California appealed to a few of Davis County's first settlers, particularly those discouraged by frontier conditions in Utah or attracted by perceived greater opportunities on the coast. Samuel Brown, one of the herdsmen with Perrigrine Sessions, was one of the first of those dissatisfied with prospects in Utah. In December 1847 the twenty-three-year-old bachelor joined a group headed for California; but the Salt Lake City marshal enforced high council policy to prevent the departure of "disaffected spirits" and refused to let them leave. Brown sought other adventures and eventually settled in Fillmore. While scouting a new cattle route to California in 1858, he and a partner were shot dead, scalped, and stripped of their outer clothes by Indians.[50]

Some Latter-day Saints headed for California with Brigham Young's blessing. Thomas Grover went west in 1849 to raise money for cattle needed to support the new colonies in Utah. While in California he visited the gold fields and collected tithing from Mormon Battalion soldiers who had reaped a bonanza when one of them participated in the discovery. He was Henry Bigler, and he later settled in Farmington for a time.

A major cause of Davis County's out-migration was the continuing expansion of Mormon settlement efforts within and beyond the corridor extending from Weber County to Utah County. Latter-day Saints founded more than fifty communities along the Wasatch Front before 1857. In that same decade, they launched almost as many villages in more distant regions, from southern California to central Idaho, from Carson Valley, Nevada, to Moab on the Colorado River in southeastern Utah.

The effort continued into the 1860s, with settlement missions claiming the land in less naturally attractive sites. Some of those who left Davis County relocated out of personal preference, others in response to invitations, or "calls," from church leaders. The sons of the founding families and the single hired hands were among those who left, after they married, to seek available farmland outside what was Utah's smallest county. Married men, established and with families, left to answer settlement missions assigned by the church or to seek more fertile land. Some of the men with plural wives kept a farm in Davis County while establishing a new home elsewhere. County residents went wherever church leaders or economic opportunities called them.

Early settlers who left Davis County could be found in all the nearby Utah counties and as part of almost every major settlement mission organized by Mormon leaders in the 1850s and 1860s. Charles C. Rich participated in the short-lived effort at San Bernardino, California, then, as a settlement leader, moved his families to Bear Lake country. The Thomas E. Ricks family spent a few years at Las Vegas and then joined relatives in Cache Valley. Farmington lost its first bishop, Joseph L. Robinson, and a half-dozen other settlers to the Iron Mission in Parowan. Other residents left Davis County with the Cotton Mission to Utah's Dixie in the southwestern corner of the future state. Thomas S. Smith and Henry W. Miller headed settlement missions to the Muddy (Moapa) Valley in Nevada. Anson Call followed them to establish a warehouse at a landing on the Colorado River. These are only a few of the Davis County settlers who participated in the far-flung colonizing efforts.[51]

When Brigham Young began sending missionaries to the Indians on the outskirts of Mormon country, three men from Davis County were among the number who responded to the October 1853 call to accompany Thomas D. Brown on the mission to southern Utah.[52] From 1855 to 1858, Davis County furnished nearly one-fourth of those sent by Young to establish or reinforce an outpost and Native American mission on the Salmon River in southeastern Idaho. The twenty-seven men who trekked the nearly 400 miles to establish Fort Lemhi, and the twenty-six additional missionaries who joined them the following spring, enjoyed a time of relative success. Under the direction of Thomas S. Smith of Farmington, they befriended Indians who spent the summer in the area, converted some, and shipped wagonloads of dried fish from the Salmon River to Utah in barrels made by the missionaries. Young visited the settlement in March

1857. Pleased with the progress, he sent another twenty-five reinforcements to the fort and set up a post at the mouth of the Blackfoot River as a halfway depot. Efforts to change the lifestyles of the Indians and occupation of the Indian land strained relationships, however. On 25 February 1858 a group of Bannock and Shoshone Indians attacked herdsmen and killed two of them, George McBride and James T. Miller of Farmington. The Indians wounded several others and drove off most of the livestock. Wounded in the attack were company leader Thomas S. Smith and Oliver L. Robinson of Farmington, Andrew Quigley, Fountain Welch, and H.V. Shurtliff.[53]

When word of the troubles reached Salt Lake City, Brigham Young immediately sent a mounted rescue expedition of more than 150 men. Horton D. Haight led the armed party, most of them young men in their late teens and early twenties. Horses, pack animals, and provisions were furnished through loans and donations. Haight recruited one-third of the number from his own hometown of Farmington, plus others from elsewhere in Davis County and beyond. The men enlisted on 9 March and served one month. Most of them carried both a long gun and a pistol. The expedition successfully accomplished its mission of moving the missionaries home, and the abandoned Fort Lemhi passed into history.[54]

Origins and Families. Those who helped establish Davis County and those who left to expand Mormon settlement efforts elsewhere shared common origins. Virtually all of them were affiliated with the Church of Jesus Christ of Latter-day Saints. Therefore, the place of birth listed for residents by the Davis County census for 1850 reflected the geographical origins of the church, the places of its congregating, and the locations from which converts were gathered. Overall, Davis County echoed the pattern for all of Utah Territory; its residents were predominantly American-born, with the remainder mostly of British origin. Since many of the children in families were born in the gathered Mormon communities of Ohio, Missouri, Illinois, western Iowa, and Deseret (the original name for Utah), it is more meaningful to limit the analysis of nativity to individuals eighteen and over. Bountiful's mix of American-born, British-born, and "Other" nativities (mostly Canadian) was close to the county average. Centerville and Farmington attracted comparatively fewer

As time and circumstances permitted, this 1850s log home in Centerville was enlarged with a rock addition, a pattern followed by many settlers in Davis County. (Utah State Historical Society)

British immigrants. Farmington stands out as especially American because of a high number of New Yorkers (almost half of its adults). Kaysville attracted a large English population, while the southern communities in Davis County were above average in Canadian-born residents. During the nineteenth century, the defining group in each town English immigrants in Kaysville, northeasterners in the other towns—furnished more than its share of community leaders and subtly influenced cultural patterns.

The census reveals another characteristic about Davis County's early settlers that helped define the first communities. As was true for almost all Latter-day Saint settlement efforts, Davis County's early residents headed west as families. Except for the mining boomtowns, the same pattern prevailed during the 1840s and 1850s in communities established in other western states. But to focus on families does not tell the entire story of Mormon settlement, including the pioneering of Davis County. While essentially all households in the county were occupied by families, a significant minority also shared the home with others. The survey of dwellings in early 1851 for the U.S. census logged 215 occupied houses in Davis County. Of these, 59 percent were occupied only by nuclear families—married couples or single parents with children. The remaining 41 percent included relatives (17 percent), or boarders (21 percent), or both (3 percent). The relatives were either parents who had lost their spouse or younger siblings of the heads of household. Many of the boarders were single men in their early twenties working as farmers, probably as hired hands on the family's farm. Some of the boarders may have been brothers or sisters of the wife. These temporary helpers and younger relatives left the home when they married and established a new household. In the meantime, the scarcity of housing in the early years made doubling up a necessity.[55]

Early Government

As was true elsewhere in early Utah, the first secular government for the Mormon communities of Davis County preceded the creation of a county government. It began as a partnership between civil and ecclesiastical organizations. In fact, the leading civil office in each jurisdiction within what later became Davis County was filled by the same man who held the key position in the local church organization. The candidates for both positions were nominated using the ecclesiastical pattern, from the top down. Orville L. Cox and Joseph L. Robinson, the bishops appointed in February 1849 to oversee the North Mill Canyon and North Cottonwood religious wards, were elected on 12 March 1849 as magistrates or justices of the peace for precincts defined along ward boundaries. Their election, in a meeting at the old bowery on Temple Square, was part of the creation of the Provisional State of Deseret. The names of the candidates had been selected more than a week earlier by church officials and presented to the public for "ratification of the people."[56]

The combining of secular and religious roles in Davis County subsequently was never as concentrated. In subsequent elections, the number of precinct offices was expanded and a number of local citizens served. After the precincts became a unit of county government in 1850, the candidates were nominated in public caucuses and elected by popular vote. This common American form of grassroots government allowed participation by all adult males. The men of the community not only chose those who would lead but often gathered in town meetings to consider and agree upon actions. For the first twenty years or so, an easy consensus prevailed in Davis County because of Latter-day Saint dominance of the political process, including the selection of candidates. Often, a single slate of officers, endorsed by religious leaders, stood for office. For example, just prior to the August 1861 election, Brigham Young and five other high church officials held a church meeting in Farmington, after which they convened a political caucus to oversee nomination of territorial and county officers. Nomination was a guarantee of election.[57]

Certain civic-minded men seemed to follow a political track as public servants. Precinct and district officers were drawn from the ranks of willing local residents who were not serving in important ecclesiastical positions. Davis County's delegates to the territorial legislature demonstrated their political interest through prior or subsequent service in offices such as justice of the peace, selectman, or county commissioner. During the nineteenth century, no Davis County LDS bishops served in the legislature; however, those active in political life generally followed the counsel of Mormon church leaders. They saw themselves as representing the general good, which they defined as the good of the LDS church and its members.

With the creation of civil government, parallel organizations were soon staffed and functioning in a symbiotic relationship. For the LDS church, the organization consisted of wards and their priesthood quorums; for the county, precincts and service districts. In a pattern resembling that of a New England town, the ward bishops and a group of adult male priesthood teachers served as a sort of town council and civil servants who looked after many personal day-to-day needs of community members. The Mormon wards of Davis County functioned as towns in this sense for more than forty years (twenty years in the case of Kaysville) before municipalities were incorporated. The wards operated side by side with a secular overlay of legal and service jurisdictions created after 1852 by the county. The precinct, road, school, and water districts formalized and secularized tasks that might otherwise have been overseen by the ward bishop and his helpers. Even with these districts, local LDS bishops often played the role of overseer and mediator. Thus, even though the bishops in Davis County did not serve in civil office after those first appointments in 1849, they did exert influence beyond their ecclesiastical roles, particularly in guiding local economic affairs. In effect, the bishops were acting as administrative officers (mayors) and judges of their unincorporated communities.

During Davis County's early years, the LDS church provided a continuity of leadership on the ecclesiastical side of this shared governmental arrangement. After some rapid turnover during the first few years because of relocations of some settlers to new settlements, the wards generally had bishops who served long terms and wielded significant influence in the management and development of their communities. North Canyon's Bishop John Stoker was called in 1850 and served Bountiful residents for twenty-three years, for example, and William R. Smith began a twenty-two-year calling in Centerville in 1855. That same year, John W. Hess became Farmington's bishop and began an assignment that lasted twenty-seven years. Kaysville's first two bishops served five- and six-year terms, but, beginning in 1862, Christopher Layton remained in office fifteen years. Until the creation of a Davis LDS Stake in 1877, these bishops served ostensibly under the Salt Lake Stake president and high council. But they actually received most of their direction from Brigham Young and his counselors in the First Presidency and from members of the Quorum of the Twelve Apostles of the LDS church. These general authorities held three or four conferences in the county each year; made other informal visits to look after private, public, and church business; and corresponded with local leaders.[58]

Organizing Davis County

When the General Assembly of Deseret created four counties along the Wasatch Front in January 1850, Davis was not one of them. Instead, the area between Salt Lake City and Ogden was split between the counties headquartered in those two cities. The Bountiful area from Stony (Stone) Creek south to the Hot Springs was included in Great Salt Lake County and called the North Canyon Precinct. The settlers from Stony Creek northward to Sandy (Kays) Creek found themselves in the Sandy Precinct and part of Weber County. The largely unsettled region north of Sandy Creek became part of Weber County's City Precinct. These three precincts replaced the four that had been created in 1849 along ward boundaries. However, before the year was out, the assembly created three more counties. One of them, formed on 5 October, was Davis County. The others, organized in early December, were San Pete and Little Salt Lake (later called Iron).

Precise demarcation was lacking for most of the early counties. Davis County stretched from a southern boundary at the Hot Springs to the Weber River on the north, with the west line along the Jordan River and Great Salt Lake. The Wasatch Mountains formed a natural divide on the east.[59] The territorial legislature more precisely defined the Davis-Weber county line in 1855. The disputed territory south of the middle of the main channel of the Weber River and due west from Kingston's Fort was given to Davis County.[60]

The general assembly named all of the early counties except Davis after natural features or existing Indian names.[61] Davis was the first of only two Utah counties to be named for Mormon pioneers (the other was Rich County, honoring colonizer Charles C. Rich, originally a settler in Centerville). In 1849 Daniel C. Davis had built a home near the middle of the county on what became known as Davis Creek. The following June, Davis died near Fort Kearney, Nebraska, while heading east to take care of family business and lead a party of immigrants to Utah. Davis had served in the Mormon Battalion as captain of Company E and as commander of a group of Mormon volunteers who had re-enlisted for six months of additional service in California. Perhaps because of this service, Davis was remembered by having Utah's fifth county named in his honor.[62]

County government in early Utah operated with a panel of selectmen and a chief justice who together made up the county court, with the term *court* used in its sense as a managing board. This commission form of government exercised certain executive and regulatory powers given to it by the legislature. A county probate judge handled wills and estates and some other judicial matters. The legislature created controversy by giving the probate judges original jurisdiction in civil and criminal cases that traditionally had been reserved for federal district courts in the territories. Territorial law allowed one man to serve as both the head of the county court and the probate judge, and that was the case in early Davis County.[63]

Because no chartered cities existed in Davis County for most of the nineteenth century, county officers performed both the functions traditionally reserved for counties and many of those given to cities. The county court looked after the conservation and use of natural resources, especially water and timber; the management of stray animals; the development of roads; and the creation of school and voting districts. The court levied taxes and issued business licenses for liquor vendors and others, such as slaughterhouses and tanneries, whose regulation was deemed in the public interest. It had legal responsibility to see that orphans and the insane received proper care. It could accomplish these tasks either by appointing responsible officers or by allowing the people to elect them.[64]

The first presiding officer (chief justice) in Davis County's governing commission was Joseph Holbrook of Bountiful, who was also the first county probate judge. He served for six years before resigning because of health concerns, and later served for another year. Serving with him initially were selectmen Truman Leonard of Farmington and Daniel Carter of Bountiful, appointed to staggered terms. James Leithead of Farmington served as court clerk. All of these men were farmers by occupation.

The county court convened in March 1852 to begin its business. It divided the county into electoral precincts and school and highway districts and also appointed watermasters. As needed, the court named officers to support its work, including a county clerk, a treasurer, a surveyor, and a tax assessor and collector. Perhaps because of their convenient proximity to the courthouse, Farmington residents were favored in these appointments during the settlement period.[65]

Utah's First Courthouse. Among the court's powers was the right to construct public buildings. It was not long before the citizens of Davis County were invited to consider such a proposal. In August 1853 the county electorate approved a proposal from a study committee appointed by the county to erect a courthouse, the first built for that specific purpose in Utah. After advertising for bids, officials hired Henry W. Miller and Daniel A. Miller of Farmington as con-

Utah's first county courthouse was completed in Farmington in 1855. For fifteen years, the adobe building served as a multi-purpose community center, then exclusively for governmental purposes until demolished in 1890. (Knowlton, Brief History of Farmington)

tractors. They appointed a three-man local supervisory committee to oversee work on the two-story adobe structure, which measured thirty-five by forty-five feet. Construction began in the spring of 1854 and was completed late the following year. A courtroom occupied most of the upper floor, while on the main level three offices and three jury rooms divided by a central hallway served court needs.[66] Beginning in 1863 various rooms on the main floor were assigned to the county assessor. In 1867 the court designated the southeast jury room for use as a county jail and purchased handcuffs and a ball and chains. Eventually those incarcerated were secured in an iron cage in this jail room.[67]

The county levied a one-quarter of one-percent property tax for two years to partially fund the $6,000 project. It raised additional money from subscriptions. The Farmington LDS Ward purchased $920 in shares. This unusual arrangement gave the ward partial ownership of the building and the right to use the upper floor when it was not needed for county business. The commissioners tried to raise the church investment by assessing another $280 for the building's use. When repeated efforts to collect the amount failed, the court cancelled the charge in 1863.[68]

The adobe courthouse served a variety of community needs in

Farmington. Among the regular uses were for dances, social gatherings, a district school, and band practices. For a few years, local merchants rented unused main-floor rooms. After the Farmington Ward finished its rock meetinghouse in 1864, it assigned its shares in the courthouse to the local school district, and in 1869 it sold the shares to the county for $450.[69]

Precinct Officers. While the heart of Davis County's civil government was centered in the courthouse, most of the services provided by county government took place through precinct and district organizations defined by the court but operated locally. While judicial functions were handled at the county level by the probate judge, precinct officers were charged with maintaining law and order locally. These officers consisted of a justice of the peace, a constable, a poundkeeper, and one or more fence viewers. Citizens elected these officials each August, with the justices serving two-year terms and the others subject to annual appointments.

The duties of the precinct justice and constable involved them in everything from cattle theft and fraudulent trading to mischief and fighting among boys. In many of these situations, local law enforcement officers consulted with the local bishop and ward teachers. Sometimes justices of the peace and LDS bishops disagreed over who should assume jurisdiction in a case. While secular solutions tended toward punishment, religious leaders sought to resolve offenses by extracting apologies and encouraging reconciliation. Civil courts levied fines or imposed prison sentences for serious offenses; Mormon church councils expelled members from fellowship through excommunication and sometimes even ordered the transgressor to leave town. Many issues were resolved by the bishops, leaving only a few difficult cases to the civil courts.[70]

The poundkeeper and fence viewers played an important role in preventing problems. Since local practices required crops to be fenced and allowed livestock to wander freely, these officials helped control stray animals and ensure that fences were secure. Fencing around common areas such as the community "Big Field" was a community rather than an individual effort, so the fence viewers also helped to see that those assigned to build and maintain these fences did their jobs properly.

The county court created new precinct boundaries in 1852 to replace the earlier ones organized by the Deseret General Assembly. The court established a North Canyon Precinct for the Bountiful area, a Farmington Precinct to serve Centerville and Farmington, and a North Precinct for the Kaysville-Layton area. As the population grew and communities became more clearly defined, the court adjusted the boundaries. Within three years, each unincorporated community had its own precinct to serve those within what essentially amounted to a Latter-day Saint ward. Elections for precinct officers coincided with the general elections, which were administered locally by three election judges appointed for each precinct by the county court.[71]

Community Schools

The history of schools in early Davis County followed a pattern dictated by the customs and practices brought to Utah by the first settlers and formalized through government action. The tradition focused on education in the basic or fundamental subjects for children through what were known as common schools; that is, a community school organized through the cooperative efforts of local citizens. Parents could pay private teachers to teach their children reading, writing, and arithmetic or they could participate in the tax-supported common schools. The common schools often were referred to as ward schools because of the way they were managed and shared boundaries with LDS wards.

The first schools in the Davis County settlements necessarily were private, established by teachers to fill the gap until other options were available. Such schools opened in 1848 in Bountiful and Centerville. Conditions were primitive, since the first teachers lived in tents or primitive huts and cabins. Private schools continued to be available throughout the settlement period in Davis County, even though communities quickly organized to provide school buildings and teachers. It was sometimes more convenient for a few families to support a neighborhood teacher than to send their children to a school in another part of the town.[72]

During the fall and winter of 1849–50 the residents of Bountiful and Farmington established common schools through a cooperative effort. Centerville and Kaysville followed a year or two later, and South Weber did the same in 1854. Parents still paid the teacher a per-student fee in cash, goods, or services, but the townspeople worked together to build the facility and hire a teacher, under the general oversight of the local LDS bishop.

In Bountiful, the citizens assumed an authority not yet formally granted them by the government. A construction committee appointed in a town meeting levied an in-kind tax to pay for securing logs and building a school. A second group, similarly appointed, hired a qualified teacher and set behavioral and curriculum standards. A third committee was given trusteeship of the school. The Bountiful building committee chose a site on Anson Call's farm, just inside what became the northwest corner of the city plat, at 400 North and 200 West.[73]

Farmington's first school was located near North Cottonwood Creek on the flats west of present Main Street at about 410 North, where the road in use at the time passed east of the present-day Lagoon resort racetrack. The small school in Farmington was probably typical of others of the period in size and format—a door at one end and fireplace in the other. It had simple windows on the two long sides, which were made by removing part of a log and filling the gap with a row of glass panes. The roof was finished with cane willows and sod. The floor and seats were made of split timbers. The Farmington school was built cooperatively but without exercising a taxing authority. It took three town meetings before Bishop Joseph L. Robinson gained the support he needed to establish the town's first school. Without that support he had no way to get the donated labor to build a structure that would double as a church meetinghouse on Sundays and for other public purposes. Robinson proposed "where it should stand and how we should build it." Finished just before Christmas, the hall was used for a picnic and dance, then turned over to teacher Harvey Green for a two-month, late-winter term.[74]

These local ad hoc organizational efforts imitated the practice for common schools in the eastern states. It did not take long, however, for Utah's early Mormon settlers to create school districts with a legal standing and taxing authority. The territorial legislature laid the groundwork in October 1851 by appointing a superintendent of primary schools and instructing him to organize a uniform school system. The following March, the legislature gave the county courts authority to create school districts. Each was to be governed by three trustees, who would levy and collect necessary taxes and hire and supervise the teachers.[75]

The Davis County Court immediately created nine school districts in the county and appointed local citizens to implement the legislative decree. This effort inaugurated a system that would function for more than fifty years. In 1860 Arthur Stayner of Farmington became the first county superintendent of common schools to provide executive oversight. Five years later the superintendent and board gained the use of an upper room in the courthouse, their first central office. In the meantime, the county court adjusted boundaries and created additional districts as needed, more than doubling the original number as the population grew. A typical early boundary ran from the foothills to the marshlands along an existing roadway. Later districts recognized neighborhoods. In time, two or more districts existed within the boundaries of each ecclesiastical ward. These new boundaries anticipated ward divisions and the creation of new communities that eventually became separate towns and cities. Even in the smaller districts, some students lived far enough from the school to be bussed in horse-drawn wagons. In winter months, the season when most students were free to attend school, the wagons were covered and warmed with a small stove.[76]

The local districts built their own schools, sometimes selling the earlier ones or moving them to a central location within the new boundaries. During the 1850s and 1860s, adobe was the most common building material for the district schools, but almost as many were built of logs. The sun-dried mud bricks took considerable effort to mold, dry, and lay up, but they could be made from local materials. In contrast, workmen had to haul logs from canyons, usually some distance from the building site, shape them, lay them up, and then fill the gaps with mud chinking. The typical school was a one-room structure, heated with a central stove. The buildings sometimes survived as residences or shops after they were no longer needed as schoolhouses.

The single-room school remained the standard throughout the

nineteenth century. Because teachers accepted students of varying ages and educational ability, the classes were eventually graded, so that each student could progress at her or his own level. The schools imported popular American schoolbooks for use as texts, including the *Lindley Murray Readers, Noah Webster's Spelling Book,* the *McGuffey's Readers* series, and *Smith's Elementary* and *Higher Arithmetic.* The reading books taught moral principles through stories, and students also read from the Bible.[77]

Initially, each district's committee set its own standards for teacher qualifications. Standards varied from district to district and ranged greatly. In addition, the committees could not always find fully qualified teachers. In 1853 the county court centralized the process by appointing a county board of examiners to review teacher qualifications. This helped to standardize credentials and expectations and minimize less-desired influences.[78]

Even though the district school system operated through committees established under county authority, the schools could not have succeeded without the support of LDS ward leaders. Latter-day Saints looked to their local bishop for direction in everyday affairs, including schools. As a practical matter, the district schools were, in essence, ward schools. Recognizing this fact, the county court in 1856 appointed Thomas Fisher as president of all the schools in the North Canyon Ward and gave him four assistants so that the two Bountiful districts would have common overseers.[79] At times, however, it became necessary for a bishop to intervene to make the system work. For example, in 1866, Bishop John W. Hess of Farmington called a school meeting when a contractor halted work on a new schoolhouse because he hadn't been paid. Some residents felt that the school tax was excessive. Apparently the bishop disagreed. He encouraged everyone to pay the tax and sent that message into the homes with the ward teachers. A few months later, residents in south Farmington wanted their own school. Hess agreed to support the proposal only if the proponents would allow him to dictate the terms and arrangements.[80]

This is just one example of how, in early Davis County, ecclesiastical and civil authorities cooperated to provide essential services. Through such efforts, the officers of church and state shaped and defined communities. They drew boundaries and platted cities so that farmers clustered along wandering stream banks could identify with religious congregations and secular communities. They pursued their objectives as shepherds of the flock and as sons of the American Revolution.

ENDNOTES

1. Erastus Snow, Journal, 9 August 1847, in *Utah Humanities Review* (1948), 282; Journal History of the Church of Jesus Christ of Latter-day Saints, 14, 23 August, 9 September 1847; Wilford Woodruff, Diary, 14 August 1847, LDS Church Archives.

2. Journal History, 17 August, 9, 22, 24 September, 7, 9 November 1847; Glen Leonard, "A History of Farmington," 18–22.

3. Some sources suggest Sessions was accompanied by his older children, but the oldest was Carlos, age six. Perrigrine's brother David and farmer Charles Foster lived with him in early 1851, U.S. Census, Utah Territory, 1850.

4. Annie Call Carr, ed., *East of Antelope Island: History of the First Fifty Years of Davis County* (Bountiful: Daughters of Utah Pioneers, 1961), 48; Les Foy, *The City Bountiful: Utah's Second Settlement, from Pioneers to Present* (Bountiful, Utah: Horizon Publishers, 1975), 45–47.

5. Isaac Haight, "Biographical Sketch and Diary," 47–49, 51, Utah State Historical Society. Haight mentions Spencer and Eldredge as partners in 1848–49, but does not name his two 1847–48 colleagues (ibid., 51).

6. Daniel A. Miller, Journal, LDS Church Archives.

7. Leonard, "History of Farmington," 27–31; U.S. Census, 1850.

8. Carr, *East of Antelope Island,* 49, 51; Foy, *City Bountiful,* 47–48; U.S. Census, 1850.

9. Carr, *East of Antelope Island,* 60–61; Mary Ellen Smoot and Marilyn Sheriff, *City In-Between: History of Centerville, Utah* (Centerville: Authors, 1975), 6–7, 195, 203–4, 225–26, 251–52, 255–56; U.S. Census, 1850.

10. Leonard, "History of Farmington," 23–27; U.S. Census, 1850.

11. Journal History, 21 June 1847; Henry H. Blood, "Early Settlement of Kaysville," 3.

12. Carr, *East of Antelope Island,* 103; Harvey and Harvey, *Map of Early Kaysville;* U.S. Census, 1850.

13. Journal History, 13, 14, 16, 22 February 1849. The boundary committee included Brigham Young and Heber C. Kimball of the First

Presidency; Apostles Parley P. Pratt, John Taylor, and Amasa Lyman; and clerk Thomas Bullock.

14. Journal History, 12 March 1849.

15. *Deseret News,* 8 February 1851.

16. Foy, *City Bountiful,* 65; Journal History, 27 February 1855.

17. Journal History, 14 May 1855.

18. Andrew Jenson, "Centerville Ward," [11], manuscript history, LDS Church Archives; Smoot and Sheriff, *The City In–Between,* 7.

19. Leonard, "History of Farmington," 82–85; Carr, *East of Antelope Island,* 108–9.

20. Journal History, 22 November 1854.

21. *Deseret News,* 21 December 1854.

22. Foy, *City Bountiful,* 67; Carr, *East of Antelope Island,* 106.

23. Journal History, 3 June 1853; *Deseret News,* 30 July 1853.

24. Leonard, "History of Farmington," 86–89; Journal History, 1 June 1854; Joseph L. Robinson, "Autobiography and Journal," 98–100, 103, LDS Church Archives. See also Steed, "The Wall Around Farmington," 109.

25. Carr, *East of Antelope Island,* 65.

26. Foy, *City Bountiful,* 73; Journal History, 13 December 1853, 5–6.

27. Journal History, 25 April 1854; Foy, *City Bountiful,* 67, 73–74.

28. Smoot and Sheriff, *City In–Between,* 7. Carr, *East of Antelope Island,* 65, says only the north wall was finished.

29. See Smoot and Sheriff, *City In–Between,* 1.

30. Carr, *East of Antelope Island,* 106; Claude T. Barnes, *The Grim Years; or, The Life of Emily Stewart Barnes* (1949; reprint, Kaysville: author, 1964), 24, 67; Blood, "Early Settlement of Kaysville," 17.

31. "Layton, Utah: Historical Viewpoints," 48–49; Collett, *Kaysville—Our Town,* 54.

32. Journal History, 13 December 1854, 4.

33. Territory of Utah, *Acts, Resolutions, and Memorials,* 269–70; Davis County, Court Minutes, 1:34–36, 1, 26 March 1855.

34. Farmington Ward, Historical Record, 12 March 1855, microfilm, LDS Family History Library; *Deseret News,* 21 December 1854, 7 November 1855; Davis County, Court Minutes, 1:41, 3 March 1856; Farmington Ward, Ward Teachers Minutes, 28 April 1867.

35. Foy, *City Bountiful,* 73–74.

36. Journal History, 17 February 1855; William Robb Purrington, "The History of South Davis County from 1847–1870" (Master's thesis, University of Utah, 1959), 36.

37. Foy, *City Bountiful,* 74; Carr, *East of Antelope Island,* 366; Journal History, 27 February 1855.

38. Carr, *East of Antelope Island,* 65; Journal History, 27 February 1855.

39. *Deseret News,* 21 December 1854; Leonard, "History of Farmington," 91–92.

40. Collett, *Kaysville—Our Town,* 42–43, 54.

41. Bell, *South Weber,* 46, 48–49.

42. Ibid., 52–54.

43. Ibid., 49, 53–54.

44. Ibid., 52, 54–55.

45. Foy, *City Bountiful,* 80–81, 103–6.

46. Smoot and Sheriff, *City In–Between,* 72–73, 84–85, 87.

47. Leonard, "A History of Farmington," 48–51; Margaret Steed Hess, *My Farmington: A History of Farmington, Utah, 1847–1976,* eds. Irene B. Olsen and Mable R. Ferguson (Farmington, Utah: Daughters of Utah Pioneers, 1976), 257–59.

48. *Deseret News,* 7 May 1862; Carol Ivins Collett, *Kaysville—Our Town: A History* (Kaysville, Utah: Kaysville City, 1976), 59, 74–75.

49. Lee D. Bell, *South Weber: The Autobiography of One Utah Community* (South Weber: [South Weber Town Council], 1990), 438, 208–9, 444.

50. Journal History, 21 June 1847, 37, 46; 26 December 1847; and 15, 18, 31 October 1858. Others had been stopped previously (ibid., 6–7 October 1849).

51. Those named and others are mentioned in the histories of Bountiful, Centerville, Farmington, and Kaysville, and in histories of other areas they settled, as well as in diaries, autobiographies, and newspaper reports.

52. Juanita Brooks, ed., *Diary of Thomas D. Brown: Journal of the Southern Utah Indian Mission* (Logan: Utah State University Press, 1972), 2. The men listed were Ira Hatch, Sessions's Settlement; Benjamin Knell, Kay's Settlement; and Lorenzo Roundy, Davis County.

53. Poll et al., *Utah's History,* 143, 362; W. W. Henderson, "The Salmon River Mission," *Utah Historical Quarterly* 5 (January 1932): 3–4, 10, 21; Journal History, 25 February 1858.

54. Milton D. Hammond, "Journal," 48–49, Utah State Historical Society. The rescue party are listed in "Captain Horton D. Haight's Company That Served in the Salmon River Expedition 1858," LDS Church Archives. See also Joseph L. Robinson, "Journal," 8, 12 March 1858, LDS Church Archives. One wall of Fort Lemhi remains today.

55. U.S. Census, 1850.

56. Journal History, 16 February, 4, 12 March 1849.

57. Davis County, Court Minutes, 1:69, 73, 97, 2:31; Journal History, 3 August 1861.

58. Foy, *City Bountiful,* 63, 307; Carr, *East of Antelope Island,* 66, 108–9; Leonard, "History of Farmington," 39–42.

59. *Constitution and Laws, 1848–50, of the State of Deseret* (Great Salt Lake City, 1850), 28–30; *Deseret News,* 19 October 1850.

60. For a fuller discussion of the Weber-Davis county line see Richard C. Roberts and Richard W. Sadler, *A History of Weber County* (Salt Lake City: Utah State Historical Society and Weber County Commission, 1997), 6–7.

61. The natural features are the Weber River (which carried trapper John H. Weber's name), the Great Salt Lake, Utah Lake (taken from the Ute—or Eutaw—Indian name), and the Little Salt Lake (later Iron County). Indian names were used for Tooele, Juab, and Sanpete counties.

62. Carr, *East of Antelope Island,* 22–24. It is possible to argue that Davis was the seventh county, since the LDS church First Presidency's "Third General Epistle" mentions Sanpete and Yoab (Juab) as having been created during the winter of 1849–50 (*Frontier Guardian* [Kanesville, Iowa], 12 June 1850); but this must have been in name only. The General Assembly of the State of Deseret defined boundaries for San Pete and Little Salt Lake (Iron) counties in December 1850, and the Utah territorial legislature created Juab County in 1852.

63. State of Deseret, *Laws and Ordinances,* 16 January 1851.

64. Poll et al., *Utah's History,* 163–64; Carr, *East of Antelope Island,* 360–61.

65. Purrington, "History of South Davis County," 82–84; Carr, *East of Antelope Island,* 361–62.

66. Davis County, Court Minutes, 1:12–13, 24, 27, 38; *Deseret News,* 21 December 1854.

67. Davis County, Court Minutes, 1:108, 110, 163, 2:84, 90.

68. Davis County, Court Minutes, 1:2, 22, 24, 31, 42, 48, 55, 74–75, 109–10.

69. Leonard, "History of Farmington," 94–95; Farmington Ward, Ward Teachers Minutes, 11 July 1869; Davis County, Court Minutes, 2:30, 35.

70. Leonard, "History of Farmington," 78–80.

71. Davis County, Court Minutes, 14 June 1852; Carr, *East of Antelope Island,* 360.

72. Foy, *City Bountiful*, 79–80; Smoot, *City In–Between*, 48; Carr, *East of Antelope Island*, 339–40.

73. Foy, *City Bountiful*, 79–80.

74. Joseph L. Robinson, "Journal," 73–74, LDS Church Archives; Jenson, "Farmington Ward," 5–6, citing Joseph E. Robinson to William M. Stewart, 25 March 1912.

75. See Leland H. Creer, *Founding of an Empire: The Exploration and Colonization of Utah, 1776–1856* (Salt Lake City: Bookcraft, 1947).

76. Foy, *City Bountiful*, 82–83.

77. Levi Edgar Young, *The Founding of Utah* (New York: Charles Scribner's Sons, 1924), 299; Foy, *City Bountiful*, 81.

78. Davis County, Court Minutes, 1:13, 13 March 1853.

79. Foy, *City Bountiful*, 82.

80. Farmington Ward, Ward Teachers Minutes, 6 November, 8 December 1866, 13 January 1867.

CHAPTER 3

DEFENDING THE KINGDOM

Residents of the communities of early Davis County defined themselves in ways other than the civil and ecclesiastical boundaries that allowed services to be administered in an orderly way. Within these defined communities, people built a sense of community through their interactions in the workaday world and through their social and religious activities. They strengthened old friendships and became acquainted with new neighbors. Through human associations, local communities solidified and gave a personal definition to the overarching goal of Utah's early Mormon settlers to build a harmonious and cooperative society.

Some activities and events that occurred during the county's first twenty years strengthened the internal bonds of local communities. Central among them were the social and recreational pastimes. Other situations—particularly political and religious aspects of life, such as participation in the county militia, patriotic holidays, group-oriented church activities, and Mormon missions—strengthened the allegiance of county residents in their loyalties. Certain challenges faced by Davis County residents in the 1850s and early 1860s threatened to dissolve communities through physical displacement and disharmony that tested unity. The Utah War, for example, an external threat, rallied most Utahns to support local leaders in what was defined as a threat to both political and religious freedom. The confrontation with the Morrisite group on the Weber River stemmed from disharmony within the LDS church. In this instance, Davis County residents opposed each other. This dilemma was resolved by government officials through legal and military actions that involved county militiamen.

Leisure Activities

The settlers of the pioneer period—before the coming of the transcontinental railroad in 1869—depended upon locally organized leisure-time activities. Providing a living occupied most of every workday for men and women, but Davis County's hardworking residents found time for socializing in their homes and halls. Settlers throughout Utah developed local cultural activities not unlike those enjoyed in the broader Anglo-American community. Salt Lake City's Social Hall, built in 1852, set a pattern followed in smaller towns. But for Davis County residents, who sometimes attended the plays presented by the Deseret Dramatic Association in the Social Hall and other cultural offerings in the capital city, it took about twenty years before they could afford local cultural halls. During the 1850s and 1860s, homes and meetinghouse/school buildings also served for dinners, dances, dramatic presentations, musical entertainments, local lyceums, and traveling lecturers. All of these relaxing and socializing occasions lifted spirits and cemented relationships.[1]

The dinner party was a popular event throughout the county. It was hosted especially by those able to build large houses that would hold groups of a dozen or more friends. After dinner, guest vocalists or instrumentalists performed popular songs of the day, including southern spirituals and Mormon folk tunes. Each community enjoyed its own local talent.[2]

In the community halls built in every town for church meetings and schools, sizable groups gathered to socialize. They danced to band music and enjoyed local or imported drama and other entertainment. Dancing was the most common community recreational

Early social events took place in community school-church buildings. Later on, specialized social halls were built, like the adobe Opera House in Farmington, affectionately known as the White Elephant. (Glen M. Leonard)

activity in the early years. A fiddler was all that was needed, and a waxed floor in the school room was much appreciated. Women brought molasses cakes or other pastries for refreshments and their partners chipped in two bits (twenty-five cents) to pay the fiddler. In some areas of the county, dancing schools offered lessons for learning or improving such skills.[3]

A few large homes in every community also offered public dancing, sometimes to the chagrin of concerned citizens. In fact, dancing—wherever the setting—raised questions of propriety for many with strict religious upbringings. Latter-day Saint leaders condoned the practice, within limits. Orson Pratt said of dancing in 1856, "Though of no harm in itself, it is a pleasant exercise, but may be . . . carried to excess." He hoped the Saints would not let dancing keep them from their studies. Brigham Young endorsed the enjoyment of music, singing, and good society in a wholesome setting.[4]

Just what constituted "appropriate" behavior was the question.

The standard square dances and quadrilles were always acceptable. After the waltz became popular, this new round dance was limited to one or two per evening. Because at times the youth became boisterous, some bishops in Davis County policed dancing parties by requiring sponsors to get prior permission. If the organizer failed to control his guests, the right to host other dances was withheld.[5]

From time to time, Davis County residents enjoyed traveling entertainments, usually a lecture or dramatic presentation. Philo Dibble, an early Bountiful settler who later moved to Springville, lectured in halls throughout Utah using paintings he had commissioned depicting incidents in Mormon history. The Wood String Orchestra of West Bountiful provided a musical accompaniment for Dibble's close-to-home lectures. At a presentation in Farmington, local resident Truman Leonard, who had participated in the Battle of Nauvoo, added his own impassioned commentary on the paintings of Joseph Smith. Farmington's choir and brass band furnished "good and sweet music" for the evening. In the late 1860s, artist Reuben Kirkham of Bountiful toured the county with his own historical panorama.[6]

A special event in Davis County's early cultural life was a concert tour of the Nauvoo Brass Band in August 1855, the first such excursion held in Utah Territory. Brigham Young authorized eight members of the Salt Lake band to visit the northern settlements to perform orchestral, brass, and vocal numbers in schoolhouses and boweries. On one of its stops, the entourage entertained fifty-two families at a bowery at Kaysville. Family tickets cost one dollar each, payable in cash or produce. Bishop John W. Hess decided that because of the devastation caused to Farmington's crops by grasshoppers, residents there "felt poor" and would not support a concert. The bishop's wife provided a dinner for the musicians, who played the bishop a tune and then moved on.[7]

Bishop Hess rectified the loss to Farmington's cultural life a year later, when he invited members of the Salt Lake band back for a musical entertainment in the courthouse. Then, to show his support for music, Hess formally organized a local group known as the Deseret Brass Band. With Salt Lake music professor Henry Pugh as instructor and William Glover as captain, the band worked hard in weekly rehearsals and was soon touring to give concerts. The band's primary role involved regular drills with the local militia. Among other honors, it was one of three bands invited to play at the 1857 Deseret state fair, and one of four participating in the 24 July celebration in Big Cottonwood Canyon in 1860; all of the other invited bands were from Salt Lake City.[8]

It was in the 1860s, after the Latter-day Saints completed their new area meetinghouses, that cultural activities blossomed in Davis County. With the first years of settlement behind them, residents found additional time and means to spend in organized leisure activities, recreation, and entertainment. New brass bands appeared in Bountiful, Farmington, and Kaysville. Other new organizations included a fife and drum corps in South Bountiful, a stringed orchestra in West Bountiful, a dramatic association in Bountiful, and a debating society in Farmington.[9]

Religious Life

Social gatherings offered a moment of relaxation from the back-bending work of tending fields and doing household chores. For spiritual uplift, Latter-day Saints in Davis County congregated on Sunday afternoons or evenings to hear sermons, to pray, and to participate in worship through music. The Sabbath service cemented feelings and loyalties within the Mormon community. No other religious organization existed in the towns during the county's early settlement years. Because the LDS church operated with a lay ministry that included all adult males in a potential missionary pool, the invitation to preach was extended widely and might involve the local bishop, his counselors, returned missionaries, others from the congregation, or visiting authorities. Messages ranged from millennial prophecies, the teachings of Jesus, and the revelations of Joseph Smith to practical advice on farming or raising children. Speakers in sacrament meetings varied in their knowledge and oratorical skills, but their effectiveness was judged more by their sincerity than presentation.[10]

To help parents properly teach their children religious and moral principles, most LDS wards in the county were hosting Sunday schools by the early 1850s. These Sunday morning gatherings had been attempted in Nauvoo and were begun in Salt Lake in 1849 by Richard Ballantyne, after which the idea quickly spread elsewhere.

The classes centered on instructions on the scriptures but sometimes included practical lessons on reading or writing. Religious and secular learning were not really separated in the county's pioneer society.[11]

Music was an important part of Latter-day Saint worship and religious activities. Ward choirs, organized as early as the 1850s, sang hymns and anthems for the Sabbath service to supplement congregational singing. Choirs also participated in other community gatherings, including holiday festivities and funerals. For accompaniment, early choirs used violins or clarinets, but they adopted pianos or organs as soon as they were available. When Kaysville's congregation lacked a skilled director, the choir borrowed one from outside the ward's boundaries. Choir members, selected for their vocal abilities, often remained loyal to the organization for years. Singers with above-average talents rendered solos for weddings, funerals, and entertainments.[12]

On Thursday afternoons once a month, Latter-day Saint adults met for a fast and testimony meeting. They brought with them food and other goods as contributions—fast offerings—to help the poor. During the meeting they testified to God's goodness in their lives. During succeeding days, the bishop and ward teachers distributed the donated offerings to widows and orphans or others unable to provide their own daily needs. Men and boys chopped wood for the fireplaces and stoves of the needy. To determine needs and to provide a watchfulness in spiritual matters, members of the ward teachers quorum visited each home monthly. This group of adult men played an important role in defining religious expectations for the community of faith and in helping meet the needs of people in the practical aspects of life.

Several times during their lifetime most Latter-day Saint men would leave their families for preaching missions. In the nineteenth century these missionaries were generally married men, usually with children. Neighbors helped care for his family while the missionary was away. Many of the elders, as the missionaries were called (referring to a priesthood office they held), traveled to places they had lived previously to call upon relatives and acquaintances there. The call to serve came typically from church leaders in Salt Lake City. At times a missionary would learn of his assignment by hearing his name read from the pulpit at a general conference. He could accept the call or request a deferment because of pressing business at home. Missions within the United States often kept missionaries away less than a year. Some men planted crops in the spring and returned from preaching in time for the fall harvest. However, an assignment to India, Hong Kong, Singapore, Chile, France, Italy, Switzerland, the British Isles, or Scandinavia—all places designated for missionary work in the 1850s—might involve an absence from home and family for two to four years. In these cases, ward teachers helped sustain the absentee's family. This acceptance of mission responsibilities impacted family life and strengthened the commitment within the Mormon community to look after one another.[13]

The Mormon Reformation

During the mid-1850s the missionary zeal that was usually reserved for those not of the Mormon faith was turned inward in a campaign known as the Mormon Reformation.[14] The foundation for the reformation was laid during the fall of 1855, when church leaders called "home missionaries" to visit members in their homes and encourage them to greater diligence in their religious duties. Soon afterward, Apostle Wilford Woodruff visited Davis County and organized local presidencies to oversee the home missionary work. With this step, organized reform work began in the congregations of Davis County.[15]

The reformation moved slowly. In the spring of 1856 Brigham Young invited church leaders at all levels to alert the people to their spiritual duties. When that effort largely failed, he sent his associates out to preach in local conferences and move the effort to an evangelical stage. Tell them, Young said, "to live their religion." Church leaders implemented the campaign in Davis County. In mid-September, Young's second counselor, Jedediah M. Grant, the president's brother Joseph Young of the Council of Seventy, and home missionaries convened a conference in Kaysville that would effectively launch a territorywide reform movement.[16]

Latter-day Saints in Davis County were accustomed to church conferences. Visiting authorities attended them as often as quarterly somewhere in the county. The purposes of the gatherings were to regulate local church affairs and to preach. Usually the conferences lasted two days, with morning, afternoon, and evening sessions both days. But the message in 1856 carried a camp-meeting fervor. Jedediah Grant, a missionary in the southern states in the 1840s, called Kaysville's members to repentance in meetings held in a bowery over a three-day weekend. The *Deseret News* titled its report of the conference the "Great Reformation."

With fervency of voice and urgency in his message, Grant encouraged a higher level of Christian living. He urged the payment of tithes and offerings and greater heed to honesty and Sabbath keeping. His preaching also paid attention to practical affairs. Grant encouraged more home manufactures. He reminded parents of their duties to their children and enjoined both physical and spiritual cleanliness. In the fervor of the experience, Grant decided to commit the congregation to do something about the messages he and his associates had delivered. Kaysville's members responded by agreeing to renew their baptismal covenants. On Monday, 15 September, Bishop Allen Taylor and more than 400 area members, virtually everyone over age eight, were immersed one by one in Weinel's millpond. With this outward symbol of compliance, members rededicated themselves to the spiritual and promised to clear away from their lives the habits of frontier lethargy. Home missionary William Willes highlighted the conference message by singing a new reformation song that ended: "For Deseret expects that all the Saints will do their duty."[17]

After Grant left his blessing on the people of Kaysville, he and his party moved on to Farmington, where transplanted New Yorkers, familiar with the revivals of the Burnt-over District, gathered in the upper room of the courthouse to hear a report of the reform meetings in the neighboring ward. Grant told Farmington residents that he wanted to put "this little village . . . to a similar test." Bishop John W. Hess concurred and the entire assembly arose to signal acceptance. A hastily scheduled conference began the next morning—a Tuesday—and continued for three days. One speaker after another stirred the congregation to an awareness of their shortcomings and a desire for a spiritual rebirth. A reported 406 local members signified their acceptance of the challenges from the pulpit by being rebaptized at the millrace north of the city wall.[18]

In Centerville and Bountiful, Grant and his companions found local church leaders willing to convene reformation conferences, but not immediately. The reformers returned a week later and held three-day conferences in each town. The conferences in southern Davis County differed in tone and results from those held earlier. Instead of instructing members in their duties and encouraging them to repent, Grant openly chastised the congregations. At Centerville, in the milder of the two conferences, he chided the people for "their minds being set upon the things of this world more than upon their religion." Joseph Young spoke "of the spiritual slothfulness and inactivity of the Saints; and urged them to honor their religion." One of the home missionaries invited the Latter-day Saints to stand to manifest their willingness to keep the commandments, and they did. But Grant told the congregation on the second day of the conference that he would not authorize any rebaptisms until they were better prepared, and he invited Bishop William R. Smith and the local ward teachers to work with the people. Grant returned two days later and received the congregation's pledge to discharge their duties and honor the commandments. The next morning, 231 people were baptized. In a final gathering in the local schoolhouse, Grant left his blessing upon the people, their lands, flocks, and other belongings.[19]

Members in Bountiful received the most direct challenge in Davis County, and it was left for the bishop, John Stoker, to "enforce cleanliness and honesty, and to cast out the works of iniquity" in preparation for a complete reformation. Jedediah Grant declared that half the congregation had never been converted in the first place. His inaugural sermon, delivered in the local bowery, charged "the people of Bountiful with being as cold as the ice of the Polar regions; that they had been in a deep sleep, and were still asleep." Other speakers endorsed the reproof as justified and recited the problems: ingratitude, avarice, covetousness, lethargy, pride, and backsliding. Grant encouraged the people to ready themselves for the work of "regeneration and salvation," and he left them to prepare for a future renewal of their baptismal covenants.[20]

Overall, the reaction to the reformation message delivered in

When the home missionaries began urging Latter-day Saints in Davis County to improve their personal lives and living conditions, many of them still lived in log homes like this one, photographed in the 1860s or '70s at an unidentified location in the Salt Lake Valley. (Utah State Historical Society)

these four communities pleased church leaders, yet they wished to effect not just promises but a change of behavior. Jedediah Grant told a gathering in the Salt Lake Bowery in October, "We want to see the spirit of the reformation in the people; we wish them . . . not only to talk about it, but to practice upon it." "The people were so sound asleep," Wilford Woodruff said in December, "that they did not realize the importance of [Grant's] mission."[71]

With Brigham Young's blessing, the campaign that had taken root in Davis County continued there and also moved throughout Utah Territory. Expectations were formalized in catechisms reviewed by the ward teachers in every home. The questions echoed all of the Ten Commandments as well as specific applications of them, such as:

> Have you cut hay where you had no right to, or turned your animals into another person's grain or field, without his knowledge and consent?

> Have you branded an animal that you did not know to be your own?
>
> Have you taken another's horse or mule from the range and rode it without the owner's consent?
>
> Have you fulfilled your promise in paying your debts, or run into debt without prospect of paying?
>
> Have you taken water to irrigate with, when it belonged to another person at the time you used it?[22]

Among the results of the Mormon Reformation was a 65 percent increase in plural marriages. This Old Testament marriage pattern, introduced by Joseph Smith in Nauvoo, had been first preached publicly in the old Salt Lake Tabernacle in 1852. A very few of Davis County's early settlers had taken plural wives before coming west. The Reformation increased that number and changed the way many families lived.[23]

The home missionaries and ward teachers accepted the responsibility in Davis County to keep the Reformation alive and, as they put it, "to prune the vineyard of dead wood." Individuals unwilling to conform to Reformation standards of righteous living were "cut off"—excommunicated from the church. Some who felt imposed upon or unwilling to change left the territory for friendlier neighborhoods. Jedediah Grant had suggested that option in his Kaysville sermons. The Latter-day Saints who were willing to recommit themselves accepted rebaptism and the behavioral standards of this intense but short-lived campaign. The Mormon Reformation—as did the practice of plural marriage—became a test of religious loyalty and commitment.[24]

Jedediah Grant's untimely death at age forty in December 1856 slowed the zeal of the Reformation and moved it into a more moderate phase. Wilford Woodruff tempered the intensity with a call for a greater tolerance and understanding. Although this dampened the cutting edge of the campaign, priesthood leaders in every community from Bountiful to Kaysville never forgot the push to perfect the Latter-day Saints, to unite them in a common religious endeavor. For years afterwards, anytime they wished to encourage greater religious commitment, they spoke of the need for a reformation.[25]

Politics and Patriotism

The Mormon Reformation created a religious enthusiasm that prepared Utah settlers for an event with both political and military repercussions. Known to history as the Utah War, the Utah Expedition, or Buchanan's Blunder—after the U.S. president who sent federal troops marching across the country to subdue a supposedly rebellious Utah—the events of 1857–58 had a traumatic impact on Davis County. Furthermore, the approach of the U.S. Army tested the political loyalties of local residents during this emotionally charged period.

The genesis of the problems that led to the Utah War lay in the form of government instituted in early Utah. Congress created Utah Territory as part of the Compromise of 1850. It was a substitute for the State of Deseret that had been requested by Brigham Young and his followers. Territorial status meant that top officials were appointed in Washington. Only half of those named were Utahns; the others satisfied the political debts of presidents. Over several years, misunderstandings and disagreements between local and imported officials led to reports to Washington, D.C., charging the Mormons with sedition, treason, disloyalty, violence, and rebellion against the federal government and the people of the United States.[26]

Both outwardly and by religious proscription most Utahns were loyal to the constituted government. The settlers of early Davis County, whether American or British in origin, celebrated Independence Day regularly in a show of patriotism for the freedoms promised by the U.S. Constitution. Latter-day Saints held the Constitution sacred, even though they sometimes denounced the "bad men" who had been elected or appointed to government office. By the mid-1850s, Fourth of July celebrations in Davis County echoed the more elaborate ones in larger cities elsewhere. On this national holiday, in at least some towns, county residents enjoyed a sunrise military salute, followed by breakfast in a local grove, speeches, toasts, and musical numbers.[27]

Salt Lake City observed a second patriotic July holiday as early as 1849—the 24 July anniversary of Brigham Young's arrival in the Salt Lake Valley. Some Davis County residents attended the celebrations of both July holidays in the capital city. Gradually, local Pioneer Day observances appeared within the county. In 1855 in Farmington, neighboring wards joined in a 24 July activity in a bowery built at the county seat especially for the occasion. The celebration was similar to Independence Day gatherings. According to Joseph Robinson, celebrants enjoyed "feasting, and dancing, several very appropriate speeches, and toasts." The celebrations of both July anniversaries honored founding fathers and cemented loyalties—to the nation and to the territory. Brigham Young, Utah's first territorial governor, symbolized this allegiance at the entrance to his Brigham Street (South Temple) estate in Salt Lake City. Atop the gate sat a carved wooden American eagle perched on Deseret's beehive. The beehive, symbolizing Deseret (a Book of Mormon term meaning "industry") soon became part of Utah Territory's logo and was eventually incorporated into the state seal. Under the beehive a third symbol identified another loyalty—a star representing Jesus Christ. In territorial Utah, Mormon leaders exercised a definite influence in local government, and members pledged their allegiance to these leaders when choices between God and Caesar were necessary.[28]

Participation in military service was one way Utah men manifested their patriotism to American constitutional government and its territorial component. En route to Utah in 1846, nearly 500 Latter-day Saints had formed a battalion in the war with Mexico. One of the reasons for that service was a show of fealty to the government, although it also benefited the Mormon church and the families of the soldiers financially. At least sixteen of the Mormon Battalion veterans located with their families in Davis County. Residents honored these men for their service in helping the westward migration.[29]

Authorized in March 1849 by the Deseret Assembly, Utah's first militia was known as the Nauvoo Legion, after the city militia organized by Illinois Mormons in 1840. Utah's citizen army theoretically included all males aged eighteen to forty-five; but in reality it depended upon willing volunteers. Most of the militia's officers had not been among the Mexican War volunteers. Among the leaders were five early residents of what would later become Davis County. The highest in rank was Col. John S. Fullmer of Farmington, who headed the cavalry regiment. Within this regiment, Captain Daniel

C. Davis of Bountiful led a company of Mountain Dragoons, with Anson Call of Bountiful as one of his lieutenants. Two county residents served as lieutenants in the foot-soldiers' regiment—Dorr P. Curtis of Kaysville in an artillery company and Jonathan H. Holmes of Farmington in the infantry company. No records survive to identify the numbers of enlisted men from Davis County; but, in 1850, an agent was asked to recruit sixty new volunteers for service.[30]

Before long, population growth and mobility made it necessary to reorganize the Nauvoo Legion. In January 1851, legislators divided the territory into nine military districts, two for Salt Lake County and one each for the other counties. Each district organized as a regiment that was subdivided into companies.[31] Daniel C. Davis of Bountiful was promoted to colonel and headed the Davis County regiment. Volunteers drilled regularly at the county seat to meet their legislative mandate to be ready at a minute's notice to repel hostile Indians or to preserve the peace. The companies established in each Davis County community held their own drills in between countywide training. For instance, Bountiful's Company E consisted of sixty men divided into six platoons of ten men each under Captain Jude Allen.[32]

Early in 1857 Utah's militia organization was again adjusted and the number of districts increased to thirteen. Colonel Philemon C. Merrill of Farmington became commander in Davis County.[33] Even though the required age for enlistment reached to age forty-five, an older group living in Bountiful and Centerville organized as a company of "Silver Greys" called the Mountain Sharps. Joseph Holbrook served as captain. The men considered themselves "home guards," ready to provide protection within the community when the younger men were away at war. This followed the pattern set up in 1849, which not only included Silver Greys for those over fifty but a "Juvenile Rifle Company" for young men under the age of eighteen.[34]

The militia did not wait long for its first call to duty. Some 2,700 guests of Brigham Young had gathered for a Pioneer Day celebration in Big Cottonwood Canyon. Among them were several from Davis County. The celebrants arrived on the afternoon of 23 July for feasting and visiting, followed by dancing on three plank floors prepared especially for the event. Cannon blasts awoke them the next morning, and that day's events included military demonstrations, singing, addresses by host Brigham Young and others, and dancing until well after midnight.[35]

Around noon, Brigham Young received word from four messengers that U.S. Army forces were marching toward Utah to quell a supposed rebellion. The couriers, including Judson Stoddard of Centerville, informed Young that President James Buchanan had dispatched 2,500 troops to escort new territorial officers to Utah. Among those accompanying General William S. Harney, the commanding officer, was Alfred Cumming of Georgia, the new governor. Brigham Young declared that the appointees were welcome if they behaved themselves, but the army must be kept out. The Mormons had not forgotten the mobbings of Missouri and Illinois by men acting under the guidance of renegade militia leaders. Utahns immediately set about preparing to defend themselves.[36]

Early in August, Brigham Young called home all proselytizing missionaries and invited settlers from the outlying settlements to join in defending the Mormon kingdom from the invading army. General Daniel H. Wells activated the Nauvoo Legion. Some of Davis County's expatriates left their far-flung settlement missions and returned home because of this directive. The Davis County militia unit stepped up its pace of military parades and drills. On 13 September a number of them heard Young deliver some impassioned remarks in the Salt Lake Bowery. He declared that the army had been ordered west illegally, and he pledged to prevent the soldiers from entering the valley. "I shall treat every army and every armed company that attempts to come here as a mob," he said.

Brigham Young discouraged a militant spirit among Utahns, however, and forbade any fighting unless absolutely necessary. He announced that he would order all improvements burned if necessary and invited anyone unwilling to participate to leave the territory in peace. Two days later, acting as territorial governor, Young declared martial law and authorized the militia to keep the U.S. Army troops from entering Utah. The Utah Legislative Assembly quickly endorsed the governor's message with a series of resolutions, published early in October. Officers in Davis County received orders to be ready to respond at a moment's notice, and they instigated weekly drills.[37]

In September, Colonel Albert Sidney Johnston replaced Harney as head of the U.S. troops heading to Utah. Johnston found his soldiers stalled on the plains of western Wyoming by indecision, bad weather, and the harassments of the Nauvoo Legion. Five special forces units of the Utah militia totaling no more than 200 men had played a decisive role in halting the army. Heading two of them were Davis County militiamen Major Lot Smith and Colonel Robert T. Burton. The forces headed by these men burned supply wagons and grass fodder and captured cattle, horses, and mules. They effectively thwarted the army's westward march and forced it to spend the winter at hastily established Camp Scott, directly south of the burned-out Fort Bridger on Black's Fork that the Mormons had torched. Davis militiamen, including a dozen from Bountiful, were part of this effort. After completing their assignment, they were released early in December to return to their homes.[38]

Lot Smith's group was perhaps the most celebrated unit of the entire war. His group of forty men left on 3 October under the leadership of four officers—Smith, Capt. Horton D. Haight, Lt. Thomas Abbott, and Lt. John Vance (all but Vance being from Davis County). General Daniel H. Wells told Smith to take "every opportunity to burn their trains, stampede their stock, and keep them under arms by night surprises, so that they will be worn out." Smith's men directly confronted the wagonmasters of the Russell, Majors, and Waddell supply trains. When the wagonmasters refused to abandon the army they had been hired to support, the Utahns helped themselves to supplies needed for their own support, then burned the wagons. The militia also drove off nearly 2,000 head of cattle and herded them to the Salt Lake Valley.[39]

The task was made easier because the men with the supply trains thought that the Mormon militia numbered between 500 and 1,000 men. Smith was under orders not to interfere with the wagon trains of Salt Lake City merchants and not to take human life. Neither side suffered any fatalities. The accidental discharge of Smith's pistol, however, wounded Orson P. Arnold in the thigh and grazed two other soldiers. A shot fired by a U.S. soldier passed through the hat of one of Smith's volunteers from Ogden.[40]

With their primary mission accomplished, Smith and his men visited Wells's camp on Black's Fork and then rode through deep

During the Utah War, Davis County's militia furnished men to help fortify Echo Canyon, seen here in a C. R. Savage photo taken after completion of the transcontinental railroad. (Utah State Historical Society)

snow and cold wind to Burton's camp on the Bear River. Here, Smith's men set up camp to watch for army deserters. In mid-December, after ten weeks of service, all but ten men who were retained as guards left for home.[41]

In a second response to the approaching army, Governor Brigham Young and General Wells fortified Echo Canyon with Nauvoo Legion units positioned to intercept the approaching forces. Davis County provided several units to support this effort. The first was dispatched in late September after Colonel Merrill received orders sped from Salt Lake calling for a detachment of lancers. A week later, a Davis County infantry detachment joined General Wells. In November, Merrill led his own regiment to Echo Canyon. The men took along provisions to last one month. In all, 1,250 Utah soldiers participated. They dug trenches across the canyon, built breastworks along the ridges above the road, and loosened stones that could be rolled down the steep slopes. With these defenses readied, Wells released all but a small guard from Echo Canyon duty about two weeks after Merrill's arrival. Johnston's U.S. forces remained stalled in Wyoming, and it was cheaper to let the Utah militiamen feed themselves at home than haul supplies into the canyon. A few guards stayed through the winter, and the Davis militia provided some of the reinforcements.[42]

The county's official militia band, the Deseret Brass Band of Farmington, also supported the defensive forces. Band members were placed on alert in mid-August and told to prepare for a three-month campaign in Echo Canyon. They escorted the infantry detachment part of the way to the canyon in September and then accompanied Colonel Merrill's regiment to the mouth of Emigration Canyon in November. Only five band members actually went into the canyon with the militia.[43]

It was during the Echo Canyon campaign that a Mormon soldier lost his life, the only military-related death during the Utah War. The victim was thirty-one-year-old William A. Simmons of Farmington, who was accidentally shot on 30 September by a comrade cleaning his gun. A tombstone in the Farmington Cemetery commemorates Simmons's death.

With the U.S. Army motionless at Camp Scott, Utahns consolidated their position in a series of official statements and resolutions passed by the territorial legislature in December in response to a formal message delivered by Governor Brigham Young. Citizens of Salt Lake County endorsed the decrees in mid-January 1858. Over the next six weeks, mass meetings convened in major settlements in various parts of the territory to endorse the pronouncements.[44] Among the first was a public meeting in the Davis County Courthouse on 18 January. Residents adopted resolutions drafted by a five-member citizens committee that vowed, "We will never submit to the rule of drunken, corrupt, and licentious officers, neither will we sustain the appointment of any but 'good' men." Accepting Young's scorched-earth policy, the assembly declared that rather than allow the invading forces to occupy their property, they would "burn and utterly destroy everything we possess."[45] The following week in Kaysville and Bountiful citizens committees drafted a more general set of resolutions supporting the declarations of Brigham Young and the legislature. Rather than submit to military rule and occupation, Utahns declared their willingness to abandon their settlements and burn their homes, barns, fields, and other improvements.[46]

In February 1858 Thomas L. Kane, a friend of the Mormons

invited to Utah by Brigham Young, arrived in Utah by way of Panama and California. He came with Buchanan's unofficial permission to negotiate a settlement. Mormon leaders expressed their willingness to make peace, so Kane headed for Camp Scott to sound out Cumming and Johnston. Taking no chances, Brigham Young ordered northern Utahns to prepare to leave their homes and move south for safety. Much of Salt Lake City had been evacuated by the time Cumming arrived there with Kane in mid-April. Preparations in the regions northward, including Davis County, were well underway, and some settlers were on the road. Rumors circulated that the evacuees would move as far as Sonora, in northern Mexico. Actually, Brigham Young had sent an exploring party looking for a new place of refuge along the White Mountain Range in the central Great Basin. Nothing suitable could be found. "The difficulty," the scouts reported from Fillmore, "was to find soil, timber, and water together."[47]

The new governor's route to the capital city brought him from Echo Canyon by way of Weber Canyon because snow blocked the more direct route through Emigration Canyon. Mounted uniformed guards from the Davis militia met Cumming at the mouth of the canyon and escorted him along the mountain road to the courthouse in Farmington, where the party arrived around midnight. The Deseret Brass Band, patiently awaiting his arrival, demonstrated its loyalty to the United States by playing "The Star Spangled Banner."

The new governor spent the night in Farmington, then headed south for a meeting with Brigham Young. That evening, the brass band followed in carriages. In Salt Lake City, the men played a few patriotic tunes. Cumming was impressed with the sincerity of the musical offering. But a non-Mormon witness who heard the band's welcome said that after Cumming was too far off to hear them, the Davis County musicians ignored their captain's instructions and vented some of their resentment toward the new appointee by playing "Doo Dah." Isaac Nash had written this ditty at the 24 July celebration in Big Cottonwood Canyon as a satirical challenge to the approaching army. Later, he had sung it in the old Salt Lake Tabernacle. The words derided the new gubernatorial appointee and his escorts and expressed undeviating support for Brigham Young. It vowed, "If our enemies do appear, We'll sweep them from the land."

While respecting American government, Utahns worried that the soldiers would be like the Missouri vigilantes who had worn military garb while mobbing the Saints there.[48]

Cumming met with Young, and the new appointee determined the falsity of the reports that had prompted Buchanan's orders. Cumming tried in vain to halt the planned evacuation of northern settlements. He then returned to Fort Scott and sent word to President Buchanan. The American president responded by issuing an amnesty. He appointed two commissioners to carry the document to Utah. Their charge: Resolve unsettled issues between Mormons and gentiles, as non-Mormons were referred to by the Latter-day Saints. The commissioners reached the state in early June.[49]

The Move South, April–July 1858

Before these negotiations were underway, and with the results of them of course as yet unknown, the residents of Davis County continued their preparations to abandon their homes. For more than six months they had anticipated the mass evacuation. Many of the county's missionaries to the Salmon River area had arrived home in September 1857, the planting season for winter wheat. They found that some of their relatives and neighbors had decided not to plant; others went ahead with the work and enclosed the fields with tight fences. Either way, food supplies were sufficient. Of greater concern as the departure neared in the spring of 1858 was what to do with surplus wheat and flour. Some residents built special boxes and made trips to Salt Lake and Utah Counties to store the grain at mills.

In late April, at the new temporary church headquarters in Provo, Brigham Young found the tithing yard there already overflowing with bins of wheat and flour. He picked a vacant city block and ordered workmen to build a temporary storehouse 150 feet long to receive the surplus. Some in Davis County didn't bother to remove their grain. They buried the grain boxes in the ground at home, along with excess furniture. Those who expected not to return sold their property at a fraction of its value or abandoned it and left without securing their fields against the cattle streaming south with people from the more northern settlements of Weber and Box Elder Counties and Cache Valley.[50]

A reporter from the *New York Tribune* visited these northern regions and wondered in print what would happen to the people. "They are moving south," he wrote, with "no inhabitable tracts of any considerable extent within seven hundred miles of their late settlements. So extraordinary a migration is hardly paralleled in history."[51]

Under Brigham Young's direction, the ward bishops supervised an orderly evacuation. This kept confusion to a minimum and helped protect individuals. An estimated 17,000 people moved out of northern Utah, including more than 2,000 from Davis County. Young encouraged the exiles to put first things first. Load your wagons with food, he counseled; then, if space remained, take along the best of your furniture and your cabin doors with their scarce hardware.[52]

Most of the settlers in Davis County relocated in Utah and Juab Counties at sites selected by the ward bishops. These refugee camps were near existing communities but did not interfere with property already claimed by earlier settlers. Not everyone reached the designated new townsites; some families joined friends and relatives in other locations.[53]

The evacuation of Davis County's communities proceeded under a common pattern. The families of Bountiful launched their move in April under the direction of Bishop John Stoker. The caravan camped just west of Salt Lake City the first day, then moved on toward their destination at Battle Creek, along the shores of Utah Lake west of today's Pleasant Grove. They set up tents, gathered willows for wickiups, or made dugouts for temporary shelter. Perhaps it was the nature of these dwellings that prompted the residents to call their camp "Shanghai." Brigham Young evaluated the situation when he visited the camp and others along the lakeshore on 23 April. He reported, "Some of the people had made themselves quite comfortable with sage brush and willow houses." Ute Indians were camped nearby, and the Bountiful exiles presented them with gifts of friendship. Both the Mormons and the Indians supplemented their diets with fish from the lake and the Provo River. With the camp established, the bishop dispatched twenty men back to Bountiful to stand ready to burn the now-abandoned city.[54]

Bishop John W. Hess left on 1 May to lead the way for Farmington's residents. Organized companies followed him with

In 1850 Charles C. Rich built this adobe home for his wives Eliza Ann and Sarah Peck in Centerville. Rich returned to Centerville from a six-year colonizing mission in San Bernardino just in time for the Move South. He sold the house to John Woolley when called by Brigham Young to settle the Bear Lake Valley in 1863. (*The City In-Between: History of Centerville*)

heavily laden wagons. He found a settlement place in Juab County on Willow Creek, between Mona and Nephi. In three weeks Farmington was deserted. Some of the exiles dropped off along the way at Provo and Springville; others moved from the temporary camps into the towns of Mona and Nephi. Hess sent at least four men back as guards, with orders to burn the town if the army tried to possess it. Buildings had been filled with straw and tinder to make the job easier. At Willow Creek, the displaced settlers built log and willow huts, hauled firewood, plowed the ground, and planted potatoes, wheat, and other crops.[55]

Bishop Allen Taylor of Kaysville had a personal concern as his community headed south toward Dry Creek, below Lehi: his wife Anna was close to delivering a child. The family set out anyway, and, with the help of an accompanying midwife, Anna gave birth just before reaching Salt Lake City. Hers was not the only birthing experience during the relocation; life went on in this and other aspects. Emily Stewart (Barnes) remembered, "We took everything we had in one wagon, which was not much except some chickens and one door, which was the only thing that was any good. Sister and I drove the cows and pigs and we walked all the way. . . . [W]e had a little place made of rushes, which sheltered us. We had good water; it was a swampy place with lots of bull rushes." Although some of the migrants camped in other places, those who stayed together found the site acceptable. They caught fish in nearby Utah Lake and salted it for later use.[56]

The residents of South Weber left home with less concern for community togetherness than was the case in neighboring towns. Some reached the southern tip of Utah Lake and camped near Goshen. Other families stayed closer to home; they simply moved up Weber Canyon and found refuge in the Mountain Green area.[57]

Johnston's Army, as the federal troops were known, marched through a nearly deserted Salt Lake City on 26 June. The Utah and federal authorities agreed to let the army set up a peaceful encampment under terms of Buchanan's amnesty. Brigham Young insisted that it be at least forty miles from the capital city. Federal officials looked southwesterly and picked Cedar Valley, where they set up Camp Floyd. The 100-acre encampment and its adjacent civilian community, now Fairfield, soon became the third largest city in Utah. The camp lasted until 1861, then disbanded in order for the troops to fight in the Civil War.[58]

Davis County exiles soon heard of the agreement and knew it meant they could go home. A few did not wait for the official instructions; they soon headed north to water neglected crops, plant winter wheat, and repair fences. Brigham Young waited for the army to pass through Salt Lake County before issuing permission for reoccupation on 30 June. Within a few days, word reached Davis County's bishops in their places of exile. It took only three or four days after that for the settlers to pack their wagons for the trip north. Some of those from Farmington took a route home around the west side of Utah Lake and visited with the United States soldiers there.[59]

The two-months' absence left its mark on the well-kept towns and farms of Davis County. When Emily Stewart (Barnes) returned to Kaysville, she remembered, "Everything at home looked forsaken—grass had grown over the pathway and the door to the little log hut stood open." Milton Hammond said he "found Farmington grown up to weeds and grass which made the place look lonesome."[60]

Losses varied among individuals. Some had secured their fences against the migrating livestock. Those who abandoned hope and made no preparations to return generally found their crops damaged. In Farmington, the protected hay and grain harvests were generally better than had been expected, but smut damaged much of the spring wheat. In Bountiful, very little winter wheat had been sown the previous fall, but volunteer growth yielded a fair harvest. The spring plantings of oats and barley survived the neglect of the evacuation to yield a good harvest. Even so, a subsequent hard winter took its toll on livestock. After the crops were in, wagons were sent from every community to retrieve the grain and flour stored out of town. The Move South and return home was a heavy sacrifice for the individuals affected. The loss of time and impact on property were a considerable price to pay for the preservation of those properties.[61] In some instances, damages extended beyond that suffered by the crops. The Robert W. Burton family returned to Kaysville to discover that someone had grazed horses in their wheatfield. Burton decided it had been Indians. The intruders also had lived for a time in the Burton home and had pulled up the wooden floor for firewood.[62]

Some of the displaced settlers never did return to Davis County. Apparently they found other places better suited to their needs. Kaysville's bishop, for example, had to replace both of his counselors. The majority of the settlers did return, however, and quickly resumed a normal lifestyle. Overall, the impact of the Move South on the 1858 harvest was minor. Besides, because of plentiful earlier harvests, many of the settlers had a two-year supply of grain on hand.[63] The removal required considerable effort, but the settlers took it in stride.

An important impact of the Utah War was psychological. Davis County's residents wanted to be loyal to the United States, but for some of them President Buchanan's decision to send an army of occupation weakened their faith in the national government, as had the reports of seditious activity from territorial officials that had prompted the order in the first place. When Newton Tuttle obtained a copy of Buchanan's "Proclamation" while returning to Bountiful as one of the torchmen, he turned the document over and vented his frustrations by writing a strongly worded letter to relatives in Bean Town, Connecticut. Speaking for many of his neighbors in the county, he denied the federal charges of lawbreaking in Utah and reaffirmed his willingness, if necessary, to abandon all he had:

> As a people, there are no more laws broken here than there are in Old Bean Town. We have the 4th of July, 24th of July, and New Years here, the same as in the rest of the world with the exception that we do not get drunk and break our shins. . . . How would you like to have Old Ireland [Buchanan's father was an Irish immigrant] send over to Bean Town a lot of petty officers with an army to back them to rule over you; and you not have the privilege of having a post master or any officer of your own townsmen, but have a pack of foreigners to make your laws for you? How would you like it? . . . If Doctor [Thomas L.] Kane had not of been sent in here last winter before the soldiers should have had our habitations, we would have burned the whole of the country and fled to the mountains. We could have used up all of the army that was sent here. If it had not been for our leaders, we would have done it.[64]

The Morrisite War, 1862

Two years after the Utah War, some residents of Davis County found themselves involved in another military skirmish. This one involved a confrontation with a group of about 200 Latter-day Saint dissenters at Kingston Fort on the Weber River. They were known as the Morrisites, after their leader, Joseph Morris. Born in England in 1824 and a convert to the Mormon church there in 1848, Morris migrated to St. Louis with his wife, Mary Thorpe. The couple spent time in St. Louis and in Pittsburgh, Pennsylvania. In both places, Morris became acquainted with the teachings of opponents of Brigham Young. During these formative years for his religious views, Morris experienced his first visions. His later doctrines of the transmigration of spirits (a type of reincarnation) echoed the teachings of Charles B. Thompson, a former Latter-day Saint living in St. Louis, who had been excommunicated for apostasy. Morris presided for a time in the Pittsburgh branch of the LDS church, but resigned over differences and moved to Utah in 1853. After a short stay in Salt Lake City, the family moved to Ephraim, where Morris's teachings were opposed by local church leaders and his wife left him. Morris then moved to Provo, where he remarried and served as a teacher in the Mormon Reformation; he then moved back to Salt Lake City.[65]

In December 1857 the thirty-three-year-old Morris sent his first letter to Brigham Young, complaining of the treatment he had received from church leaders in Utah County. In a second letter in October 1858 Morris presented himself as a prophet and deliverer of the Latter-day Saints. He challenged Young's prophetic authority while proposing that Young retain his administrative role in the church. In addition, Morris chided the Mormon church for excessive materialism and attacked the practice of plural marriage. Young ignored both letters, judging them to be the work of an illiterate, weak-minded man.[66]

Morris was not a very impressive individual physically, but he attracted followers because of his spiritual sensitivities. Of wiry, muscular build, he stood about five-foot six-inches tall. His handsome face featured an uncut beard, and his flowing black hair hung in soft curls about his head and neck. In England, Morris had labored on a farm and as a coal miner from his youth. Like Brigham Young, Morris had received little formal education. Severe burns in a mining accident may have affected his outlook on life. In St. Louis, Morris worked as a fireman on a steamboat. In Utah he sought work wherever he could find it, mostly as a farm laborer or hod carrier. He knew the toils of life and yearned for deliverance through the promises of religion.[67]

Letters to Brigham Young continued in 1859 and 1860, with Morris placing emphasis on the Second Advent of Christ and the beginning of the millennium. In some of his correspondence, Morris revealed that he had a demanding and militant spirit. He predicted a doomsday destruction of those who refused to follow him. Soon, Morris began a preaching mission in Utah. Rather than reform the Mormon church, however, he was now hinting at forming his own separatist community. Morris saw himself ushering in Christ's millennial kingdom on earth with a people who had been purified by the Mormon Reformation. He demonstrated his belief in continuing revelation by issuing a steady flow of written revelations—more than forty by February 1861. He intended to lead his people back to

Jackson County, Missouri—an early center of the Mormon church—to build the City of Zion.[68]

In the spring of 1860, Morris moved to Slaterville, in Weber County. Within months, local church leaders there invited him to leave. They also excommunicated thirty-one Latter-day Saints who accepted Morris as prophet. Morris made one last attempt to call Brigham Young to repentance, then moved forward with plans to establish his own church. Forced from Slaterville, Morris found a receptive audience in South Weber, at the time a settlement of fewer than one hundred Latter-day Saints. Among his earliest significant converts was Richard Cook, the South Weber LDS bishop, whose conversion influenced others to take seriously Morris's claims. Over the next several months, Morris attracted a following of nearly 200 people. Many of them moved to South Weber. Most residents who rejected Morris's teachings remained in the community.[69]

The growth of Morris's following prompted Brigham Young to send Wilford Woodruff and John Taylor to investigate the new prophet at Kingston Fort. Their visit in February 1861 led to the excommunication of seventeen members of the South Weber Ward who said they accepted Morris as a prophet, seer, and revelator to the church. Among them was Bishop Richard Cook. The Morrisites clustered in and around the ten-acre Fort Kingston, living in tents and wagon boxes. Many of them built new homes of wattle, made by interlacing willows and plastering them with mud. For meetings, they set up a large tent and bowery inside the fort.[70]

On 6 April 1861 Morris organized the Church of Jesus Christ of Saints of the Most High, known soon by a shortened title, the Morrisite church. By midsummer, membership reached 300, and Morris encouraged all members to gather to Fort Weber, where all property was consecrated to the church in preparation for Christ's Second Advent. A year later, the Morrisite church counted 507 baptized members, many of them Danish immigrants. Several hundred more were unbaptized believers. The organization included a First Presidency, with Morris and counselors Richard Cook and John Banks (an able English missionary and a friend of Morris from Pleasant Grove), and twelve apostles. The talented and outgoing

William Kendell an early Morrisite Apostle and his family were living in Uintah, at the mouth of Weber Canyon, when this photo was taken in July 1869. One of the first six persons to affiliate with Joseph Morris, Kendell was apparently "cut off" for refusing to consecrate all of his property. (Utah State Historical Society)

Banks, who had had a falling out with Brigham Young in 1858, played a key role as an orator for the naturally quiet Morris.[71]

As 1861 drew to a close, tensions within the Morrisite camp increased. Morris believed that Christ would come that year, and his followers, many of them poor, generally had not prepared adequate foodstuffs to sustain them beyond that time. Relationships were strained as well with the normally tolerant non-Morrisite community. Stigmatized as heretics and apostates in the larger community, the Morrisites were harassed by some local rowdies, who jeered at them and threatened to burn the fort. Disagreements between the Morrisites and their Latter-day Saint neighbors over livestock and the theft of some Morrisite horses increased tensions. The Morrisites appointed sentries to watch their herds, guards for firewood-collecting excursions into the canyons, and nightwatchmen around the camp. Their prophet's revelations defined all Latter-day Saint leaders and members as enemies of God and the Morrisites. Morris predicted a direct confrontation between the two groups to usher in the millennium. A directive in November 1861 even instructed his followers how to act if Utah authorities attempted to arrest him.[72]

Under these circumstances, some of the Morrisites became fearful for their safety. Morris tried to calm them with reassurances of divine protection; however, a few became disenchanted and left. His counselors disagreed over policy and administrative duties and with the meaning of Morris's revelations. Reprimands from the prophet did not solve the problem of disunity. A greater challenge to the unity of the Morrisite community was the failure of Morris's revelatory promises that the Lord would come unto His people before year's end. One revelation after another during December 1861 postponed Christ's appearance from one designated day of deliverance to another. However, when the New Year dawned without the expected millennium, only a few Morrisites departed; the majority remained at Fort Kingston through the cold and stormy winter of disappointment. A January revelation declared, "I shall not tell my people to prepare for me any more. . . . I shall come as a thief in the night."[73]

The anticipated confrontation with Mormon authorities came in 1862 over two legal issues that involved Davis County officials. One of these involved taxes, the other an incident over a load of wheat. Joseph Morris told his people to ignore the law of the land, since the law of God took precedence. The Morrisites therefore refused to pay their property taxes. County officials sent Sheriff Lot Smith to attach property in lieu of payment. In one incident, Smith attempted to take the horse of David Parks, but left when Parks intervened with the backing of several armed men. Smith then filed a complaint against Parks for resisting an officer.[74]

Latter-day Saint leaders counseled their members to avoid all dealings with the Morrisites. This made it difficult for the Morrisites to get their grain milled. Finally, they found a miller in Kaysville willing to turn their wheat into flour. In the spring of 1862, three Morrisite defectors living in Kaysville intercepted a load of flour and forced the teamster to abandon his team and wagon with its cargo. One of the defectors was William Jones, who had fled the Morrisite camp without his family. Several times, with no results, Jones had urged the Morrisite teamster to bring his wife and children to Kaysville. Soon afterward, an armed posse of about twenty Morrisites captured the three defectors, hauled them to the fort, and locked them in a log house at Kingston. A revelation on 8 May condemned them to die at a time to be designated later by the Lord.[75]

Seeking release of the captives, friends and family of the prisoners quickly filed a complaint with Chief Justice John F. Kinney of the Third District Court. On 22 May, Kinney ordered the Morrisite leaders to set the men free. The territorial marshal asked Judson L. Stoddard to deliver the habeas corpus writ. Stoddard took Thomas Abbott and Wells Smith with him. The three Davis County couriers were allowed inside the stockade, where Stoddard read the document to the assembled townspeople. John Banks, as spokesmen for Morris, refused to accept it. Stoddard tried again to hand the writ to Banks, but it fell to the ground and was burned by live coals brought from a nearby house.[76]

Morris appeared to be preparing for battle. By the time of Stoddard's visit, Morris had organized 142 soldiers into seven companies as the beginning of the "Army of the Kingdom." The men did not expect to fight their neighbors but, rather, to serve in a millennial world army after Christ's Second Coming. According to Morris's revelations, his people would witness a grand pageant on 30 May, the "Foreshadowing of the Kingdom of God Day." Soon afterward, an angelic army of the Lord would destroy the wicked and usher in the millennium.[77]

Stoddard claimed that he had been met by about sixty men from this Morrisite army when he attempted to delivered the writ. Most of them carried pistols, rifles, shotguns, or swords. On 10 June, Stoddard filed an official complaint against the Morrisites, explaining to Judge Kinney their reaction to his visit. Stoddard requested an armed posse to assist in a second attempt to deliver the writ. On the same day, two other Davis County residents, H. O. Hansen and Philo T. Allen, filed complaints describing the capture and detention of the prisoners. Judge Kinney acted immediately on Allen's affidavit and ordered the arrest of Joseph Morris, John Banks, Richard Cook, John Parson, and Peter Klemgaard. Territorial Marshal Henry W. Lawrence was absent from Utah on private business, so the responsibility fell to his chief deputy, Colonel Robert T. Burton. Acting Governor Frank Fuller authorized the use of militiamen as a *posse comitatus.* The posse included several hundred men drawn from ten different Latter-day Saint wards. Those called up from Davis County joined as the militia moved northward from Salt Lake City toward Kingston. According to Jacob Miller of Farmington, Davis County recruits doubled a 200-man force that came from Salt Lake, and another 100 men joined from Weber County. Burton hoped that the posse's massive size would intimidate Morris and cause his peaceful surrender.[78]

Though the posse acted under civil authority, it did so with the concurrence of Mormon church leader Brigham Young. Officially, the militia marched north to enforce a court order to arrest the five Morrisite leaders on charges of holding the defectors without due process of law. Members of the posse and its leaders also understood the religious aspects of the case, however. Morris and his council were seen not just as lawbreakers but as apostates. Similarly, the Morrisites did not view the challenging army as a federal posse. They were involved in a religious war; the opposing Mormons were seen as an evil force about to trigger Armageddon.[79]

Early on the morning of 13 June 1862, Burton positioned his forces on a high bluff south of Fort Kingston. He commandeered a Morrisite herdboy and sent him with a message to Morris demanding immediate surrender. Privately, Morris dictated a revelation promising safety for his people and the destruction of their enemies. He then gathered his followers in the bowery for prayer and to hear the writ and their prophet's latest revelation. While John Parson was reading the revelation, Burton ordered two warning shots from his vantage point 200 feet above the valley. The first cannonball flew over the fort. The second struck plowed ground and ricocheted into the crowded bowery, killing two women and breaking the lower jaw of a young girl. With the confusion caused by the unexpected attack, Richard Cook shouted to the Morrisites to flee to their homes and prepare to defend themselves.[80]

The Morrisite position was virtually indefensible. The flimsy fort was surrounded on the south and west by the high bluff controlled by Burton's men. Another 100 volunteers from Ogden perched across the swollen Weber River atop another bluff to the north that gave them a view inside the fort. Burton posted riflemen on the east and west sides of the fort. The riflemen on the downriver side took a posi-

Mary Anderson was hit in the jaw with a cannon ball when the posse attacked the Morrisite compound. She is seated with her husband, Neils, and surrounded by their eight children in this family photograph taken many years later. (Utah State Historical Society)

tion behind the mud walls of the old fort; the other group found a hiding place in brush along the river upstream. When the men started shooting, two Morrisite families came out, waving a white handkerchief. They were placed under guard. The Morrisites then released the prisoners they had taken in Kaysville. The Mormon soldiers interpreted this as an attempt to end the hostilities, but Morris saw it as part of a larger scheme in which all "hypocrites" would leave the fort, leaving only the "true and faithful."[81]

Most accounts say that the militia's artillerymen fired first and that the Morrisites only returned the fire. Militiaman Jared Smith was the first soldier killed. He died from a shot in the chest received when he rose up to see what a shot he had just fired had accomplished. When Burton reported this fatality and the resistance of the Morrisites, Acting-Governor Fuller instructed him to enforce the order to arrest the Morrisite leaders. Heavy rain during most of

Saturday, 14 June, hindered the posse; however, damage to the Morrisite fortification and to the homes inside discouraged the water-soaked inhabitants. They could not build fires or dry out soaked clothing or bedding. A number of the Morrisites surrendered.[82]

Clear weather on Sunday allowed Burton to storm the fort. His men prepared a battery out of three wagon wheels laced with willows and used it as a shield to advance toward the fort. Hungry and with little remaining ammunition, the Morrisites watched the advancing army, expecting a miraculous delivery. Their prophet had received a revelation that morning promising that the time of Christ's coming had arrived. The revelation directed them to continue their defense, which they did. Burton's men rushed a vacant home along the west perimeter of the fort, but in doing so they lost a second man, John Peter Wahlin. When the posse rolled their battery up against the fort, the Morrisites in adjacent homes fled to the far side of the fort. Resistance melted. When a bugle sounded in the fort, the Morrisites assembled and raised a white flag of surrender. Burton and his men entered the fort and collected the Morrisite arms.[83]

Burton had been sent to arrest Morris and four associates. He called for their unconditional surrender and told Morris he wanted all the men who had taken up arms against the posse. Undaunted, Morris invited his followers to die with him. A number of men moved toward him to accept the invitation. Burton interpreted the movement in the crowd as an attempt to recover their arms or to find a place of defense. When Morris ignored Burton's order to stop, the colonel fired several shots from his revolver. Morris fell dead. Other members of the posse also fired. John Banks suffered a fatal wound to the neck. Two women also died. "Even when Morris was shot and fell lifeless to the ground we did not think him dead," a Morrisite witness later said. "We considered him invulnerable, or that if he should be killed he would be immediately restored to life." But with the death of their prophet, resistance ended. The posse left Fort Kingston with ninety Morrisite men as prisoners. Judge Kinney placed them under bond to appear in the spring 1863 session of the court. The bodies of Morris and Banks were viewed by thousands at Salt Lake City. Morris's robe, crown, and rod lay by his side.[84]

At the court session in March 1863, seven Morrisite men were convicted of murder and sentenced to prison. Sixty-six others received $100 fines for resisting arrest, and two were acquitted. Utah Territory's new governor, Stephen S. Harding, who had arrived the previous July, subsequently concluded that the Mormons had been too heavy-handed in their treatment of the Morrisites and issued a full pardon. Harding was supported in his decision by the non-Mormon community. Among them were the soldiers of Colonel Patrick E. Connor, who had arrived in Utah in November 1862 and established Fort Douglas on the hill above Salt Lake City to watch over the Mormons.

Chief Justice Kinney and most Latter-day Saints condemned the pardon. A grand jury composed mostly of Mormons declared the governor "not only a dangerous man, but also as one unworthy the confidence and respect of a free and enlightened people." Latter-day Saints petitioned President Abraham Lincoln to remove him from office. Non-Mormons countered with a petition for Judge Kinney's removal. Lincoln transferred Harding to Colorado as chief justice there and removed Kinney from his post. Utahns then rewarded Kinney with an appointment to Congress, the only non-Mormon to serve as a territorial delegate until the 1890s.

In 1879 a jury equally represented by Mormons and non-Mormons tried Robert T. Burton and pronounced him not guilty of murder in the death of one of the two women killed during the assault at Kingston Fort. The women were no doubt accidental casualties in the confusion surrounding the event. Politics in the territory had taken a turn in the years after the Utah War. While locally the Mormons dominated, territorial officials represented the non-Mormon community. This division reinforced local feelings about government and heightened the tensions that played out over the next quarter-century.[85]

The winter of 1862–63 proved difficult for the Morrisites left behind at Kingston Fort. The wives and children of the arrested men were in a desperate condition, lacking even the basic necessities. Many Latter-day Saint neighbors provided food, clothing, and shelter, and Brigham Young sent a doctor to care for the wounded. Some of Morris's followers rejoined the Mormons; others left the territory, including Morrisite apostle Mark A. Forscutt, who later became an influential missionary, editor, chorister, and hymn writer for the Reorganized Church of Jesus Christ of Latter Day Saints.[86]

The pardon of the convicted Morrisites created a hostile environment for them in Utah and led to other legal challenges. Many of the Morrisites held to their faith in an imminent Second Advent and had come to see Joseph Morris as a forerunner of the expected millennium, but they lacked a clear leader. Even with the supportive political climate in Utah, the Morrisites concluded that their best prospects for peace lay in removal elsewhere. A portion of them, including Richard Cook, traveled to Carson City, Nevada, in the spring of 1863 with a military supply train from Fort Douglas. At the same time, Colonel Connor sent a second train to Soda Springs, Idaho, to establish a colony. Other Morrisites accompanied these troops and established a settlement there. A few Morrisites remained in Utah, while others moved to California, Washington, and elsewhere. The scattering of the Davis-Weber Morrisite colony led to factionalism and competing leadership within the movement. This disunity persisted among the Morrisites despite the appearance over the years of a number of claimants to Joseph Morris's leadership. Eventually death and affiliation with other churches brought an end to the Morrisite church in the 1940s.[87]

ENDNOTES

1. James B. Allen and Glen M. Leonard, *The Story of the Latter-day Saints* (Salt Lake City: Deseret Book, 1992), 284–85.

2. For example, see Truman Leonard, Journal, 4, 21 February 1857, LDS Church Archives; Thomas S. Smith, Journal, 21 February, 7 July 1857, LDS Church Archives.

3. Les Foy, *The City Bountiful,* 97; Truman Leonard, Journal, entry for second week of October 1856, LDS Church Archives; Annie Call Carr, *East of Antelope Island,* 450.

4. *Journal of Discourses* (Liverpool: S.W. and F.D. Richards, 1854–1886), 3:293–94; Brigham Young, sermon, 6 July 1864, in *Deseret News,* 15 July 1864.

5. Farmington Ward, Teachers Minutes, 22 February 1863, 18 December 1864, 12 February 1865.

6. Carr, *East of Antelope Island*, 267, 423; Leonard, Journal, 30 December 1856.

7. *Deseret News,* 29 August 1855.

8. *Deseret News,* 20 August 1856; Kate B. Carter, ed., *Heart Throbs of the West* (Salt Lake City: Daughters of Utah Pioneers, 1939–51), 4:135–37; Journal History of the Church of Jesus Christ of Latter–day Saints, 3 October 1857, 24 July 1860.

9. Foy, *City Bountiful,* 97–99; Carr, *East of Antelope Island,* 432, 442–45.

10. Examples can be found in minutes of ward meetings preserved in the LDS Archives and in some individual diaries of county residents.

11. Margaret Steed Hess, *My Farmington,* 281; Carol I. Collett, *Kaysville—Our Town,* 81; Foy, *City Bountiful,* 81; Carr, *East of Antelope Island,* 319.

12. Hess, *My Farmington,* 276–79; Collett, *Kaysville—Our Town,* 22.

13. Allen and Leonard, *Story of the Latter–day Saints,* 288; Foy, *City Bountiful,* 102.

14. See Gustive O. Larson, "The Mormon Reformation," *Utah Historical Quarterly* 26 (January 1958): 46–53; and Thomas G. Alexander, "Wilford Woodruff and the Mormon Reformation of 1855–57," *Dialogue: A Journal of Mormon Thought* 25 (Summer 1992): 25–39.

15. *Journal of Discourses* 4:60–61, 72; Alexander, "Wilford Woodruff," 26–27.

16. Alexander, "Wilford Woodruff," 27; *Deseret News,* 1 October 1856.

17. Glen M. Leonard, "History of Farmington to 1983" (M.A. thesis, University of Utah, 1963), 55; *Deseret News,* 24 September 1856.

18. *Deseret News,* 1 October 1856; Leonard, "History of Farmington, 55.

19. *Deseret News,* 8 October 1856.

20. Ibid.

21. *Deseret News,* 7 January 1857; *Journal of Discourses* 4:146.

22. From an 1856 manuscript in the LDS Archives, quoted in Paul H. Peterson, "The Mormon Reformation of 1856–1857: The Rhetoric and the Reality," *Journal of Mormon History* 15 (1989): 70. Other versions of the catechism, most of them without the practical applications quoted here, are in Juanita Brooks, *John D. Lee: Zealot, Pioneer Builder, Scapegoat* (Glendale, California: Arthur H. Clark, 1972), 193–94; Brooks, *Mountain Meadows Massacre* (Norman: University of Oklahoma Press, 1962), 12; and Larson, "The Mormon Reformation," 53–55.

23. Alexander, "Wilford Woodruff," 33–34. The specific impact of the

Reformation on polygamous marriages in Davis County has not been studied. Findings from a study of the 1880 census are reported in a later chapter of this history.

24. Leonard, "History of Farmington," 55–56; *Deseret News,* 24 September 1856; Peterson, "The Mormon Reformation," 71–72, 76; Alexander, "Wilford Woodruff," 30.

25. Alexander, "Wilford Woodruff," 31–33, 35–36; Leonard, "History of Farmington," 56.

26. Thomas G. Alexander, *Utah, The Right Place: The Official Centennial History* (Salt Lake City: Gibbs Smith, 1995), 117–24.

27. Leonard, Journal, 1 July 1857; Milton D. Hammond, Journal, 4 July 1857, Marriott Library, University of Utah.

28. Joseph L. Robinson, Autobiography, 73 (1849), 101 (1853?), 106 (1855), LDS Church Archives; Linda Thatcher, "The State Symbols of Utah, *Beehive History* 12 (1986): 8.

29. Carr, *East of Antelope Island,* 499.

30. *Ordinances of the General Assembly of the State of Deseret* (Great Salt Lake City, 1851), 12–13, 15–17; *Deseret News,* 5 October 1850.

31. *Ordinances of the General Assembly,* 33.

32. Joseph L. Robinson, Journal, 100, entry for 25 March 1854, LDS Church Archives; *Ordinances of the General Assembly,* 15–17; Foy, *City Bountiful,* 109–10.

33. *Deseret News,* 29 April 1857.

34. Carr, *East of Antelope Island,* 494,; Journal History, 26 May 1849, 3.

35. Thomas S. Smith, Journal, July 1857, LDS Church Archives.

36. Alexander, *Utah, The Right Place,* 126.

37. Leonard, "History of Farmington," 65–66; Foy, *City Bountiful,* 109–10; *Journal of Discourses* 5: 228–34; Richard D. Poll, et al., eds., *Utah's History,* 167–68; *Deseret News,* 7 October 1857.

38. Alexander, *Utah, The Right Place,* 128–29; Foy, *City Bountiful,* 112–13.

39. "Narrative of Lot Smith" (written 1882–83), in LeRoy R. Hafen and Ann W. Hafen, eds., *The Utah Expedition, 1857–1858: A Documentary Account*. . . (Glendale, CA: Arthur H. Clark, 1958), 220–25, 231–32, 236–37.

40. Ibid., 227–28, 232, 235, 242.

41. Ibid., 243–46.

42. Leonard, *Farmington,* 65–66, 68; Hafen and Hafen, *The Utah Expedition,* 196.

43. Hugh O'Neil, "Deseret Brass Band of Farmington," in Carter, *Heart Throbs of the West,* 4:135–37.

44. Journal History, 15 December 1857, 6–7, 12 January, and various entries during February 1858.

45. *Deseret News,* 27 January 1858; Journal History, 18 January 1858.

46. Andrew Jenson, "Kaysville Ward," manuscript history, LDS Church Archives; Journal History, 27 January 1858.

47. Alexander, *Utah, The Right Place,* 134–35; Richard D. Poll, "The Utah War," in Allan Kent Powell, ed., *Utah History Encyclopedia* (Salt Lake City: University of Utah Press, 1994), 607; Journal History, 22 April 1858. A complete history is Clifford L. Stott, *Search for Sanctuary: Brigham Young and the White Mountain Expedition* (Salt Lake City: University of Utah Press, 1984).

48. Journal History, 15 April 1858; Hafen and Hafen, *The Utah Expedition,* 287; Otis G. Hammond, ed., *The Utah Expedition, 1857–1858* (Concord: New Hampshire Historical Society, 1928), 288; Thomas E. Cheney, ed., *Mormon Songs from the Rocky Mountains: A Compilation of Mormon Folksongs* (Austin: University of Texas Press, 1968), 84–86. A version of "Doo Dah" from *Deseret News,* 17 February 1858, and another antifederalist song (Cheney, no. 33) are found in Claude T. Barnes, *The Grim Years; or, The Life of Emily Stewart Barnes* (1949; reprint, Kaysville: Inland Printing, 1964), 69–70.

49. Alexander, *Utah, The Right Place,* 135; Poll, "The Utah War," 607.

50. Leonard, "History of Farmington," 70–71; Journal History, 22 April 1858.

51. Reprinted in *Latter–day Saints' Millennial Star* 20:469.

52. This estimate of numbers is based on an extrapolation of the 1850 and 1860 census figures for the five affected counties. The 1860 census reported 22,087 people in Salt Lake and counties to the north. Ten years earlier, the count was 8,477. Assuming a steady growth, the population in 1857 would be about 16,565. Some estimates have placed the evacuees as high as 30,000, but that would involve all Utah residents in 1857. Brigham Young's advice was given in a sermon (Journal History, 28 March 1858).

53. See Journal History, 25 April 1858.

54. Foy, *The City Bountiful,* 114–15; Andrew Jenson, "Bountiful Ward," manuscript history, LDS Church Archives; Journal History, 23 April 1858.

55. Leonard, "History of Farmington, 70–73.

56. Collett, *Kaysville—Our Town,* 71–72; Barnes, *The Grim Years,* 69.

57. Lee D. Bell, *South Weber,* 67.

58. Audrey M. Godfrey, Camp Floyd," in Powell, *Utah History Encyclopedia,* 66–67.

59. Leonard, "History of Farmington," 73.

60. Milton D. Hammond, "Journal," Marriott Library, University of Utah, 56; Barnes, *The Grim Years,* 69.

61. Leonard, "History of Farmington, 74; Foy, *City Bountiful,* 122.

62. Collett, *Kaysville—Our Town,* 74.

63. Ibid., 71. The two–year supply is mentioned in Foy, *City Bountiful,* 121.

64. Newton Tuttle to his brother and sister, 27 June 1858, original in private possession, reproduced in Foy, *The City Bountiful,* 121–22.

65. C. LeRoy Anderson, *For Christ Will Come Tomorrow: The Saga of the Morrisites* (Logan: Utah State University Press, 1981), 37–44; G.M. Howard, "Men, Motives, and Misunderstandings: A New Look at the Morrisite War of 1862," *Utah Historical Quarterly* 44 (Spring 1976): 113–14.

66. Anderson, *Saga of the Morrisites,* 14–15, 31–34; Howard, "The Morrisite War," 114.

67. Howard, "The Morrisite War," 113; Anderson, *Saga of the Morrisites,* 37, 43, 71.

68. Anderson, *Saga of the Morrisites,* 45–49, 57–60, 64–65.

69. Ibid., 55–58, 65; Howard, "The Morrisite War," 115–16.

70. Anderson, *Saga of the Morrisites,* 65–68, Howard, "The Morrisite War," 116–17, 120.

71. Howard, "The Morrisite War," 117–19, 131; Anderson, *Saga of the Morrisites,* 69–73.

72. Anderson, *Saga of the Morrisites,* 74–88, 91–92; Howard, "The Morrisite War," 119–22.

73. Anderson, *Saga of the Morrisites,* 89–95, 99; Howard, "The Morrisite War," 123–24.

74. Anderson, *Saga of the Morrisites,* 101–2.

75. Ibid., 100–106, 108; Howard, "The Morrisite War," 124.

76. Anderson, *Saga of the Morrisites,* 106–7, 113.

77. Ibid., 109–10.

78. Ibid., 112–20; Howard, "The Morrisite War," 124–25.

79. Anderson, *Saga of the Morrisites,* 117–18, 132–34; Howard, "The Morrisite War," 132.

80. Anderson, *Saga of the Morrisites,* 120–24, 132; Howard, "The Morrisite War," 125–26.

81. Anderson, *Saga of the Morrisites,* 128–33.

82. Ibid., 133–36.

83. Ibid., 136–40.

84. Ibid., 140–44, 155–56.

85. Ibid., 144, 148–51, 155–56; Howard, "The Morrisite War," 126–31; Alexander, *Utah, The Right Place,* 147.

86. Anderson, *Saga of the Morrisites,* 147; Richard P. Howard, *The Church Through the Years* (Independence, MO: Herald House, 1993), 2:25, 129, 189, 199.

87. Anderson, *Saga of the Morrisites,* 151, 159–62, 228–29.

CHAPTER 4

LIVING ON THE LAND

In its present definition, Davis County is the smallest in area of Utah's twenty-nine counties. With fewer than 300 square miles, it is noticeably smaller than the second and third smallest counties, neighboring Weber and Morgan, with their 600 or so square miles. Within Davis County, the Great Salt Lake on the west and the steep Wasatch Range on the east taken together reduce the habitable area by almost one-third. Furthermore, Antelope Island—dry, and isolated by the briny lake—was useful in the nineteenth century only as a range for cattle. For all practical purposes, Davis County exists as a narrow strip of land east of the lake measuring twenty-three miles from north to south and varying in width from three miles at the Farmington-Centerville boundary to fifteen miles at the county's northern border.[1]

Reference to this contiguous land area does not entirely define the county's size. For hundreds of years, the shallow lake's meandering shoreline has reached into some of the adjacent lowlands, leaving alkaline sediments and creating marshy areas unsuitable for agriculture and many other uses. As they have done for ages, however, these wetlands do sustain native and migratory birds and other wildlife. On the gently sloping ancient lake terraces and foothills between the saline flatland and the mountain slopes Mormon settlers found a fertile soil rich in humus, moistened naturally by a sparse sixteen inches of water in an average year. In its native state, grasses and sagebrush covered the lower vegetation zone. Cottonwoods appeared along the streams and scrub oak on the upper benchlands. It was in this environment along the eastern shore area of the ancient lake that the Numic peoples had cultivated gardens, gathered seeds and berries, and stalked game. In this same area the new settlers established irrigated farms, planted orchards and gardens, and grazed livestock.[2]

Humans and the Land

For the Weber Utes of the early nineteenth century, the east-shore land was a resource to be used communally but not claimed individually. Small bands occupied definable sites, with designated living and farming areas, sacred places, and burial grounds. They hunted wildlife, gathered berries, and raised corn and squash. These peoples undoubtedly loved the place of their homeland and respected the land and its resources.[3]

The Latter-day Saints who occupied these same lands beginning in the late 1840s also came to call the land home. But they defined the use of natural resources differently. They brought with them the patterns of Anglo-Saxon property ownership as refined in the early American colonies and tempered by a pattern of cooperative economics drawn from their religious worldview. The early Mormon settlers of Davis County accepted the guidance of their religious leaders in the allocation of scarce resources, including land, timber, and water. In many aspects of daily life, they survived by helping one another. They cooperated to tame the wilderness, to provide for their needs, and to minimize the impact of natural and human hazards.

Through the entire pioneer period, the chief economic interest of Davis County's residents was agriculture. Most of the men farmed either as a full-time occupation or as a sideline. Agriculture provided the raw materials for other industries, including gristmills, tanneries, and creameries. It supplied work for farm laborers and for some skilled workers. Older boys helped their fathers with chores, irrigation, and harvesting of the crops. Many women worked in the fields alongside their husbands. In addition, women tended the gardens, helped with the dairying, prepared meals, and made clothing for the family. Girls helped in household duties, gardened, and sometimes herded livestock.[4]

Merchants appeared gradually on the scene in Davis County, at first as a sideline, and later as a full-time occupation. Similarly, skilled workers in clothing production and other crafts sometimes worked both in their specialized skill and as farmers in order to provide for their families. Blacksmiths, coopers, and millers were among those most likely to find a full-time need for their services. The census reports of occupations in 1850 and ten years later suggest the steady evolution from an essentially agrarian economy to one more diverse. In the 1850 census report four times as many residents listed themselves as farmers as all other occupations combined. Ten years later, however, farmers accounted for only half the working adults.[5] By 1870, at the end of the settlement period, economic diversification was firmly established on a solid agrarian base.

Residents turned often to neighboring Salt Lake County and, at times, to Weber County for some services and products, making it less necessary to develop such sources inside Davis County. The availability of highly specialized services and trades and the presence of import merchants in Salt Lake City allowed agriculture to remain a more dominant occupation in Davis County than it might otherwise have been. And the county prospered as an agricultural mecca. Near the end of the pioneer period, a reporter traveling with Brigham Young on one of his regular visits to the northern settlements observed with a note of optimism, "There is an air of thrift and plenty about Davis county that assures the traveler that the farmers of that favored section are well-to-do. It would be difficult to find a richer spot of ground in the Territory; even the weeds along the sides of the road attain a rank luxuriance that is not seen elsewhere."[6]

The patterns of the workaday world common to most men in early Davis County centered around the seasonal cycle of the farmer. A typical year followed a pattern known to farmers over countless centuries. As soon as the soil dried sufficiently in the spring, the farmer would hitch a harrow behind a horse or ox and break up the clods that had been turned by a plow the previous fall. This was followed by the sowing of wheat or other grains, broadcast style, and the planting of garden crops in rows. During the growing season, the challenge was to nurture the crops to provide the largest possible yield. Row crops were hoed to control weeds, then furrowed and irrigated to moisten the summer-dried soil. Farmers used flood irrigation on grain and hay fields. Gathering the harvest often involved hired hands or cooperative efforts among neighbors. It took many hours to scythe the grain, bind and haul it from the field, and then separate it on a threshing floor. After field crops were stored away, the farmers turned to fall plowing. As the weather cooled, they obtained firewood from the canyons. Winter months were spent repairing equipment and tools and caring for livestock. In all seasons, the daily chores of a farmstead continued.[7]

Securing and Surveying Farmland. The first Latter-day Saint settlers claimed their homesites and surrounding farmlands and described them by terms of metes and bounds. Inevitably, without the benefit of a surveyor, claims of this type created the potential for misunderstanding among neighbors. When such disputes arose, it was often the LDS bishop and his council who were called upon to propose a fair resolution. Sometimes parties called in outside help; for example, in 1850 Brigham Young accompanied surveyor William Lemon to Bountiful to resolve a boundary feud.[8]

Latter-day Saint bishops in Davis County saw to it that those emigrants arriving soon after the first settlers also received land. Under a policy established by Brigham Young in July 1847, land was alloted without charge, the only obligation being that a farmer "must be industrious and take care of it." Thereafter, with certain restrictions, landowners could sell or trade their property.[9] To avoid land speculation, individual claims in Utah were kept small and productive, typically from five acres to forty acres. Only a few squatters claimed more than sixty acres, and rarely was a full section—160 acres—or more claimed.[10]

Because fertile soil was vital to their survival as farmers, settlers in Davis County sought the best irrigable agricultural land available. By the end of 1850, the 149 farmers of Davis County reported more than 2,000 acres of farmland under cultivation, or about 28 percent

Because millers kept a portion of the flour they ground for clients as payment for their services, they became important flour merchants during times of shortage. The large rock mill that Frederick Kesler built for Franklin D. Richards at the mouth of Farmington canyon is Davis County's only surviving pioneer grist mill. (Utah State Historical Society)

of their total holdings. The average size of a farm was fifty-two acres, only slightly above the average for the territory. An average of fourteen acres of this was improved and thirty-eight acres unimproved, including pastures and foothills. Holdings in the county ranged in size from ten acres to 185 acres. The farms in Centerville and Farmington, the narrow part of the county, averaged just over forty acres, those in Bountiful and Kaysville around sixty acres.[11]

Within a few years, and until dry farming and canals made the northwestern portion of the county more agriculturally productive, all that remained of this limited pool of land was the shared pasture and grazing land. Some families filed on more than they could immediately use. In Brigham Young's view, this was speculation on future sale, even though landowners may have seen it a reserve for their maturing sons or as a commercial opportunity manageable with hired help. During the Mormon consecration movement in the late

1850s, some bishops asked local farmers to relinquish their fertile but uncultivated land. In one Davis County community, thirty landless residents received property through this redistribution effort.[12]

Until January 1848 the Great Basin was part of Mexico's Upper California province and no government officials were nearby to regulate immigrants' claims to the lands used by the Numic peoples and their predecessors. The Latter-day Saint settlers established their own governmental system, first under the Council of Fifty and high council, then under the Provisional State of Deseret. The first step at regularizing property lines east of the Great Salt Lake was taken between 1848 and 1850, probably working through the county from south to north. An official surveyor visited each cluster of farmers to establish common fields and to describe existing individual claims. Following the pattern established in Salt Lake County, and imitating a practice used by Latter-day Saints in Far West, Missouri, each community surveyed a "Big Field." It included many smaller private farms enclosed by a single, community fence. According to Nathan T. Porter, at least one field in Centerville was surveyed in 1848. The general surveys in Bountiful and Centerville probably took place in 1849.[13] The typical process can be illustrated with information available on what happened in Farmington. In mid-November 1849 William M. Lemon of Salt Lake City enlisted the help of local assistants. Together they created garden plots along the west banks of North Cottonwood Creek as well as a community field farther west and south.[14] Edward Phillips remembered that he helped Lemon survey west Kaysville in 1850.[15]

These first land surveys in Davis County were underway when government agent Captain Howard Stansbury arrived in Utah for a scientific survey of the Great Salt Lake and surrounding lands. His 1850 map clearly identifies the surveyed parcels as a continuous strip extending from Bountiful through Farmington, with additional patches for the three clusters of settlers in the Kaysville-Layton area. The land between Holmes Creek and Kay's Creek was surveyed later that year.[16]

After Utah became a territory in 1850, government surveyors continued the process of defining land ownership. In 1855–56 territorial surveyors established section lines and laid out townsites. County surveyors confirmed the boundaries of farmlands that had been divided into individual parcels. The Mormon squatters had staked out their farms by placing a pole at each corner. They registered their claims with the surveyor for a small fee and received a certificate as evidence of ownership. Territorial law required the owner to fence the surveyed land within one year or the title would be nullified and the land become common property subject to claim by others. Owners could sell land with a written quit-claim deed registered with the county recorder.[17]

Only after the United States government established a land office in Utah in 1869 were federally recognized titles secured. Once the office was functioning, Davis County's landowners individually filed their claims to confirm the titles they had obtained over the previous twenty years. To make certain of the accuracy of the new claims, county officials paid Utah Surveyor General Jesse W. Fox to resurvey all section lines.[18]

Crops and Livestock. The farmlands of Davis County proved fruitful right from the first harvests. For the year ended 1 June 1850, with 2,075 acres under cultivation, the county's farmers reported harvesting more than 13,000 bushels of wheat, nearly 7,000 bushels of potatoes, and more than 2,000 bushels each of oats and corn. These were the major field crops and were used primarily for human consumption. The crops averaged out per household at eighty-eight bushels of wheat, forty-six bushels of potatoes, sixteen bushels of oats, and fourteen bushels of corn. Two-thirds of the farmers harvested wild hay to help feed their livestock during the winter, with an average yield of more than six tons per harvester. The yield typically ranged from one ton to a dozen, with highs of forty and seventy tons from two large fields.[19]

Most farms in early Davis County included livestock—both working stock and animals that helped feed and clothe the pioneer families. The most common working animals were oxen, needed to prepare the fields for planting. The 1850 census reported 616 oxen in the county, enough for each farm to have four. Of course, they were not evenly distributed, but only 20 percent of farms reported having no oxen. Almost all of those who reported no oxen owned one to three horses. Eighty percent of all households in the county owned at least one horse. Very few families owned mules; of the forty-four head reported, ten belonged to John Barnard in Centerville, eight to his neighbor Justin Stoddard, and six to Eric Hogan of Bountiful.[20]

All but five homes in the county (all of them in Bountiful) reported owning milch cows. Most homes kept at least one cow to provide fresh milk for drinking. Other families owned several cows in order to make butter and cheese. A typical family kept two or three cows. Enough butter was produced in Davis County during the year period ending 1 June 1850 to provide 107 pounds per household. Cheese production averaged eighty pounds per family. About 40 percent of the households reported owning "other cattle," presumably beef cattle. Most of the owners reported having at least a single animal to as much as a herd of a dozen or so.

Other useful animals serving the needs of Davis County's pioneers were pigs and sheep. Nearly 70 percent of the county's residents kept swine in 1850. The average was two pigs per household, and the number seldom exceeded four or five. Bacon, ham, and lard were typical products. Sheep were owned by only 15 percent of the residents, and the herds were typically small. The exceptions were Alonzo Buckland's herd of 250 sheep and Joel Ricks's herd of 125. The other owners averaged twenty head each. The spring shearing yielded a reported 1,800 pounds of wool for use in making yarn and cloth.[21]

Food Processing and Production

Gristmills. The earliest businesses in Davis County supported the agrarian economy by processing grain for human and animal food and by providing materials for housing. Getting a commercial milling operation underway to grind corn and wheat into meal and flour was a high priority for pioneers. During the first years, residents hauled their wheat to Salt Lake City to the small City Creek gristmill opened in 1848 by John Crismon or to John Neff's large flouring-mill operation finished later that summer at Mill Creek. Recognizing the need for service closer to home, Samuel Parrish built a crude gristmill at Centerville in 1848 to provide temporary service.[22]

By the mid-1850s three of Davis County's towns had their own full-scale gristmills. The first was a frame structure built for Willard Richards at the mouth of North Cottonwood Canyon in Farmington. It began operating before 1 September 1852 and was replaced a few

The couple in this 1907 photograph are posed in front of the abandoned Heber C. Kimball rock and adobe grist mill, opened in Bountiful in 1860. (Utah State Historical Society)

years later by a handsome—and more expensive than anticipated—three-story rock building built for Franklin D. Richards, Willard's nephew. It opened not far from the original site in April 1860, outfitted with new equipment and grinding stones.[23]

In Bountiful, Heber C. Kimball began a gristmill in 1852 and opened it the next year. This may have been a small mill, because the larger, more efficient three-level adobe building on North Mill Creek seems to have been built in 1859–60. It measured forty-eight feet by thirty feet, the largest in the county.[24] In 1854 John Weinel, a German-born miller who had worked for several years with John Neff, began serving residents of the Kaysville area with his small mill on Spring Creek, just outside the fort. He served patrons as far away as South Weber. Settlers in that community also sometimes took their grain to mills on the Weber and Ogden rivers.[25]

These first gristmill operators eventually had competitors, who saw the opportunity to meet a growing demand for their services. By the mid-1860s Farmington's stream powered two new mills. The "Red Mill"—a frame structure painted red—was built by Charles Bourne and Henry Steed near the mouth of the canyon, and an adobe mill owned by Thomas Steed operated on the city ditch just inside the mud-wall fort's northeast corner.[26] In Kaysville, Christopher Layton teamed up with Salt Lake businessman William Jennings in 1866 to build a turbine gristmill not far from Weinel's pioneer mill. Business was sufficient to keep both in operation for a time.[27] Anson V. Call and several associates in the cooperative association at Stoker opened a new gristmill on Deuel Creek in May 1867. Though named the Centerville Rock Mill, the large facility served a clientele extending into the north Bountiful area.[28]

Most owners of the early water-powered gristmills turned to experienced millwrights to design and construct their facilities. Heber C. Kimball hired Frederick Kesler, one of Utah's best-known mill builders. Appleton Harmon installed the milling equipment.[29] Henry Lyman Hinman built the two Steed mills in Farmington and, with his sons, Henry and Morgan, built other mills elsewhere.[30] John Weinel built his own mill over a three-year period, using native stones for the foundation, local timber for the framing, and red brick from Bountiful for the walls of the twenty- by-forty-foot mill. Anson Call's rock mill was built by a millwright named Lancaster.[31]

The buildings and their machinery followed the patterns of gristmills built elsewhere in the United States. The larger mills built for Franklin Richards and Heber Kimball by Frederick Kesler had three levels. They followed Kesler's preferred style, with a stepped gable roof, known as the clerestory monitor pattern.[32] Weinel and Call (and possibly Willard Richards) built smaller structures—a main floor over a basement level, where the cog pits held the gear wheels. These buildings had a simple gable roof. For fifteen years, Weinel's mill used hard, porous millstones hauled from the Oquirrh Mountains near Bingham Canyon; imported stones later replaced them.[33] The principal products of the mills were a course meal (from corn or wheat) and fine whole-wheat flour. By-products included feed for livestock, pigs, and chickens, including shorts, middlings, and offal.[34]

Even though mills were strategically placed to try to ensure a steady flow of water, variations in annual snowfalls and streamflows impacted the millers' work. Heber C. Kimball reported in August 1855 that water was so scarce he was not able "to grind over 7 or 10 bushels in the twenty-four hours."[35] Other appropriation of water could also jeopardize milling. Because irrigation depleted a stream, by common agreement the mill had first claim to the water. If farmers attempted to access the stream above the mill, the county court and Latter-day Saint church officials stepped in to enforce the milling rights. On the other hand, if the miller lost the valuable liquid by failing to keep his millrace in repair as the water exited, the farmers complained. Both problems surfaced from time to time during Davis County's early years.[36]

The day-to-day operation of each of the county's mills was entrusted to a skilled miller. Only in the case of John Weinel's mill in Kaysville was the mill built and operated by an owner who was himself a miller. As his pay, the miller retained a one-third portion of the grain he milled. Because community members interacted regularly with the miller and depended upon him for an essential service, he usually was trusted as a friend, and the building where he worked was viewed as a community landmark. In addition to their economic and social contributions, most mills also played a religious role in the community. Latter-day Saints used the millpond for baptisms and the miller's home as a dressing room and a place for confirmations.[37]

Molasses mills. If corn meal and wheat flour provided the bread to sustain life, sugar supplied the sweetener. Yet it was many years before large-scale sugar factories appeared in Utah. Besides a little wild honey that some were able to gather, the initial solution in every community was to squeeze the juice out of carrots, pumpkins, watermelons, or parsnips and then boil out a molasses sweetener. By the 1850s, molasses was being produced from sugar cane and sweet sorghum (a sweet-stalked, corn-like grass). Every Davis County town had several small molasses mills functioning during the pioneer period. Some were turned by horses; many others used water-powered crushers. For consumption, women mixed the fresh molasses with peaches or crabapples to make a candied fruit preserve. Some of the sweetener was stored in barrels for winter use. A thickened syrup could be pulled to make candy.[38]

These local mills may not have survived had Brigham Young's hopes for a sugar beet industry succeeded. Experiments with sugar beets began in Utah in 1850. Despite a huge investment in equipment and attempts over several years to refine the process, the effort failed.

Young then shifted his emphasis to the production of sorghum cane. He distributed free seed to encourage the commercial production of molasses by farmers.[39]

As was the case with other mills in Davis County, it was necessary to obtain permission from the county court to divert water from local canyon streams to power the molasses machinery. The court set specific restrictions with each grant to protect local irrigation and culinary needs.[40] The court also left to local ward bishops the resolution of problems created by conflicting claims caused by its willingness to grant multiple permits on the same stream or main water ditch in a town.[41]

A few molasses producers in each community followed Brigham Young's counsel and became suppliers to neighbors and to merchants. In some instances, especially after sugar cane was introduced locally in the 1860s, these businessmen supplied a substantial number of customers, including some in adjacent towns. Settlers preferred the higher-quality cane sweetener to their own homemade substitute. The local molasses industry was phased out in the final years of the century after Utah-made beet sugar became available through a processing factory in Lehi.[42]

Kitchen gardens. Every family supplemented the basic farm crops of wheat and other grains, hay, potatoes, and corn, with vegetables and fruits grown in a backyard garden on their city lot. Settlers also gathered some wild berries and used wild game. Kitchen gardens provided squash, turnips, carrots, and other crops for winter storage and a variety of summer foods. Pioneer women also raised herbs for seasoning foods and for medications.[43]

Apples were quite easy to grow. Many families also raised peaches, plums, and cherries. All of these fruits could be dried for storage. Apples were used as well for cider and vinegar. The backyard produced other food besides that grown in gardens and small orchards. Chickens and pigs provided meat. Butter, eggs, cheese, and milk were often produced in quantities that gave a family surplus for use in paying tithes and offerings or for bartering for dry goods from merchants or services.[44]

Challenges of nature. The task of turning a newly settled land into a productive agricultural Eden challenged the hardworking early set-

After Davis County's farmers became settled, they often built barns after an English pattern seen in this example owned by Charles A. Miller in Farmington. The large doors (behind the shed) open on a central threshing floor, with side aisles for stock or hay. (Charles G. Miller)

tlers of Davis County. They fought crickets and grasshoppers, weeds, wolves, and fires. They faced the vagaries of climate and weather, including threats of frost, wind, and drouth. From one season to another, in order to survive on the food they raised, the first generations maintained a constant vigilance against nature's challenges.

The earliest Davis County settlers experienced the cricket invasions of 1848 and 1849. "The crickets came like the locusts in the days of Moses," Perrigrine Sessions reported. Like the settlers in Salt Lake County, farmers harvested diminished crops those years, the damaged mitigated by swarming seagulls that ate some of the insects. Over the next several years, the number of crickets in Davis County was reduced and the threat they posed to agriculture largely disappeared.[45]

Grasshoppers threatened tender spring plants throughout the pioneer period. At least six times before 1870 these insects seriously damaged crops in Davis County. Hardest hit were the crops of 1849, 1854, 1855, 1860, 1868, and 1870. The combined impact of insects, late frosts, cold winds, summer hailstorms, smut, and drouth resulted in a substantial variation from year to year in the yield of crops.[46] Even in the same year, the damage could vary from field to field. In 1868, for example, while most grain and hay crops in the county dropped by one-third because of losses to grasshoppers, some farms suffered a near total crop loss.[47]

During the summer of 1855, after two years of grasshopper invasions, a severe drouth further diminished the supply of wheat and created one of the most severe grain shortages recorded in pioneer times. Joseph L. Robinson lost his entire wheat crop to grasshoppers in 1854. The following year he planted three different times and still only harvested twenty-eight bushels instead of the expected 400. "The winter of 55 and 6," he recalled, "was what we called the hard winter." Because the grasshoppers had stripped the pastures of their grass, hundreds of cattle, horses, and sheep died from malnutrition while foraging on the hostile range during that cold winter of heavy snow and hard winds.

Water was so scarce in 1855 that few backyard gardens survived. The following spring, awaiting the harvest of 1856, families rationed the meal they had ground from their corn, oats, and wheat. Wheat supplies were estimated at no more than fifteen bushels to a family.[48] "We all lived on weeds and roots and many nearly starved to death," Emily Stewart Barnes remembered. "We had to go early in the morning to gather nettles to eat. . . . We also gathered some sego roots and pulled some wild onions to eat." Settlers everywhere in the county felt the brunt of that bad farming year. For food they depended upon rationed flour and meal, a little meat, and wild greens and roots cooked in milk.[49]

A combined community campaign proved the best way to face the challenge of the "iron clads," as the grasshoppers were called by the settlers. When pulling brush drags over the insects failed during the insect onslaught of 1868, the citizens of one Davis County town "turned out *en masse* with spades, shovels, and pounders, and caught the enemy from one to four inches thick under the shelter of weeds . . . and slaughtered some millions," according to one account. To expand the slaughter, men, women, and children worked to prepare water-filled ditches. Driving the hoppers into the ditches, the citizens scooped them up with sacks and baskets, and then smashed them or burned them with straw. As one grim-humored reporter put it in a mock toast to the grasshoppers, "Peace to their ashes if they are mashed, and to their ashes if they are burned."[50] Natural processes dispatched many of the insects when they migrated to the Great Salt Lake and were killed by the saltwater. "Their bodies formed little islands 2 feet deep, 3 to 4 feet across, so firm, a dog could walk without sinking," Anson Call wrote. Winds spread the decaying mass along the shore, and it was reported that "the stench was unbearable" for many weeks.[51]

Another challenge to both crops and clean communities were the noxious weeds of the region. After twenty years in Utah, area citizens decided it was time to join forces in eliminating the most troublesome weeds from fields and meadows and from along fences, hedges, and roads. Residents joined in an unsuccessful effort to eradicate mustard, sourdock, sunflower, parsnip, cocklebur, and other nuisance weeds, though they did reduce their number somewhat.[52]

The pioneers of Davis County very quickly discovered the impact of the weather when high pressure built in Wyoming and a low-pressure system settled into the Great Salt Lake Valley—the result was a bank of clouds near the crest of the Wasatch Mountains and strong canyon winds. "The first night we arrived there was a heavy east wind," Daniel Miller of Farmington reported in the fall of 1848. Conditions that could create winds of near hurricane force existed most often during the late fall and early spring. The east winds piled snow in drifts, unroofed houses and barns, tore off shingles, uprooted trees, overturned carriages, scattered haystacks, and wreaked damage to fences and sheds. The best the settlers could do to protect their homes was to tie down roofs with molasses barrels, discarded millstones, or logging chains.[53]

In February 1864, while John Rigby of north Centerville was away getting medicine for his fifteen-month-old son John, the wind unroofed his family's house. His wife of two years, Elizabeth, tried to get to a neighbor's house with the child, but the two were pinned against a fence and died in the sub-zero temperatures. These are the only known deaths from an east wind in Davis County.[54]

Fire was a constant threat to property and life in early Davis County. Sparks from fireplaces and their chimneys could destroy houses, barns, and fields quickly, with little hope of human intervention saving the structures. A bucket brigade was the only system available to fight a fire, and often that could not be organized in time to douse the flames. In 1860, one family lost a straw stack, several tons of hay, a mule, and 116 sheep when a windstorm carried sparks from a fireplace twenty rods to the straw stack. Besides the threats they posed to homesteads and property, fires also sometimes damaged grazing lands and the mountain watershed. For example, fires started by Indians and whites swept most of the canyons of Davis County clear of timber and underbrush in 1855, a summer of dry, hot weather.[55]

The wildlife of Davis County was generally not a threat to human life, but some animals could be a nuisance; others could be a source of food. Emily Stewart Barnes remembered, "There were many wild animals; some of them are: rattlesnakes, blow snakes, blue racers, lizzards, ground hogs, wolves, porcupines, skunks, rabbits, mink and deer in the mountains, as well as wild ducks and all kinds of birds." When wolves became a threat to livestock and fowl, the county court offered a bounty for each wolf killed.[56]

Managing Timber Resources

Even though the weather and wildlife challenged the pioneer generation, it was from the natural resources—the land, the timber, and the water—that they received sustenance and protection. Along with policies for distributing land, the first settlers managed the access to and harvesting of timber in the canyons to serve community interests and allocated mill rights along the major canyon streams. Trees and water were considered community property in Mormon society, and they were managed for the common good. Officials appointed individuals to develop canyon roads for community use and often gave these same people the first rights to build sawmills and gristmills on the canyon streams.[57] In addition, Latter-day Saint leaders reminded sawmill operators that, because the timber was community property, "every mill in the Territory is legally bound to give one tenth of all they saw to the tithing office."[58] This corporate timber tithe was used in public buildings, given to the poor, or traded for other goods.

Limited timber resources existed in the mountains east of Davis County. Among the forested areas harvested was one stretching from Mueller park toward Bountiful Peak, captured in this 1906 Shipler photograph. (Utah State Historical Society)

The first stewardships over canyons and their resources were granted by Mormon leaders; later ones were granted by civil governments. In 1849 the rights to the major canyons in the first areas of settlement were assigned to members of the Quorum of the Twelve Apostles and a few others. Heber C. Kimball held the rights to North Mill Creek Canyon in Bountiful and Willard Richards had the rights to North Cottonwood Canyon in Farmington. Kimball also received rights to convey water from the next canyon north to ensure sufficient flow to power mills. These men were expected to build canyon roads, then recover their costs by charging a toll of twenty-five cents per wagonload of logs or firewood removed from the canyon. They also held the exclusive right to build mills on the canyon streams. The Deseret Assembly (and later the territorial legislature) confirmed these rights. In February 1851, legislators authorized county judges to grant timber, mill, and water rights for the remaining canyons.[59]

The Davis County canyons with unassigned useable resources were claimed within two years. The selectmen (commissioners) assigned them upon request, usually to a group of business partners. Those given the rights to build mills of various kinds and to cut roads into the canyons acted quickly on their opportunity and responsibility to meet community needs.[60] In 1855 the court authorized the bishops in each Latter-day Saint ward to issue and monitor additional canyon grants and to supervise the use of the water flowing from the canyons.[61]

The question of rights at times became confused. Brigham Young insisted that the timber itself was community property, available for free use by anyone who wished to cut or collect it, subject only to a toll for using the canyon road. Unless the owners of existing saw- or gristmills or others in the community objected, the court could grant multiple milling permits on a single stream. The county court expected the bishops to settle disputes over the use of canyon water for milling and to resolve questions of access and use of the canyons and their valuable timber.

Building Materials and Construction

Sawmills. As had been the case in Nauvoo, the construction industry was second only to agriculture in importance during Utah's early years of Mormon settlement. The first settlers secured their own materials, and the most accessible timber was cottonwood. Even with a log home, however, some sawn lumber was needed to finish doors, windows, and floors. John Marriott's response was to dig a hole in the ground in early Kaysville and create a saw pit. Then he and Robert W. Burton fashioned lumber for their own homes and those of their neighbors along Holmes Creek. One of the men climbed down into the pit while his partner took the top end of the steel saw, and together they sliced the logs lengthwise to fashion rough boards. Makeshift operations like this also existed in other parts of Davis County until more sophisticated sawmills could be erected.[62] Given the demand for lumber, those who received the rights to manage canyon resources quickly hired men to build wagon roads and water-powered sawmills. Bountiful had the county's first sawmill, followed by one in Farmington and another in Kaysville.

In Bountiful, Norton Jacob, William Wallace, and E. Whipple had a sawmill operating on North Mill Creek Canyon by June 1849. Built for Heber C. Kimball, eventually the successful operation became known as Whipple's sawmill. William Atkinson and his son-in-law M.W. Merrill set up an independent operation to make shingles, and they produced 17,000 during the winter of 1853–54.[63]

In Farmington, Willard Richards launched the most energetic program in the county when his agent Andrew Lamoreaux advertised in August 1850 for fifty workers to build a sawmill, a millpond, and a millrace. He also sought men to begin chopping and sawing logs at a site four miles into North Cottonwood (Farmington) Canyon. Work on a road into the steep canyon was already underway. Richards drew $2,300 from the central tithing office to help pay for the project. It was almost a year before the mill produced its first timber and shingles, because it took that long to finish the mill and get the steep, winding road and bridges in a condition to allow wagons with timber to reach the mill. In the meantime, Richards's agents set up a shingle mill at the mouth of the canyon. By late January 1851 they were selling pine shingles in exchange for cash, beef, wheat, and potatoes. Richards offered to buy for resale shingles produced by others.[64]

A third pioneer sawmill was set up at the east end of Grove Creek, later known as Bair Creek, east of Kaysville. A three-man partnership organized by John Bair secured the mill rights from the county court in 1852. The sawyers also soon gained exclusive rights to the saw timber in South Holmes Creek Canyon when it was found that a single canyon could not supply logs in sufficient numbers to make the mill commercially viable.[65]

A few other sawyers joined these pioneer county entrepreneurs during the next decade. Typically, payment for services was made in shares, with one-third of the customer's logs kept by the miller for sawing and finishing the timber. The local industry did well for a time, but steam mills, diminished local timber sources, and imported lumber gradually forced the closure of local timber and shingle mills.[66] By the end of the pioneer period, the county's mostly shallow canyons and sparsely timbered mountainfaces had been stripped of their trees. It became essential to seek other sources. Imported materials became widely available in local lumberyards soon after the arrival of the transcontinental railroad in 1869.[67]

Providing Shelter. The timber industry helped provide the basic need for every resident for shelter. Living in wagons, tents, dugouts, and wattle-and-daub summer homes served the purpose temporarily while settlers awaited the time and means to prepare a more secure dwelling. Logs harvested in nearby canyons provided the building materials for the first permanent homes. Builders selected trees for their evenness, then notched the ends of the logs where they intersected. They then filled the cracks between the logs with a moist clay. A blanket or hide filled the framed doorway. Within a few years, "dobie" pits appeared at convenient places in every town, as adobe bricks—sun-dried clay and mud bricks—became a popular material for house walls. A roof of planks and sod—eventually replaced by shingles—kept rain out sufficiently to make a comfortable home. Plank flooring, simple windows, and a fireplace completed the home. Both logs and adobe bricks provided excellent insulation from the summer's heat and the winter's cold. Because of its insulating value, adobe continued to be used as a wall liner after lumber was available in adequate quantities and quality to build frame homes. Another popular local building material was stone. Gathered from fields or the highlands near the mountains, the rocks were laid up in walls stabilized with a lime mortar obtained near the hot springs at the southern county border or in Weber Canyon.[68]

The county's first kiln-fired bricks were produced in Bountiful when Joseph Holbrook hired John Dale to establish a brickyard in 1849. Dale's bricks were used as far north as Kaysville. Other brickmakers later worked in the Bountiful-Woods Cross area and, after 1870, in Kaysville. It was not until the later decades of the century that fired bricks became commonly available.[69]

The county's first residents furnished their homes meagerly, using the few pieces of furniture most of them had hauled west in wagons, and supplementing them with locally made or imported items. Cooking utensils and chairs were among the items commonly brought to Utah by immigrants, along with trunks and boxes containing clothing and dishware. Marriner W. Merrill of South Bountiful reported that he and his wife, Sarah, set up house in 1854

John W. Young's barn in Centerville was one of many in the Farmington and Centerville area built entirely of common fieldstone. (Utah State Historical Society)

in a one-room log home with "one old bedstead, one baking skillet (borrowed), one frying pan (borrowed), my chest for a table, two three-legged stools, two knives, two forks, six small tin spoons, etc., but we were happy and felt at home."[70]

After providing for a home, landowners next turned their attention to barns, sheds, granaries, and other improvements. They patterned these farm buildings after those they or others had built elsewhere in the United States or in England. A typical barn was built of square timbers, planks, and shingles produced by local sawmills. For fasteners the builders used wooden pegs and locally made spikes and nails. Most buildings sat upon rock foundations. Some barns and granaries were built entirely of the plentiful native field stones. Friends and neighbors joined in the work and enjoyed the hearty food and socializing that accompanied a "barn-raising bee."[71]

For more than thirty years, Davis County farmers used a fencing policy they had known before their migration to Utah. It was based on the notion that if everyone worked together the load would be lighter. Cultivated fields needed to be fenced, because it was the tradition to let livestock wander freely. Rather than build a fence around each field, settlers cooperated in building one long perimeter fence enclosing the private fields of a large number of farms. This large enclosure was called the "Big Field." If several such fields existed in the community, they were designated by location, such as the "Big West Field." Farmland not enclosed in this way because of its location was privately fenced, and some private corrals and fences were built to enclose livestock. Bountiful's 315-acre Big Field was fenced in the spring of 1850 under the supervision of two men appointed at a town meeting held in the schoolhouse.[72] Other communities made similar arrangements.

Latter-day Saint bishops provided general oversight for the fencing of land in Davis County for at least the first dozen years. Each spring, the bishop appointed committees to oversee the building or repair of cooperative fences around one or more large agricultural tracts. The committees monitored the work of volunteer laborers, considered requests for new fences, handled complaints of damaged sections, and watched to see that sheep and roving cattle were kept out of the crops. After the crops were harvested, the fences were abandoned until the following spring. In 1865 this arrangement was formalized under a county cattle law adopted by a vote of 445 to 36. This shifted the responsibility away from ecclesiastical oversight and gave the existing practice a legal civic basis. Thereafter, the local fencing committees drafted formal contracts that were signed by the owners of the enclosed land.[73]

Managing Water Resources

The water that flowed from the canyons along the Wasatch Front in Davis County served three major purposes. First, mill operators needed water to power their machinery to saw lumber, grind grain, and produce sorghum. Secondly, farmers quickly learned that Utah soils needed added water in the form of irrigation to coax the crops to the fall harvest. Both purposes were essential for survival—providing housing and food for settlers. In the first years, the streams also supplied culinary water.

The county's water supply was derived from melting snows in the nearby mountains. The depth of the previous winter's snowfall influenced this supply. Canyon streams began flowing each spring around

An outdoor summer kitchen, like the one seen here behind a home in Centerville, made cooking and canning tolerable during hot weather. Note also the water tap at the right and the ground-level doors to the cellar under the building at left, where fruits and vegetables were kept cool. (Utah State Historical Society)

the end of March and continued until late summer, dwindling with the onset of fall in September. Supplementing the water supplied by the aboveground watershed were the natural springs that issued from gullies in the benchlands. In later years, farmers dug artesian wells to tap underground water sources.[74]

In time, most families found a more convenient source for culinary water—a well located as near the house as a reliable supply could be found. Each community had its specialists in digging wells and lining them with rocks. More than 150 wells were dug in Bountiful alone, ranging in depth from 60 to 100 feet.[75] Utah's sparse rainfall made a roof-collection system, using barrels placed under downspouts on the roof, an unreliable system for obtaining culinary water.

Some early settlers were skeptical about allowing new settlers to claim land because of the limited amount of water. Bishop Kay discouraged some applicants in 1854 with the words, "I should be glad to have you settle here; there is plenty of land but no water." In Bountiful, some of the early settlers began looking for other places to live.[76] Careful management, the nurturing of natural springs, and the digging of wells made it possible in most years to meet the needs of the expanding settlements. But if little snow fell during the winter, water could become scarce, leading to smaller stream flows, diminished yields of summer crops, and higher prices for foodstuffs and commodities. When a dry summer followed a mild winter in 1863, territorial officials froze prices to protect the poor against speculators. Crops were light again the following year because the streams dwindled in June. Joseph Holbrook told the *Deseret News* that "he sowed twenty bushels of oats, planted fifteen acres of corn and ten of sugar cane this year, and that he does not expect to get a bushel of oats or corn nor a pint of molasses, owing to the drouth."[77]

Distribution Systems. Because water was scarce, even in good years, landowers cared about the methods of its allocation and distribution. In developing a water-management system, the Mormon settlers set aside the familiar doctrine of riparian rights. That law, used in the eastern United States, required that users maintain the stream flow undiminished in volume. This worked well for water-powered machinery but not for irrigation agriculture. Therefore, in Utah, water was appropriated for industrial, agricultural, and culinary use under new principles adopted in 1852 that allowed water to be used up. With minor variations, sixteen other western states later adopted this same principle of "prior appropriation." Utah's interests in benefiting as many users as possible minimized litigation and softened the rights of the first claimants. Secondary and tertiary rights and rules were established to set priorities in dry years. Everyone in each class was treated alike and shared the available water. Ownership rights were also influenced by Brigham Young's policy of community ownership. Throughout the pioneer period it was customary for water rights to pass with the land to a new owner. Not until after Young's death did the legislature separate land and water rights.[78]

The first party of Mormon pioneers in the Salt Lake Valley commenced the practice of irrigation in Utah on 23 July 1847, diverting the waters of City Creek by blocking the stream with clumps of sod and digging diversion ditches. Davis County farmers also applied the simple diversion system on their own farms. The first canals, laterals, and ditches for the Big Field farms were built by cooperative effort. Hitching oxen to a plow, the men marked out a channel, then widened and deepened the ditch with scrapers and shovels. They flooded their fields and furrowed their row crops to control the moistening of the soil. Within a few years a network of distribution ditches had spread out across the foothills and along the borders of the farmlands to disburse the water.[79]

Once established, this cooperative network of ditches, large and small, needed maintenance. Individual landowners took care of their own ditches, keeping the weeds out of the channels and securing the ditch banks. If farmers shared a ditch, or when the streambed itself needed care, the work was shared cooperatively. This was true also with the city water sects that carried water to the backyard orchards and garden plots within each town. These sects were authorized by the county court and developed by court-appointed committees. Needs for upkeep of the city sect were resolved in discussions during Latter-day Saint priesthood meetings, a weekly gathering of men that effectively served as a town meeting. Every spring, the ward teachers supervised the work of cleaning and reinforcing the main channels serving the town.[80]

Watermasters. Of special importance in the regulation of agricultural water was the watermaster system, which was developed to give farmers fair access to extremely limited water supplies. In the water-scarce Midwest, sodbusters of the late nineteenth century homesteaded the land under the belief that the rain would follow the plow. In early Utah, a similar expectation prevailed. Latter-day Saint settlers established a complex system of canals and ditches and then regularly reported an increase in water supplies to irrigate their farms. Clearing the natural streambeds of clutter and an annual scouring of irrigation ditches also helped conserve water.[81]

The key figure in water allocation was the local watermaster. Appointed watermasters managed the use of the water by assigning water turns to protect both individual and community rights. The system was launched only a month after Brigham Young's arrival in Utah, when the Salt Lake High Council appointed Edson Whipple to superintend "the distribution of the water over the plowed lands" in Salt Lake City.[82] The pattern set up by Brigham Young in the Salt Lake City LDS wards in April 1849, of bishops overseeing such affairs, was adopted in Davis County as wards were created there. In 1851 the new territorial legislature gave incorporated cities the authority to appoint watermasters. The following year, county courts gained the same privilege, along with the power to assign timber and mill rights.[83] Davis County was the first to act on this new law, in March 1852. Salt Lake County followed in April, and Weber County in June, with Box Elder and Cache Counties making such appointments in 1856 and 1860.[84]

Before designating agents for the area's sixteen canyon streams, the Davis County Court consulted with the four local Latter-day Saint bishops. Watermasters nominated by the bishops were local farmers living along the streams whose waters they would supervise.[85]

For ease of administration, the court soon created water districts that included one or more streams, and they chose boundaries already in use by school and road districts.[86] Beginning in 1855 the court named separate watermasters for the east and west ends of the major branches of the creeks in the Kaysville-Layton area. Over the next decade, the practice grew in many communities of naming separate watermasters for each major ditch spreading out from the larger streams.[87] In South Weber, for example, since all irrigation water came from the Weber River, it was only the ditches or canals that needed regulating. The most important was the South Weber Canal, built by fourteen farmers in 1852 along a four-mile-long channel used later by the Bambrough Canal.[88]

For ten years, the court made annual appointments of the watermasters nominated by the ward bishops. Then, to simplify the process, in 1863 Judge Thomas Grover named a single head watermaster in each community—the ward bishop—and allowed him to appoint the district watermasters.[89]

In 1865 a territorial law challenged the involvement of religious leaders in the irrigation management process. At the same time, the law recognized the importance of the cooperative irrigation system. It authorized a new type of irrigation district with self-governing authority. To create a district, a group of water users would petition the court. The stockholders then would elect a board of trustees to build and maintain water diversion projects and manage them. This secularization of water management helped prepare the way for Utah's transition to a more diverse population—the influx of non-Mormons—with fewer social strains.[90]

In Davis County the new law had little initial impact. It simply prompted a temporary reversion to civil appointment of the watermasters. For two years—1865 and 1866—Judge Joseph L. Holbrook appointed the nominated watermasters himself. But after that brief respite, and continuing until 1875, the court once again appointed the bishops as general watermasters and allowed them to manage the selection of local watermasters.[91] In the late 1860s some of Davis County's bishop-watermasters allowed the local choices to be made by nomination in a priesthood meeting. This shift was a weak nod toward the 1865 territorial law but preserved ecclesiastical influence. More typically, the general watermaster simply "called" the watermasters for each creek or ditch and the priesthood quorum sustained his actions.[92] It was not until 1876 that water management in Davis County moved more definitely toward democratic self-government within the irrigation districts. Beginning in that year, the court created a water district for each community and appointed watermasters nominated locally in a secular mass meeting.[93] Haight Creek, which served settlers in two towns, had its own water district.

The watermaster assigned each farmer times and length of water use. Generally, it was the watermaster who resolved questions of missed or misappropriated water turns. Only when a dispute crossed town/ward boundaries or when petitioners wanted to adjust a grant previously mandated by the court did the county judge step in to resolve questions. The court did offer a general guideline during the drought year of 1863 "that in times of scarcity of water the oldest improved Farms shal[l] have the preference." Also, in one dispute involving the use of water from Haight Creek (the boundary between Farmington and Kaysville), the court and local bishop referred the matter to the LDS First Presidency.[94]

Another duty of the watermaster was to supervise new construction and routine maintenance of the main ditches. Each water user was expected to turn out for work duty on the appointed date or to

Layton's first brick home was built in 1870 by Elias Adams, a brickmaker. His son rigged up a pulley system to transport buckets of water to the house from a spring in a nearby hollow. (Rebecca A. Nalder) (*Layton, Utah: Historical Viewpoints*)

hire someone else to do his work. Widows were exempted from this duty. If residents failed to heed the call, watermasters could appeal to the bishop, who had one last recourse. As Bishop John W. Hess put it, "If men would not do their duty and quit finding fault he would try them for fellowship," that is, threaten to disfellowship them from the Mormon church.[95]

Dams and Canals. Most farmers managed with the water available during the seasonal flow of the particular stream they used. But Elias Adams, one of those using the waters of the north fork of Holmes Creek, decided in the spring of 1852 to create a pond to preserve the early stream flow for later use and thus extend his irrigation season after the streambed went dry. Using shovels, Adams and his sons created a bank four feet high and forty feet long and stored enough water to irrigate his nearby farm. Early in 1863, under the direction of the Kays Ward bishop, local residents hauled in additional soil in wheelbarrows to raise a new dam to a height of fifteen feet on top of the earthen dam. Unfortunately, this work was done in winter and melting ice under the dam weakened its base. The new dam washed out the following June. The community gave up on the project, but Adams steadily reinforced the surviving original dam and created a useful pond. This first Davis County reservoir built for irrigation purposes was also the earliest reservoir in Utah.[96]

Several neighbors imitated Adams's efforts to conserve water. Robert Knell and others gained county permission in 1857 to dam the north fork of Kays Creek. A dam existed on the south fork of Holmes Creek before the fall of that year and a road crossed it. The county court approved these and other attempts to husband water, including the use of waste water from irrigated farms. The judges held the builders of the dams liable for any damage caused by washouts.[97] The widespread use of reservoirs would become a common practice only after the end of the pioneer period, however, due to the engineering problems and the limited availability of equipment and manpower.

One other early effort to provide more water received the active endorsement of Brigham Young and his counselors. They promoted a canal to carry water from the Weber River along the benchline to a point just above Heber Kimball's millpond in Bountiful and then to Davis County's southern boundary. A route south to Kay's Creek had been explored a few years earlier. The territorial legislature incorporated the Davis County Canal Company in January 1856, and, at a meeting in the county courthouse in August, community leaders accepted the LDS First Presidency's challenge to build the canal. Territorial surveyor general Jesse W. Fox and his assistant had just completed a survey of the proposed route. It would take "much labor . . . and perhaps some tunneling and flumeing," they reported. Engineers decided to tunnel through the sand ridge, expecting to find a compacted clay material. Instead, they found loose sand. It was dangerous for workers and prohibitively expensive to create a lined channel and protective roof. The Utah War delayed a decision on the project, and the idea would not be revived for many years. By then, the local economy would be undergoing a transition that would move Davis County from the agrarian pioneer era of cooperation to a time of independent business partnerships and individual entrepreneurship.[98]

ENDNOTES

1. Ward Roylance, *Utah: A Guide to the State* (Salt Lake City: Utah: A Guide to the State Foundation, 1982), xvi. Roylance gives the size in square miles of the six smallest counties as: Davis, 297; Weber, 581; Morgan, 603; Daggett, 682; Piute, 754; and Salt Lake, 764. Tillable land in Davis County is around 200 square miles, or about 128,000 acres.

2. Deon C. Greer et al., eds., *Atlas of Utah,* 28–31.

3. Ibid., 77.

4. Glen M. Leonard, "A History of Farmington, Utah, to 1890," 96.

5. Ibid., 36.

6. Journal History of the Church of Jesus Christ of Latter–day Saints, 17 August 1868. A similar observation appears in Edward L. Sloan, ed., *Gazeteer of Utah, and Salt Lake City Directory* (Salt Lake City: Salt Lake Herald Publishing Co., 1874), 65.

7. Glen M. Leonard, "Truman Leonard: Pioneer Mormon Farmer," *Utah Historical Quarterly* 44 (Summer 1976): 251–52.

8. Record of Members and Historical Record of Farmington Ward, 1851–65, Book A, 29 December 1851, microfilm, LDS Family History Library; Journal History, 4 May 1850.

9. *Wilford Woodruff's Journal, 1833–1898: Typescript,* ed. by Scott G. Kenney (Midvale, Utah: Signature Books, 1983–85), 3:236.

10. Leonard J. Arrington, *Great Basin Kingdom: An Economic History of the Latter–day Saints, 1830–1900* (Cambridge, MA: Harvard University Press, 1958), 51–52; "The Settlement of Bountiful" manuscript, 1912, 4, 46, LDS Church Archives; Andrew Jenson, "Centerville Ward," [11], manuscript, LDS Church Archives.

11. Analysis of information in U.S. Bureau of the Census, *Seventh Census,* Territory of Utah, Davis County, Schedule 3 "Productions of Agriculture," manuscript, LDS Church Archives.

12. Clifford Westenskow, "The Economic Development of Davis County, Utah" (M.S. thesis, Brigham Young University, 1946), 56–59; Leonard, "A History of Farmington," 99.

13. An 1849 survey in Centerville is mentioned in Mary Ellen Smoot and Marilyn Sheriff, *City In–Between: History of Centerville,* 7. Porter is quoted in Jenson, "Centerville Ward," [11].

14. Kate B. Carter, ed., *Heart Throbs of the West,* 2:270–71, 4:328; Historical Record, Farmington Ward, 29 December 1851.

15. Andrew Jenson, "Kaysville Ward," entry for 1850, manuscript, LDS Church Archives.

16. See Howard Stansbury, *Exploration and Survey of the Valley of the*

Great Salt Lake of Utah (Washington, D.C.: Government Printing Office, 1852), map; Jenson, "Kaysville Ward," entry for 1850.

17. *Acts, Resolutions, and Memorials . . . of the Legislative Assembly . . .* (Great Salt Lake City: Joseph Cain, 1855), 66–67, 6 March 1852; Gustive O. Larsen, "Land Contest in Early Utah," *Utah Historical Quarterly* 29 (October 1961): 312–13.

18. Lawrence L. Linford, "Establishing and Maintaining Land Ownership in Utah Prior to 1869," *Utah Historical Quarterly* 42 (Spring 1974): 139–43; Davis County, Minutes of the Davis County Court, 1 July 1869, Davis County Clerk's Office, Farmington, Utah.

19. Seventh Census, Utah Territory, Davis County, "Productions of Agriculture."

20. Ibid.

21. Ibid.

22. Hubert Howe Bancroft, *History of Utah, 1540–1887* (San Francisco: The History Co., 1891), 279, 327.

23. *Deseret News,* 4 September 1852; "Farmington Grist Mill," an account listing work done by Kesler and Laub, 1 November 1857, to December 1858, LDS Church Archives; Journal History, 5 April, 20 November 1860.

24. Wallace N. Cooper II and Allen D. Roberts, "Report on the Isaac Chase Mill (Brigham Young's Lower Mill), ca. 1852–79, Liberty Park, Salt Lake City, Utah," typescript prepared for Salt Lake City Department of Parks and Recreation, January 1980, 26; Annie Call Carr, *East of Antelope Island: History of the First Fifty Years of Davis County,* 379–80.

25. Inez Barker, *John Weinel, Miller: Early Pioneer and Operator of the First Flour Mill in Kaysville, Utah* (Kaysville: Daughters of Utah Pioneers, 1983), 1–3, 7; Kate Carter, ed., *Treasures of Pioneer History* (Salt Lake City: Daughters of Utah Pioneers, 1952–57), 2:422.

26. Margaret Steed Hess, *My Farmington: A History of Farmington, Utah, 1847–1976,* 342.

27. Henry H. Blood, "Early Settlement of Kaysville" (1912; typescript reproduced by Kaysville Historical Society, 1995), 12.

28. Journal History, 15 May 1867. Dates of "about 1854" and "about 1860" are suggested in Smoot and Sheriff, *City In–Between,* 35; and Carr, *East of Antelope Island,* 382.

29. Carr, *East of Antelope Island,* 379–80; Cooper and Roberts, "Report on the Isaac Chase Mill," 26.

30. Carr, *East of Antelope Island,* 382. Margaret Steed Hess, *My*

Farmington, 340, misidentifies the Hinmans' mill with the Richards sawmill and both Richards's gristmills.

31. Barker, *John Weinel, Miller,* 7, 10, 19; Carr, *East of Antelope Island,* 380; Journal History, 15 May 1867.

32. Cooper and Roberts, "Report on the Isaac Chase Mill," 38.

33. Barker, *John Weinel, Miller,* 7–8, provides a useful description of Weinel's mill. For photos of Davis County mills see Barker and various town histories.

34. Barker, *John Weinel, Miller,* 8; Cooper and Roberts, "Report on the Isaac Chase Mill," 37.

35. Heber C. Kimball to Franklin D. Richards, in Journal History, 31 August 1855, 3.

36. Journal History, 25 July 1864; Davis County, Court Minutes, 7 December 1863, 5 September, 5 December 1864, 7 March, 5 December 1865; Farmington Ward, Teachers Minutes, 21 June, 28 June 1868.

37. Hess, *My Farmington,* 340–42; Foy, 86; Smoot and Sheriff, *City In–Between,* 35; Carol Ivins Collett, *Kaysville—Our Town: A History* (Kaysville, Utah: Kaysville City, 1976), 36–40; Barker, *John Weinel, Miller,* 12, 24; Carr, *East of Antelope Island,* 379–83.

38. Lester T. Foy, *The City Bountiful: Utah's Second Settlement from Pioneers to Present* (Bountiful, Utah: Horizon Publishers, 1975), 90–91; Smoot and Sheriff, *The City In–Between,* 38; Hess, *My Farmington,* 340; Collett, *Kaysville—Our Town,* 34; Carr, *East of Antelope Island,* 397, 411.

39. Arrington, *Great Basin Kingdom,* 116–20.

40. Examples are in Davis County, Court Minutes, 2 December 1861, 1 June 1863, 1 June 1868.

41. Davis County, Court Minutes, 7 September 1863; Joseph L. Robinson, Autobiography and Journal, 30 August 1863, microfilm, LDS Church Archives.

42. Carr, *East of Antelope Island,* 238, 277, Farmington Ward, Teachers Minutes, 21, 28 August, 25 September 1870; Arrington, *Great Basin Kingdom,* 120.

43. Carr, *East of Antelope Island,* 154–55.

44. Ibid., 136, 156.

45. Foy, *City Bountiful,* 48–49; Carr, *East of Antelope Island,* 64.

46. For further analysis see Leonard, "A History of Farmington," 111–12; and Foy, *City Bountiful,* 49–50.

47. Arthur Stayner to editor, 4 August 1868, in *Deseret News,* 12 August 1868.

48. Robinson, Autobiography and Journal, 105–10, entries for May

1855–summer 1856; *Deseret News,* 2 May 1855; Heber C. Kimball to Franklin D. Richards, in Journal History, 31 August 1855, 3; *Deseret News,* 29 August 1855, 8.

49. Quoted in Claude T. Barnes, *The Grim Years, or The Life of Emily Stewart Barnes,* 44, 53; Carr, *East of Antelope Island,* 65, 173; Lee D. Bell, *South Weber: The Autobiography of One Utah Community,* 48.

50. *Deseret News,* 20 May 1868; Journal History, 17–18 May 1868.

51. Anson Call, Diary, in Carr, *East of Antelope Island,* 372.

52. *Deseret News,* 20 May 1868.

53. Hess, *My Farmington,* 417; Foy, *City Bountiful,* 52–55; Collett, *Kaysville—Our Town,* 46–47; *Deseret News,* 23 November 1864.

54. Carr, *East of Antelope Island,* 238; Foy, *City Bountiful,* 54; Hess, *My Farmington,* 417.

55. Journal History, 16 November 1860; Heber C. Kimball to Franklin D. Richards, in Journal History, 31 August 1855, 3.

56. Barnes, *The Grim Years,* 33; Foy, *City Bountiful,* 71.

57. Arrington, *Great Basin Kingdom,* 50–54.

58. *Deseret News,* 14 May 1853.

59. *Laws and Ordinances of the General Assembly* (Great Salt Lake City: Willard Richards, 1851), 8 and 15 January, 4 February 1851; Journal History, 8 January 1851.

60. For examples see Davis County, Court Minutes, 19 September 1853, 30 January 1854.

61. Davis County, Court Minutes, June term, 1855.

62. Collett, *Kaysville—Our Town,* 10; Foy, *City Bountiful,* 85.

63. Foy, *City Bountiful,* 70–71, 85; Davis County, Court Minutes, 4 December 1854; Carr, *East of Antelope Island,* 150.

64. *Deseret News,* 24 August 1850; Journal History, 15 December 1858; 31 May, 14 June 1851; 25 January, 8 February, 17 May 1851.

65. Davis County, Court Minutes, 30 October 1852, 4 December 1854.

66. Carr, *East of Antelope Island,* 150, 383–84.

67. Farmington Ward, Teachers Minutes, 2, 6, 9 June 1867; William R. Purrington, "History of South Davis County," 24, 71–72.

68. "The Settlement of Bountiful," 17–24; Carlos Sessions, "Colonization of Home Town of Sessions Settlement Now Called Bountiful," quoted in ibid., 45–46; Carr, *East of Antelope Island,* 150.

69. Foy, *City Bountiful,* 89; Collette, *Kaysville—Our Town,* 35–37.

70. "The Settlement of Bountiful," 17–18; Barnes, *The Grim Years,* 28; George W. Givens, *In Old Nauvoo: Everyday Life in the City of Joseph* (Salt

Lake City: Deseret Book, 1990), 182–88; Marriner W. Merrill, Journal, quoted in Carr, *East of Antelope Island,* 151.

71. Leonard, "A History of Farmington," 106.

72. Ibid., 100–2; William W. Willey, "A Short History of Bountiful," 7, manuscript, 1914, LDS Church Archives.

73. Leonard, "A History of Farmington," 102–5.

74. Carr, *East of Antelope Island,* 52–53.

75. Foy, *City Bountiful,* 69; Carr, *East of Antelope Island,* 159.

76. Collett, *Kaysville—Our Town,* 40; Foy, *City Bountiful,* 69–70.

77. Foy, *City Bountiful,* 51–52; *Deseret News,* 27 July 1864.

78. Arrington, *Great Basin Kingdom,* 52–53; Richard W. Sadler and Richard C. Roberts, *The Weber River Basin: Grass Roots Democracy and Water Development* (Logan: Utah State University Press, 1994), 21–23; George Thomas, *The Development of Institutions under Irrigation, with Special Reference to Early Utah Conditions* (New York: Macmillan, 1920), 43–47, 53–55); Larsen, "Land Contest in Early Utah," 313.

79. Arrington, *Great Basin Kingdom,* 41, 53; Carr, *East of Antelope Island,* 108, 158–59, 173.

80. Leonard, "History of Farmington," 116.

81. Lowry Nelson, *Mormon Village* (Salt Lake City: University of Utah Press, 1952), 47 n. 30; Blood, "Early Settlement of Kaysville," 5; Carr, *East of Antelope Island,* 105.

82. Journal History, 22 August 1847.

83. "First General Epistle," *Latter–day Saints' Millennial Star* 2 (1 August 1849): 228–30; Sadler and Roberts, *Weber River Basin,* 19–20.

84. Thomas, *Development of Institutions,* 58–59. Claims that the idea for watermasters originated in Davis County may be a misreading of this quick action by the Davis County Court (see Westenskow, "Economic Development of South Davis County," 12).

85. Leonard, "History of Farmington, 113; Davis County, Court Minutes, 22 March 1852, 27 January 1862; Carr, *East of Antelope Island,* 360.

86. Foy, *City Bountiful,* 71; Davis County, Court Minutes, March 1853.

87. Davis County, Court Minutes, March term, 1855, 7 March 1865.

88. Carr, *East of Antelope Island,* 173; Bell, *South Weber,* 149 (chart), 151–52.

89. Leonard, "History of Farmington," 113–14; Davis County, Court Minutes, 27 January 1862; 6 February 1863, 4 March 1867.

90. Thomas, *Development of Institutions,* 53–55, 117–24; Roberts and Sadler, *Weber River Basin,* 20.

91. Leonard, "History of Farmington," 113–14; Davis County, Court Minutes, 4 March 1867; Farmington Ward, Teachers Minutes, 30 May 1869, 26 June 1870.

92. These observations are based on information from the Farmington Ward, Teachers Minutes, 30 May 1869, 26 June 1870, and 8 June 1873.

93. Thomas, *Development of Institutions,* 59; Leonard, "History of Farmington," 113–14.

94. Leonard, "History of Farmington," 114; Foy, *City Bountiful,* 70; Thomas, *Development of Institutions,* 66–67, 84–87; Davis County, Court Minutes, 1 June 1863, 7 March 1870; John W. Hess to First Presidency, 14 February, 24 February, 25 March 1871, LDS Church Archives.

95. Leonard, "History of Farmington," 115; Farmington Ward, Teachers Minutes, 16 July 1865.

96. Frank D. Adams, ed., *Ancestors and Descendants of Elias Adams, the Pioneer, 600–1930* (Layton, Utah: Author, 1929), 111–14; Collett, *Kaysville—Our Town,* 41.

97. Davis County, Court Minutes, 2 March, 7 September 1857; Thomas, *Development of Institutions,* 70–71.

98. Purrington, "History of South Davis County," 63–65; *Deseret News,* 20 August 1856, 10 October 1860.

Chapter 5

An End to Isolation

Managing natural resources proved to be much easier and more successful for the first settlers of Davis County than their attempts to shape commerce and industry for the common good. The land, the water, and timber all had some degree of scarceness, so it became imperative that users of these resources work together to conserve and share these earthy elements essential for survival.

In contrast, manufactured goods offered by local merchants were available freely to those willing and able to pay the price. The problems here centered around commerce, costs, and the availability of cash or marketable exchange goods. Davis County's Mormon settlers sought to avoid poverty and promote prosperity in their communities by spreading out the profits from merchandizing and manufacturing. They did so by implementing cooperative commercial ventures and pledging to support them rather than independent mercantile efforts. But market forces worked against this sharing of economic resources, and conflicting values challenged their ability to live a cooperative isolationist economic policy.

When the Mormon settlers built wagon roads and railroads they intended to encourage immigration of church converts and interaction among church members. They promoted good mail and telegraph service to unify their society. But these networks of transportation and communication, this reaching outward, worked against the inward-focused tendencies of their economic ideals. Imported goods competed with poorer quality local manufactures, and competitive commerce smothered cooperative economics. The transcontinental railroad worked not only to smooth the inward flow of Mormon converts but also of gentile (non-Mormon) miners and merchants. This leavening weakened both the resolve and the ability to nurture an agrarian, self-sufficient cooperative community.

The residents of Davis County, like their neighbors elsewhere in territorial Utah, made a good-faith effort to achieve both an expanding transportation and communication network and an inward-oriented commercial structure. These efforts dominated the shaping of the communities of the county during the 1860s and 1870s—the decades surrounding the coming of the transcontinental railroad.

Transportation and Communication

Roads. When the first Mormon settlers arrived in Davis County, they found a faint network of Indian trails. A few California-bound emigrant parties had followed the best known of these trails from the mouth of Weber Canyon south along the foothills to Farmington Canyon and then along the lowlands to the Jordan River. This became the county's first described route. The segment north of Farmington was known locally as the Indian Trail or the Mountain Road; it later was the basic route of U.S. Highway 89.[1]

Another route came into use along the county's western border to serve emigrants headed north around the Great Salt Lake to California. The general path in north Davis County no doubt had served Indians who lived along the lakeshore before it became a distinct wagon road. In the fall of 1848 Samuel Hensley, en route to California, recognized it as a better route than the Hastings Cutoff, notorious as the route of the Donner-Reed party two years before. From Salt Lake City Hensley followed the main-traveled route, which took him along the lowlands west of Bountiful and continued through to Farmington. He then turned northwesterly to Hector

Haight's herd station at the lake's edge. From west Kaysville his route followed the edge of the bluffs bordering the lake through what became Syracuse. He passed through Weber County by way of Ogden City and then continued on to Brigham City, where he crossed the Bear River and turned west to join the California Trail at City of Rocks in present-day southern Idaho. Hensley met returning members of the Mormon Battalion along the Humboldt River and sent them toward Salt Lake City along this route instead of toward Fort Hall and then south.[2]

Known locally as the Emigrant Road or, in north Davis County, as Bluff Road, this route served hundreds of California-bound Forty-niners. These adventurers knew it as the first stretch of the Salt Lake Cutoff or Salt Lake Road. The eastward-bound Mormon soldiers in 1848 camped for the night at Herd (now Haight) Creek. This waystation also served as a stop-over point for many of the Forty-niners. For Utahns, the Emigrant Road was simply an alternative route through northern Davis County.[3]

Neither the Mountain Road nor the northern portion of the Emigrant Road enjoyed immediate acceptance as designated highways. As the first Mormon settlements grew into towns, two other routes gained official recognition and tax support for grading and maintenance. They both were north-south routes more convenient for local travel. In 1850 the Deseret Assembly created a state road from Ogden to Provo, with a branch from Salt Lake City to Tooele, and gave it a 142-foot right-of-way. In southern Davis County it followed a route through lowlands west of the present Denver and Rio Grande Western (D&RGW) railroad line route below Centerville and Farmington. North of Farmington it went along the route of present-day Utah Highway 106, including the Main Streets of Kaysville and Layton, and then moved northwesterly through northern Davis County and on to Ogden along a route known as Highway 1, later designated as U.S. Highway 91. Later on, the southern portion of the state road was rerouted along 500 West in Bountiful and what became Interstate 15 to Farmington.[4]

The second official road was sanctioned by Davis County. It was laid out in 1852 to connect Bountiful with Centerville and Farmington, with various additions to the north added later. The original route appears to have followed 200 West in Bountiful, continuing in an almost straight line to Farmington. After a few years, increased settlement suggested the need for adjustments; therefore, in 1859 the county court annulled the entire county system. The selectmen appointed a three-member committee to identify a single good wagon road and declared that any abandoned roadways would be sold as surplus property.[5]

Determining a route that would satisfy all interested parties proved difficult. The selection committee's proposal was rejected by the court for failing to heed the spirit of its instruction. Determined to involve broad citizen input, the county court asked the Mormon bishops to convene local mass meetings and to personally examine various routes to find one that was both inexpensive and practical. This time, the court accepted the recommendation. With minor variations, the route followed an existing local road from the South Weber fort over a sand hill to the Little Fort in Layton and on to Kaysville. It continued along "the main traveled road" through Farmington to north Centerville. It jogged west one block in Centerville and then continued on through south Davis County. Even after construction began, however, this approved route required some adjustment in order to satisfy local interests.[6]

The route underwent additional changes in later years. In the early 1870s, residents of southern Davis County approached county officials about relocating the county road between Bountiful and the Hot Springs. Apparently, they could not decide the issue, so the court sent Bishop Christopher Layton of Kaysville and a companion to discuss the matter with Brigham Young. The Mormon leader recommended orienting the road at right angles along surveyed property lines. This had not been what residents intended, but the county surveyor and Bishop John Stoker of Bountiful decided on the new route and it was opened. Two years later, the LDS bishops of Farmington, Centerville, and Bountiful wrote to Brigham Young on behalf of residents asking that the old road be reopened. The original route followed the natural terrain at the foot of the mountains, they noted. The bishops acknowledged that this road ran "diagonally across some surveys . . . [but] was located and in general use long before the farms were taken up." The new route, they explained, took a zigzag course and was hilly, rocky, and sloped in such a way that it was difficult to haul loose hay without losing the load. Bishop Anson Call delivered the letter in person and received verbal advice from Young. The diagonal route was restored.[7]

Transportation in Davis County tended to orient itself along the most heavily traveled routes—the state and county roads extending on a north-south orientation between Salt Lake City and Ogden. To meet local needs, residents laid out local streets connecting to these official routes and, in the Kaysville area, extending to the Mountain Road. In the southern half of the county, east-west streets ran due east and west. By the early 1850s many of the streets were permanently in place at irregular intervals along pre-existing farm boundaries and were being used as reference points for district boundaries.[8]

The pattern established in northern Davis County reflected the influence of natural features. Kaysville-Layton area residents found it more convenient to ignore the compass grid and let their connector roads parallel the local streambeds. These routes extended in a northeasterly direction from the lower roads to the Mountain Road. The earliest of these ran from the Kaysville fort up 200 North and along South Holmes Creek. Except for the streets inside the Kaysville city plat, only a few local roads in northern Davis County before 1870 followed the compass quadrants.[9]

The construction and maintenance of designated roads was a county responsibility, accomplished through road-district supervisors. Following the boundaries previously created for schools, the Davis County Court in 1853 organized nine road districts and appointed committees to raise taxes and supervise the work on state, county, and local roads and bridges. The district committees accomplished their tasks with the direct support and encouragement of Latter-day Saint ward leaders.[10]

Funding came from both property and poll taxes. At first, citizens paid a separate road tax on their property. In 1859 the county set aside for roads one-fourth of the regular county property tax (then at 0.25 percent).[11] The poll tax required every able-bodied male over eighteen to work on the roads one day each year. In 1862, lawmakers increased the poll tax to two days' labor and redefined eligibility as healthy males between twenty-one and sixty-three years of age.[12] Residents could opt to pay the poll tax in cash or to hire a surrogate to do the work. Cash was assessed at 12.5 cents per hour, later raised to 15 cents and figured at $1.50 per ten-hour day.[13]

Taxes collected for roads in Davis County were initially expended at the discretion of the local supervisors. In early 1853 the county court assigned two-thirds of the funds to the heavily traveled north-south routes.[14] Only one type of road in Davis County depended upon users' fees; this was the private canyon road, built under a territorial or county charter. Developers recovered their construction and maintenance costs by charging tolls on timber wagons.

Very few of the designated roads of the pioneer era existed as more than well-traveled, graded but otherwise unimproved wagon routes. In summertime even the most-used roads were mere dusty lanes, often marred with ruts. Wet weather turned them into muddy quagmires. Wheels could sink to the hubs, and straining teams sometimes broke single and even double wagon trees trying to extract the mired wagons. By the late 1860s Utah Territory claimed only thirty-two miles of improved graveled roads.[15]

In Kaysville an attempt was made in 1867 to improve a wagon road south from Kay's Creek through Kaysville to Haight's Creek. The territorial legislature incorporated the Kaysville Wagon Road Company to do the work. The company was allowed to charge a toll for ten years to recover its costs, and the road then would revert to the state. A newspaper reporter inspecting the site after two years found it no better than the rest of the route. Spring rains had turned the dirt tracks into fifteen inches of mud.[16]

Mail Services. The need of the first settlers to communicate within Utah and beyond led to the creation of mail services. Before a formal postal system was functioning, travelers carried letters as a courtesy. Distribution within the community would take place personally or at the close of Sabbath meetings. This informal network continued even after the federal government established Utah's first post office in Salt Lake City in March 1849.[17] At that time, the U.S. mail left Salt Lake City only four times a year, traveling on routes east to the Missouri River and west to Sacramento. In 1850 Congress organized internal territorial mail service, with a southern route to Sanpete Valley and a northern route to Ogden.[18]

The government contract for delivering mail to Davis County was awarded in 1851 to Phineas H. Young & Son. The company's two-horse stage carriage left the Salt Lake City post office every Monday and Thursday at 7:00 A.M. and reached Brownsville (Ogden) at 6:00 P.M. The stage made the return trip on Tuesdays and Fridays. Passengers, who paid two dollars each way, subsidized the mail service. This twice-weekly schedule remained in place throughout the pioneer period. After mail service was extended northward, first to Brigham City in the late 1850s and then into Idaho, the return trip passed through Davis County on Wednesdays and Saturdays.[19] Thomas J. King arranged for a twice-weekly mail and passenger coach for the county in 1862. By the late 1870s, daily mail service in both directions was in place between Salt Lake and Kaysville.[20]

The first mail was left at designated local stage stops and distributed informally. In February 1854 Congress authorized a post office for Kay's Ward and named David Nelson postmaster. That same year, post offices were approved for Centerville and for Stoker (Bountiful). Aaron B. Cherry and David Sessions served as the respective postmasters. Ira Blanchard was named postmaster in Farmington in 1855. Thereafter, coaches made stops in each of these four towns in Davis County. The post offices were kept in the homes of the postmasters, a common practice in nineteenth-century America. Some offices later moved in with area businesses or had their own small building.[21] In all instances, patrons called at the post office for their mail.

Service to South Weber was more difficult because of the town's location off the main mail route. Residents received mail through informal deliveries or at nearby towns. A South Weber post office operated in 1863–64, but from then until the coming of the railroad residents traveled to Riverdale for their mail.[22]

Pony Express. For eighteen months beginning in April 1860 the Pony Express followed a route across the country from St. Joseph, Missouri, to Sacramento, California. The route did not pass through Davis County, so Pony Express mail dropped off in Salt Lake City or Ogden was delivered to Davis County through the regular bi-weekly stagecoach deliveries. Persons or companies willing to pay the high cost could receive Pony Express mail through a connecting route at the mouth of Weber Canyon. Riders from Ogden intercepted the Pony Express at the Echo Junction Station and carried mail down Weber Canyon to an express station on Ogden's 25th Street. The riders had a Davis County hand-off point at Uintah. From that point, mail was carried by local riders to post offices in Davis County. Their pace was slower than that of riders on the cross-country route, so it was not called an "express." Several young men from the county worked as riders for the famous, but short-lived, pony mail.[23]

Telegraph Service. The Pony Express soon faced a competitor in the transcontinental telegraph. When the lines from the east and west were connected in Salt Lake City in October 1861, the days of the cross-country pony service were numbered. With the transcontinental line in place, Brigham Young announced plans for a territorial line from Cache Valley to St. George, with a branch line from Nephi into Sanpete County. The Civil War, which had prompted construction of the national line, made supplies impossible to get for local extensions, however, so work on the Deseret Telegraph was not commenced until the fall of 1865.

"We should bring into requisition every improvement which our age affords . . . to render our intercommunication more easy," a circular from Brigham Young to the LDS bishops said. The residents of each valley built the line under the direction of local Latter-day Saint leaders. They selected and surveyed the route, cut the twenty-two-foot poles, placed them seventy feet apart along the route, and strung the wire. Kaysville residents built six miles of the line, and residents of other communities in Davis County did their proportional share of the work. Local contributions paid for the project, and residents supplied a share of the teams and wagons that hauled the supplies and equipment to Utah.[24]

To learn how to use the new communications system, young men and women selected for the job by each town attended a telegraphy school in Salt Lake City. The local telegraphers were ready when the system was put into operation through Davis County. The line opened for business between Ogden and Salt Lake City on 1 December 1865 and at other Utah stations over the next six weeks. A specialist loaned by the Western Union company visited Centerville during a snowstorm on 4 December to install and connect telegraphy equipment there. The new communications system was an immediate boon to businesses, church and government officials, and individuals. Salt Lake City's *Deseret News* was able to publish more immediate information, including news and weather reports from one end of the territory to another.[25]

Transportation Services

Stagecoach Lines. Passenger service from the east and west to Salt Lake City was established by stagecoach companies organized to carry the mail under government contracts. The Butterfield Overland Mail began service in 1861. Ben Holladay then entered the business but sold out to Wells, Fargo & Company in 1866. The initial east-west routes did not pass through Davis County; but, as noted above, local passenger service was available on coaches carrying the mail to northern Utah. When Wells, Fargo & Company expanded its service northward to the Montana mining camps, it contracted for services at stops located every eight to ten miles through Davis County, the usual distance for securing fresh horses along mail routes.[26]

Stage stations operated along the main road in Centerville, Farmington, and Layton and on the Mountain Road through Fruit Heights to South Weber. Some of these stops served the Wells Fargo line; the others served other stage companies. Each stopover offered food for drivers and passengers, feed for horses, and fresh animals. At Centerville, William Reeves built the Wells Fargo station in 1866. Thomas Hunt provided livery service for Wells Fargo in Farmington in a building erected near his hotel just east of the adobe courthouse.[27] John Green and Joe Harris built log barns in 1857 on what later became Layton's Main Street and furnished prairie hay for local mail stages. Isaac "Ike" Brown cared for the horses there. The Wells, Fargo & Company stages taking the old Mountain Road en route to Montana used a stop maintained by Grandison Raymond just north of present Green Road in Fruit Heights. The county's northernmost stop, operated by John Hill, was located at South Weber.[28]

A Mormon traveler northbound from Salt Lake City in 1869 described the ride along the Mountain Road to the railroad depot at Uintah as rough and dusty. "The driver . . . recked not [took no heed] of rocks, ditches, nor creeks, but went clean through or over them

The "Livery and Feed Stable" at Farmington was still serving travelers in 1912, more than a half century after Thomas Hunt began the business for Wells Fargo. (Utah State Historical Society)

without hesitation or remorse, bumping the passengers provokingly," he reported. "Uintah was the most miserable looking place on the whole route," he added. It is . . . a little town, covering a couple of acres or so, built of boards and canvas. . . . Every house seemed to be a grogshop, 'restaurant,' or gambling den, none of them by any means inviting."[29]

Wells, Fargo & Company did a brisk business on the Overland Trail and on its Salt Lake-to-Montana route. Local passengers had difficulty booking seats out of Salt Lake City. Even local stage companies filled available seats early. With the arrival of the transcontinental railroad, Wells Fargo set up an office at Uintah. Within months, however, the company sold its stage business. A Salt Lake City partnership headed by Jack Gilmer bought the northern route and operated from the terminus of the Utah Central Railroad in Ogden to Helena, Montana.[30]

Travelers aboard stagecoaches or trains and other people passing through Davis County on horseback or in wagons or carriages sometimes needed overnight accommodations and food for themselves or their animals and repairs to their vehicles. Stagecoach stops were a specialized service to meet the needs of customers of the stage lines. But these were not the only services available for travelers. Early Davis County also had a few strategically located hotels that, together with blacksmith shops in every community, met transient and local needs. These inns served as both a home for the owner's family and a hostelry offering meals and a bed to travelers. Nor was it uncommon for private homeowners to host strangers passing through, a traditional practice in the nineteenth century.

In the 1850s, when Brigham Young and his touring party visited Utah settlements regularly to hold church meetings and consult with local leaders, the travelers carried tents, bedding, and food with them. Within a few years, however, Davis County had a few homes in each settlement large enough together to accomodate Young and his traveling companions. By the 1860s, the inns of Davis County had become places of choice for overnight stays.[31]

The distance between Salt Lake City and Ogden made the Farmington area a natural place for overnight stopovers. Three hotels opened there during the 1850s. The first evolved naturally at the homestead of Hector C. Haight, who provided an inn, blacksmith shop, stables, pasturage, and fresh livestock on his farm located conveniently along the Salt Lake Cutoff (the Bluff Road) near the Great Salt Lake. Advertised in an 1851 emigrants' guide, *Mormon Way-bill to the Gold Mines,* as Blooming Grove, it was a popular campground for California emigrants as well as others traveling the lower road. In 1857, on Farmington's Main Street, Haight built a two-story adobe house with rooms to take in guests. It became known as the Union Hotel, and it still stands, south of the rock meetinghouse. On the north corner of the same block (now the church parking lot), Thomas Grover hosted visitors in a two-story adobe house called the Inn or the Halfway House.[32]

Travelers through the county could find formal accommodations in at least two other towns as well. Christopher Layton built his four-room Prairie House near Kay's Creek in 1858 on what became Layton's Main Street. He sold it three years later, after which it seems

One of the early hotels serving travelers through Davis County was Hector C. Haight's adobe inn on Farmington's Main Street. (*East of Antelope Island*)

to have been used by stagecoach passengers. His toll bridge at the Kay's Creek crossing made wagon travel easier (although at a price). In Bountiful, a large adobe home built by Perrigrine Sessions on the main-traveled road along 200 West doubled as a hotel, post office, and community dance hall. A sign at the entrance announced "Refreshments." This led residents to call the place the Tavern.[33]

The Coming of the Railroad

The Transcontinental Line. The driving of the golden spike at Promontory, Utah, on 10 May 1869 marked the completion of the transcontinental railroad and ushered in a new era for Utah Territory. Elsewhere in the United States railroad lines had been expanding transportation and commercial opportunities for decades. Utah's leaders had lobbied Congress since 1852 for the transcontinental line. They applauded when Abraham Lincoln signed authorizing legislation in 1862, and residents welcomed the benefits they received through the connecting iron road. Through Brigham

Young's influence, northern Utahns got railroad construction contracts that brought jobs and money into the territory. Davis County residents helped push the Union Pacific line from Echo Canyon through the challenging Weber Canyon to Ogden. The coming of the rails made immigration to Utah faster and cheaper and reduced freighting costs dramatically. The easier movement of people and goods helped Utah's economy grow in the 1870s and 1880s.[34]

In Davis County, LDS ward bishops took subcontracts from Brigham Young on the Union Pacific project in Weber Canyon. They recruited laborers to do the grading and the masonry work on bridges during the summer and fall of 1868 and again the following spring. Several Bountiful men supplied railroad ties. Farmers and livestockmen sold meat and other supplies to the railroad crews. An especially lucrative business was furnishing feed for the work horses. An observer in central Davis County in January 1869 noted, "It is not uncommon to see ten to fifteen loads of hay off for the railroad at one time. Hay fetches $50 per ton with $10 per day for hauling. Greenbacks pass freely."[35]

Grading was hard work. The men used picks and shovels to break the ground and horse-drawn scapers and dump carts to move the soil. Work crews welcomed entertainment furnished by local residents. On at least one occasion the Kaysville Brass Band serenaded the men who were laying the tracks. As a reward, they were invited to ride in a boxcar on the Union Pacific construction train when it first emerged from the mouth of Weber Canyon.[36]

The Utah Central. The connected transcontinental Union Pacific and Central Pacific lines served only a few of Utah Territory's residents directly. By offering land for a depot and shops, Brigham Young convinced the two rail companies to establish their junction in Ogden rather than in the gentile town of Corinne. To accomplish this, the Central Pacific bought the forty-seven miles of line between Corinne and Ogden from the Union Pacific.[37] This placed the terminal in a Mormon city instead of the railroad boom town. Young already had plans for adding routes to serve communities north and south of Ogden.

The first connecting railroad was a thirty-seven-mile line called the Utah Central, built through Davis County largely by local labor-

Engineer Robert Bolt stopped his southbound engine at a point between Ogden and Farmington at 11:15 A.M. on 10 January 1870, and Utah Central's Ogden agent, John Reeve, faced the camera from the step of the passenger car as a photographer recorded for history the first train to pass through Davis County. (Utah State Historical Society)

ers recruited by the ward bishops. Brigham Young organized the cooperative railroad company on 8 March 1869. Christopher Layton was Davis County's sole representative on the five-member board of directors. Surveying and grading started in mid-May, and tracks were laid beginning in September. Crews were hindered only when they were delayed by the slow arrival of rails and spikes shipped from Omaha. By early December, passenger service was open from Ogden to Farmington. To celebrate construction of the road to the half-way point, Brigham Young and a group of church leaders rode in horse-drawn carriages from Salt Lake City to Farmington. The trip took two hours. Then, in a new railroad passenger car pulled by a steam engine, they glided along the completed line to Ogden in just one hour. A reporter said that the men did not miss the tedious horse-drawn drive over Sand Ridge. They expressed delight that the railroad had been planned and constructed by Utah residents—an example of what cooperative community spirit could accomplish.[38]

Workers completed laying the tracks to Salt Lake City by late December. On a cold, foggy 10 January 1870, Brigham Young drove a polished spike made of Utah iron in ceremonies witnessed by thousands at the end point of the line at North Temple Street and Third West. Hailed as the "Pioneer Line of Utah," the Utah Central went into immediate operation, with daily service between Salt Lake and Ogden. After a few years, trains were making the round trip twice a day. The first fares matched those charged for the stagecoach—two dollars for the full distance, pro-rated for other stops. As traffic increased, the fares were halved.[39]

The construction and successful operation of the Utah Central depended heavily upon the efforts of Davis County residents. As president of the Mormon railroad company, Brigham Young invited local leaders to plot the route of the Utah Central through the county and to determine the site of a depot in each town. He expected the townspeople to build the grade and support the railroad with their patronage. From Young's perspective, the UCRR was a cooperative community project. "The Utah Central Railroad is not being built by a company solely to make money or for its own benefit," the *Deseret News* weekly editorialized, "but for the good of the people and . . . by the common consent of all concerned."[40]

Railroad officials carefully observed the building process during a two-day working trip through the county in June 1869. More than one hundred land owners and local leaders joined in selecting a route and sites for depots in the south half of the county. A depot site in the Bountiful area was picked at the northwest corner of Daniel Wood's farm and was named Wood's Crossing. Even though local tradition of a later date suggests that the name was derived because Wood was upset with Brigham Young for bisecting his fertile land, evidence from the time suggests otherwise. During the public discussion, Wood actually offered to donate the land for a depot if the tracks would bisect his property and stay clear of the lane at its east border. The unanimous vote of townspeople present placed the depot on Wood's land. Wood left four months later on a short-term mission to Canada—before the rails had been laid. When he returned in

March 1870 he seemed well pleased that he could travel home by train. "We arrived at Woods Cross 20 minutes to 9 o'clock," he wrote in his diary after a ninety-five-minute ride from Ogden. "We landed right on our own farm."[41]

The decision in Centerville followed the same town-meeting pattern. Landowners and citizens selected a site agreeable to UCRR officials one-quarter mile west of the settlement. It was close enough for access "but sufficiently far off to prevent the occurrence of accidents to children or cattle from their straying on to the track."[42]

In Farmington, the process revealed the influence of local citizens. Bishop John W. Hess had scouted three possible routes. His personal preference was the westernmost, "through a barren piece of land" that preserved good farmland closer to town. After visiting the site, Brigham Young agreed and predicted that this more direct route between Centerville and Kaysville would save ten thousand dollars over other options. Young then "called upon the people to learn from them whether they wanted Farmington to come to the railroad or the railroad to come to Farmington." Citizens wanted the convenience of closeness. The route they chose invaded the fertile lands about a half mile west of the rock meetinghouse. Bishop Hess and President Young deferred to the common will.[43]

The management group traced the route to Kaysville and stopped for the night. The following morning, railroad officials and local residents agreed on a depot site right against the western borders of the townsite, no more than a hundred rods from the adobe meetinghouse. Brigham Young led his party to the engineer's camp two miles north of Kaysville. From there to the north county line, three survey crews had completed their work. Grading had been completed for most of this surveyed route. Railroad officials continued to Ogden for church meetings, observing along the way teams pulling scrapers to shape the cut that rose from the Weber River to the bench land. The workmen's goal was to bring the cut within the maximum slope of forty feet to the mile.[44]

From Kaysville to the southern county line, each community was given its own section of the route to grade. Ward bishops recruited construction crews and paid them—sometimes in borrowed cash furnished by the railroad company, but more often in railroad stock.

Money was difficult to obtain, and, besides, the company was a cooperative that paid dividends to its stockholders. Young men without steady work and recent emigrants welcomed the work. Some who had incurred debts to the Perpetual Emigrating Fund (which helped immigrants come to Utah) took credit on their accounts.[45]

Sawmills in Weber and Tooele Counties furnished most of the ties for the railroad. However, some ties came from North Millcreek Canyon, where contractors built Bountiful's first steam-powered lumber mill just for that purpose. Timber from Tooele County was hauled out of canyons there on bobsleds during the winter, and in the spring of 1869 it was transported on wagons to the shore of the Great Salt Lake. The ties had been cut sixteen feet long. In June 1869 a 300-foot raft made of one thousand of these double-length ties was assembled. Eighteen men poled the raft along the edge of the lake to Farmington, a trip of three days. The lengths were then hauled on wagons to the track site and cut in half.[46]

Completion of the $1.25-million Utah Central line left the company short on funds for operation; it also needed a wider right-of-way. Once again officials turned to local residents in Davis County communities. "It appears that they want us to deed 50 feet of land on each side of the railroad to the Company," Bishop Hess told his local priesthood quorum. The families visited by the ward teachers agreed to donate the requested property. In addition, seven Farmington citizens subscribed nearly $6,000 in cash for Utah Central bonds, and prosperous residents in other towns did likewise. The Davis County Court also refunded the company's 1870 tax and reduced the assessment the following year to help.[47]

The Utah Central was the first of what became a Utah railroad network. The Mormon-built Utah Northern Railroad route from Ogden through Brigham City and Logan to Franklin, Idaho, was added between 1871 and 1874 and the Utah Southern line to Provo in 1871–1873. The local railroads were consolidated in 1880 as a subsidiary of the Union Pacific Railroad Company. This company extended the lines in both directions. In 1899 the route became known as the Oregon Short Line. This expansion gave Davis County residents easy railroad access to visit friends and relatives elsewhere in the territory and beyond.[48]

A second major railroad company built a line across Utah from the Colorado border through Price and north to Ogden in 1881–1883. Routed through Davis County west of the Utah Central, the Denver and Rio Grande Western line was built by a Colorado company primarily to serve long-distance traffic. Davis County residents boarded workmen during the construction period, and some landowners took contracts for building the grade. The resulting competition with the Union Pacific line lowered shipping rates in the state. Among the benefits to Davis County was that coal could be hauled directly from newly developed mines in Utah's Carbon County at a savings over the previous monopoly shipments from other coal sources by Union Pacific rail car. By 1900, D&RGW's subsidiary, the Utah Fuel Company, supplied 90 percent of Utah's coal. Smaller companies halved this dominance by World War I, the competition once again reducing coal prices for consumers.[49]

The Utah Central Railroad changed the way Davis County residents received and sent mail and telegraph messages and it created new options for transporting goods and passengers. In addition, the railroad had social consequences and opened up economic opportunities. Jobs made available for local residents included those of crewmen, station clerks, and maintenance men. During the years of heavy grasshopper infestations, the train company hired local youths to keep the tracks clear. The insects became so thick at times that the wheels would spin and impede the forward movement of the train.[50]

Almost immediately, the transcontinental trains replaced stagecoaches as the primary carriers of out-of-state mail. Southbound Utah Central trains hauled inbound letters for Davis County residents to depots in each of the four communities along the route. Couriers sent by the local postmasters retrieved the packets and delivered outbound mail to the railroad station. Residents of South Weber received mail at the Uintah post office along the transcontinental route.[51] The Deseret Telegraph soon moved its offices into the UCRR stations, making them important communication as well as transportation centers.[52]

The railroad did not immediately put the upper stagecoach route out of business. Railcar passengers headed to Salt Lake City from the east could save time by disembarking at Uintah and catching a southbound stage along the Mountain Road rather than continuing into Ogden on the train for connections with a stage or the Utah Central train. Eventually, however, the stage stations in Davis County were closed and the buildings adapted for other uses. Centerville's station became an amusement hall named after operator William Reeves; it later was known as Elkhorn Hall.[53]

Cooperative Commerce and Agriculture

Mormon immigrants to Utah after 1869 could disembark from their transoceanic ship or Mississippi steamer and make the entire journey across the continent by railcar. According to one travel writer, the five-day trip from New York City to Salt Lake City on five connecting lines cost $119. The ease of railroad travel and the promotional efforts of the railroad companies encouraged non-Mormons to settle in Utah. The establishment of mining also led to diversification—of peoples, employment patterns, and religion. The arrival of larger numbers of gentiles changed the social character of Utah. At first, the Latter-day Saints resisted the change, with defensive economic and social programs. Eventually, however, as the pioneer generation died off, accommodation became the watchword.[54]

Economic patterns among Latter-day Saints in territorial Utah reflected a religious worldview that encouraged a unity of effort for the common good. From the beginning of settlement in Utah, Brigham Young encouraged settlers to provide for themselves by producing as much of their own food, clothing, and other material needs as possible. This emphasis encouraged farming, ranching, and agrarian-based industries. Young specifically discouraged mining. He nurtured a home industry movement to minimize the flow of capital out of the territory by importing only those essential products that could not be made in Utah. Community leaders in Davis County were part of this movement to encourage self-sufficiency.[55]

The 1850s Consecration Effort. Not long after the establishment of communities in Davis County, Mormon leaders reintroduced Joseph Smith's 1830s plan for consecrating property to the church. The California gold rush had tempted Latter-day Saints with wealth, and non-Mormon merchants were threatening the home-industry movement with their imported goods. To counter these threats, to strengthen commitment, and to curb inequality in land holdings, Mormons were invited in 1854 to sign a formal deed conveying to the church their land, buildings, and marketable personal property, including livestock, furniture, and tools. The program called for the local bishop to return most of the property to the member to manage as a stewardship for the support of his or her family.[56]

Mormon leaders introduced the principle of consecration at the general conference in April 1854. They followed up with an epistle from the First Presidency and sermons in the old Salt Lake Tabernacle. Davis County residents who heard the conference talks repeated the message in local meetings. The response varied from family to family. Surviving records suggest that about one-third of Latter-day Saint families formally consecrated their property. In Davis County, that amounted to fewer than 200 of the 540 families living in the county in 1858, when the movement ended.[57]

The limited number who filled out deeds of consecration may have been a factor in launching the Mormon Reformation, but the onset of the Utah War diverted attention away from both efforts. The economic program did not move beyond the initial consecrations, nor did not the church take control of the deeded property. The consecration movement proved to be only a symbol of religious dedication to the principle of unity, an idea that would be revived later in the cooperative and united order programs.[58]

The Cooperative Movement, 1868–1874. In the first years after settlement, Davis County residents bought most of their hardware, selected clothing items, and other imported goods in Salt Lake City. Gradually, enterprising individuals in each community began offering goods carried west by immigrant companies. These first county merchants began with small inventories in rooms in their homes while continuing their full-time occupation as farmers.

For a number of reasons, church leaders initially opposed all importation of goods. First, such goods were expensive and drained cash out of Utah's economy. Second, Brigham Young considered the markup on most imported goods to be price gouging. Finally, to counteract both of these effects, church leaders encouraged local manufacturing. Beginning in 1860, however, Young allowed a limited amount of inbound freighting by Latter-day Saints in conjunction with the church immigration wagons. Five years later, he opened the trade wider as part of an effort to control prices and keep capital from leaving the territory. He allowed members to organize freighting companies and urged Latter-day Saints to boycott non-Mormon merchants.[59] With this liberalized importation policy, new stores opened in every Davis County town. This marked the beginning of full-scale mercantile operations in the county.

About this same time, Mormon church leaders in Salt Lake City decided to build a wall against the local non-Mormon merchants. With Mormon imports increasing, they organized a boycott of the gentile merchants and in the fall of 1868 set up a wholesale and retail operation in Salt Lake City known as Zion's Cooperative Mercantile Institution (ZCMI). More than a dozen men spread out from headquarters to urge creation of similar general stores elsewhere. The result was more than 150 local retail co-ops in Utah. Horace S. Eldredge and William Clayton were the delegates sent to Davis County to preach the benefits of cooperation.[60]

The message from headquarters was magnified in Davis County through local preachings by the bishops, other ward leaders, and the priesthood teachers who visited each Latter-day Saint home. They explained that the policy of mercantilistic exclusiveness included two aspects: first, members were encouraged not to patronize gentile merchants, because these businessmen were said to be not always willing to support ward schools and other "public" programs; second, members should buy from cooperative stores and local manufacturers.[61]

With the encouragement of Mormon leaders, merchants in each Davis County community except South Weber followed the Salt Lake City example by organizing a local retail cooperative. During the early months of 1869, merchants in each of these towns merged their existing operations and received credit on the books of the new store. The officers were usually elected from among the leading stockholders. In Centerville and Bountiful the local bishops were elected as cooperative presidents. Leading merchants of Farmington and Kaysville headed the stores in those places. South Weber had no existing merchants and thus created no cooperative.

The story of the emergence of commerce and the creation of co-op stores differs little from one Davis County town to another. In

Kaysville, probably the first to offer imported goods was John Bennett. By 1863, residents could buy goods from William Blood, Ebenezer A. Williams, and John R. Barnes, who were hauling goods westward by wagon train from the railhead on the Missouri River. These four merchants merged their operations in 1869 to form the Kaysville Co-operative Mercantile Institution. Barnes, the firm's largest stockholder, became superintendent. Christopher Layton, a former partner with Blood, was elected president. The company was capitalized with nearly $8,000 in stock.[62]

By 1869 Farmington had one well-established storekeeper, John Wood, who had expanded his operation from a room in his rented log house in 1855 to a small frame building. He became president and superintendent of the Farmington Co-operative Mercantile Institution. Wood's only competitor was Frederick Coombs, an English immigrant of 1861, who was managing a store for a Mr. Bershome in a rented room in the adobe courthouse. When that store closed for lack of patronage, Coombs moved to Morgan as an employee of Gergor Cronin; but he soon returned to Farmington to oversee a Cronin branch store in the courthouse. A report in 1870 credited Coombs with doing as much business as did the co-op. However, Cronin's store closed after local church leaders repeatedly reminded Coombs and the Farmington Latter-day Saints of their responsibility to support the cooperative movement. Coombs then went to work for the church-sanctioned store.[63]

Among the early merchants in Centerville were John Holland and Nathan T. Porter. Holland soon moved to Weber County, but Porter remained to participate in the creation of Centerville's cooperative store when it was capitalized in March 1869 with $2,000 in stock. Bishop William R. Smith became president, with Porter as vice-president, and Joel Parrish as manager. John Adams, who had been freighting goods from the east, was hired as clerk. Brigham Young had encouraged Utah's co-ops to employ women as store clerks. Hardy men, he said, should be producers—hoeing potatoes or harvesting timber. Davis County's early retail outlets ignored the church leader's counsel.[64]

During the canvass for the 1850 census, only one Davis County resident listed "merchant" as his occupation. Thus, twenty-five-year-old David Floyd, an unmarried boarder, may have been the first in that business during his stort stay in Bountiful. Enoch Tripp kept a small stock of goods in Perrigrine Sessions's house. Abram D. Boynton, a storekeeper before migrating to Utah, was another early merchant. In 1860 Anson Call and Joseph Holbrook became partners in the mercantile trade. They established Bountiful's first full-fledged store. A small step toward cooperation in Bountiful came in November 1865, when a mercantile association was organized with community support. Holbrook was named president, with Anson Call and Sidney B. Kent as directors. These businessmen were responding to the new freedom to import merchandise. The organization's stated purpose was to purchase goods in the east, freight them to Utah, and sell them to residents of the North Canyon LDS Ward. It was this association that formed the basis of Bountiful's retail cooperative in March 1869. Call served as one of five directors, and Bishop John Stoker became president.[65]

The cooperative stores in Davis County operated under policies and procedures defined by Brigham Young and his associates in discourses at the Mormon church's general conferences. Additional counsel came through meetings of the School of the Prophets, a group of influential Latter-day Saints organized in 1867 to discuss religious and political matters and to promote economic self-sufficiency. Arthur Stayner of Farmington belonged to the select group, which met from time to time until 1874 in confidential meetings in Salt Lake City. Stayner's voice was heard regularly in local gatherings in support of home industry.[66]

Through public pronouncements in general and local conferences, the intent of the cooperative movement was made clear to every Utahn. Latter-day Saints were expected to show their loyalty to the church by supporting the cooperative stores with their purchases (and investments) rather than buying from competing private merchants, especially non-Mormons. To assess community support, at least one Davis County bishop asked the ward teachers to survey members about their shopping habits. They found that about two-thirds of the families were lending at least a share of their support to the ward store.[67]

Like the cooperative stores found elsewhere in Utah Territory,

Davis County's mercantile operations suffered from several common problems. The principle of cooperation implied a broad investment in the business, with investors sharing in the profits. In fact, however, only a few owners held a large portion of the stock in virtually every cooperative venture in Utah, including those in Davis County. The intended dispersion of profits among many residents thus could not be achieved. Another common problem was that competing merchants continued to operate in many communities. Despite preachments to the contrary, residents succumbed to the temptation to buy imported manufactured goods from these merchants rather than inferior locally made goods from the church stores and factories. Added to these factors was the matter of financial stability. The national economic panic of 1873 negatively impacted a number of Utah's cooperatives and forced their closure. Those in Davis County survived the depression, however.[68]

Related to these challenges was another financial problem that may have been more severe than all the rest. Many residents of Davis County had little extra cash and depended upon a barter economy. Because of this, the co-ops often extended credit under a good-neighbor policy of trust. Surviving records from the ward store in Farmington reveal that the inability to collect on these accounts kept the business constantly on the verge of bankruptcy. Arthur Stayner, one of the directors, finally convinced the Farmington board of directors to quit offering credit. Bishop John W. Hess sent the ward teachers out to collect on the overdue accounts, but they had little success. The good-hearted store manager gradually extended additional credit, and the store carried a heavy load of unpaid bills.[69]

Even with the economic challenges faced by the cooperative stores of Davis County, they remained in business during difficult times. They offered a variety of goods, including some sought-after imports, and netted sufficient income to keep the stocks replenished.

Bountiful's cooperative store made an effort to expand beyond the mercantile business during the short-lived cooperative movement. A few months before the Bountiful Co-operative Mercantile Institution (BCMI) came into being, local citizens had organized a Co-operative Agricultural and Manufacturing Society. As with other such societies, this one presumably intended to establish manufac-

An unidentified group of wagon passengers pause in front of the brick store built in 1873 for Bountiful's Co-operative Mercantile Institution. (*The City Bountiful*)

turing businesses. It appears, however, that it stepped aside to allow the new Bountiful mercantile institution to take the lead in all cooperative efforts. During the summer of 1873 the BCMI opened a brickyard, operated by William Garrett. The company used some of the bricks to build a large, new general store on Main Street.[70]

"Let us have co-operative brick yards and co-operative everything else that benefits the people, and that has a self-sustaining and independent tendency," the *Deseret Evening News* said when its reporters first learned of Bountiful's plans to make bricks.[71] Other cooperatives in Davis County did not establish manufacturing businesses until after Brigham Young raised the stakes by introducing a new form of communal economics.

The United Order, 1874. Near the end of April 1874, many residents of Davis County attended a special meeting in the new Mormon Tabernacle in Salt Lake City to hear Brigham Young explain a new economic order. In its ideal form, the "United Order" introduced in that meeting anticipated an all-inclusive communal arrangement, with the entire economy owned cooperatively. The residents of Orderville, in southern Utah, came closest to achieving that ideal, including a common kitchen and standard clothing styles. Brigham City's successful cooperative movement, with a variety of manufacturing enterprises tending towards a self-sustaining economy, became a model for the kind of united order program attempted in Davis County.[72]

All Latter-day Saints were encouraged to join the local united order, but, as with the cooperatives, membership was a personal decision. Those who chose to participate in the economic aspects of the program in Davis County were not asked to deed property to the order like with the Law of Consecration. Rather, they indicated support by investments of time and resources in existing cooperative stores and by entering into new cooperative businesses established under church direction. In its practical application in Davis County, the United Order was merely an expansion of the cooperative movement marked by the founding of one or more new businesses to do such things as make shoes, tan hides, or make brooms.[73]

Those who joined a united order pledged to maintain certain religious standards similar to those preached during the Mormon Reformation twenty years earlier, and they agreed to support church cooperatives. The fourteen rules published as guidelines included pledges to patronize united order businesses, refrain from criticizing the managers of the order, give a full day's work for the credits recorded on the cooperative's books, and avoid the extravagant fashions and lifestyles of the world.[74]

Brigham Young took a personal interest in launching the United Order. In a series of visits to Davis County in May and June 1874, he and other church leaders organized the new order in each community where cooperatives existed. Many of the officers involved in running the cooperative stores were carried over to run the new organizations, but new names also appeared on the rosters.

In Farmington, the new organization in May placed Bishop John W. Hess in the president's post, with other bishopric members as vice-presidents and secretary. Over the next few months, these leaders discussed a communal option with local residents. Lacking support for a comprehensive system, they concluded instead to expand existing cooperative projects by adding a tannery, shoe shop, and broom factory. "It was not the people's property that was wanted," said Hess, "but it was their whole faith in this thing."[75]

The Kaysville United Order was probably organized around the same time as the visit to Farmington, but details have not survived. Christopher Layton remained president of that order for a year; he was succeeded in 1875 by Rosel Hyde.[76]

Centerville leaders anticipated a large crowd in late June when Brigham Young, his counselors, and two apostles organized that town's united order. The bishop scheduled the gathering for the Young Men's Hall, a structure larger than the local meetinghouse. Even that building was inadequate, however. Some citizens listened from outside to the morning preaching meeting and the afternoon organizational session. Bishop William R. Smith and other officers who had headed the cooperative store were carried over in the new organization, supported by an expanded board of directors. Centerville's Mormon women lent their support to the home industry movement in 1875 by voting in their Relief Society organization to give their business to Elizabeth Whitaker in a milliner business.[77]

The reorganization in Bountiful took place early in June, at a meeting in the tabernacle. Anson Call was named president, replacing Bishop John Stoker, who had headed the co-op. The new leaders of the Bountiful United Order attempted to build the business and expand offerings. Most notably, in 1875 they hired Charles R. Jones to open a tailoring department in the firm's new Main Street store.[78]

The Davis County United Order, 1876. The several united orders in the towns of Davis County manifested a renewed energy to win patrons and investors. Their enthusiasm sparked such a spirit of competition between the projects in neighboring towns that it caught the attention of Mormon church officials in Salt Lake City. In the spring of 1876, Brigham Young appointed Joseph F. Smith, a member of the Quorum of the Twelve Apostles, to coordinate ecclesiastical and economic activities in Davis County. Young asked the new "president" over the area's Latter-day Saint wards to bring competing united order businesses in the county under a central organization. In addition, Smith was asked to promote efficiency through the cooperative purchase and use of farm equipment.[79]

Some potential conflicts had already been resolved locally. When

Centerville announced plans for a cheese factory in 1875, Farmington residents dropped their plans for a similar facility. However, tanneries and shoe shops in Kaysville and Farmington vied for scarce hides and looked wherever they could to find customers for their crude locally made shoes.[80]

Investors in Farmington had been especially agressive. They rallied local residents in 1874 to build a new adobe building for their Union Tannery and then outfitted it with vats, a bark mill, tools, and supplies. Hides and the right kind of bark were difficult to find; yet, after struggling for a year, the co-op built a new shoe shop and reached out to other communities for support. Operators talked some Kaysville area livestockmen into selling them hides. Bishop John W. Hess secured pledges from the bishops of Bountiful and Centerville to direct raw materials toward the Union Tannery. However, this local initiative was preempted by a new umbrella organization coordinated from church headquarters.[81]

In March 1876 the Davis County United Order was incorporated, with three directors from each of the four participating wards. These ward representatives managed the businesses in their own communities under Joseph F. Smith's general oversight. The firm's headquarters was in Farmington, and that town's cooperative businesses dominated the new organization, transferring assets valued at more than $12,000. Other communities contributed less to the consolidation. Together, they added goods and stock valued at just under $3,000. A $1,300 investment by the church's general tithing office and a small private purchase of stock brought the total capitalization to just under $17,000.[82]

Amalgamation failed to solve the problems inherent in the local tanning and shoe businesses. Scarce hides and bark were the most critical problems. Some local livestockmen continued to send their hides outside the county for processing. County tanneries sought hides as far away as Cache Valley. Local producers also could not find satisfied buyers for their products. Higher-quality imported leather and shoes dominated the market. Despite efforts to improve the tanning process, the county manufacturing businesses lacked sufficient income to meet operating expenses. Directors closed the corporation in November 1880, marking the end of the United Order manufacturing effort in Davis County.[83]

Cooperative Agriculture

As noted in an earlier chapter, the earliest economically cooperative efforts in Davis County grew out of the need to manage limited natural resources—land, timber, and water—for the general good. In addition, settlers hoped to save time and money through collaborative efforts to meet certain agricultural needs. Farmers worked together to build common fences, and they hired community herders for their sheep and livestock. Through these New England-style cooperative efforts, they learned to depend upon one another.

The first formally organized cooperative efforts in agriculture emerged in the mid-1850s in an effort to improve yields in both crops and livestock. For intercommunity cooperation, county residents formed a branch of the Deseret Agricultural and Manufacturing Society, which had been organized in Salt Lake City in 1856. Directors were elected from the county's four towns. The organization recommended planting specific varieties of grains, fruits, and vegetables. To encourage excellence, the county organization followed the example of the parent society by sponsoring annual exhibits so that producers could show their best crops, livestock, flowers, and manufactured items. The Davis County residents who won top prizes in the annual fair held each September in the Farmington courthouse often then took their specimens to Salt Lake City, where they were regularly listed among the prizewinners at the territorial fairs. Those fairs were scheduled to coincide with the October general conference of the Mormon church.[84]

With the encouragement of the society, ward bishops and local agents of the parent society shared advice on agricultural matters with men during their weekly priesthood meetings. Bishops saw themselves as appropriate leaders in such matters and were supported by the citizens in this role. For example, in 1868, when residents adopted a countywide plan to sell hay to the mail stations, they appointed the bishops as their agents in the respective communities.[85]

One of the efforts of the county agricultural society and local church leaders was to encourage livestockmen to improve the breeds of their cattle and sheep to increase the production of milk, meat, and wool. The improvement effort expanded to include beekeeping and fisheries in 1871, when delegates to a county convention in Farmington organized a specialized society, the Davis County Branch of the Deseret Fine Stock and Bee Association. A nominating committee of bishops or their representatives picked five men for each of seven committees to encourage the improvement of horses, horned stock, sheep, bees, fish, swine and fowls, and general agriculture.[86]

Davis County livestockmen, like others in Utah, obtained some fine breeds of beef cattle by trading with California immigrants who needed horses and provisions. Later on, they sought out Short-horn, Devon, Hereford, Jersey, and Ayrshire cattle. To improve their sheep breeds over those brought with them from the east or purchased in New Mexico, they imported the Merino, long-hair, and fine-hair breeds from California, Canada, Ohio, and Kentucky.[87]

Cooperative Livestock Herds. Davis County's first settlers came to the area as herders. For a few years, some of them continued to use the county as a range for surplus cattle and horses from the Salt Lake City area. They attacted business by word of mouth and through advertisements in the *Deseret News.* As populations grew, however, uncultivated bottomlands and foothill rangelands in Davis County were restricted to permanent residents. In 1856 the county court made ward bishops responsible for supervising the use of these common areas. The court guaranteed non-Mormons equal rights with "the people." In each community, the bishops and ward teachers organized separate herds for the domestic cattle (milk cows and working oxen), surplus cattle (those not needed on a daily basis), and sheep. The districts hired herders and paid them with grain or cash. Boys often cared for the domestic cattle, adults for the surplus and sheep herds. These community arrangements worked well for more than a dozen years.[88]

From spring to fall, domestic herds were pastured within ward boundaries on designated bottomlands to keep the milk cows and oxen available to their owners. Around mid-October each year, after the crops in adjacent fields had been harvested and tight fences were no longer maintained, cattle were allowed to roam free on the lowland pastures until the spring planting season. In some towns, residents organized a community herding arrangement for horses similar to that for the domestic cattle.[89]

To accomodate the herds of surplus livestock, residents soon sought rangeland outside the heavily settled areas of southern and central Davis County. They found such grazing lands in northern Davis County, in Weber, Morgan, and Box Elder counties, in Cache Valley, and in the Malad Valley of southern Idaho. Livestockmen in south Bountiful used summer ranges at Silver Creek and Parleys Park in Summit County and in Tooele County's Skull Valley. The first general use of the distant, virgin ranges was forced by the drouth and grasshopper plague of 1855. That year, Joseph Holbrook sent the Bountiful ward cattle herd to Bear River Valley, hoping to preserve the townspeople's investment. Nearly half of the weakened cattle died during the hard winter.[90]

In normal seasons, to prevent the overgrazing of local ranges, everyone was required to send their surplus stock to the "big range." Each April, the hired herders would meet at a collection point, accept the cattle that had been branded by their owners, and drive the cattle to the summer range. Any surplus stock found on local grazing lands afterward was declared a stray and locked in the local pound. Owners could claim these animals only by paying a fee. Similar arrangements existed for community sheep herds. Working together under the direction of a church-appointed committee, sheep owners built a local collecting pen, gathered the animals each spring, and sent them off with a hired herder. Some groups summered their sheep on mountain ranges east of town. Others found grazing land in Weber or Morgan counties.[91]

The Miller brothers, Henry W. and Daniel A., found an ideal grazing site on Fremont Island, where upwards of 2,000 sheep could roam freely without a herder. Beginning in 1859, and continuing for a quarter century, the Millers ferried sheep from Farmington to what became known as "Millers Island." They used a succession of flat-bottomed boats to transport the sheep back and forth across the lake. "The meat of this flock tasted more like venison than mutton," according to Seymour Miller, and it brought a handsome price on the spring market.[92]

Herding arrangements for surplus cattle and for sheep took new

This abandoned boat is believed to have been Jacob Miller's cattle boat, used in the late 1870s to haul sheep and cattle from Farmington to the island ranges of the Great Salt Lake. (Utah State Historical Society)

forms during the cooperative movement of the 1860s and 1870s. In the spirit of cooperation, citizens of Kaysville, Farmington, Centerville, and Bountiful organized the Davis County Co-operative Stock Institution in February 1871, with a capital investment of one million dollars. Organizers promised high-quality care and protection against theft and reminded owners of the need to protect crops from loose stock. Elected officers included leading men from every community, including some LDS bishops. The board hired Horton D. Haight to manage the operation; he was assisted by trusted appraisers for horses, cattle, and sheep.[93]

The county livestock cooperative became part of the Davis United Order three years later. To accomodate the huge cattle herds, the organization established its own ranch at Blue Creek in Box Elder County. "No country can produce fatter or better flavored beef and mutton," claimed a report in the *Salt Lake Herald.* In addition, officers negotiated for shares on Antelope Island, which had been reserved up to that time for the exclusive use of the Mormon church's Perpetual Emigrating Fund Company. To transport sheep and supplies to and from the island, in 1879 officials engaged Jacob Miller of

Farmington to build and operate a sixteen-by-forty-foot sloop-rigged sailboat.[94]

As with other cooperative organizations, the livestock co-op faced its share of challenges. The society at first tried to care for the herd by rotating herding assignments among participating livestock-men. In 1875, officers hired a permanent caretaker to oversee operations. After another year, however, the cooperative disbanded and distributed the cattle to shareholders according to their investments. The responsibility for community herding returned to the local level. The Davis County Co-operative Mercantile Institution took over the grazing lands of the discontinued livestock co-op and for the next four years made them available to the local surplus cattle herds.[95]

Cooperative sheep herds also existed for a short time in Davis County in the early 1870s. The loosely organized community herds were affiliated with local cooperatives or united orders, but they failed to meet the expectations of directors. For a time, sponsors considered establishing a woolen factory in Farmington to save the cost of shipping the wool produced in the county to Provo's factory. When the unprofitable cooperative sheep herds were disbanded, the sheep were returned to the individual shareholders.[96]

The Privatization of Cooperatives

Transcontinental railroad connections made increased amounts of imported merchandise available in Utah, including Davis County. This influx of goods challenged the home industry movement and eventually supplanted much of the local production. Most imported goods came from San Francisco or St. Louis. The products were usually cheaper than those made locally, and the quality was often better. In Utah during the early 1870s imports greatly outnumbered exports. They were paid for with cash received from California immigrants, soldiers, and passengers on the stage lines. By the 1880s, half of the goods shipped into Utah were consumer products; the other half was mining equipment. Utah's export trade finally reached a balance with imports only because of the mining industry. Agricultural products could not compete with those of the West Coast because of freight costs and distance. Products brought into the territory for resale included dry goods, groceries, clothing, lumber, agricultural

When the United Order disbanded, the Kaysville Cooperative continued under private ownership. Its major investors started Barnes Bank in part of the co-op building on Main at Center Street, seen in this 1895 photograph. (Utah State Historical Society)

implements, wagons, furniture, livestock, wool, leather and leather products, hides, and tallow.[97]

The cooperative mercantiles, shops, and herds failed due to this competition and the lack of local support. The spirit of cooperation had less appeal to the people of Davis County than did the spirit of independent enterprise and their hunger for the goods they could not produce locally. Latter-day Saints did not blame anyone but themselves for the failure. In their view, cooperation would not succeed until those who participated in the effort were personally of a moral character willing to make it work. The Mormon Reformation and the rules of the United Order were attempts to help people govern their lives so they could unite harmoniously in economic and social enterprises. Unlike the Owenites, another nineteenth-century group attempting to live a communal lifestyle, according to one historical assessment, "a Mormon did not enter a commune to *become* good, but because he *was* good. . . . Faith was the instrument of change—not institutions."[98]

Not long after Brigham Young's death in 1877, the remaining united order cooperatives in Davis County paid off their investors and either became private businesses or ceased operation. The general stores financially had been the most successful of the cooperative efforts in Davis County, and all four of them survived under private ownership. For many years these stores appealed to the loyalty of Latter-day Saint shoppers by keeping the name "co-operative" in their title.

The united order manufacturing companies shared many of the same economic challenges faced by the co-op stores, plus one additional hurdle. The tanneries, shoe shops, broom factories, and tailoring shops specialized in a single product, and their locally made commodities could not always compete in quality with eastern factory goods. For this reason alone, few of these enterprises survived the demise of the united order movement.

Brickmaking in Davis County did well, since bricks were not a product easily imported. That industry continued in the private sphere beyond the 1870s in both Bountiful and Kaysville. Tailors and broom makers could also compete in local markets and did so until mass-produced products undercut them in variety and price. The leather industry in Davis County did not survive. Both the Barnes and Stewart Tannery of Kaysville and the Union Tannery of Farmington soon ceased operation.[99]

As noted earlier, the county livestock cooperative disbanded in 1876, after five years of deficit operation. The cooperative ranch in Box Elder County was sold at a private sale for a modest sum, along with a few remaining head of livestock and some wagons. The firm realized a greater return when it sold its ferry and its livestock, land, and equipment on Antelope Island to private buyers.[100]

With the end of the Davis United Order, herding was managed once again as a community effort in Davis County. But within a few years even that disappeared. One reason for the transition to private herds was a change in fencing practices. Community fencing of Big Field croplands ended and farmers began enclosing their individual lands. In addition, communities built fences around some of the remaining common pastures. Serious ranchers purchased or leased private ranges outside the county. For others, in the late 1880s private herding arrangements once again became available for those needing the service.[101]

The management of irrigation water followed the pattern of other agricultural cooperatives. To remove the Mormon church from the management process, each existing irrigation district in Davis County organized as a non-profit irrigation company. The farmers in each of these corporations owned shares that defined the amount of water they could use. Together they named a watermaster, who apportioned the water by setting times for each water turn, just as such men had done under the court-ordered, church-supervised system. The new irrigation companies lasted well into the twentieth century. They finally disbanded and sold their water rights when Weber River water was piped into the county along the mountainside, increasing water supplies and making pressurized irrigation possible.

ENDNOTES

1. Carol Ivins Collett, *Kaysville—Our Town: A History,* 54; Dale Morgan, *The Great Salt Lake* (New York: Bobbs–Merrill, 1947), 159.

2. Morgan, *Great Salt Lake,* 216; Clayton Holt, *The Community of Syracuse, 1820 to 1995: Our Heritage* (Syracuse: Syracuse Historical Commission, 1994), 9–13.

3. For the precise route see L. A. Fleming and A.R. Standing, "The Road to 'Fortune': The Salt Lake Cutoff," *Utah Historical Quarterly* 33 (Summer 1965): 248–71.

4. Annie Call Carr, ed., *East of Antelope Island: History of the First Fifty Years of Davis County,* 146.

5. Davis County, Court Minutes, 6 June 1859, Davis County Clerk's Office.

6. Ibid., 13, 18 June 1859; Leslie T. Foy, *The City Bountiful: Utah's Second Settlement, from Pioneers to Present,* 64.

7. Davis County, Court Minutes, 30 September, 31 December 1872, 3 March 1873; John W. Hess, William R. Smith, and Anson Call to Brigham Young, 1 September 1874, LDS Church Archives.

8. Foy, *City Bountiful,* 64–67; Glen M. Leonard, "A History of Farmington, Utah, to 1890," 46.

9. "Kays Ward or Kaysville, As It Was October 27th, 1862, as remembered by Joseph Barton," in Collett, *Kaysville—Our Town,* 42–43, 54.

10. James V. Barber, "The History of Highways in Utah from 1847 to 1860" (M.A. thesis, University of Utah, 1949), 29–30; Foy, *City Bountiful,* 68.

11. Davis County, Court Minutes, 8 March 1859.

12. Barber, "History of Highways, 29–30.

13. Davis County, Court Minutes, March 1854, and 8 March 1859.

14. Ibid., March 1853.

15. Janice P. Dawson, "A Brief Look at the Development of Early Roads and Highways," 1, manuscript, in possession of Janice P. Dawson, Layton; Carr, *East of Antelope Island,* 135; Barber, "History of Highways, 149.

16. Myron W. McIntyre and Noel R. Barton, eds., *Christopher Layton* (n.p.: Christoper Layton Family Organization, 1966), 115, 236 n. 51; Betty M. Madsen and Brigham D. Madsen, *North to Montana!: Jehus, Bullwhackers, and Mule Skinners on the Montana Trail* (Salt Lake City: University of Utah Press), 131–32.

17. Hubert Howe Bancroft, *History of Utah, 1540–1887* (San Francisco: The History Co., 1891), 769.

18. William Mulder and A. Russell Mortensen, eds., *Among the Mormons: Historic Accounts by Contemporary Observers* (New York: Alfred A. Knopf, 1958), 236; Kate B. Carter, ed., *Heart Throbs of the West,* 12:54.

19. *Deseret News,* 29 November 1851, 4; 16 November 1864, 3.

20. Carter, *Heart Throbs,* 1:184; *Deseret Evening News,* 30 December 1878.

21. "Collett, *Kaysville—Our Town,* 63; Journal History of the Church of Jesus Christ of Latter–day Saints, 21 December 1854, 3; Margaret Steed Hess, *My Farmington: A History of Farmington, Utah, 1847–1976,* 315.

22. Lee D. Bell, *South Weber: The Autobiography of One Utah Community,* 138–39.

23. S. George Ellsworth, *Utah's Heritage* (Salt Lake City: Peregrine Smith, 1972), 248–50; Bell, *South Weber,* 136; Foy, *City Bountiful,* 127–31; Carr, *East of Antelope Island,* 55, 487, 492.

24. Leonard J. Arrington, *Great Basin Kingdom: An Economic History of the Latter–day Saints,* 199–200, 228–29; *Deseret News,* 9 November 1865; Journal History, 11 December 1866, 21 January 1867; Collett, *Kaysville—Our Town,* 80; Foy, *City Bountiful,* 132.

25. *Deseret News,* 9 November 1865; Journal History, 11 December 1866, 15 January 1867. Kaysville's telegraph office apparently did not open until 1867 (Carr, *East of Antelope Island,* 391).

26. Ellsworth, *Utah's Heritage,* 247, 251–52; Madsen and Madsen, *North to Montana!,* 106–7.

27. Carr, *East of Antelope Island,* 68–69, 483, 492; Mary Ellen Smoot and Marilyn Sheriff, *The City in–Between: History of Centerville, Utah,* 317.

28. Collett, *Kaysville—Our Town,* 58; Carr, *East of Antelope Island,* 393; Bell, *South Weber,* 80–81, 299.

29. Journal History, 16 August 1869, 2.

30. Ibid.; Madsen and Madsen, *North to Montana!,* 173–75.

31. Journal History, 25 August 1868.

32. J. Roderic Korns and Dale L. Morgan, eds., *West from Fort Bridger: The Pioneering of the Immigrant Trails across Utah, 1846–1850,* rev. by Will Bagley and Harold Schindler (Logan: Utah State University Press, 1994), 301; Joseph Cain and Arieh C. Brower, *Mormon Way–bill to the Gold Mines* . . . (Great Salt Lake City: Willard Richards, 1851), 29; Steed, *My Farmington,* 312–15.

33. McIntyre and Barton, *Christopher Layton,* 101–2; Carr, *East of Antelope Island,* 124, 484, 470; Foy, *City Bountiful,* 64–65.

34. Richard D. Poll, Thomas G. Alexander, Eugene E. Campbell, David E. Miller, eds., *Utah's History,* 218–19, 221; Ellsworth, *Utah's Heritage,* 252–55.

35. Foy, *City Bountiful,* 132–33; Collett, *Kaysville—Our Town,* 88; Journal History, 10 January 1869.

36. Collett, *Kaysville—Our Town,* 88.

37. Ibid., 88–89.

38. Bancroft, *History of Utah,* 756–57; *Deseret Evening News,* 3, 12 January 1870, 22, 23 December 1869; Journal History, 2 December 1869.

39. *Deseret Evening News,* 11, 28 January 1870; 24 October 1882.

40. *Deseret News* (weekly), 16 June 1869.

41. Ibid.; diary quoted in Arlene H. Eakle, Adelia Baird, and Georgia Weber, *Woods Cross: Patterns and Profiles of a City* (Woods Cross: Woods Cross City Council, 1976), 6–7.

42. *Deseret Evening News,* 11 June 1869.

43. *Deseret News* (weekly), 16 June 1869.

44. Ibid.

45. Collett, Kaysville—Our Town, 91.

46. Foy, *City Bountiful,* 133; Journal History, 25 June 1869; Morgan, *Great Salt Lake,* 296.

47. Farmington Ward, Teachers Quorum, Minutes, 4 June 1870; Davis

County, Court Minutes, 9 September, 20 October 1870, 5 June, 12 October 1871.

48. Poll et al., *Utah's History,* 219–20, 440, 735; Ellsworth, *Utah's Heritage,* 257–59.

49. Carr, *East of Antelope Island,* 485; Poll et al., *Utah's History,* 383, 435–36.

50. Carr, *East of Antelope Island,* 237.

51. Collett, *Kaysville—Our Town,* 58; Bell, *South Weber,* 139.

52. Carr, *East of Antelope Island,* 412; Collett, *Kaysville—Our Town,* 80; Hess, *My Farmington,* 324.

53. Collett, *Kaysville—Our Town,* 58; Smoot and Sheriff, *City In–Between,* 166.

54. John Codman, *The Mormon Country: A Summer with the "Latter–day Saints"* (New York: United States Publishing, 1874), 211; William Robb Purrington, "The History of South Davis County from 1847 to 1870," 51.

55. Leonard J. Arrington, Feramorz Y. Fox, and Dean L. May, *Building the City of God: Community and Cooperation among the Mormons* (Salt Lake City: Deseret Book, 1976), 89.

56. Feramorz Y. Fox, "The Consecration Movement of the Middle 'Fifties," *Improvement Era* 47 (February–March 1944): 146–47; also in Arrington, Fox, and May, *Building the City of God,* 68–75.

57. Joseph L. Robinson, Autobiography and Journal, LDS Church Archives, 100–1, entries of 6 and 17 April 1854; Fox, "The Consecration Movement," 121, 187; Arrington, Fox, and May, *Building the City of God,* 65–66; consecration deeds, LDS Church Archives.

58. Fox, "The Consecration Movement," 188; Arrington, Fox, and May, *Building the City of God,* 65–66, 77–78.

59. Arrington, Fox, and May, *Building the City of God,* 79–86.

60. Ibid., 90–91, 101; Journal History, 10 October 1868.

61. Leonard, "History of Farmington," 128–30.

62. Doneta M. Gatherum and Kent C. Day, comp., *Kaysville and Layton General Stores* (Kaysville and Layton: Kaysville–Layton Historical Society, 1987) 4, 11; Collett, *Kaysville—Our Town,* 94–95; Carr, *East of Antelope Island,* 393–95.

63. Hess, *My Farmington,* 6, 30, 231–32, 304–6, 342, 379; Leonard, "A History of Farmington," 127–28.

64. Carr, *East of Antelope Island,* 68; Smoot and Sheriff, *City In–Between,* 32, 188–89, 227, 233; Arrington, Fox, and May, *Building the City of God,* 88, 98.

65. U.S. Census, 1850; William Wallace Willey, "A Short History of Bountiful," manuscript, 1914, LDS Church Archives, 23; Foy, *City Bountiful,* 95, 141; Carr, *East of Antelope Island,* 415–18, 421.

66. Leonard, "History of Farmington," 126; Steven R. Sorensen, "School of the Prophets," in Daniel L. Ludlow, ed., *Encyclopedia of Mormonism* (New York: Macmillan, 1992), 1269–70.

67. Leonard, "History of Farmington, 130.

68. Arrington, *Great Basin Kingdom,* 335–45; Leonard, "History of Farmington," 131.

69. Leonard, "History of Farmington," 131–34.

70. Journal History, 20 December 1868; Foy, *City Bountiful,* 141; *Deseret Evening News,* 2 July 1873.

71. *Deseret Evening News,* 11 June 1873.

72. *Deseret News,* 13, 15 May 1874; Arrington, *Great Basin Kingdom,* 330–37.

73. Leonard, "History of Farmington," 137–38.

74. Among other places, the list is available in Mulder and Mortensen, *Among the Mormons,* 393–98.

75. Leonard, "History of Farmington," 136–38.

76. Collett, *Kaysville—Our Town,* 94.

77. *Deseret Evening News,* 24 June 1874; Collett, *City In–Between,* 113.

78. Foy, *City Bountiful,* 141–42.

79. *Salt Lake Herald,* 9 June 1876.

80. Leonard, "History of Farmington," 141; *Deseret News,* 29 June 1874.

81. Leonard, "History of Farmington," 140–43.

82. Ibid., 143, 146.

83. Ibid., 144–46.

84. Leonard J. Arrington, "The Deseret Agricultural and Manufacturing Society in Pioneer Utah," *Utah Historical Quarterly* 24 (April 1956): 167–68; Leonard, "History of Farmington," 109.

85. *Deseret News,* 27 August 1862, 3 August 1864; Leonard, "History of Farmington," 109–10.

86. Journal History, 20 March 1860, 2; *Deseret News,* 21 January 1871.

87. Bancroft, *History of Utah,* 729–31.

88. *Deseret News,* 27 July 1850, 17 April 1852; Leonard, "History of Farmington," 118–20.

89. Leonard, "History of Farmington," 118–20; Farmington Ward, Teachers Minutes, 26 April 1867.

90. Leonard, "History of Farmington," 118; Carr, *East of Antelope Island,* 162–63; Arrington, *Great Basin Kingdom,* 150–51.

91. Leonard, "History of Farmington," 118, 120–23.

92. David H. Miller and Anne M. Eckman, eds., "Seymour Miller's Account of an Early Sheep Operation on Frémont Island," *Utah Historical Quarterly* 56 (Spring 1988): 162, 169 n. 30, 170.

93. Journal History, 22 February 1871, 2.

94. Leonard, "History of Farmington," 119, 121–22; *Salt Lake Herald,* 9 June 1876, 3; Peter G. Van Alfen, "Sail and Steam: Great Salt Lake's Boats and Boatbuilders, 1847–1901," *Utah Historical Quarterly* 63 (Summer 1995): 202–3.

95. Leonard, "History of Farmington," 121–24.

96. Ibid., 123–24.

97. Bancroft, *History of Utah,* 759–61.

98. Arrington, Fox, and May, *Building the City of God,* 8–9, 12–13.

99. Collett, *Kaysville—Our Town,* 93; Leonard, "History of Farmington," 144–45.

100. Leonard, "History of Farmington," 122–23.

101. Ibid., 123.

CHAPTER 6

CHALLENGES AND CHANGE

The last thirty years of the nineteenth century were a time of significant change for Davis County and for Utah. The Mormon church's abandonment of the dream of a unified, cooperative economic community was one part of the transformation. Other transitions took place in political and social life. Of special significance was the diminished influence of the Church of Jesus Christ of Latter-day Saints in the direct conduct of government. Related reforms appeared in the official discouragement of new plural marriages in 1890 and the end of church management of local schools.

Some of the modifications that marked the end of Utah's territorial period were imposed by outside forces—notably politicians and reformers. Many Americans believed that the way Mormons lived challenged basic national values. Theocratic government, a cooperative economy, plural marriage, and a church-dominated educational system had to be abandoned if Utah were to be granted statehood. For a time, the Latter-day Saints defended their ways. Their experiences before coming to Utah had taught them to distrust government officials not of their faith. They believed in education that fused secular and sacred knowledge. They sought group unity in the political, social, and economic aspects of their lives. In the end, however, under increasing pressure from without and a shifting of attitudes within the church, the Latter-day Saints accepted change so that Utah could become a state.[1]

The Road to Statehood

Six times in a forty-year span Utahns petitioned the federal government for statehood. Delegates from Davis County participated in each constitutional convention and extolled the benefits of statehood. In 1864, for example, the county sent John Stoker, Philo Allen, Thomas S. Smith, Christopher Layton, and William R. Smith as representatives.[2] The final appeal for statehood in 1887 eventually succeeded in large part because federal anti-polygamy legislation over the years had prepared the way. The laws threatened the temporal power of the LDS church by challenging its political and economic influence and the practice of plural marriage. After the United States Supreme Court sustained the constitutionality of one of these laws in 1879, an aggressive judicial campaign against the Mormon church and those practicing polygamy led to an eventual end of the practices that had offended the nation.[3]

Statehood came in 1896, six years after church members voted to accept President Wilford Woodruff's Manifesto ending new plural marriages. Residents in Davis County celebrated the political achievement with gusto. One community launched its celebration of the 4 January statehood proclamation by ringing school bells and firing a forty-five-gun salute in honor of Utah becoming the forty-fifth state. A patriotic program followed. The local militia stood at attention while the band played, residents offered speeches on Utah's past and future, and a choir sang "America" and "Utah, We Love Thee." Similar events were staged at meeting places elsewhere in the county.[4]

Politics and Plural Marriage. Citizens of Davis County were very much a part of the transition from the old theocracy to the new democracy. Old ways had become entrenched. In political matters, most residents, but not all, supported the Mormon People's party against its gentile rival, the Liberal party.[5] Many residents had lent their energies to promote Mormon economic exclusiveness, and not a few men had formed polygamous families.

The 1880 census captured a picture of the extent of plural marriage at its peak in Utah. Among Davis County's 5,222 Latter-day Saints, 1,140 men, women, and children resided in polygamous families. This amounted to 21.8 percent of the Mormon population, slightly above the average for the state. Within the county, involvement ranged from 19 percent in South Hooper and Kaysville wards to 32 percent in West Bountiful. East Bountiful and Centerville were close to the county average, and Farmington reported nearly 27 percent in polygamous households. South Weber, perhaps influenced by its anti-polygamist Morrisite background, counted only one large plural family, constituting 5 percent of local Mormons. Perhaps the best explanation for these variations within the county is that personal circumstances seemed to make a difference.[6]

What it meant to be one wife among several, a husband with plural wives, or a child in a multiple family must have varied from one family to another as well. Two-thirds of Utah's participating men in plural marriages had only two wives, another 20 percent took a third. Those few men who married five or more wives in Davis County were a definite exception. Among this group were Daniel Wood, John W. Hess, Christopher Layton, Thomas Grover, and Thomas E. Ricks. A woman in a monogamous marriage averaged eight children, a plural wife less than six. Husbands counted an average of fifteen children from their various wives.[7]

When a husband could afford to do so, he provided separate living quarters for each wife and her children, sometimes in different settlements.[8] The best-known report of the plural wife experience in Davis County is Annie Clark Tanner's reminiscence, *Mormon Mother.* Her husband, Joseph M. Tanner, a prominent Salt Lake City attorney and educator, had six wives and a farm in Canada. He seldom visited Annie in Farmington and left her to provide much of her own support and to raise their eight children. Less well known is Josephine Streeper Chase of Centerville, whose diary reveals her involvement in the daily routines of life and offers glimpses into her feelings as the second wife of George Ogden Chase.[9] Other glimpses into the stresses and strains of multiple families and the cooperative arrangements that developed in many successful families can be gleaned from other personal and family histories.[10]

Most polygamous marriages were reasonably successful. In some of these families under one roof the wives specialized as cooks, seamstresses, or teachers and shared the housekeeping and baby-sitting duties. In around 10 percent of the cases, a man married sisters. Jealousies did create strains in families, and divorce or separation became an answer when the patriarchal marriage system resulted in unhappy relationships.[11]

Because of their religious commitment to plural marriage as a divinely sanctioned practice, Latter-day Saints did not submit easily to the legislative bans on plural marriage. The Mormon judges in local probate courts refused to prosecute under the Morrill Antibigamy Act of 1862. When the Cullom Bill came before Congress in 1870, with a provision to shift criminal matters to federal authorities, some 5,000 Mormon women joined an indignation meeting in the Salt Lake Tabernacle. Similar protest sessions were held throughout the territory, including Farmington, Centerville, and Kaysville. When Mormon Apostle Orson Pratt and the Rev. J.P. Newman, a Methodist preacher and U.S. Senate chaplain, met in Salt Lake that August to debate the topic "Does the Bible Sanction Polygamy?" some Mormon priesthood quorums in Davis County canceled meetings so they and their wives could hear the exchange.[12]

Beginning in 1884, Utah Chief Justice Charles S. Zane and his associates in the Utah federal courts began an aggressive judicial crusade to enforce a tougher anti-polygamy bill, the Edmunds Act. Under this law, citizens convicted of unlawful cohabitation were subject to six months' imprisonment and/or a $300 fine. The law also took away a polygamist's right to vote or hold public office. In compliance with this part of the law, Ezra T. Clark resigned his office as Davis County treasurer and his son was appointed in his stead.[13]

A number of Davis County polygamists were among the thousand or more men who served terms in the territorial penitentiary in Sugarhouse near Salt Lake City, leaving the care of farms and livestock to their wives and older sons. Other men adopted a passive form of resistance and escaped prosecution by going into hiding, or what they called "on the underground." A few confronted arresting

A decade or so into his thirty-year term as bishop of Kay's Ward, Peter Barton (seated at center) served a six-month's sentence in the territorial penitentiary for practicing plural marriage. (Utah State Historical Society)

officers directly. A number of the older pioneers escaped this latest trouble through a circumstance that did not go unnoticed. "The Marshalls are making a heavy raid on our Poligamists," Joseph L. Robinson wrote in his diary. After noting three recent arrests, he listed six polygamists who had escaped this fate and added: "It is very remarkable if not strange the Lord has removed by death several of our Brethren from their grasp."[14] No comprehensive list of Davis County residents imprisoned for polygamy is available, but some are identified in various town histories.

Those who served prison terms described themselves as "prisoners for conscience sake." These citizens felt unjustly denied their constitutional guarantees for free religious practice. But in 1879 the U.S. Supreme Court had decided otherwise. A half-dozen or so from each community in Davis County served time in prison. Some of the men complained of ill-fitting prison clothes, inadequate bedding during cold weather, and poor-quality food. Visitors were permitted, however, as was correspondence with families.[15] B.H. Roberts, a Centerville blacksmith who became a teacher, historian, and Mormon church authority, escaped immediate sentencing by leaving for a mission to England. That decision cost him the bail he had posted. When he returned two years later, he surrendered to the court and served four months in prison.[16]

Friends or relatives often offered refuge for those who chose to hide. A number of Mormon church authorities found safe houses in southern Davis County; some of them had plural wives living in the area.[17] Church president John Taylor spent the last few months of his life in hiding in west Kaysville with the monogamist family of Thomas F. Roueche, the city's first mayor. Personal guards known by code names kept watch by patrolling the nearby road on horseback. With many church leaders in hiding, Latter-day Saints found themselves isolated from the direct contact they had enjoyed before. "We are living now when we must stand or fall for ourselves," Bishop Jacob Moroni Secrist told a priesthood group in Farmington. "We have no visits from Apostles [or] Presidents. . . . [We] should do our duty day by day. Some [of the] best men have died; others are on the U.G. [underground] and younger heads of families must prepare for responsible duties."[18]

Some Davis County residents found secure hiding places in secret spots in their own homes or barns or with helpful neighbors. Haystacks, corn fields, and trap-doors sometimes were used to hide. Residents of Bountiful set up daytime watchmen at the point of the mountain and signal men atop the tabernacle to warn of approaching lawmen. They also created a hide-out at Buckland Flats east of town. The polygamists in every town depended upon trusted friends to help them remain free, and they feared snitchers who might tip off the federal marshals.[19]

For some, the answer was to leave the territory. These exiles served proselyting or genealogical missions for the church. A few accepted settlement missions or set up new homes and farms in safe places on their own initiative. Some found refuge in Mexico, Canada, or closer to home along the Little Colorado River in northern Arizona or in Wyoming's Big Horn Basin.[20]

Such adjustments were not easy for families. Christopher Layton, successful Kaysville farmer and businessman, reluctantly agreed to accept a settlement mission to southern Arizona in 1883. His tenth wife, Elizabeth Williams, and an increasing number of family members joined him in exile. Layton subsequently served as president of the St. Joseph LDS Stake in Arizona for fifteen years, and made his last of numerous trips back to Utah shortly before his death in 1898. To preserve his freedom, Truman Leonard of Farmington spent some time in Logan doing ordinance work in the LDS temple there. He then left two wives and most of his children behind and, with his second wife, Margaret Bourne, established a second home in Alberta, Canada. Leonard abandoned his adopted place of refuge after six years, returning to Utah in 1894.[21]

The decision to stop taking new wives halted the judicial crusade against the Mormons, but it did not end the practice of plural marriage. Most Davis County polygamous families honored their marriage commitments and lived out their lives in a plural relationship. Some believed the ban to be only a temporary measure. Wrote one Davis County resident after the October 1890 conference, "We have to shut down on plural marriages for a season, and Uncle Sam will have to howl."[22] Within a generation, however, the ban became permanent and well established.

Incorporation of Towns. The end of Mormon church control over civil affairs gave Davis County's communities a broader margin for self-government. Those towns which became incorporated entities held open elections and levied taxes to pay for city services. Their biggest initial responsibilities were maintaining streets, managing the distribution of water within the city, and enforcing laws. Councilmen in each city appointed a justice of the peace, city marshal, street supervisor, sexton, and other needed officers. Recorders and treasurers were elected, as were the mayor and five councilmen. Most city business was accomplished by organizing the councillors into standing committees. Typical were committees on elections, the local cemetery, irrigation, streets, police and fire, prison, sanitary conditions, finance, public grounds, municipal laws, and the judiciary, which were the primary services offered by city governments.[23]

Of Davis County's first five communities, only one—Kaysville—

succeeded in its effort to incorporate during Brigham Young's lifetime, although at least one other town—Farmington—tried. Kaysville became the county's first full-fledged city on 15 March 1868. By then, at least sixteen other cities had been incorporated in the Territory of Utah.[24]

A desire for civic independence emerged early in the Kaysville area. When Bishop William Kay left for Carson Valley, Nevada, on a settlement mission in 1856, some residents of Kay's Ward proposed a name change for the ecclesiastical unit. They chose the name "Freedom." Brigham Young is said to have responded, "When did Kay's Ward get its freedom?" Even after this presumed rejection, the name Freedom was sometimes used when referring to local civic matters. When incorporation came more than a decade later, the city of 1,400 residents was named Kaysville, after its first Mormon bishop. Thomas F. Roueche became the first mayor and, with breaks between, subsequently served three other terms. Roueche and his five councilmen were all Latter-day Saints. None had been a top local church official, although Roueche and Rosel Hyde later served as counselors to bishops (a position Hyde held when he later served as mayor). Their credentials as civic-minded individuals were sufficient and emphasized the intent to separate the affairs of church and state. The new city emphasized its secular orientation by naming the streets running east and west after trees and the north-south streets First Street through Eleventh Street.[25]

With the approach of statehood, the largest of the old communities in Davis County followed Kaysville's example. Farmington and Bountiful sought and were granted territorial approval to incorporate in 1892. Centerville waited until 1915, and then organized as a town under county authority. South Weber became a town in 1938.[26]

Farmington church leaders had initially toyed with the idea of incorporation at about the same time Kaysville was organized and again three years after Brigham Young's death. Hector C. Haight raised the possibility in a February 1868 priesthood meeting, and the men voted to petition the legislature for a city charter. A week later, the quorum was informed that Haight had discussed the matter with "the *President,* [who] said if the people wished it, it would be all right. But he did not see any advantages to be derived from it." The group

The steepled county courthouse can be seen at the far left of this 1896 overview of Farmington, not long after the town's incorporation. Just across the wide State Street is the LDS Academy, and at the right edge of the photograph is the transplanted Lake Park dance pavilion at Lagoon Resort. (Utah State Historical Society)

then rescinded their previous vote. Arthur Stayner observed that "he was now satisfied there is sufficient power in the priesthood to govern and control us." It was Stayner who sponsored a resolution in 1880 that a committee check the laws to see if Farmington would qualify for incorporation as a town. No report exists of that finding; but, for whatever reason, nothing happened.[27]

The city government in Farmington finally came into being on 15 December 1892, with James H. Wilcox as mayor. He and the city council implemented secular government for the community of 1,100 people. "Our council are grinding out wholesale and wholesome ordinances," a reporter noted a few weeks later. Enforcing the new laws governing stray dogs and cattle and prohibiting Sunday ball games and profanity proved more difficult than their enactment, however.[28]

Bountiful launched its new civic venture two weeks after Farmington, on 28 December 1892, in a meeting at the home of the newly appointed city attorney. The first mayor was Joseph Lamoni Holbrook, oldest son and namesake of the county's first probate judge. Councilmen and officers were drawn from all geographic regions of the Bountiful area. They set about to protect the community's moral foundations with laws regulating liquor stores and pool halls, and they tackled the challenging task of making limited water serve an increasing number of users. Some old-timers were skeptical about leaving behind a form of priesthood government that had served Bountiful well for a half-century. They were not alone. Disincorporation was actively discussed in many Utah cities in 1893. Even so, with city governments functioning, Davis County's residents were reported to be pleased to no longer be considered "country Jakes" to Salt Lake's urban dwellers.[29]

During their first years, Davis County's new city governments first met in homes and then in rented rooms in local halls or business buildings. In 1889 Kaysville became the first of the three to build its own city hall. After twenty years in rented spaces, the city council bonded for $5,000, hired local architect William Allen to prepare plans, and secured bids from contractors. Allen designed a one-story brick building, typical of the times and adorned with an impressive front entrance and tall wooden tower.[30]

For more than a dozen years, Bountiful officials rented the vestry room of the brick hall owned by the local Relief Society. They next used the Commercial Club Room in the Bountiful State Bank Building. In the 1930s the city council purchased and adapted a business building at 150 North Main for its uses.[31]

By 1898 Farmington's council was meeting in the county courthouse for its Monday evening meetings. But the members regularly considered other options, and as official records multiplied, they began a search for a permanent location. In June 1917 the city purchased a ten-year-old brick office building erected at First North and Main Streets by the Davis LDS Stake. It came conveniently equipped with meeting rooms and a walk-in safe.[32]

As the pioneer period drew to a close, Davis County officials also sought better office facilities. In 1890, the county built a new court-

The landscaped grounds offered such a picturesque setting for Davis County's handsome second courthouse and new jail that this scene appeared in *Art Work of Utah* in 1896. (Utah State Historical Society)

house to replace the adobe structure that had served well for thirty-five years but was found to intrude into the surveyed street. Kaysville architect William Allen designed a picturesque, two-story brick building reflecting classical styles popular at the time. Measuring sixty-one-by-fifty-two feet, the new building doubled the space previously available for county administrators, justices, and school officials. The new courthouse cost $12,500, more than twice that of the original building. According to Jacob Miller, local builders finished the job after the original contractor failed in business.[33]

The following year, a separate jail containing three cells and an office was built just east of the courthouse. Commissioners decorated the courthouse grounds with an iron fence, ornamental shrubs, and a row of poplar trees along Court House Street (now State Street). They furnished the janitor with a double-geared power lawnmower to keep lawns neatly trimmed.[34]

Political Changes. Along with the transition in the 1890s to local municipal governments and statehood came an increase in partisan political activity, an increased involvement of women in public life, and a change in local militias. Elections had been a regular part of the life of Utah men from the beginning of settlement, especially the annual August precinct elections. Voters supported nominations for territorial and county offices in an annual caucus organized by Mormon church leaders and held at the county seat. During these years candidates generally ran unopposed.[35]

The first steps toward partisanship and a breakdown of direct church influence and gender barriers occurred in Utah's political life in the 1870s. The formation of the Liberal party was a non-Mormon effort to challenge Mormon church political control. In response, Mormon candidates ran under a People's party banner. The creation of this two-party system impacted Davis County politics only slightly. During the 1880s, the Liberal party in Bountiful drew enough support from non-Mormons, anti-Mormons, and from Latter-day Saints who disagreed with theocratic influence in politics to win some elections in that district; however, the People's party dominated elections elsewhere in the county. To ensure the victory of Mormon candidates, local church leaders in Davis County actively encouraged men and women voters to go to the polls. They invited Latter-day Saints to acquaint themselves with the issues and the candidates in order that they could vote intelligently.[36]

Women in Utah gained the right to vote when the territorial legislature enfranchised them in February 1870. Eastern reformers and non-Mormons in Utah had been lobbying Congress to do this, expecting that polygamous wives would use the ballot to free themselves from the "repressive" plural marriage system. Mormon leaders surprised the reformers by supporting suffrage. Their objective was statehood. Utah's polygamist wives rallied in favor of the "peculiar principle"—polygamy. In 1872 the LDS Relief Society launched the *Woman's Exponent,* which editor Emmeline B. Wells made an advocate both for suffrage and plural marriage. Davis County's Relief Society members became subscribers and supporters of suffrage.[37]

The pace of campaigning picked up noticeably during the 1880s, when Latter-day Saint leaders attempted to distance themselves from direct involvement in politics in order to convince Congress that Utah was ready for a secular government under statehood.

Candidates for congressional and territorial office from both parties canvassed for votes in Davis County. For the congressional rallies in 1882, nearly 500 county residents assembled at Farmington for the People's party gathering. Around eighty showed up when the Liberal party met. Arriving in Farmington by train, the candidates joined rallies at the Social Hall that involved speech making, band music, and the firing of cannons. People's party candidates emphasized their role as representatives of the majority's right of self-government. They accused their opponents as being agents of "despotism and serfdom." The Liberal candidates countered by defining themselves as the true voice of the people.[38]

As the anti-polygamy campaign picked up steam in the 1880s, dissatisfaction with the political condition in Utah Territory led to some tentative shifts toward a nationalization of politics. A few second-generation Mormons organized a short-lived Democratic Club in 1884 to try to open a way out of the church-state impasse. The Manifesto of 1890 opened the way for partisanship. With the approval of the LDS First Presidency, the Republicans organized in 1891, the Democrats revived their organization in the territory, and the People's party dissolved. Latter-day Saints were encouraged to affiliate with national political parties in order to eliminate the Mormon-gentile division. Because Republicans had led in the attacks on plural marriage, Mormons gravitated naturally to the Democrats, and church leaders had to encourage a more even division among the two parties.[39]

Voters in Davis County preferred Democratic candidates in the elections for county, territorial, and national offices during the transition period from 1892 to 1896. Generally around 75 percent of eligible voters turned out. Typical of the voting pattern during this period was the 1895 territorial senate race, where Democrat John R. Barnes garnered 611 votes, Republican E. P. Ellison received 434, and People's party candidate E. McLaughlin claimed 26. This pattern was consistent at all levels of government in the county. Notable exceptions were the Layton Precinct, which went two to one for the Republicans, and South Weber, where the People's party claimed half the votes and the other parties split the remainder.[40]

Elections in the incorporated cities during the 1890s tended toward fusion tickets. In Bountiful and Farmington, nonpartisan citizen's nominating conventions created tickets that included mostly Democrats. Republicans were included as opponents in some races, but they seldom won election. Kaysville's ballot was openly partisan. When Farmington offered names under two party headings in 1897 it was actually an attempt at a nonpartisan face-off: "The Democrats nominated two Republicans on their ticket and the Republicans, a few days later, placed the names of five Democrats, one-half the number to be elected, on their ticket," according to a local report. Over the next few years, Farmington alternated between Republican and Democratic tickets—both always a mix of both parties' candidates.[41] Whatever the look of the ballot in these three cities, however, it was generally the Democrats who scored victories during the 1890s.

Davis County's women organized in 1890 to support the suffrage movement. The Edmunds-Tucker Act of 1887 had robbed territorial women of the franchise they had received in 1870, and they wanted it back. General Relief Society leaders set up a countywide Woman's Suffrage Association, headed by Lucy A. Clark, who won annual reelection until the organization achieved its goals and disbanded. Chapters were soon functioning in each county community.[42] With education as their focus, the local groups studied civil government and how it operated. They encouraged women to prepare to vote intelligently and teach their children the principles of government. "Women should not be taxed without a voice" was a common theme in the meetings. Apostle Francis M. Lyman told one organizing meeting, "I have always felt that government was just as safe in the hands of our sisters as with the brethren, and those were the sentiments of President Young." Speaking out for equal rights, Lyman expressed his opinion that qualified women could serve as judges, police ("women are more courageous"), jurors, in elected office, and, if they wished, in the military.[43] With the breakdown of the rift between Mormon and non-Mormon politicians, Davis County's women followed the example of the LDS general Relief Society by moving from the People's party into the two national parties. Working within these parties, they helped prepare for statehood by seeking the right to vote and to hold office.[44]

Brigham H. Roberts of Centerville, a Davis County delegate to the statehood constitutional convention of 1895, spoke out against giving women the vote. The sentiment reported in the county was that "about eighty per cent of the male but not quite that per cent of the female population . . . endorse the course taken by delegate Roberts." But the suffragettes enlisted the oratory of Franklin S. Richards and Orson F. Whitney to counter Roberts's influence. Women's suffrage ultimately was included in the new state's constitution. Davis County's women once again went to the polls in 1896 (as did women in Idaho and Wyoming), twenty-four years before the Nineteenth Amendment nationalized women's suffrage.[45]

One of those enfranchised women had her name on the ballot. Lucy A. Clark, the county's suffrage leader, stood as the Republican candidate in the state's Third Senatorial District, comprising of Davis, Rich, and Morgan Counties. Facing the challenges of anti-Republican sentiment and some hesitance of voters to accept an expanded role for women, Clark lost to her Democratic opponent, rancher Aquila Nebeker. Accepting women as candidates for legislative office on an equal basis with men in state elections proved difficult for some, but three women did win seats in Utah's first state legislature.[46]

Some Latter-day Saints in Davis County also resisted the shift from a political system based on unity and founded on mutual trust, persuasion, and consent. They disliked a process that encouraged diversity and that insisted on majority rule. It took time to accept a two-party system in which religious differences were set aside and people of different faiths—or no religious faith—worked together for common political goals. The People's party did not immediately disappear from Davis County politics. It was still holding conventions on the eve of statehood, even though its minority candidates drew very few votes.[47]

By the time Utah became the forty-fifth state, grassroots partisan politics had replaced top-down theocratic rule in Davis County. Both Democrats and Republicans were organized at the local level, with women sharing leadership roles in the parties. County conventions met annually at the county courthouse to name about twenty delegates to state gatherings in Ogden, Provo, or Salt Lake City.[48]

With the increase of political partisanship, candidates for statewide races staged rallies in every Davis County community along the route of the Utah Central Railroad. A report just before the November 1896 election noted, "For the past week, everything has been politics, politics, politics. The great parties are sending out their missionaries in this county and each disciple professes to carry the war into the 'enemy's camp.'"[49] Partisans debated the issues of the national parties—immigration, monetary policies and standards, government spending, and pork barrel politics. One Davis County observer noted, "With the Silverites, the Republicans, Democrats and Populists we hope to have a good time."[50]

Among the political changes brought about during the struggle for statehood was the disbanding of Davis County's militia units and the creation of a new system under the Utah National Guard. Over a twenty-year period, Utah's Nauvoo Legion had participated in a number of engagements against Utah Indians, including the Black Hawk War of 1865–68, which involved more than 140 Davis County soldiers. The Utah War of 1857–58 had rallied the entire militia to confront the invading American forces led by Albert Sydney Johnston. During the Civil War, Captain Lot Smith and some three dozen Davis County militiamen for a time protected telegraph lines and the mail route leading to California. Following the war, Smith became head of the militia in Davis County.[51]

In September 1870 the territorial governor ordered the militia to cease its annual musters. Many Utah Mormons were uneasy, fearing that officials in Washington might choose a military solution over other options to combat polygamy being discussed in Congress. Almost immediately some U.S. troops stationed in Utah County, drunk with whiskey, went on a rampage of vandalism and harassment. In the wake of this incident, and with public militia activities suspended, the burden of military readiness fell to individuals. The men of Davis County were counseled by Mormon church and civic leaders to secure private arms and ammunition if they had not already done so. "Now is the time to prepare for war!" Lot Smith told one group. But the political crisis did not lead to armed conflict. The Nauvoo Legion's military commanders reinforced the ban against drills, but it effectively remained in a state of waiting until it was officially disbanded seventeen years later by the Edmunds-Tucker Act.[52]

A few months after the Utah National Guard was created in the

Davis County's militiamen shifted their allegiance from the territorial Nauvoo Legion to the Utah National Guard in 1894. Bountiful's artillery unit is seen in this 1899 photograph. (Mabey Collection, Utah State Historical Society)

spring of 1894, local military units were formed in various communities. In Davis County, they came into existence with a good deal of local enthusiasm. Band music, reminiscing about the Mormon Battalion, patriotic speeches, and pledges of loyalty to the United States were all part of the organizing meetings. The units purchased uniforms, held combined drills with other units, equipped themselves with arms furnished by the federal government, and presented themselves for inspection by Governor Caleb W. West and his staff.[53]

In 1898 the United States became involved in Cuba and the Philippines in what is known as the Spanish-American War. This conflict gave Latter-day Saints an opportunity to express their loyalty to the nation. When Congress declared war on Spain, the American flag was hoisted at the county courthouse and at schools in Davis County. Memorial services during the summer remembered the 266 men killed in the blowing up of the U.S. battleship *Maine* in February in Havana harbor. Local citizens donated money for a monument. In a show of patriotism, three National Guard units from Salt Lake City joined those from Bountiful and Farmington for an encampment during the Labor Day weekend. The companies attracted nearly 8,000 spectators for their sham battle at Lagoon Resort.[54]

Some in Utah questioned the war resolution passed by Congress. Public debates in Salt Lake City compared the reasons for enlisting with arguments for conscientiously objecting to the war. Most residents north of the capital city seemed willing to support the war effort. With the encouragement of Latter-day Saint leaders, two dozen men from Davis County were among the 663 who responded to Governor Heber M. Wells's call for a battalion of 500 enlistees. Davis County farmers lent their support by selling hay to an Ogden supplier shipping goods to San Francisco for military use.[55]

Second-generation Pioneers

During the last thirty years of the nineteenth century, Davis County's population nearly doubled. When the Utah Central Railroad opened for business in 1870, the number of county residents was 4,450. At the end of the century, census takers counted some 8,000 residents living between the Hot Springs and the Weber River. Davis County, however, had dropped from its position as fifth-most populous county in 1860 (with 2,904 people) to seventh place a decade later. It was number ten in 1900. This diminished standing reflected the growth of some of the outlying counties. They were experiencing in-migration that included some of the overflow of second-generation pioneers from Wasatch Front settlements. In addition, during the late 1870s a hundred new Mormon settlements appeared outside Utah to create new farms for young men.[56]

During this time of expansion, several new communities emerged in Davis County. Some were created by settling new land, repeating the process begun in 1847. Others defined themselves by withdrawing from the jurisdiction of existing communities. In the northwestern region, for example, new settlers homesteaded the more difficult areas on what was known as the Sandridge. They took up farming despite a scarcity of water and began what eventually would become five new towns—Syracuse, Clearfield, West Point, Clinton, and Sunset. Meanwhile, farmers north of Kaysville's city plat withdrew to create the beginnings of Layton; and the settlers in the western and southern portions of Bountiful became two distinct entities that later defined themselves as three cities—West Bountiful, Woods Cross, and North Salt Lake.

In almost all of these places, water and the possibilities of agriculture were the defining factors in the story of their creation. In northwestern Davis County, the lack of mountain streams delayed settlement. When homesteaders entered the area in the 1870s and 1880s, they depended first upon springs and wells. The area blossomed when canals later brought water from the Weber River. The issue in the Bountiful area was more the allocation of canyon streams than the development of new water sources, although that too became a necessity as populations grew.

The early settlers of Davis County, and those across the Weber County line, had grazed cattle on the grasslands extending from the Syracuse and Clearfield region northward. They referred to it as the Big Range. With permission from Brigham Young, William H. Hooper, a former Mississippi River steamboat captain, built a herd house in 1854 and hired two young men from Farmington to manage his business. Other private and community groups also used the area as a winter range or for surplus livestock. All of the herdsmen used the only major spring in what would become west Syracuse. The watering hole was named after herdsman John F. Stoddard and later after landowner William H. Miller, but it was popularly called Jacob's Well. Hooper moved his herds to Tooele County in the mid-1860s as the first settlers arrived on the Big Range. The families of James Hale, Levi Hammon, and Henry Gwilliams were early arrivals on the Davis County side of the range—all were experienced pioneers transplanted from other towns along the Weber River.[57]

The region attracted only a few scattered settlers until the late 1870s, when a younger generation needed land to farm. Territorial surveyors had marked section corners in 1855 to create plats measuring one mile square (640 acres). Beginning in 1876, couples staked out claims under the Homesteading Act of 1862 or bought land in the alternate sections along the lines given by the government to the transcontinental railroad companies. Families built log and adobe cabins and dug shallow wells for culinary and irrigation water. Most of the settlers chose the well-drained clay soil just below the bluff, where well water satisfied their basic needs. The land holdings were larger than those of the pioneer settlements—80, 160, or even more acres, compared with the 20-acre and 40-acre parcels in the areas settled in the 1850s. Within twenty years, a five-mile strip along the Great Salt Lake was supporting an estimated three dozen families. Informally, the settlers called the place Willows. Outsiders nicknamed it Hoboken, and it was the beginning of what would become Syracuse. Farther north, the area straddling the Weber County line was known as Hooper.[58]

Above the bluff, between the Emigrant Road and the Utah Central tracks, the land was undulating, dry, and covered with sagebrush, rabbitbrush, and grass—good for grazing cattle. The sandy soil was an alluvial delta of the Weber River, fertile but lacking water. Settlers began arriving on this rangeland, known as the Sandridge, in the late 1870s. Proving up a homestead required five years' occupancy, but living on the land only during the summer months still counted as a whole year. Some of the first settlers set up temporary summer shelters in the area and returned to their home base elsewhere for the winter. They came from South Weber, Riverdale, Hooper, Kaysville, Farmington, and Bountiful. Most claimants on the Sandridge were younger couples just getting established. Among them were Richard and Emily Hamblin, English immigrants living with a relative in the Layton area; Alma and Catherine Tolman of Bountiful; and Richard and Elizabeth Venable, midwesterners who met in Kaysville, married, and set out "to conquer . . . 160 acres of virgin wilderness on the Sandridge."[59]

After clearing the land, the Sandridge homesteaders planted winter wheat in the fall months and depended upon natural precipitation to produce a crop. They hauled culinary water in barrels from Kaysville or Hooper. Attempts to dig shallow wells on their farms yielded brackish water at a depth of forty feet. Anxious to stop hauling water, they tried again. Sunk to depths approaching one hundred feet, the wells produced useable culinary water. Despite the challenges of taming this fertile but dry land, by the mid-1880s eleven families had established claims on the Sandridge. As the population grew on the bench, the lowlands below the bluff began to be called the Bottoms. A competitive spirit evolved between the two areas, contributing toward the development of separate communities.[60]

The settlers in Hooper and Hoboken on the Bottoms and those on the Sandridge east of the Bluff Road established farms; however, unlike pioneers in the older towns in Davis County, they had no incentive to survey town plats to create a central identity. They built homes on their large farms and opened local roads along selected section lines. A sense of community solidified, however, when the private schools moved out of homes into simple school buildings in the mid-1880s. The early part of this same decade saw the establishment of Latter-day Saint Sunday Schools for children living in the four quadrants of northwestern Davis County. As these Sabbath schools and public gatherings met in the new school buildings, these buildings became community centers, repeating the process developed by the early settlers of the county.

In 1877, Mormon leaders created the Davis LDS Stake, with William R. Smith of Centerville as president. Until this time, the South Weber Ward had been under the umbrella of the Weber Stake and the wards from Kaysville south were under the nominal supervision of the Salt Lake Stake. Most bishops, however, took difficult matters directly to Brigham Young. With the creation of the new stake, officials organized the South Hooper Ward for members in Davis County who lived between the county line and the Syracuse Road (Antelope Drive, at present-day 1700 South). Settlers south of this boundary remained in the Kaysville Ward.[61]

The Syracuse Road was a precinct line, but it sliced through a natural cluster of homesteads of residents who found it more convenient to meet in the local schoolhouse than to travel in either direction for worship services. In 1882, Latter-day Saint leaders acknowledged this fact. The stake presidency created a South Hooper-Kaysville Branch, with William Beazer as presiding elder, to serve members in the Syracuse-Clearfield area. Members in the West Point, Clinton, and Sunset areas remained in the South Hooper Ward.[62]

This adjustment solved half of the geographical problem. An

The prosperity of the 1890s prompted the construction of new meetinghouses in a number of the rural LDS wards. Among them was this handsome Syracuse church designed by Kaysville architect William Allen and furnished with benches made by Barton and Sons, also of Kaysville. (Utah State Historical Society)

emerging sense of community continued to develop around the schools and Sunday schools. This created a distinct identity separating the Clearfield area from Syracuse. Similarly, a clustering in the Clinton-Sunset area (known variously as Summit or the Basin) grew apart from the west section of the South Hooper Ward (West Point). As populations warranted, local residents appealed to leaders of the Davis Stake for separate wards. The South Hooper-Kaysville Branch became the Syracuse Ward in 1895. Twelve years later, Clearfield gained its own ecclesiastical administration. Meanwhile, the Summit Ward was created in 1896 to serve the Clinton-Sunset area. A separate Sunset Ward emerged in 1916.[63]

The 1890s saw the evolution of one other new community on the rural outskirts of Kaysville. The Kaysville Ward, as organized in 1851, had included settlers clustered along two major canyon streams—Holmes Creek, near the platted city, and Kay's Creek, a few miles to the northwest. The northern group lived in an uncharacteristically scattered condition for a Mormon community, having spread out onto nearby rangeland with homesteads from the first farm sites along the two branches of Kay's Creek. Even though it lacked a town plat, the Layton area acquired a separate identity because of the emergence of a distinct commercial center along the state road at Gentile Street beginning in 1882. When a U.S. post office opened in 1886, the community gained a name. Layton was granted its own Mormon ecclesiastical unit in September 1889, six months after the county commission created a separate Layton precinct. Known initially as Kaysville Second Ward, it consisted of about 200 settlers. Daniel B. Harris was the first bishop, and the congregation met in a small frame building at 962 Church Street. At the request of independence-minded members, the new unit was renamed Layton Ward in 1892.[64]

The Layton Ward soon spun off a second church unit. In 1895 the 143 Latter-day Saints clustered around Gentile Street west of Flint Street became the West Layton Ward. David E. Layton served as bishop for thirty years. The congregation met for services in a brick school that had been built in 1892 near the halfway point on Gentile Street. A brick meetinghouse was completed nearby in 1897. These building became a focal point for this rural neighborhood, which survived on dry farming and stock raising. The West Layton homesteaders had emerged as a separate neighborhood after 1882, when Gentile Street was opened as a public lane west to the Bluff Road. The street name referred to two non-Mormon settlers who were living near the top of the street. West Layton did not develop as a separate town but thrived as a Layton neighborhood.[65]

The formation of new ecclesiastical jurisdictions for identifiable congregations proved much easier than the creation of civic independence for the new communities. Not long after Kaysville's incorporation in 1868, the people in the Layton area asked to be included in its boundaries. To accomodate them, the city expanded from about five square miles to twenty-three square miles. Despite the expanded boundaries, the city did not extend police patrols or street maintenance to the farm areas. Layton residents protested this with legal challenges and opposed Kaysville City's decision in 1889 to borrow $5,000 to build a city hall in the northwest corner of the city plat.

The Farmer's Union mercantile store formed the core of a small commercial center at Main and Gentile Street during the time of the Layton de-annexation movement. (Utah State Historical Society)

Court rulings in three challenges to the city's right to levy property taxes and collect fees for business licenses produced mixed results. In 1898, city officials attempted a reconciliation by offering police patrols and road maintenance in Layton; however, they were rebuffed by the tax protesters, who said they were not part of the city.[66]

At this point, the ongoing controversy seemed unsolvable, so Bishop Peter Barton invited higher church officials to intervene. In January 1899, three LDS apostles met with about thirty of the local disputants. Former mayor Hyrum Stewart spoke for the city and businessman Ephraim P. Ellison for the Layton citizens. Following an open but friendly meeting, the apostles acknowledged their lack of jurisdiction and suggested that the parties submit a compromise plan to the district court. A conciliation committee went to work on a proposal to pro-rate unpaid taxes and draw a new city boundary. Discouraged by its efforts, the committee finally invited public mass meetings in Kaysville and in Layton to resolve the difficult tax issue.[67]

While negotiations were continuing, the state supreme court ruled in a Grantsville City case that cities did, indeed, have the right to tax all property within their boundaries even if a particular area received no direct benefit. The court also specifically nullified contrary rulings in earlier Kaysville cases. This decision vindicated Kaysville City's taxing authority but complicated the conciliation effort. Most of the Layton businessmen finally agreed to buy city licenses, and residents expressed a willingness to pay a share of back taxes. In 1900 the city paid off the remaining debt on the city hall. With that obligation resolved, the district court authorized Layton residents to withdraw from the corporate limits of Kaysville. The justice concluded that the Layton area was "but an ordinary farming community and had no necessity for city government." After fifteen years of controversy and litigation, Layton became an unincorporated part of Davis County on 1 March 1902.[68]

In an ironic quirk five years later, the controversial Kaysville City Hall was seriously damaged when its bell tower toppled in upon the building during a windstorm. The city sold the rubble for ten dollars and bought the Kaysville LDS Academy at 100 North 300 West to serve as a replacement.[69]

Concerns over the equitable distribution of water were at the center of a civic separatist movement in south Davis County. But those who wished to leave Bountiful City after its incorporation in 1892 were also keenly conscious of belonging to distinct geographical communities. For twenty years the various residents had been cooperating in separate south and west school districts, voting precincts, and ecclesiastical divisions. They had also developed cooperative sharing of irrigation water.[70]

Bountiful's settlement had actually begun in the region of moist, clay soils toward the Jordan River, in a place called for a time Willow Settlement. Herdsman Perrigrine Sessions's first campsite was in this area in 1847. Eastbound Mormon Battalion members Meletiah and Orin Hatch stopped long enough to clear springs and farmland in the area the following fall. Overwintering in 1848–49 in the South Bountiful-Woods Cross area were the families of George W. Bradley, Eric G. M. Hogan, Thomas S. Smith, Joseph Holbrook, Anson Call, and others. In 1849 the emerging settlement grew with the arrival, among others, of the families of William Henrie, John Moss, Reuben Perkins, Christian Hyer, and Ira S. Hatch. All were initially farmers. Each settler claimed from twenty to forty acres of land, which they irrigated from local springs or the shared waters of Mill Creek Canyon and North Canyon.

Some of the first settlers moved into Bountiful proper with the intention of maintaining their western farms. A few relocated outside the Bountiful area, and others stayed behind on their farms to become the founders of a new community. The main emigrant road along 500 West became a line of demarcation between the settlers on the southwesterly bottoms and those in Session's Settlement on the drier soils closer to the platted townsite nestled against the foothills. Bountiful's first post office and the Utah Central Railroad depot were at Wood's Crossing in this southwestern district, but it was other factors (noted below) that eventually gave the region its definition as a separate community.[71]

Meanwhile, in the area immediately west of the city fort, a sense of community began to emerge for a second region along and below 500 West—this one north of 400 South in what became known as West Bountiful. Many of the first settlers in this area built homes along 800 West, which formed a natural, though linear, neighborhood. The farms here tended to be larger than many of those in east Bountiful that shared the waters of Mill Creek and Barton Creek. Among those pioneering settlement along the Eighth West corridor were the families of James Fackrell, Sr.; James Fackrell, Jr.; Israel Barlow; Daniel Wood; William S. Muir; James Kipper; John Pack; Joseph Bates Noble; and Benjamin Ashby.[72]

Like their fellow citizens in the Layton and Syracuse areas, residents of Bountiful living away from the city's platted center established neighborhood schools. The original school district boundary of 1852 bisected the Bountiful area into two districts, north and south of 500 South. That boundary was used for other civic purposes as well. The county retained the 500 South boundary when it created separate rural school districts for the two western Bountiful neighborhoods in 1859. A year later, the West Bountiful community built a one-room adobe building on 800 West near 300 North. In 1870, Latter-day Saints in the area began meeting in the schoolhouse for some religious meetings. A second adobe school at 1500 South served South Bountiful residents for their educational, religious, social, and public gatherings. Both rural groups had been holding Sunday Schools for children since the late 1860s.[73]

Following the creation of the Davis LDS Stake in 1877, the North Canyon Ward was divided into three units to recognize the existence of the emerging religious communities below 500 West. These Latter-day Saint wards created a formal identity for residents, and this sense of community carried over many years later into town governments. The new West Bountiful Ward extended from Pages Lane (1600 North) southward to the school/precinct line at 500 South. William S. Muir was named bishop. The new South Bountiful Ward, under Bishop William Brown, served Latter-day Saints in the southwestern portions of Bountiful. The remaining region around the platted city center became the East Bountiful Ward, with Anson Call as bishop. The East Bountiful Ward met in the tabernacle. The West Bountiful Saints quickly built a small adobe meetinghouse on a lot across 800 West from their new school. The South Bountiful Ward invested more time and money to erect a 60-by-30-foot concrete building, which was completed in 1880. Both the West Bountiful and South Bountiful wards built handsome brick meetinghouses in 1904.[74]

These three religious communities were in place when Bountiful became a city in 1892. The city's incorporation did not win universal acceptance. Under ecclesiastical and county administration before that time, much of the work to maintain streets had been done by volunteers working to pay off their county taxes. The management of water resources had been an entirely voluntary effort accomplished by watermasters appointed by the LDS bishops under county authority. In contrast, the new Bountiful City used hired help and added new taxes to pay for it. Some residents refused to pay. Also, municipal officers faced difficult challenges: the city pound keeper could not keep stray livestock out of unfenced property; not all businesses paid for licenses; urbanites wanted the city to repair deep ruts in city streets and to keep neighbors from piling wood or extending corrals into the road right-of-way. Rural residents complained of the dust stirred up by sheep being herded from their Wasatch Mountains summer grazing lands to their winter range in Skull Valley. Bountiful residents chaffed at the municipal regulations and especially disliked how the city managed the distribution of water. The most perturbed citizens circulated a petition in 1893 asking the city council to disincorporate part of the city; however, the appeal lacked the required number of signatures.[75]

More than anything else, the city council heard protests over the allocation of water, the handling of waste water, and water turns being cut short by upstream farmers anxious to begin their own watering turn. City officers worked to improve conditions. They repaired bridges, cleaned ditches, and extended culverts. Watermasters did what they could to monitor the water turns. To improve the measurement of the water, the city installed new headgates on Barton Creek, Stone Creek, and Mill Creek. Dissatisfaction continued, however. Two city councilmen and a sub-watermaster on the west Mill Creek ditch resigned in one confrontation with farmers.[76]

Once again, the opponents of incorporation organized. John Waite gathered signatures from the northwestern residents of the area and S. S. Howard contacted people in southwest Bountiful. The resulting petitions led to a vote during the November 1895 election. The vote was 181–79 in favor of detaching the city's southern and western sides. Bountiful's new western boundary followed a section line at 400 West. On the south, the line was drawn about where Mill Creek crossed Main Street at 700 South. The separation of the southwestern and west side settlers from the city recognized the viability of the communities previously defined by school districts and the West Bountiful and South Bountiful LDS wards.[77]

The rural communities of West Bountiful and South Bountiful remained unincorporated for a generation. The creation of formal town governments began in the 1930s. The West Precinct became known first as the town, and, later, the city of West Bountiful. Bountiful City itself expanded into much of the eastern portion of the South Precinct, leaving the area below 500 West to become the City of Woods Cross and the region beyond 2600 South to emerge as North Salt Lake City.[78]

Diversity in Education and Religion

The Protestant reformers who lobbied for anti-polygamy legislation in Congress mounted a direct attack on Utah's religious culture during the final decades of the nineteenth century by setting up churches and schools in the territory. Organized as a mission effort, the Utah outreach programs of the 1880s offered worship services and a Protestant Bible education in Sunday Schools. On weekdays, the schools taught a basic educational curriculum and set up extracurricular youth clubs. The mission churches and tuition-free schools hoped to diminish the Mormon influence within families in an attempt to give women a way out of polygamous marriages and children an alternative to the Mormon-dominated school system.[79]

Transforming Education. Latter-day Saints in Davis County struggled with the challenges offered by the Protestant mission schools. Because the existing district schools received some tax money for their construction, they were nominally public. Yet because most students were Latter-day Saints whose parents paid their tuition, there was some expectation of a Mormon religious thread to the teaching. District schools also lacked standardized schedules and teachers' certification. Attendance was voluntary. The alternative Protestant schools attracted a significant following with their well-trained teachers and free tuition.[80]

District school trustees responded by encouraging their own teachers to meet territorial school recommendations by getting certified. The Protestant challenge also prompted discussion favoring free public schools. This notion did not win immediate acceptance in Utah—especially not in Davis County. Proponents of the status quo cited Brigham Young to bolster arguments opposing "any thing like free schools as known by the world."[81]

At one time or another before 1890, Protestant church groups operated about 110 mission schools in Utah. Schools existed for as long as fifteen years in Bountiful, Centerville, Farmington, Kaysville, and Layton; and they attracted a number of Latter-day Saints students. Education in these schools led to few, if any, conversions away from Mormonism, however. In that aspect, at least, they failed to meet their sponsors' objective.[82]

The mission schools in southern Davis County enjoyed moderate enrollments; those in the north end appeared to do better. In Bountiful, the presence of an active group of supporters for the Liberal party ensured some success for a school organized in 1881 by

Among the Congregational church mission schools built in Utah was Bliss Hall, the first Protestant school in Bountiful. (Utah State Historical Society)

the Congregational church. This school was one of twenty-eight established in Utah by that church's educational arm, the New West Education Commission. Within a year, the sponsors had completed a multipurpose brick building at 170 West 400 South for the school and a church. They named it Bliss Hall after a New England minister. The school probably attracted students from families already outside of or at odds with the Mormon church. Most Bountiful-area students remained in the five district schools or in one of several private schools.[83]

The Centerville Free School was organized by an American Protestant mission not remembered by name in local histories. The sponsors erected a rock building with a vestibule and spacious classroom at 385 East 100 South. The mission effort may have been weakened when Miss Abbey Benedict, the first teacher, married a Latter-day Saint and moved to Ogden.[84]

Farmington Latter-day Saints faced competition to their two district schools when the Congregational church's New West Educational Commission opened a school in a small rock building on 100 North at 80 East.[85] Local residents knew it as the Liberal School or the "outsider's school." Classes got a head start in 1882 by opening before local trustees in Farmington's central district had hired a teacher. Some families enrolled their children in the free school and were hesitant to transfer them later. Other parents claimed that they couldn't afford tuition. Bishop Jacob M. Secrist and the LDS home teachers immediately offered financial support for the poor and encouraged loyalty to "our schools." In 1885 the competing schools engaged in some kind of legal battle. The Congregational school retained sufficient enrollment to continue operating until at least 1897.[86]

The Presbyterian church established a mission school in Kaysville in the late 1870s. It was taught by a mission teacher from Ohio, who was later joined by a second instructor. It was one of twenty-nine schools opened in Utah Territory by the Presbyterian church during the last quarter of the nineteenth century. Classes met in an adobe building at 80 East Center Street until completion in 1888 of a brick church just to the east. The Kaysville Presbyterian school attracted as many as forty students. During the politically charged 1880s, local Latter-day Saint leaders saw the mission school as a threat to the faith of their congregation. Ella McDonald, one of the school's teachers, reported in 1883, "Those who send their children to school and voted the Liberal ticket are under trial by the church with a view to retraction and discipline."[87]

An Episcopal school in nearby Layton received financial support through regional Bishop Daniel S. Tuttle and his successor, Bishop Abiel Leonard. Under Tuttle's general supervision, Henry Ellis purchased land in 1888, built a brick building at 319 West Gentile Street, and hired Miss Hatty Prout as teacher. As one of only two schools supported by the Protestant Episcopal church in Utah, it met a specific local need. Enrollment reached forty in 1891, with the core support drawn from families "outside of the Mormon Church." A year later, Ellis branched into auxiliary education with the Boys' Circle, a club for young men devoted to lectures, debate, and politics. He and his wife also started a sewing club, the Girls' Pansy League, for young women.[88]

Most of the mission schools in Utah closed with the phasing out of plural marriage and overt political activity of the Mormon church. The creation in 1890 of a tuition-free, tax-supported public educational system with stricter standards for teachers hastened the end of

Protestant as well as private alternatives. This development pleased the Protestant missions—the establishment of free, public schools fulfilled one of their goals. Some of the unemployed Protestant schoolteachers were hired by the public schools. The abandoned buildings served various needs—as a district school in Layton, as homes in Farmington and Bountiful, and as a LDS Relief Society Hall in Centerville.[89]

Some of the Latter-day Saint wards in Davis County responded to the proliferation of mission schools in the late 1880s by building their own church schools. The short-lived academy movement helped the LDS First Presidency deal with anti-polygamy laws that restricted property holdings at church headquarters. They simply diverted church contributions to local use. The academies taught the fourth through eighth grades. The new Mormon schools taught regular academic subjects plus a course in Bible history.

Like the mission schools, the academies closed with the inauguration of free public schools in the 1890s. Another factor in their closing was the national economic depression of the 1890s—the Panic of 1893. A Davis County reporter noted, "Free district schools, and, the oft repeated trio of words, scarcity of money, are seriously operating against the church schools, but it would look rather inconsistent in us to build such expensive structures and then not use them." The buildings in Davis County were sold at discounted prices to local school districts.[90]

The academies in Farmington and Kaysville occupied two-story brick schools built according to the same general floor plan, except that Farmington built the right wing from the main entrance and Kaysville the left wing.[91] The Farmington Academy opened in 1889 at the rock church a few months before completion of its new building at 80 West State Street. For five years the school served fourth- through eighth-grade students. Even though it was billed as the *stake* academy, most of the students lived in Farmington; a few came from north Centerville. School District 6 in Farmington purchased the building in 1895 for $5,000 and installed the first hot-air furnace in town. The building was demolished in 1910 and its school bell preserved by the Daughters of Utah Pioneers.[92]

The academy in Kaysville was located on the northeast corner of

100 North and 300 West. It offered ungraded classes for what would later be called junior high school students. The academy served students in the Kaysville and Layton areas from 1889 until 1893. District 8 rented the building for a time after that, and then Kaysville City purchased it as a city hall. It was torn down in 1936.[93]

Apparently the other communities in Davis County did not join the academy movement. Instead, they built new brick district schools and used those until the consolidation of area school districts centralized education.

Religious Options and Mormon Auxiliaries. Many of the Protestant schools in Utah Territory existed in conjunction with Sunday Schools or worship services held under the auspices of the sponsoring church. During the last quarter of the nineteenth century, eighty-eight Protestant and Catholic church congregations were established at one time or another in Utah Territory. Three of them were in Davis County. These churches operated in conjunction with the schools, under the expectation that their small congregations would grow through local conversions.[94]

In Bountiful, Bliss Hall housed both day and Sunday schools from the time of its completion in 1882. Nine years later, the Reverend David Pebles began holding worship services there. The Congregational church was formally organized locally in 1897 and has continued to serve its members since then.[95] A decade after starting a mission school in Kaysville, area Presbyterians hired local architect William Allen to design a church to replace the adobe school and serve a small religious congregation. The handsome red-brick building was completed in 1888. The Reverend E.M. Knox conducted Sunday services and his wife taught school.[96]

Henry Ellis, the Episcopal lay reader who organized the Layton mission school, was the first to offer an alternative to Latter-day Saint religious services in that community. Ellis and his family had left England expecting to find an interest in the Church of England among British immigrants to Utah. However, the English Latter-day Saints in the Kaysville-Layton area had already dissented from Anglicanism to affiliate with the United Brethren before meeting the Mormon elders and converting to the LDS church. They befriended Ellis but remained Latter-day Saints.

Carpenters remodeled a store on Layton's Main Street for St. Jude's Episcopal church after the group's brick building on Gentile Street was destroyed in a fire. (*Layton, Utah: Historic Viewpoints,* from University of Utah Library Special Collections)

Ellis pursued his goals under the Kay's Creek Mission—soon renamed St. Jude's. His Sunday School served sixty enrollees, but only two confirmed members appeared on the records of St. Jude's Episcopal Church. Attendance at meetings was sparse. Ellis extended regular services to Hooper in 1893, but ill health soon forced his curtailment of this service. Thereafter, visiting ministers from Salt Lake and Ogden delivered the sermons. Two teachers kept a diminished Sunday School going. In 1901, carpenters remodeled and added a vestry and bell tower to the William Hyde store near 60 North Main Street to replace the church's brick building on Gentile Street after it burned. Ellis continued as lay reader until 1916, when St. Jude's closed. In a show of respect for Ellis, Layton citizens elected him justice of the peace. He served from 1894 until shortly before his death in 1918.[97]

While Protestants were offering options for worship and school in Utah's Mormon country, the Church of Jesus Christ of Latter-day Saints itself placed a new emphasis on supplementary programs to its regular preaching and priesthood meetings. British Latter-day Saints had known of Sunday Schools in their homeland, and Englishman Richard Ballentyne introduced the idea in Salt Lake City in 1849. By the mid-1850s, the Farmington and Kaysville wards were teaching children faith-promoting stories from the Bible and the Book of Mormon in Sunday morning gatherings. Wards in the Centerville-Bountiful area organized their own such groups in 1868. As noted earlier, Sunday Schools appeared in emerging communities elsewhere in the county beginning in the mid-1870s.[98]

The Latter-day Saint women's auxiliary, the Relief Society, had its origins in 1842 in Nauvoo, Illinois; however, it ceased operation two years later. Some of its purposes were met in other ways in Salt Lake City in the 1850s. Brigham Young revived the organization in 1867 and encouraged churchwide participation.[99] Under Young's direction, Eliza R. Snow, who would later become general president of the organization, visited the four largest wards in Davis County in 1868–69 to create local organizations. The founding local presidents were Elizabeth Barlow in Bountiful, Mary Ann Harmon in Centerville, Sarah Harvey Holmes in Farmington, and Ann Barnes Smith in Kaysville. Organizations appeared in other wards in the county soon after the creation of the Davis Stake in 1877 and appointment of a stake Relief Society presidency headed by Sarah H. Holmes. The women who joined the Relief Society met weekly for religious and practical instruction. They organized charitable relief for the poor, practiced principles of frugal living, and supported home industry.[100]

It was a sign of their strength as self-sufficient organizations that the county's Relief Societies were able to provide their own meeting places. The Relief Societies in Bountiful and Farmington met in the old multipurpose school/church buildings, as did the women's groups in the newer communities. These buildings became known as the "Ladies Hall" or Relief Society Hall when that became their primary use. The women in Centerville fitted out a donated home for their use in 1870 and purchased the Free School building when it became available. Kaysville's women built their own red-brick Relief

Society Hall on land donated by Bishop Allen Taylor at 75 North Main in the city's commercial block.[101]

With the arrival of the railroad, and the cultural challenges it posed, Mormon leaders launched new groups for youth and children. The purpose of these Mutual Improvement Associations (MIAs) was to counter external influences by reinforcing in the younger generation the beliefs of their converted parents. The first groups for young women and young men began under Brigham Young's direction in Salt Lake City. Eliza Snow carried the Young Ladies (later Young Women's) MIA concept to other places. Independent young men's literary groups and clubs preceded the centrally sponsored Young Men's MIA. The two youth groups encouraged a retrenchment from worldly fashions among young women and functioned as lyceums, or discussion groups. Participants read literary classics, debated contemporary public issues, and discussed religious subjects. Grass-roots study groups for young men appeared in Centerville and Farmington in the early 1870s. By the end of 1878, a year after Brigham Young's death, the YWMIA and YMMIA were functioning in all of the old settlements in Davis County. They became a part of later wards soon after their creation.[102]

A children's organization, known originally as the Primary Mutual Improvement Association and later simply as Primary, emerged from the concerns of Farmington resident Aurelia Spencer Rogers. Anxious to teach Mormon history and beliefs, and hoping to instill social graces and curb youthful rowdyism, she turned to her bishop for help. He referred the proposal to church president John Taylor, who sent Eliza Snow to develop the concept. On 11 August 1878, in Farmington's rock church, officers were selected and an organization established. Two weeks later, Primary President Aurelia Rogers began holding meetings for the children. The idea quickly spread to other Mormon wards. Primaries were functioning in the older Davis County wards within three years and in the far north county wards by 1891.[103]

With the creation of the Latter-day Saint auxiliaries, all ages and genders were made part of an organized effort to involve members in the church's effort to create not just a religion but a religious society. The church had not yet achieved its goal of a people worthy of its

Zion. The first Mormons were dying off, and, with them, so too were many of the early patterns of Latter-day Saint life. The early members hoped to pass the torch to their children. In organizing the Davis Stake in 1877, Brigham Young admonished the bishops, "We expect to see a radical change, a reformation, in the midst of this people." He intended not just a perfecting of the spiritual aspects of Mormonism but a new emphasis on cooperative economics and political unity as well.[104]

The auxiliary organizations outlasted Brigham Young and the contemporary United Order movement. They became part of a new era in Latter-day Saint history created by the transformation of Mormon political, economic, and religious life. The decision to include social graces, contemporary issues, and literature among the topics taught in the weekday auxiliaries made them useful agents in helping to socialize those who were growing up in a new time. The death of the founding generation of Latter-day Saints marked the end of the original formulation of Mormon life as a closed society. An institutional church emerged to sustain a people prepared to live more openly and in a different way in a changing world. Davis County remained an essentially Mormon, rural community well into the twentieth century. But those who reached adulthood beginning in the 1890s lived and worked differently for the next half century than had their predecessors who had settled and first defined the towns of Davis County.

ENDNOTES

1. Richard D. Poll, Thomas G. Alexander, Eugene E. Campbell, and David E. Miller, eds., *Utah's History,* 243, 270–71.

2. Farmington Ward, Teachers Quorum Minutes, 30 April 1882; *Deseret News,* 17 August 1864.

3. Poll et al., *Utah's History,* 243–44, 250–73. See also Thomas J. Alexander, "Federal Authority Versus Polygamic Theocracy: James B. McKean and the Mormons, 1870–1875," *Dialogue: A Journal of Mormon Thought* 1 (Autumn 1966): 85–100.

4. *Davis County Clipper,* 3 January 1896; *Salt Lake Tribune,* 7 January 1896.

5. Farmington Ward, Teachers Quorum Minutes, 18 January 1874.

6. Lowell "Ben" Bennion, "The Incidence of Mormon Polygamy in 1880: 'Dixie' versus Davis Stake," *Journal of Mormon History* 11 (1984): 28–30, 36–38.

7. Stanley S. Ivins, "Notes on Mormon Polygamy," *Western Humanities Review* 10 (Summer 1956): 236.

8. Poll et al., *Utah's History,* 290–92.

9. See Annie Clark Tanner, *A Mormon Mother: An Autobiography;* Fae Decker Dix., ed., "The Josephine Diaries: Glimpses of the Life of Josephine Streeper Chase, 1881–94," *Utah Historical Quarterly* 46 (Spring 1978): 167–83.

10. See, for example, Annie Clark Tanner, *A Biography of Ezra Thompson Clark* (Salt Lake City: Tanner Trust Fund, University of Utah Library, 1975): 39–40, 59–62; Leslie T. Foy, *The City Bountiful,* 137–39; and Arlene H. Eakle, Adelia Baird, and Georgia Weber, *Woods Cross: Patterns and Profiles of a City,* 26.

11. Ivins, "Notes on Mormon Polygamy," 234; Poll et al., *Utah's History,* 290–91; Eugene E. Campbell and Bruce L. Campbell, "Divorce among Mormon Polygamists: Extent and Explanations," *Utah Historical Quarterly* 46 (Winter 1978): 4–23.

12. Poll, et al., *Utah's History,* 249; *Deseret News,* 18 January 1870; Journal History, 2 March 1870; Beverly Beeton, "Woman Suffrage in Territorial Utah," *Utah Historical Quarterly* 46 (Spring 1978): 111, 115; Farmington Ward, Teachers Quorum Minutes, 14 August 1870.

13. Poll et al., *Utah's History,* 258–59, 261–65; Edward B. Clark, *Autobiography of Edward B. Clark* (Farmington, Utah: Author, 1953), 22.

14. Leonard J. Arrington, *Great Basin Kingdom: An Economic History of the Latter–day Saints, 1830–1900,* 359–60. One confrontation is recounted in Davis Bitton, *The Redoubtable John Pack: Pioneer, Proselyter, Patriarch* (Salt Lake City: Community Press, 1982), 176–77; Joseph L. Robinson, Autobiography and Journal, 26 September 1886.

15. Carol Ivins Collett, *Kaysville—Our Town: A History,* 96–97; Mel Bashore, "Life Behind Bars: Mormon Cohabs of the 1880s," *Utah Historical Quarterly* 47 (Winter 1979): 22–41.

16. Andrew Jenson, *Latter–day Saint Biographical Encyclopedia* (Salt Lake City: Andrew Jenson History Co., 1901), 1:205–6.

17. Mary Ellen Smoot and Marilyn Sheriff, *The City In–Between: History of Centerville, Utah,* 114.

18. Poll et al., 263–64; Collett, *Kaysville–Our Town,* 101–2; Farmington Ward, Teachers Quorum Minutes, 5 September 1886.

19. Foy, *City Bountiful,* 136–37; LaRue Hugoe, and Edith Deppe, *West Bountiful: A Pictorial History, 1848–1988,* 80.

20. Foy, *City Bountiful,* 136–37. For the outlying colonies see F. LaMond Tullis, *Mormons in Mexico: The Dynamics of Faith and Culture* (Logan: Utah State University Press, 1987), 56; and Brigham Y. Card et al., eds., *The Mormon Presence in Canada* (Logan: Utah State University Press, 1990).

21. Myron W. McIntyre and Noel R. Barton, eds., *Christopher Layton,* 141, 145, 183, 243 n. 70; Glen M. Leonard, "Truman Leonard: Pioneer Mormon Farmer," *Utah Historical Quarterly* 44 (Summer 1976): 258–60.

22. Robinson, Autobiography and Journal, 4 October 1890.

23. Collett, *Kaysville–Our Town,* 83; Foy, *City Bountiful,* 150; *Davis County Clipper,* 14 February 1896, 14 January 1898.

24. Collett, *Kaysville–Our Town,* 83; Hubert Howe Bancroft, *History of Utah, 1540–1887,* 450.

25. Collett, *Kaysville—Our Town,* 64, 83–85, 204, 214.

26. Smoot and Sheriff, *The City In–Between,* 174; Lee D. Bell, *South Weber: The Autobiography of One Utah Community,* 241–42.

27. Farmington Ward, Teachers Quorum Minutes, 9, 16 February 1868, 21 March 1880.

28. George Quincy Knowlton, *A Brief History of Farmington, Utah,* ed. Jannetta K. Robinson ([Farmington]: Privately published, 1965), 8; Glen M. Leonard, "A History of Farmington, Utah, to 1890," 101; *Davis County Clipper,* 9 March 1893, 25 July 1895.

29. Foy, *City Bountiful,* 149–50; *Davis County Clipper,* 21 September 1892, 12 January 1893.

30. Collett, *Kaysville–Our Town,* 105, 109.

31. Foy, *City Bountiful,* 151, 182, 205–7, 228.

32. *Davis County Clipper,* 25 February 1898; Farmington City Council, Minutes, 3 February, 23 December 1908, 7 February, 20 March, 6 November 1912, 7 March, 4 April, 15 June, 5 July 1917.

33. Peter L. Goss, "William Allen, Architect–Builder, and His Contribution to the Built Environment of Davis County," *Utah Historical Quarterly* 54 (Winter 1986): 56–58; *Salt Lake Herald,* 22 December 1889; Jacob Miller, Journal, in possession of Elna Miller.

34. Margaret Steed Hess, *My Farmington: A History of Farmington, Utah, 1847–1976,* 14; *Davis County Clipper,* 10 June 1892, 18 May, 14 December 1893.

35. Bancroft, *History of Utah,* 482; Journal History, 3 August 1861.

36. David L. Bigler, *Forgotten Kingdom: The Mormon Theocracy in the American West, 1847–1896* (Spokane: Arthur H. Clark, 1998), 276–79; Foy,

City Bountiful, 145; Farmington Ward, Teachers Quorum Minutes, 11 February, 17 March 1872, 20 April 1879.

37. Beeton, "Woman Suffrage in Territorial Utah," 102–3, 106–9, 112, 118.

38. *Deseret Evening News,* 24 October 1882; *Salt Lake Herald,* 21 October 1882.

39. Poll et al., *Utah's History,* 270–71; Thomas G. Alexander, *Utah, The Right Place: The Official Centennial History,* 201–3.

40. *Davis County Clipper,* 7, 14 November 1895. The pattern is evident also in 1894 and 1896 elections, reported in the *Clipper,* 8 November 1894, 6 November 1896.

41. *Davis County Clipper,* 26 October, 2, 9 November 1893, 31 October 1895, 15, 22, 29 October, 5 November 1897; Journal History, 3 November 1899, 7.

42. *Davis County Clipper,* 19 October 1893, 13 December 1894, 27 December 1895; Annie Call Carr, ed. *East of Antelope Island: History of the First Fifty Years of Davis County,* 171.

43. Farmington Woman's Suffrage Association, Minutes, 13 April 1892, LDS Church Archives.

44. Alexander, *Utah, The Right Place,* 203–4.

45. *Davis County Clipper,* 4 April 1895; Beeton, "Woman Suffrage in Territorial Utah," 119–20; Jean B. White, "Woman's Place Is in the Constitution: The Struggle for Equal Rights in Utah in 1895," *Utah Historical Quarterly* 42 (Fall 1974): 344–69.

46. Jean Bickmore White, "Gentle Persuaders: Utah's First Women Legislators," *Utah Historical Quarterly* 38 (Winter 1970): 33.

47. Farmington Ward, Teachers Quorum Minutes, 2 August 1885; Donald Bruce Gilchrist, "An Examination of the Problem of L.D.S. Church Influence in Utah Policies, 1890–1916" (M.S. thesis, University of Utah, 1965), 141–42; *Davis County Clipper,* 5 September 1895.

48. See, for example, *Davis County Clipper,* 25 March, 9 April, 21 September 1892, 25 July 1895.

49. *Deseret News,* 31 October 1896.

50. *Davis County Clipper,* 11 October 1894, 4 September 1896; quote from *Deseret News,* 14 October 1896.

51. Richard C. Roberts, "The Utah National Guard and Territorial Militias," in Allan Kent Powell, ed., *Utah History Encyclopedia,* 596–97; Carr, *East of Antelope Island,* 494, 499–500; Collett, *Kaysville: Our Town,* 77–78, 119; Journal History, 19 May 1866.

52. Bancroft, *History of Utah,* 656–61; Farmington Ward, Teachers

Quorum Minutes, 25 September 1870, 1 October, 24 December 1871; quotation in ibid., 24 September 1871.

53. *Deseret Evening News,* 7, 25 June 1894, *Davis County Clipper,* 2, 9, 16, 30 August, 15 November, 20 December 1894.

54. *Davis County Clipper,* 22 April, 29 July, 2, 9 September 1898.

55. Roberts, "The Utah National Guard," 597; James B. Allen and Glen M. Leonard, *The Story of the Latter–day Saints,* 442–43; Poll et al., *Utah's History,* 424; Carr, *East of Antelope Island,* 500; *Davis County Clipper,* 13, 30 May 1898.

56. Powell, *Utah History Encyclopedia,* 432; Arrington, *Great Basin Kingdom,* 353–54.

57. Clayton Holt, ed., *The Community of Syracuse, 1820 to 1995: Our Heritage, Centennial Edition* (Syracuse: Syracuse Historical Commission, 1994), 15–16; Carr, *East of Antelope Island,* 187.

58. Holt, *Community of Syracuse,* 21–28, 112, 16, 29–41.

59. Ibid., 26, 43–52; Carr, *East of Antelope Island,* 187.

60. Holt, *Community of Syracuse,* 44–52; compare Carr, *East of Antelope Island,* 74–75, 187.

61. Holt, *Community of Syracuse,* 117; Lynn M. Hilton, ed., *The Story of Salt Lake Stake of the Church of Jesus Christ of Latter–day Saints: 125–Year History, 1847–1972* (Salt Lake City: Salt Lake Stake, 1972), 25.

62. Holt, *Community of Syracuse,* 16–17, 118–19.

63. Ibid., 117–18; Carr, *East of Antelope Island,* 77–78, 189; Ivy M. Johnson and Ethel S. Mitchell, comps., *Out of the Sifting Sands: Clinton, 1870–1942* (Clinton, Utah: Clinton Ward/Lake View Stake, 1942), 4, 6. For the parallel story just across the Weber County line see Richard C. Roberts and Richard W. Sadler, *A History of Weber County,* 164–72.

64. Janet P. Dawson, "The Separation of Layton from Kaysville," in *Layton, Utah: Historic Viewpoints,* eds. Dan Carlsruh and Eve Carlsruh (Layton, Utah: Kaysville–Layton Historical Society, 1985), 55, 59; Collett, *Kaysville—Our Town,* 102.

65. Carr, *East of Antelope Island,* 202–5; G. Ralph Dibble, Carmen Dibble, and Stanley S. Cunningham, eds., *West Layton/Layton 2nd Wards,* 1895–1955 (Layton: Layton 2nd Ward, 1995), 3–10.

66. Dawson, "Separation of Layton from Kaysville," 55–67.

67. Ibid., 67–70.

68. Ibid., 70–75.

69. Ibid., 74–75; Collett, *Kaysville–Our Town,* 116–17, 120.

70. Eakle, Baird, and Weber, *Woods Cross,* 4–5.

71. Carr, *East of Antelope Island,* 145–48; Eakle, Baird, and Weber, *Woods Cross,* 3–5, 16, 21.

72. Carr, *East of Antelope Island,* 192–94; Hugoe and Deppe, *West Bountiful,* 1–28.

73. Carr, *East of Antelope Island,* 194–95, 158, 167–69; Foy, *City Bountiful,* 82; Andrew Jenson, Bountiful Ward, manuscript history, map, LDS Church Archives; Hugoe and Deppe, *West Bountiful,* 93.

74. Foy, *City Bountiful,* 143; Hugoe and Deppe, *West Bountiful,* 154–55.

75. Foy, *City Bountiful,* 149–50, 152–54.

76. Ibid., 150.

77. Ibid., 154.

78. Eakle, Baird, and Weber, *Woods Cross,* 3–5; *Davis County South Directory Map* (Bountiful: Carr Directories, 1997).

79. T. Edgar Lyon, "Religious Development in Utah," *Utah Historical Quarterly* 35 (Fall 1967): 295–96.

80. Ibid., 295.

81. Farmington Ward, Teachers Quorum Minutes, 13 October 1878, 14 November 1880.

82. Lyon, "Religious Development in Utah," 294–98.

83. Ibid., 296; Foy, *City Bountiful,* 139, 199–200, 269.

84. Smoot and Sheriff, *The City In–Between,* 71–72, 156–57.

85. It was referred to as the "N. W. [New West] School" in Farmington Ward, Teachers Quorum Minutes, 10 October 1897. A reference to the "Congregational mission" is found in *Davis County Clipper,* 2 May 1897.

86. Hess, *My Farmington,*347–48; Farmington Ward, Teachers Quorum Minutes, 15 October, 10 December 1882, 8 December 1883, 5 December 1884, 17 January 1885, 10 October 1897.

87. Lyon, "Religious Development in Utah," 296; Collett, *Kaysville–Our Town,* 193; Carr, *East of Antelope Island,* 112–13; Doneta Gatherum, "Early Protestant Churches in Kaysville/Layton," in Carlsruh and Carlsruh, eds., *Layton, Utah,* 193–94; McDonald's statement is from *The Earnest Worker,* May–September 1883, quoted in ibid., 193.

88. Carr, *East of Antelope Island,* 131; Lyon, "Religious Development in Utah," 294; Gatherum, "Early Protestant Churches in Kaysville/Layton," 187–89.

89. Lyon, "Religious Development in Utah," 298; Gatherum, "Early Protestant Churches in Kaysville/Layton," 190; Hess, *My Farmington,* 348; Foy, *City Bountiful,* 139–40; Smoot, *City In–Between,* 157.

90. *Davis County Clipper,* 7 September, 26 October 1893.

91. *Salt Lake Herald,* 22 December 1889, 3; Karl G. Maeser to Wilford Woodruff, 26 September 1889, LDS Church Archives.

92. Hess, *My Farmington,* 349–50; Maeser to Woodruff, 26 September 1889; *Davis County Clipper,* 14 December 1893, 15 March 1894, 30 May, 4 July, 25 July, 15 August 1895.

93. Collett, *Kaysville—Our Town,* 116–17.

94. Lyon, "Religious Development in Utah," 294–98.

95. Foy, *City Bountiful,* 269, 139.

96. Carr, *East of Antelope Island,* 112–13; Collett, *Kaysville—Our Town,* 193.

97. Gatherum, "Early Protestant Churches in Kaysville/Layton," 187–93; Doneta Gatherum, "St. Jude's School First Occupied Layton Elementary Site," *Davis News Journal,* 7 March 1984.

98. Details of the Sunday School and other LDS auxiliaries in Davis County can be found in Carr, *East of Antelope Island,* passim; Foy, *City Bountiful,* 142–43; Hugoe and Deppe, *West Bountiful,* 193, 201; Smoot and Sherrif, *City In–Between,* 161; Hess, *My Farmington,* 281–92; Collett, *Kaysville—Our Town,* 81–82; Bell, *South Weber,* 439–41; and Holt, *Community of Syracuse,* 117–20.

99. Jill Mulvay Derr, Janath Russell Cannon, and Maureen Ursenbach Beecher, *Women of Covenant: The Story of Relief Society* (Salt Lake City: Deseret Book, 1992), 62, 70–71, 75–79, 86–88.

100. Hess, *My Farmington,* 346; Foy, *City Bountiful,* 151; Smoot and Sheriff, *City In–Between,* 154–57; Collett, *Kaysville—Our Town,* 47, 81, 121; Allen and Leonard, *Story of the Latter–day Saints,* 345; and see note 98, above.

101. See previous note.

102. Allen and Leonard, *Story of the Latter–day Saints,* 345–47, 384; and note 98.

103. Allen and Leonard, *Story of the Latter–day Saints,* 384; Leonard, "A History of Farmington, Utah," 59–64; and see note 98.

104. *Journal of Discourses,* 26 vols. (Liverpool: Franklin D. Richards and others, 1853–1886), 19:43; Leonard, "A History of Farmington, 60–61.

CHAPTER 7

THE NEW AGRICULTURE

The second-generation settlers who claimed homesteads in Davis County's neglected northwestern region during the closing decades of the nineteenth century witnessed a significant economic change in the county during their lifetimes. Their pioneering of the dry farms on the Sandridge was only the beginning of a new agricultural emphasis that placed the focus on commercial sales. Related changes included the introduction of new crops, an increasing mechanization, and development of new sources for irrigation water. Many Davis County farmers found opportunities in commercial crops such as sugar beets, fruit, and vegetables. Others launched specialized livestock and dairy industries. To sustain these changes, businessmen and farmers created new marketing organizations. They worked hard to improve the quality of their products and thus increase profits.

As was true in earlier decades, Davis County's farmers depended upon various support industries. Flour mills and blacksmithing shops were common to both the settlement years and the period bridging the end of the cooperative movement and the First World

War. The new commercial agriculture could not have existed without sugar factories and canneries, and farmers depended upon the railroad to distribute processed goods. Hay and grain continued as staples in the county; but, by 1920, because the commercialization of agriculture had introduced new crops, the rural landscape looked different than it had when the Utah Central Railroad first crossed the county in 1870.

Not all signs pointed to progress and growth. Farmers and ranchers faced many challenges. Early frosts and droughts could limit productivity, and destructive winds, insects, and diseases in crops and livestock threatened profits. Also feared were the possibilities of fires and floods. On the economic front, the Panic of 1893 hit businesses hard nationwide, but most of Davis County's farmers survived the ensuing scarcity of money. The difficult years of the 1930s again slowed the process of change in agriculture but did not stop it. Along with other Utahns and fellow Americans of the Progressive Era and the Great Depression that followed, the residents of Davis County faced both opportunity and opposition with optimism.

Economic Transitions on the Land

The shift from small, self-reliant agriculture to large-scale commercial production marked a watershed in Davis County's agricultural history. The economic system espoused by Brigham Young had focused on group unity. Its manifestations were home industry, cooperative institutions, and the United Order. All of these were organized within a religious principle of self-reliance. As one local historian noted, "Families lived mainly by their own production and exchanged with their neighbors. Every farm was a little kingdom by itself."[1]

Brigham Young's successor as church president, John Taylor, eased away from the United Order in 1878 without giving up the goal of building a religious society that was unified in its economic, political, and social life. He offered help to the struggling cooperatives by organizing the Zion's Central Board of Trade. This board served as a coordinating council to establish policies that would protect the shared interests of Mormon farmers, merchants, and artisans. It also targeted the needs of consumers. Leading citizens from a dozen regions gathered at semiannual board meetings in Salt Lake City and carried guidelines back to local boards organized in their counties, including Davis. The central and local boards promoted home industries. They regulated prices and eliminated middlemen in order to foster consumer-oriented commerce. They also encouraged progressive practices in agriculture, manufacture, and commerce. The county trade organizations recognized the vitality of individual initiative while preserving the long-term idealistic goal of a cooperative society. The boards disbanded in 1884 as a result of the anti-polygamy campaign. At that time, the earlier united order projects were being privatized, agriculture was becoming more commercialized, and specialized industries were emerging. The new ways of making a living began to dominate Utah's economic landscape. The shared goal of unity gave way to a friendly competition and a focus on individual profit-making.[2]

Zion's Board of Trade encouraged the development of eighteen specific enterprises. One of these, silk production, resulted in a good-faith but limited effort in Davis County. Two others, the salt and sugar industries, had greater economic impact on the county's economy. The silk industry was promoted as a cooperative church program and was intended to foster self-sufficiency. Its operation fell to women within a few families.[3] The collection and refining of salt in Davis County, as will be noted later, flourished initially as a private enterprise. Paradoxically, local businesses were forced out of the market through competition with a monopolistic salt company launched by leaders of the LDS church. In contrast, Mormon church nurturing of a struggling sugar industry sustained Davis County's sugar beet farmers for a half-century. Following a commercial model used elsewhere in the industry, church-supported processing plants contracted with farmers to supply the sugar beets. While the production of silk, salt, and sugar did enjoy some success in Davis County, one other new crop failed. When county farmers joined the Mormon effort to produce cotton in the territory, northern Utah's short growing season quickly ended the experiment.[4]

The Silk Industry. From the earliest time of settlement, Brigham Young encouraged immigrants to bring mulberry seeds and silkworms to Utah. One of the first to respond was California convert

The women of Davis County were noted for their involvement in the silk industry. In this view, an unidentified group of Utah women and girls display the stages of silk production, from worms to cocoons, silk thread, and finished products. (Utah State Historical Society)

Thomas Whitaker, a Centerville resident. He had silkworm eggs shipped from London several times before his efforts succeeded. Finally, in 1862, he raised 1,400 worms and offered to share them with others to spread sericulture in Davis County. When his wife, Elizabeth, presented a silk vest of her making to Brigham Young, the Mormon leader encouraged the Whitakers to focus on the silk business. They resisted, however, not confident they could make a living from sericulture.[5] Four years later, Young encouraged the formal establishment of a silk industry through the Deseret Agricultural and Manufacturing Society. Seen as a work suited to women, children, and the aged, and as a means to generate additional income, it was organized in various parts of the territory through local cooperatives. If women wanted fancy formal wear, Young advised, they should make their own from locally produced silk in the spirit of home industry.[6]

Neither that counsel nor Young's 1868 invitation to Relief Societies to promote the venture appealed to many women in Davis County. The work of feeding the silkworms on a strict schedule required special dedication, and reeling the fine silk threads was tedious. Lorinda Robinson of Farmington was one of those who did respond. She secured worms, planted mulberry groves, and began producing silk.[7] Her husband's diary gloried in her progress by the spring of 1876:

> My wife Laurinda is now doing what she has been telling us that she could do. She is manufacturing silk from the silk worm eggs. And the mulberry leaf. She has actually done the work. Hatched the eggs, fed the worms, prepared the cocoons, reeled and prepared an abundance of sowing silk. And Brother Joseph Hadfield of Farmington has wove a considerable of silk handkerchiefs and dress goods, but she prepared it for the loom. The first silk ever made in the mountains. A triumph.[8]

Personal visits in the county by Relief Society General President Eliza R. Snow in the late 1870s finally expanded the cottage industry into at least some additional homes. The society's educational efforts were centered on the Deseret Silk Association, organized in 1875 with Zina D.H. Young as president. When the association offered to buy silkworm cocoons from the women at two dollars a pound, production in the territory doubled. Mulberry trees, grown to provide the green leaves on which the worms fed, sprouted in groves near the Bountiful Tabernacle, the Farmington rock church, and along creeks and lanes elsewhere in the county.[9]

The few women in every community in Davis County who set aside a room for the silkworms gained the support of local LDS bishops and priesthood quorums. The men were responding in part to the promotional efforts of silk missionaries sent from Mormon church headquarters by Brigham Young. The first of these was George D. Watt, who began his mission in October 1868. A few months after visiting Davis County, the English-born Watt moved his three families to a 160-acre homestead in northeast Kaysville.[10]

The silk produced in early Utah was used mostly for specialty items such as ribbons, fringes, shawls, scarfs, neckties, hosiery, embroidery thread, and portieres. The women of Davis County were held up to others in northern Utah as leaders in the production of dresses from local silk.[11] The record of their accomplishment is impressive. In 1877 Nancy A. Clark of Farmington made a dress from fourteen yards of light slate-colored silk that she had produced and reeled. Clark donated the dress to the Salt Lake LDS Temple construction fund. A patron then purchased it as a gift for Eliza R. Snow. Bishop Edward Hunter certified that Clark had produced the first dress piece of silk material in Utah. Joseph Hadfield wove the fabric on his hand loom.[12]

Clark was not alone at the pinnacle of silkmaking—fashioning a fancy dress of the material. Another dress made in Farmington was given to Aurelia S. Rogers.[13] Local histories record several other silk dresses made in Davis County, including those produced by Jane Wilkie Hooper Blood and Louisa Egbert of Kaysville and by Emily Jane Smith Burk of Farmington. Josephine Robinson Rose and her daughter Lorinda Attwood Robinson of Farmington won prizes at the territorial fair and at the Chicago World's Fair. Some of these women not only raised the worms and reeled the thread but also spun the silk.[14]

During the 1880s Zion's Board of Trade encouraged a mechanization of silk production. The Utah Silk Association and others set up factories in the Salt Lake Valley to produce high-quality threads on water-powered reeling machines. Before then, Davis County silk was reeled locally on hand-powered looms or sold commercially to mills in Provo. Joseph Hadfield, Davis County's premier reeler and weaver of silk for local growers, had learned the trade before leaving England in 1853. Besides weaving most of the dress-patterned silk pieces made in the county, he produced the silk fringe used in the St. George LDS Temple in 1877.[15]

The industry continued steadily for a decade, then slowed in the 1890s after many of the mills closed. Silk making revived when the Utah Silk Commission, a state agency organized in 1896, offered a bonus of twenty-five cents per pound for cocoons. This incentive doubled production. Davis County was one of fourteen counties where such bounties were paid. When the commission discontinued the bonus in 1905, however, area silk production ended. In an economy no longer isolated from the world, it was less trouble to secure imported silk or to do without. Davis County's silk industry died with the passing of the pioneer generation that had tried mightily to become self-sufficient in the production of food, clothing, and other necessities.[16]

Sorghum to Sugar Beets. An industry with a longer life and deeper impact on Davis County's economy than silk was that of sugar production. For most of the nineteenth century, Utahns depended upon sorghum molasses as a sweetener. Since sugar cane was a strictly tropical plant and sweet sorghum could not be grown easily in Utah's short summers, settlers looked for alternative sweeteners. The modern production of sugar from beets was in its infancy in France and Germany in the early part of the nineteenth century. This did not stop the Deseret Manufacturing Company, organized by John Taylor, from making the first attempt to process sugar beets in Utah. At considerable cost, the firm imported equipment from France and set it up in one of Salt Lake City's public works shops in 1853. The effort yielded only molasses, however. Another group tried again with the same equipment in a factory in Sugar House in 1855–56. They also lacked the know-how to get the required vacuum pressure needed to crystallize the syrup. With the onset of the Utah War of 1857–58, the beet sugar experiment was dropped.[17]

During the 1860s and 1870s, Utahns developed a thriving cottage industry for producing syrup from sweet sorghum. A cousin to broom corn, the plant was commonly called sorghum cane in Utah, or even "sugar cane," although technically it was not a cane plant. In 1868, fifteen sorghum mills in Bountiful were producing syrup, along with four in Centerville, three in Farmington, and others in Kaysville and South Weber. Centerville's Nathan T. Porter, a Vermont native, had produced 2,000 gallons of syrup from what he called "Chinese sugar cane." Bishops John Stoker and Christopher Layton received the commendation of a specially called Davis County agriculture meeting that year for promoting the raising of pure sorghum seed. The bishops had assigned specific farmers to nurture isolated fields at the mouth of North Canyon in Bountiful and on Kaysville's east bench. The intent was to prevent the preferred Early Red Imphee and old sorghum seed from mixing with broom corn and other related plants.[18]

By the late 1870s, some in Davis County were successfully producing small quantities of sugar from what was called the "amber cane." Arthur Stayner became interested in refining the sorghum syrup into sugar commercially when the territorial legislature offered a $2,000 prize (later increased to $5,000) for the best 7,000 pounds of homemade Utah sugar. He built a small factory southeast of the courthouse in Farmington and installed machinery, vats, and furnaces. Stayner, one of Davis County's delegates to Zion's Central Board of Trade, became the first Utahn to prove that commercial quantities of sugar could be produced. After experimenting for two years, in 1882 he produced sugar from a five-acre sorghum field, but it fell short of the legislature's minimum quantity. Continuing his efforts, Stayner developed a pilot sugar-manufacturing plant in Spanish Fork in 1887 and claimed the legislature's prize.[19]

After that facility had made brown sugar from grain sorghum, Stayner and others visited operating sorghum and sugar beet manufacturing plants in Nebraska and California to explore commercial options. Stayner gained the financial support of Salt Lake City businessmen to organize the Utah Sugar Company. Mormon church leader Wilford Woodruff agreed to invest church funds in the company's first venture, a fully equipped sugar factory. Stayner had favored sorghum, a more traditional American sugar-producing crop, but the sorghum grown in Utah did not produce a quality juice. The company therefore chose sugar beets, which had been successfully grown in California for twenty years. In 1891 California sugarmaker E.H. Dyer built a $400,000 facility in Lehi for the Utah investors. It was the first to use American-made equipment and the first to process sugar beets grown on irrigated farms.[20]

Thus began a major agricultural industry that impacted north Davis County for more than half a century. Private investors built a factory in Ogden in 1898. By 1920 a dozen more factories were operating in Utah, including one in Layton. To ensure financial security, the plants subsequently became part of the Utah-Idaho Sugar Company, organized in 1907, or the Amalgamated Sugar Company, formed in 1915.[21]

The thinning and weeding of sugar beets required much hand labor. At season's end, these workers in northwestern Davis County are topping the mature beets and hauling them by team and wagon to the railroad loading dump. (*The Community of Syracuse*)

Farmers in north Davis County were among the first to ship beets to the new Utah-Idaho Sugar Company plant in Lehi. By 1895, Syracuse farmers themselves were shipping more than 1,500 tons south by railcar. By the turn of the century, with an estimated 160 acres in beets, most of the Syracuse farmers had shifted their contract to the closer Amalgamated Sugar Company plant built in 1898 in Ogden. Those in the Kaysville-Layton area continued to ship their beets to Lehi, but the drayage cost them two dollars a ton, which reduced their return by as much as one-third. Mass meetings beginning in 1913 resulted in the formation of the Layton Sugar Company. It was incorporated in April 1915, with Jesse Knight of Provo, E.P. Ellison of Layton, and David Eccles of Ogden as officers. Ellison and Eccles had been among the original directors of the Ogden Sugar Company. By that fall, the Dyer Construction Company had completed a $500,000 plant on a forty-eight-acre site along the Denver and Rio Grande railroad tracks in west Layton.[22]

The first campaign in October and November 1915 processed 25,000 tons of beets from about 2,500 acres in Kaysville and Layton. A drought that summer had hurt the crop, but the yield still was 150,000 pounds of refined sugar. The first bags were on Davis County store shelves by early October. Meanwhile, field supervisor David E. Layton secured contracts for the following year for an additional 450 acres from Syracuse, Clearfield, and West Point farmers at a guaranteed five dollars a ton for the beets. South Weber farmers remained with the Ogden plant. During the 1917–18 sugar beet harvest season, the Layton plant received 44,000 tons of beets. The factory employed 300 men in round-the-clock shifts.[23]

An expanding sugar beet industry in Davis County created a need for field workers. To help farm families, the Layton Sugar Company hired laborers, provided housing for them near the factory, and built a school and church. The first laborers were Japanese. Later, Filipino and Mexican workers were hired. The company also built a boarding house for factory workers. Designed by William Allen, it opened in 1918, but was little used after the 1930s and was vacated in the 1940s. The factory itself survived the Depression of the 1930s, but the construction of military bases in the Davis-Weber area during the two world wars preempted farmland and decreased sugar beet production. Post-war housing construction also reduced agricultural land, and increasing costs of labor and fertilizer hurt farmers. The company and its major stockholder, the LDS church, sold out to Utah-Idaho Sugar Company in 1959. The new owner closed the Layton factory, and the remaining farmers shipped their beets to plants in Garland or West Jordan. The company used the Layton buildings for storage and limited processing until 1963. The factory was demolished in 1972.[24]

The New Agriculture

Until Mormon church-sponsored cooperative economic endeavors faded in the 1880s, Davis County farmers centered their efforts on producing enough food to sustain their families. They traded surplus products from their traditional family farms for manufactured necessities. Mormon cooperative manufacturing enterprises and community irrigation systems were natural adjuncts to the patterns of the conventional farm village. This accent on home industry and self-sustaining agriculture stressed the common good rather than personal financial gain.

During the last decades of the nineteenth century, Davis County

Alfalfa became a major cash crop for Davis County farmers. Thomas M. Roberts and his sons Cliff, Rex, Cal, and Phil worked a fifty-acre farm in West Bountiful and drove milk cows to the eastern foothills each day to graze. (*History of West Bountiful*)

farmers became more interested in cash crops. This commercial approach to agriculture transformed the way farmers looked upon their work. Because hay and grain fields yielded surpluses, they became the first commercial farm products in the county. Westering emigrants and railroad construction crews purchased these crops, along with fresh horses and beef cattle. Some county residents specialized in the production of these marketable products and developed successful commercial operations.[25] Other crops followed, as did an increased interest in efficiencies to lower costs and scientific advancements to increase yields.

A key component in all market-centered agriculture was a quality product. Davis County farmers sought to improve their marketable crops and livestock to meet that need. They did so through new or better seeds or breeding stock and by using improved farming practices. When alfalfa seed from Chile began to thrive in California in the 1860s, its cultivation spread to other western states. Because of its deep roots, the plant (also known by its British name lucerne) was well-suited for dry farming, including Davis County's Sandridge area. Christopher Layton introduced alfalfa to Utah Territory in 1870. The new crop soon replaced native grasses in the livestock feed market, including Davis County.[26]

The importation and local breeding of riding horses, draught horses, beef cattle, milch cows, and sheep became an established business in most Davis County communities by the late 1880s. The number of men raising livestock and the number working as livestock dealers grew steadily over the next thirty years. Some dealers specialized in sheep. Their offerings to support local woolgrowers included the buying and selling of wool, sheep, and popular Merino rams. Other livestock merchants specialized in horses and cattle, but many of them also dealt with sheep. A few dealers or consortiums acquired and offered specialized stock or services. Registered Percheron draught horses were such an offering, as were imported Holstein milch cows.[27]

Another improvement on Davis County farms was the construction of new barns to store hay, horses, harnesses, wagons, and machinery. Local newspapers publicized new construction and even published sketches on how to build a barn.[28] Barn building was not new to the county, however. The early settlers had brought the knowledge and skills with them and had been erecting familiar-looking barns for years. But beginning in the 1890s and continuing for thirty years, a new generation of commercial farmers invested some of the proceeds of their prosperity in the construction of handsome new hay barns, cow barns, horse barns, and milking barns, or combination barns for many purposes.[29]

Of special help to Utah farmers in the early twentieth century were the county agricultural extension agents and the county extension home economists. These public officials in Davis County were part of a nationwide educational effort to help improve farming practices, financial management of farms, gardening and food preparation, nutrition, and health. The program began when Congress created the Cooperative Extension Service in 1914 by the Smith-Lever Act. In Utah, this service was introduced by the Department of Agriculture through the Utah Agricultural College in Logan, founded in 1888 as a land-grant institution. As one of its programs, the college created an Agricultural Experiment Station on a thirty-five acre parcel in Farmington in 1920 to test soils, fertilizers, field crops, vegetables, and fruits. Utah had the first county agents in the United States. Their roles included advising 4-H leaders and vocational agricultural teachers. At Davis High School the program sponsored a chapter of Future Farmers of America.[30]

Utahns were as interested in improving their use of water as they were in improving crops and livestock. The region's irrigation agriculture was not unique in western America, and local farmers found much to learn from others involved in commercial farming that depended upon irrigation. In September 1891 the first international irrigation congress was organized in Salt Lake City to share information. Within a few years, Davis County irrigation companies were sending delegates to the meetings of a regional irrigation congress that met each year in a different western state. While serving as president of Utah State Agricultural College in 1914, Dr. John A. Widtsoe published a nationally acclaimed book, *Principles of Irrigation,* that provided scientific information to help farmers.[31]

Not every Davis County farmer depended upon irrigation ditches to raise a commercially successful farm crop. The large homesteads between Kaysville and the north county boundary were well suited to dry-farm production of grain. Winter wheat, planted in the fall and harvested in early summer, generally yielded adequate harvests without irrigation. Christopher Layton pioneered the raising of grain without irrigation and was soon joined by others, including Kaysville farmers John Marriott, John Thornley, George D. Watt, John Flint, and Elias Adams. By the late 1920s just over half of all wheat in Utah was being raised on dry farms. Davis County farmers improve their yields by imitating the success of the much larger grain farms in the Midwest. Most Utahns abandoned the seeds they had used in the 1890s and adopted the Turkey and other Kansas red wheat varieties. They sought technical help in dry-farm publications, including Dr. Widtsoe's *Dry Farming* (1910), and from county agricultural extension agents.[32]

When canals brought water to the Sandridge, the number of acres devoted to wheat increased, as did the yields. By the turn of the century, agents for grain dealers and shippers were buying carloads of grain in Davis County for export. Wheat became Utah's most important cash crop for farmers and was second only to hay in acreage planted. As they had done with winter wheat, Davis County farmers adopted scientific farming methods and new varieties of soft, white spring wheat. The standardizing of seeds helped ensure a uniform product for flour production.[33]

During the late 1920s, Davis County farmers were planting about 5,000 acres of cropland to wheat each year, another 1,200 acres to barley, and more than 600 acres to oats. They realized an average yield of 28.6 bushels of wheat to the acre. Restricted in farming acreage by its geography, Davis County could not compete in acreage with the more expansive grain farms of Box Elder, Cache, Utah, and Juab Counties. In all, eleven Utah counties cultivated more land for wheat, but only four counties ranked above Davis County's yield per acre. By 1925 Davis County had no surplus; rather, it imported some wheat to meet local needs. More than half of the wheat became poultry feed, and most of the rest was milled for flour and cereals, with a small amount reserved for seed. Along with other Utahns, county grain farmers prided themselves on the high quality of their crop.[34]

Mechanized Agriculture. It was not just in its livestock and crops that Davis County farmers sought improvement. Even though they were isolated from farmers in the eastern United States, Utahns kept abreast of new agricultural technology and knowledge. Within five years of settlement, Davis County's farmers were benefiting from labor-saving machinery such as horse-powered machines to thresh grain and mow hay. Machinist Arthur Walton arrived in Bountiful in 1851 with a cumbersome thresher that he had brought from Maine; Christopher Layton had one in operation in the north end of the county the following September.[35]

The number of these useful machines increased rapidly during the next decade. Many of them were shipped in from California; some were made in Utah. Owners used the threshing equipment on their own larger-than-average grain fields and also hired out their services to others. By the late 1860s, some of the county's local threshing and mowing machines were traveling as far as Cache Valley for work. The arrival of the transcontinental railroad hastened the mechanization of agriculture by opening new markets that made possible a more rapid shift from self-sufficient family farms to commercial operations. New crops and expanding markets became the common trend.[36]

The big machines at the end of the century, though a distinct improvement, were still cumbersome and slow. The larger ones were powered by four or five teams of horses walking in a circle pulling the long spokes of the sweep that powered the thresher. A ten-man crew kept busy loading and hauling the shocks, feeding the thresher, sacking the grain, and stacking the straw. The arrival of steam threshers speeded the process of removing the wheat from the shocks, which were cut and bound by mechanical headers. Stoddard Brothers of South Hooper introduced this modern improvement to the north end of the county in 1906 and harvested 900 bushels of wheat with their thresher the first day.[37]

Blacksmiths. Throughout the pioneer period and well into the twentieth century, the blacksmiths operating in Davis County provided services for farmers and travelers. Amos P. Stone, an immigrant of 1850, was the first to fire up a forge in Bountiful. Not long afterward, John Mower and William Camp also were offering blacksmithing services.[38] The head of one of Centerville's founding families, Osmyn M. Deuel, brought his equipment with him from Nauvoo and set up shop in the spring of 1848.[39] Andrew L. Lamoreaux, a millwright, and Hector C. Haight, a farmer and livestockman, were offering smithing services to residents of the Farmington area soon afterward. These men also sought to attract emigrants with advertisements in the *Deseret News* and the *Mormon Way-bill to the Gold Mines.* English convert Robert W. Burton arrived in Kaysville in 1851 and set up a blacksmith shop to serve the needs of residents of that area.[40]

Within a few years, each Davis County town had several men operating forges to fashion iron into needed products. Blacksmiths worked closely with local farmers to help make and assemble farm implements such as plows, harrows, levels, scythes, and cradles. In addition, they made nails, hand tools, hinges, latches, chains, hoes, rakes, chisels, and wagon tires. They fashioned and nailed into place shoes for horses and oxen. Blacksmiths also sharpened axes and repaired tools, carriages, and wagons. Their cluttered shops provided a social function as well. Located at convenient spots around each town, they often served as community gathering places for men. The Farmington blacksmith shops became such a popular stopping place for travelers that in the early 1860s the bishop and ward teachers asked the smithies to cut back on their work on Sundays. The men agreed to observe the Sabbath.[41]

The blacksmiths were well-known in their time and not forgotten by later generations. In some instances, sons of the first blacksmith kept the family business going for more than half a century. Examples are New Yorker Ira Oviatt and his sons, Dee and Lewis, of Farmington, and Henry Rampton, a second-generation English blacksmith who settled in Bountiful. Rampton's sons continued the tradition: Fred stayed in his father's shop, while Henry, Jr., worked in Centerville, Walter served clients in Farmington and then Layton, and George moved to Syracuse.[42] The last of the traditional blacksmithing operations disappeared from the county and were replaced by welding shops when gasoline-powered machinery finally took over for draught horses around the end of World War II.

Flour Mills. The transition in flour milling was not unlike that of other mechanized aspects of the new agriculture. New forms of power and mechanical improvements of machinery impacted the millers as well as the farmers of Davis County. To keep abreast of improvements meant replacing water power in the mills with steam or electricity and substituting metal rollers for milling stones. Owners of the county's pioneer mills had few economic incentives to upgrade their old equipment. Thus, they were caught short when entrepreneurs built new commercial flour mills to produce flour for export. In 1886, eighty-seven Utah mills were listed by Cawker's *Biennial Flour Mill Directory.* Most of these first-generation mills, including the half-dozen in Davis County, would soon be gone.[43]

Kaysville miller John Weinel was one of the nineteenth-century mill operators who tried to improve his equipment as new machinery became available. He replaced his wooden waterwheel with a steel one shipped from the east in 1869. He then discarded his native grinding stones for two superior stones brought west by the railroad from St. Louis. Weinel did not make the change from water power to steam or electricity, nor did he install metal rollers to increase productivity; after Weinel's death in 1889, those who ran the mill could not compete with new, modern plants. They limited their output to chopping animal feed. The mill closed after strong winds in 1906 caved in the west wall and made the building unsafe.[44]

The demise of other pioneer mills in the county followed a similar pattern. Unable to compete due to their antiquated equipment, all of the old mills closed in the decades surrounding the turn of the century when new technology made traditional methods inefficient. Around 1890 William D. Major found other uses for the Kimball Mill building in Bountiful. He opened a confectionery inside the mill and maintained the millpond for swimming and ice skating. In Centerville, James Miller simply abandoned the old Anson Call mill. A few years later, Henry Steed and Charles Bourne closed their North Cottonwood gristmill in Farmington. Fred Coombs and Jonathan D. Wood kept the nearby Rock Flouring Mill going into the early 1900s. For a time, the sturdy rock walls housed an electric power generating plant and then served as an ice house before becoming a private residence then a restaurant, then, once again, a home.[45]

Replacing the old area mills were two up-to-date facilities designed for commercial production using steam rollers. Investors strategically built these new mills adjacent to the Union Pacific Railroad tracks in northern Davis County. The builders were a younger generation, most of them successful commercial farmers or livestock growers. Ephraim P. Ellison, H. Gibsons, and others organized the first of these new-generation plants in 1890. Their business was known as the Layton Roller Mills. It was located just south of the Farmer's Union on Layton's Main Street. By 1903 the mill was the most productive in the state; in a twenty-four-hour day, it could turn out 440 sacks of flour.[46]

The success of Layton's mill may have prompted other investors to build a second modern mill in 1905 four miles to the south. The Kaysville Milling Company, organized by John R. Barnes and associates, built its five-story mill along the Union Pacific tracks at the west edge of Kaysville. This mill, too, produced flour widely recognized for its quality. After fire destroyed the building in 1920, it was rebuilt and the business was merged with the Layton company to form the Kaysville-Layton Milling Company. Henry H. Blood served as president and Ephraim P. Ellison as vice-president. The expanded operation developed a regional market in four western states and reached out with sales in Alabama and Georgia. During the 1940s, Rasmussen Grain Company owned the Layton mill. After sixty years in business,

The Kaysville Milling Company was strategically located on a railroad line to ensure access to commercial markets outside Davis County. (Intellectual Reserve, Inc., courtesy LDS Church Archives)

that facility closed in 1951 following a disastrous fire. Not long afterward, the Kaysville mill became part of the welfare program of the Church of Jesus Christ of Latter-day Saints. With the end of local milling options, many county wheat farmers shipped their grain to Weber County, which had become one of the ten top milling centers in the United States.[47]

Livestock. The creation of a commercial livestock industry was a natural outgrowth of community herding arrangements. Some local ranchers had formed private partnerships before the Mormon church encouraged everyone to band together in a local cooperative. When co-op herding ended in the late 1880s, opening the way for private partnerships, local ranchers created commercial livestock companies. Those who had specialized in sheep or cattle raising during the pioneer period led the way in forming corporations to produce and market meat, leather, and wool.

Settlers were first attracted to Davis County because of its suitability for grazing cattle. But much of the richest grassland was soon turn into cultivated cropland, leaving the county's ranchers to seek ranges elsewhere. The local foothills, mountain ranges, and lowland pastures served small-scale needs but were not adequate for commercial operations. The same kinds of ranges used by the cooperative herders—in western and northern Utah and beyond Utah borders—served the new companies. Ranchers in the county coordinated with Weber County residents the stock drives that passed through both counties in order to prevent losses along the way and limit the mingling of herds on the range.[48]

The commercialization of ranching operations was especially evident in the Woods Cross area, where as many as eight different livestock companies operated. The giant Deseret Livestock Company, organized in 1891, included among its ninety-five original stockholders members of the Moss, Atkinson, Hatch, Parkin, Nelson, Howard, Rampton, and Moyle families. The extended Hatch family created two other livestock companies, one for cattle and the other for sheep. One of the other consolidated firms was the Bountiful Live Stock Company, created in 1899 by a merger of the Howard, Cleverly, Mantle, Ellis, Egan, and other family herds.[49] Partnerships in livestock businesses in Layton included the Adams and Thornley families and the Dawsons and Websters. Beef cattle specialists in Layton included the Morgans, Ellisons, Nalders, and Greens. In addition, many farmers in Davis County became stock raisers on the side; they might buy thirty head of beef cattle—a railcar load—to feed over the winter and then send to market.[50]

A specialized support industry developed early in the twentieth century to assist in the marketing of livestock. In Davis County, buyers and sellers used the services of the Salt Lake Union Stock Yards in North Salt Lake or the Ogden Union Stockyards in Weber County. Both were strategically located along railroad lines. By the end of World War I, these yards were shipping thousands of cattle and sheep daily. Two large, meat-packing plants in Ogden provided another outlet for beef cattle. Supporting the operation of the stockyards were other companies offering necessary services. In North Salt Lake, these included two livestock brokerage firms, two commission companies, and two feeding yards. In an effort to learn and share knowledge among industry colleagues, some Davis County livestockmen attended the first U.S. cattlemen's congress, a fifteen-state gathering held in 1892 in Ogden.[51]

Within Davis County, the county commission opened a cattle road from Farmington through West Bountiful along 1100 West as a route for the spring and fall sheep movement. The Deseret Livestock Company alone moved more than 50,000 sheep back and forth from summer ranges in the upper valleys of Rich, Summit, and Morgan Counties to the desert ranges of Skull Valley in Tooele County as the seasons changed. With careful management, it was possible to provide more than three-fourths of a sheep's feed by grazing. Deseret Livestock endeavored to buy land for grazing. The resulting cattle and sheep operations opened many jobs for herding, shearing, and haying. The company sold its spring and fall ranges in Davis County in 1930 because their small size made them unprofitable.[52]

Islands in the Great Salt Lake also served as herding grounds. During his lake survey in 1849–50, Howard Stansbury had recognized the high quality of the major islands for grazing. Until 1877 the LDS church-owned Island Ranching Company used Antelope Island for its cattle, horses, and sheep, including those of the Perpetual Emigrating Company. Because the Mormon church held only squatter's rights to the land, however, its claims were challenged in the 1870s by homesteaders. Most of those who filed claims were miners who kept only small farms and gardens to prove their rights. A few, like George and Alice Frary, sought long-term residences and established ranches and small farms. It was not long before land ownership on Antelope Island became consolidated. During the last dozen years of the nineteenth century, ownership was divided about equally between John H. White's company, White & Sons, and John E. Dooly's Island Improvement Company. During this time, White & Sons managed both ranch properties. The firm raised purebred Hereford and Galloway cattle to supply beef to wholesalers in Davis County and Salt Lake City. For thirteen years, White's ranch foreman, James W. Walker, lived on the island with his wife and their three children. In 1893 White purchased seventeen head of Texas buffalo that William Glassman of Ogden had brought to Utah. Raising and selling the animals became a sideline on the island. In 1903, Dooly's son-in-law Ernest Bamberger purchased White's interest, thus uniting the operations in the Island Improvement Company.[53]

As the livestock industry grew, an essential part of the ranchers life was fattening the beef and swine for market. Dairy cows and sheep also needed sustenance during winter months, and this created a local market for hay and other fodder crops. Alfalfa was by far the most popular animal feed. By 1930, most of the alfalfa produced in Davis County was used locally to support a burgeoning livestock and dairy industry.[54]

Dairies and Creameries. During the early years of the pioneer period, a typical family depended upon its own cow for milk and butter. Any surpluses would be traded to neighbors without cows or hauled to nearby urban markets. It wasn't long before settlers could buy dairy products from farmers who kept a few cows as a sideline. With the commercialization of agriculture, specialized farmers opened larger dairies or local creameries to serve a broader customer base. Over time, fewer and fewer families found it necessary to keep their own cows.[55]

Dairying in the Syracuse area expanded after the formation of the South Hooper Cheese Factory in 1893. Organized by a group of local farmers, it was soon processing about 2,000 pounds of milk daily. The cans of milk were hauled from the individual farms to the South Hooper plant on a specially built horse-drawn milk wagon. The company sold much of its cheese to the Adams and Keisel regional wholesale and retail firm headquartered in Ogden. The factory added a butter plant in 1897. That same year, the factory made a 700-pound cheese for a float in the Pioneer Jubilee parade in Salt Lake City. The plant continued under local management until it was purchased in 1928 by the Weber Central Dairy Association, a new cooperative marketing group.[56]

The other center for major dairy operations was at the opposite end of the county. In South Bountiful in the 1870s, Joseph and Eric Hogan set up Spring Farm Dairy, later known as Bonneville Dairy. Others soon entered the dairy business: Samuel S. Howard organized Bountiful Dairy in 1879, and the Farmer's Dairy, a three-farm partnership, appeared in the 1880s. In Woods Cross, Ike Atkinson teamed with the Hatch family to develop a commercial dairy based on a

Holstein herd. Before 1920, however, separate Atkinson and Hatch dairies were operating, along with a Moss family dairy. These dairies served the south Davis County and Salt Lake City markets. Consumers could buy directly from the dairies, or have milk, buttermilk, cream, and butter delivered to their homes.[57]

A number of Davis County residents became sideline dairymen. In west Layton, for example, as many as one-third of the farmers milked six to ten cows. Most South Weber farmers had herds of similar size. Some of these producers sold their milk to large processing plants, and some funneled their milk into local dairies; but most supported creameries. Beginning in the 1890s, one or more creameries were set up in South Weber, Layton, Kaysville, Farmington, Centerville, Bountiful, and West Bountiful. Some of them operated under a sole proprietorship; others incorporated with support from multiple stockholders. One of them was the South Weber Creamery Mercantile and Manufacturing Company, formed in 1895.[58]

During their heyday, the creameries served an important role as middlemen between producers and consumers. Typical of many was the creamery built in 1893 by Eli Manning in north Farmington to serve residents of the area. At the end of each week, "Mr. Friday," as Manning was called by Bountiful observers, drove his loaded wagon to Salt Lake City to deliver his surplus sweet cream butter to merchants serving urban buyers.[59] Similarly, many north Davis creameries hauled their surplus products to Ogden. After the turn of the century, the Bamberger Interurban Railroad diverted much of the raw milk from local creameries by transporting it directly to Salt Lake City or Ogden processing plants. This quickly drove most small creameries out of business, and eventually all of them closed. The regional processing plants marketed products to customers either through delivery vans or local merchants.[60]

Utah's Garden Spot. Beginning in the late 1880s, commercial agriculture expanded in other ways to utilize Davis County's fertile soils. The area became home to a market garden industry that provided fresh produce for buyers in Salt Lake City and Ogden and cash crops to farmers of vegetables and fruit for local canneries. The county celebrated its role as the "Garden Spot of Utah" with a float under that name in Salt Lake City's Pioneer Jubilee parade in 1897.

A pair of "Then and Now" floats represented Davis County in the 1897 Pioneer Semi-centennial Parade in Salt Lake City. This one celebrated the "Garden Spot of Utah," while the other float featured a sagebrush landscape under the title "Davis County 1847." (Utah State Historical Society)

Those who depended upon a bounteous harvest of fruits or vegetables for their income found themselves at the mercy of late spring or early fall frosts, dry summers, and other natural conditions. But they met these challenges—as well as the need to recruit field laborers—and developed an important new agricultural industry in the county.[61]

Farmers in Davis County turned to commercial vegetable gardening when they discovered that by diversifying their commercial crops they could guarantee at least some income in the event of frost, disease, or insect damage. When yields were good, vegetables and fruits were extremely profitable crops—every acre planted returned more than five times as much value to the farmer as a similar acreage planted in hay or grain.[62]

Thomas Briggs is credited with pioneering commercial gardening in Davis County. His attempts to start seeds in hot beds in the windows of his Bountiful home inspired others in the area to create their own in-house nurseries. In 1875 a group of these gardeners elected Briggs as head of a growers company to market produce in Salt Lake City. The company lacked the capital to succeed at that time, but market gardens increased gradually until by the turn of the century they were a leading source of income for many farmers.[63]

By 1910, four dozen or so vegetable and fruit growers in south Davis County were shipping produce commercially, much of it to markets in other states. They revived the idea of cooperative marketing in 1911 by organizing a gardeners and fruit growers association. Soon known as the Growers Exchange, the organization purchased seed and other farm items in bulk and set up a farmer's market at 140 West on 400 South in Salt Lake City for direct sales to urban customers. During the harvest season, the farmers would hitch up their teams before dawn each morning to haul their produce to the market. They offered their goods in stalls rented from the Growers Exchange, then returned home to harvest produce for the next day's market. The association erected its own building in 1918 and adopted the name Growers Market. The building served as the nerve center for the produce growers until it was demolished in 1972 to make way for a Hilton hotel.[64]

A new focus on specialization began when a cannery opened in Woods Cross in 1892 and contracted with market gardeners in Davis County to grow tomatoes. By 1894 the Woods Cross Canning and Pickling Company had fifty-five employees and was producing 8,000 cans of tomatoes and 700 bottles of catsup per day during the fall processing season. The firm later added other products to its line. It built a tomato cannery in Clearfield in 1902 and ten years later acquired the plant that had been operating since 1903 as the Layton Canning Company. Woods Cross Canning Company also operated a pea cannery in Heber City. By 1912 the company was Utah's second-largest commercial cannery. Its canneries were at their peak during the 1920s and 1930s. The company's Woods Cross and Layton plants remained in business until the 1950s; the Clearfield cannery operated until 1975.[65]

The first plant of the Woods Cross Canning and Pickling Company found a ready market for local garden products, shipped by rail to customers in a wide region. (Utah State Historical Society)

Most of Utah's canning industry operated in Weber, Davis, and Cache Counties. Before the Woods Cross Canning Company expanded, farmers in Syracuse and Hooper processed their tomatoes on local farms or supplied crops to Utah's first cannery, organized in Ogden in 1886. In response to the expanding supply in the Weber-north Davis region, new plants were built in Hooper in 1892 and in Roy six years later. A temporary facility set up in 1893 on a farm in Syracuse served farmers in that area until investors organized the Syracuse Cannery Company in 1898. The firm built a plant alongside a railroad spur at 4000 West. This prompted a rapid expansion of tomato growing in the northern end of the county. D. C. Adams, co-owner of the Syracuse Resort, purchased the company in 1901, expanded the plant, and increased contracts with farmers to 200 acres. The Syracuse Canning Factory expanded its operations very soon after it opened to include products besides tomatoes, which

George C. Wood, Sr., and his six sons stand in their commercial watermelon field southeast of Woods Cross in about 1910. (Intellectual Reserve, Inc., courtesy LDS Church Archives)

remained its leading product. It canned squash as soon as the two-month tomato campaign ended and built a pickling tank to process cucumbers. The cannery also processed apples, prunes, pears, peaches, plums, and beans. The other canneries in the county likewise kept a diversified list of branded goods flowing to market to keep their plants profitable.[66]

The success in Syracuse spurred John R. Barnes and associates to build the Kaysville Canning Company in 1902. When the Syracuse plant closed following the death of owner D. C. Adams in 1910, Barnes lined up investors to build another factory in Syracuse—the Davis County Canning Company at 2000 West. The new factory was merged with the Kaysville company two years later and adopted the Kaysville brand name. The Syracuse cannery operated until it was destroyed by fire in 1923. The cannery in Kaysville processed tomatoes, beans, peas, and other vegetables for more than half a century.[67]

During their heyday, canneries in Davis County exported large quantities of canned fruits and vegetables, provided stable incomes for contracted farmers, and offered seasonal employment for many other residents and migrants. The Woods Cross and Kaysville brands were widely known and respected in many parts of the United States. The Davis County canneries were part of a much larger Utah industry, including the canneries in neighboring Weber County, where more than twenty were in operation in the 1920s.[68]

Other major cash crops for county farmers included potatoes, peas, and onions. The pattern in Syracuse was typical of other areas of the county and along the Wasatch Front. The first commercial vegetable crop in Syracuse was potatoes. By the mid-1890s good quality potatoes were being shipped to outside markets. A report in 1904 noted that ten railcars of Syracuse potatoes were on their way to Colorado and beyond. The first commercial peas were being grown on forty acres at that time and hauled to Ogden for canning. As more farmers began raising that crop, pea viners were built near the farms to remove the peas from their pods before delivering them to a cannery. The onion business was launched about the time World War I began and became a mainstay for many farmers. After West Bountiful and Layton farmers perfected the sweet Valencia onion, it became a favorite in markets nationwide. Eighth West in West Bountiful became known as "Onion Street" because so many farmers were raising the crop. There were some farmers in almost all of the flatland farming areas of the county who found potatoes, peas, and onions commercially attractive. In a good year, the irrigated alkaline soils of Davis County could produce twenty tons of tomatoes to the acre, 250 bushels of potatoes, or around 600 bags of onions per acre.[69]

Orchards, Nurseries, and Apiaries. Contributing to Davis County's reputation as Utah's Garden Spot were the county's commercial orchards. Families had planted fruit trees around their homes very early during the settlement years. Mormon settlers found the county's temperate climate well-suited to growing apples, peaches, and plums. Some families also raised pears and pie cherries. Besides supplying family needs, the trees often produced a surplus. Local merchants would accept dried fruit in exchange for clothing or other goods and then ship the fruit to western mining camps to redeem it for cash. A few families marketed commercial quantities of dried fruit locally or in Ogden or Salt Lake City. In the Bountiful area, Newton Tuttle and Israel Barlow pioneered the commercial production of dried plums and peaches. Fruit and molasses (that is, peaches preserved in molasses) could be traded for coal in Summit County. Residents in Park City purchased these products as well as vegetables, dairy products, and eggs from south Davis County farmers. In the 1880s merchants throughout the county aggressively advertised their services as shipping agents for local farm products.[70]

The sale of fresh fruit also began early. For example, Joseph Robinson of Farmington expanded an existing orchard in 1859 by planting fifty-two apple trees and the same number of peach trees. One of his best markets in the mid-1880s was Summit County. One of Davis County's most productive fruit areas was along a half-mile-wide strip of land below Bluff Road in Syracuse and South Hooper (West Point). Three major fruit growers in this area were serving national markets in the 1890s with their high-quality canned fruits, jellies, and preserves. Gilbert Parker, who was raised on a farm in Wellsville, grew apples, peaches, plums, and cherries on a twenty-five-acre orchard in West Point. William H. Miller, a sheepman and farmer, specialized in Missouri Pippin apples and Bartlett pears, and he also raised Jonathan and Winesap apples. He shipped his first harvest of more than a thousand bushels of Pippins in 1898 to eastern markets. Daniel C. Adams and his silent financial partner Fred Keisel of Ogden owned a bathing resort and a salt plant before planting fruit and vegetables on the 200-acre lakeside property. Adams planted pear and French prune trees in 1893, and within a few years he was shipping his produce to out-of-state markets. Adams sold fresh fruit, canned prunes, canned grape butter, bottled pears and peaches, and various jellies and preserves. He later expanded by adding apples, asparagus, cucumbers, pumpkins, squash, cherries, and grapes.[71]

Orchards were also found along the benchlands of Davis County. Commercial operations thrived along Mountain Road in east Layton and Fruit Heights and on the rocky benches of Farmington, Centerville, and Bountiful. Some growers specialized, but many raised a variety of fruits to hedge against the weather and disease and to serve a broader market. Typical of the diversified

Orchards flourished in northwestern Davis County in the 1890s and lined the eastern foothills. This 1906 view is near Mueller Park east of Bountiful. (Utah State Historical Society)

approach was New Englander Grandison Raymond, Sr., an early orchardist in Fruit Heights, who produced cherries, peaches, plums, apricots, apples, and berries. In later years, Fruit Heights became known for its high-quality cherries and peaches, raised by a half-dozen growers.[72]

Each area of the county had its pioneers in commercial fruit cultivation and its successful producers. In South Weber, Joseph Bambrough put twenty acres of pasture land into fruit trees, and his success prompted others to try orchards of various sizes. Among them was Swedish immigrant Charles A. Fernelius, who produced choice apples and cherries. English emigrants William and Esther Bosworth of Kaysville marketed fruit, berries, and vegetables as far away as Evanston, Wyoming. Farmington's Thomas F. King operated a ten-acre "peach ranch," featuring seven varieties that matured one after another from July to October. In the early 1890s, his fruit was selling for from sixty cents to one dollar for a twenty-pound box. A half-dozen other growers could be named in Farmington, and many more were tending orchards as a main source of income in the area from Centerville to Bountiful.[73]

Davis County fruit farmers were their own nurserymen, growing and grafting their own trees and selling saplings to neighbors. Newton Tuttle and Israel Barlow, Sr., did this in Bountiful. Barlow was remembered for his ingenuity in budding several varieties of apples onto one tree and in growing apricots and plums together.[74] Kaysville's pioneer horticulturist was Levi Roberts, an 1850 settler who took slips from every newly arrived variety of fruit he could locate to graft into his trees. Thomas Whitaker, a pioneer in producing silk in Utah, led out in nursery work in Centerville. In time, successful nurseries and some florists appeared in the city. The first nursery was founded by Samuel Smith, who moved to Centerville from Logan in 1885. Smith Brothers' Nursery became a leading supplier of trees, shrubs, and flowers in the county. It was later sold to P. A. Dix. Other companies soon followed in Centerville. Porter-Walton Company was in business early in the century, along with florists William Barber and John Reading. By the mid-1910s Charles Boylan was working as a florist in Farmington and Emil Lund had launched his long career as manager of Lindgren Conservatories, wholesale and retail florists.[75]

While Centerville enjoyed the largest concentration of nurseries, it was in Farmington in 1910 that Robert Miller, a New England transplant, established what became Utah's largest wholesale floral company. Miller Floral specialized in growing cut flowers, especially roses and carnations, plus ferns and potted plants. Local stockholders purchased the company in 1925. After Miller left Utah, Elijah B. Gregory and Golden J. Barton managed the operation. The floral expanded its hothouses to serve an expanding list of intermountain and national retail florists. By 1968, Miller Floral was the largest wholesale floral west of Denver, employing fifty workers in its twenty-one greenhouses, enclosed by 300,000 square feet of glass. It was shipping 1.5 million roses and 1 million carnations, plus gladioli, snapdragons, irises, sweet peas, chrysanthemums, and other flowers. The company underwent three ownership changes in the 1960s. The floral closed in the 1970s, but its owners under a new corporate name built new greenhouses near Draper to continue the tradition of raising high-quality flowers and potted plants for the retail market.[76]

Besides landscape trees and plants, Davis County's nurserymen provided imported varieties of berries for home use. In the first years of settlement, women gathered wild chokecherries, currants, elderberries, raspberries, and serviceberries.[77] Domestic varieties appeared in home gardens as soon as plant starts could be imported. Some of the small fruits became commercial crops. In the 1890s, Maren Mitchell, a Danish immigrant, helped her husband, James, make payments on their house in Clinton by raising and selling gooseberries, raspberries, currants, rhubarb, and dried apricots door to door in Ogden.[78] Clearfield's Richard and Emily Hamblin and their sons brought plants from St. George and became specialists in raising strawberries. The family supplied much of Ogden with the fruit. Hamblin, known to some as the "Strawberry King," shipped as many as 100 cases a day to Evanston, Wyoming.[79]

One noteworthy horticultural contribution in Davis County was the development of the Gleason Early Elberta peach. Kaysville physician Dr. Sumner Gleason, who also raised fruit and operated a small cannery, nurtured the variety after he found it growing on a tree in his orchard. He actively promoted the peach and eventually convinced a Clearfield nursery to market it. Orchardists in Fruit Heights also may have had a hand in the development or expansion of the stock of the original tree for commercial marketing under Gleason's name.[80] For his efforts, Gleason won a $500 prize from the Stark Brothers nursery in Missouri for the best early Elberta peach. The peach was included in Stark's 1914 catalog and became widely used.[81]

The county's nurserymen also sold to residents the quick-growing Lombardy poplars to shade roadways and temper the winds. In the 1880s, these tall trees became a widely-used feature in Davis County. As Doritt Brough remembered it, "Up until the advent of the automobile and surfaced roads an almost unbroken row of poplar trees lined the west side of what is now Highway 91 from Layton to Bountiful. When roads were deep with dust and travel was slow this shade was deeply appreciated."[82] Some towns lined the main street of their business district with Lombardies; more commonly, the trees marked rural lanes and streets.

One other minor business related to agriculture was that of beekeeping. A number of Davis County orchardists kept bees to ensure good pollination of their fruit trees. Farmers and tradesmen took up beekeeping as a financial sideline. The efforts of these apiarists helped pollinate local orchards and alfalfa fields as the bees collected nectar for their hives.[83] The resulting honey found a ready market along the Wasatch Front. Like other agricultural efforts that helped the community, bee culture was promoted both from the pulpit and in agriculture meetings. "There can be no doubt about its being a paying business if managed rightly," a Farmington correspondent reported for the *Deseret News* in 1878; "E. T. Clark . . . began with two swarms six years ago; they now number fifty-seven."[84] Davis County apiarists in the early twentieth century included Joseph Adams and Samuel J. Adams of Layton, Timothy B. Clark of Farmington, and George Gerritt of Bountiful.[85]

Irrigation and Canals. Except for the dry-farm grains, all of the new commercial crops depended upon irrigation. The incorporation of community irrigation systems and the construction of new canals made possible the area's orchards and market gardens and an expansion of farming to include alfalfa and sugar beets. A forty-year period of expanding irrigated acreage peaked in 1910 in Utah and then slacked off. Davis County ranked among the top twelve Utah counties in total irrigated acreage.[86]

The successful effort to irrigate Davis County's northwestern prairie came after a change in Utah territorial law. In 1865 a new law allowed the creation of water districts, and many mutual irrigation companies were formed. Under this law, water users conducted business by vote, appointed a watermaster, and, as they had always done, turned out every spring and fall to clean the ditches. The watermaster apportioned the stream flow according to the shares owned by each member.[87]

In Davis County, the county court authorized the water-distribution change in 1876. Farmers in Kays Creek (Layton) had apparently held an election and named their own watermaster, and Joel Parrish of Centerville proposed to the court that the other county areas be allowed to do the same. After much discussion, the court agreed. It created eight water districts and ordered each district to

Irrigation made Davis County's market gardening possible. The Philadelphia Commercial Museum documented agriculture along the Wasatch Front in 1902, but did not record a specific location for this typical garden. (Utah State Historical Society)

hold an annual election each February and to report the results for county certification. This effort speeded the shift from Mormon church to user management. In at least one community, the bishop assisted with the transition by allowing time in priesthood meetings for electing the district watermaster and selecting overseers for individual creeks. The eight districts created in 1876 were Bountiful, Centerville, Farmington, Haights Creek, South Fork of Holmes Creek, North Fork of Holmes Creek, Kays Creek, and South Weber River.[88]

An 1880 law reinforced this trend to replace community interests with individual property rights. The new law separated water rights from the land. County water commissioners resolved all disputes. During the next twenty years, commissioners in Davis County ruled on ownership claims to fifteen streams and issued 306 certificates of ownership. Some disputes inevitably arose. According to news reports, disagreements over water and stock in water companies in Davis County at times came close to fist fights.[89]

The 1880 law encouraged the creation of private irrigation companies. This move completed the conversion from ecclesiastical to private oversight of water resources. In Davis County, incorporation began with the formation of the North Canyon Water Company in 1893. Over the next decade, most other water users in the county took similar steps, and, by another ten years, more than twenty streams and ditches were under this system of governance. Other parts of the state were moving in the same direction; by 1913, 168 water companies were functioning in Utah. The move from cooperative to corporate water management was complete by the outbreak of World War I.[90]

Even as this transformation was taking place, state water laws shifted again. The state legislature created the office of state water engineer, and in 1903 it enacted a law to increase state supervision of water resources. Sparse funding hindered implementation of the new laws, so in 1919 Utah moved back to public control of water resources. The law reestablished the Mormon system of irrigation districts. This emphasized local cooperative management under the irrigation companies, but with state instead of Mormon church supervision.[91]

As noted in an earlier chapter, the farmers who homesteaded on the Sandridge in Davis County's northwestern region depended upon deep wells for culinary water and did without irrigation water. Their neighbors in Hooper and South Weber had diverted water from the Weber River in the 1850s and 1860s to water farm crops, and the Sandridge farmers tried to develop their own Weber River canal system. The Davis Canal Company had already failed in an 1856–57 effort to tunnel through the sand at the mouth of Weber Canyon. It was a quarter of a century before the task was accomplished by taking a long detour around the sand hill and into Layton. Brigham Young had seen the potential. He said in 1864, "Davis is the richest county for grain and fruit that we have, and if a portion of the Weber were brought out, thousands of acres of good land now on the open prairie might be brought into cultivation." The Hooper Canal was extended into Syracuse in 1875 to supplement the flowing wells below the Bluff, but this did not solve the need south of the Syracuse Road or on the dry-farm homesteads on the Sandridge.[92]

The project that brought water to these areas began with the organization of the Central Canal Company, which was reorganized in 1884 as the Davis and Weber Canal Company. Organizers included Feramorz Little, William R. Smith, William Jennings, Anson Call, and William H. Hooper. The company used horse-drawn scrapers to build more than twenty miles of earthen ditch to carry irrigation water from the Weber River to higher-elevation land in Sunset, Clearfield, and as far as Kays Creek in east Layton. The canal worked well during the early months of the growing season; however, during the late summer months, when the river's level dropped, it could not supply all the water needed by stockholders. To provide more water, from 1896 to 1899 the canal company built a rock-and-soil-fill storage dam sixty-eight feet high in the Red Rock Gorge of East Canyon Creek, about twelve miles south of Morgan. Within three years, the dam was raised twice, increasing its capacity from 3,800 acre-feet to 13,800 acre-feet.

The enlarged reservoir watered 12,000 acres in Davis County, and it led to a rapid expansion of commercial farming. In 1913 the company lined the canal with concrete to preserve water, and three years later a larger, reinforced-concrete dam was built. With the supply increased to 28,000 acre-feet, farmers from Clinton to West Layton were able to grow good crops of alfalfa, potatoes, tomatoes, and sugar beets. Various local ditch companies were incorporated to channel the water from the canal to local farms under the watch of a local watermaster. In the Syracuse-Clearfield area, irrigated agriculture increased from about one-fourth of the land in 1906 to almost all of it by 1920. It was the increase in irrigation water from East Canyon Dam that allowed northwestern Davis County to blossom as a commercial agricultural center.[93]

Nature's Riches

While Utah's flatlands attracted farmers, the hills and mountains surrounding the populated valleys offered a different commercial opportunity. The territory's mining boom of the 1870s and 1880s attracted national attention and piqued the interest of at least a few Davis County residents. If silver could be found in Parley's Canyon, they reasoned, why not in Farmington Canyon? If copper threaded

This persistent Davis County miner was still hoping to strike it rich when Harry Shipler photographed him in 1902 at his Farmington Gold & Copper Mining and Milling Company. (Utah State Historical Society)

the soils of the east face of the Oquirrh Range, what might await discovery along their own west-facing Wasatch Mountains or on Antelope Island? Those who took up the challenge scoured the hillsides and explored the canyons between the Hot Springs and the Weber River seeking the ore that brought instant wealth to owners of the mines circling Salt Lake County. But, in the end, Davis County's argonauts found commercial gain only in the county's most obvious cache of minerals—the briny waters of Great Salt Lake—and then only for a short time.

During the Utah mining boom, prospectors picked at rocks and dug exploratory shafts at various places in Davis County. All claims in the county were filed under the Farmington Mining District. Striking it rich was an idea that attracted both established settlers and newcomers. Patsy Morley, a former Irish prizefighter, became a legend in Farmington for his untiring efforts to strike it rich in a mine on the bench just north of Steed Creek. For twenty years, the old bachelor made daily trips to his mine from a back-room apartment in an old Main Street business building, hoping that each day would bring the lucky strike. When he finally gave up, Morley left town as unceremoniously as he had arrived.[94]

More typical of the attempts to extract ore in Davis County were those of Farmington flour miller Henry Southworth. For a few short years, Southworth and his son worked at least four mines part-way up Farmington Canyon. Because the men shipped a little ore from one tunnel, they attracted investment from a mining company; but the mine lacked commercial potential. Similar results dogged the miners who staked claims in other canyons above Farmington, Kaysville, Centerville, and Bountiful. In all instances, after a few years of hard work, the claimants abandoned their efforts. A South Weber attempt to mine coal likewise ended in failure. The only material extracted for profit from Bountiful's hillside was rock, which was quarried for a time beginning in 1893 by the Bountiful Rock Company.[95]

The county's most promising mining boom followed the discovery of copper and silver on Antelope Island in the late 1880s. Prospectors dug dozens of test holes and organized several mining companies. Five operators joined forces in 1899 as the Great Salt Lake Mining Company; four others continued independent operations. One mine yielded ore containing 26 percent copper, and, before long, more than fifty miners were at work on the island. They expected to discover yields like those of the Bingham Canyon copper mine in the Oquirrhs, directly across the lake to the south. Antelope Island's most promising vein played out quickly, however, and the shortlived boom ended.[96]

Another potential commercial resource was discovered along the lake's east shoreline in 1883, when artesian-well drillers hit an underground pool of natural gas at the 550-foot level in north Centerville. Nothing was done to develop the gas on the land of Ephraim Garn for another decade, however. At that time, the American Gas Company bought out the owner's rights, and in February 1895 the company agreed to supply fuel to the Salt Lake and Ogden Gas and Electric Company. Manufactured gas had been used to light Salt Lake City streets since 1872. The Davis County natural gas replaced this earlier source; but, within a year, customers were complaining about unreliable pressure in the lines. The service company reintroduced manufactured gas to supplement the Centerville fuel for about a year; then, early in 1898, it returned wholly to the more reliable product. Thus, after only three years of commercial use, Davis County's marsh-gas wells were capped. The first street lighting in Davis County was furnished in Bountiful by Lakeshore Gas and Oil Company beginning in 1902.[97]

Like earlier indigenous peoples who lived along the shores of the Great Salt Lake for centuries, Mormon settlers found the lake a ready source for salt. Harvested by individuals and cooperatively, salt was used to season or pickle foods and to prepare meats for winter storage. The easily harvested compound soon became a successfully exported product for Davis County's entrepreneurs. Residents of South Weber filled their wagons with salt from the lakeshore sloughs, cleaned it, and sold it to Ogden residents. People elsewhere in the county likewise quickly moved beyond the bucket-at-a-time collection of salt for personal need. Hauling off a wagonload, they would sell the product locally at fifty cents for a heaping bushel.[98]

Salt gathered from the lakeshore contained impurities that gave it a bitter taste. The salt could be purified by boiling off the excess minerals. At least one company had vats boiling daily along the south shore of the lake in the 1850s and 1860s. The families in Davis County who collected salt locally did their own boiling and skimming. In the early 1870s two developments hastened the growth of commercial salt production. First, the lake rose to such an extent that it covered most of the natural salt beds. Not long afterward, the mines of Nevada and Montana began using a chlorination process to reduce their ores, and this created a new market for salt. Utahns responded to both opportunities. New salt production companies appeared in the 1880s, including ones in Davis County. Using pumps and ponds, the salt makers produced salt and shipped it by wagon and railcar to local and out-of-state markets.[99]

The county's first salt company was organized in Syracuse in 1880 by George Payne. Three years later, in Farmington, Isaac Sears, "Mac" MacKeg, and James Mellus organized the Deseret Salt Company. These two pioneering companies served both the local and

An artist for *Harper's Weekly* captured the look of the early salt industry along the shores of the Great Salt Lake during the summer of 1887. (Utah State Historical Society)

mining markets with crude salt. Their methods were simple. Using horse-powered pumps, they piped lake water into ponds for controlled evaporation. As the salt crystalized, workers shoveled it into piles within the pond, then carted it out in large wheelbarrows to continue drying. Loaded into sacks, the salt for export was hauled by wagons or the railway to out-of-state ore-processing plants.[100]

In 1885 Payne sold out to William W. Galbraith, who marketed the product under the "Syracuse" brand, a name he "borrowed" from a well-known salt company in Syracuse, New York. A year later, Galbraith sold the saltworks to Adams and Keisel, who added a lakeshore resort to the property. The resort used the Syracuse name, as did the Ogden and Syracuse Railway, a spur built in 1887 by the Oregon Short Line Railway to serve the resort, the salt works, and local farmers. These uses of the Syracuse name gave the surrounding community, previously named Hoboken, its permanent name. Noting the success of the Syracuse salt works, the Gwilliam Brothers of South Hooper soon opened the county's third salt works. It became known as the Crystal Salt Company in 1892.[101]

The expansion of Utah's salt industry and a decrease in needs at western silver mills led in the early 1890s to over-production of the product. All but the largest Utah salt companies were sold or closed. Hastening the demise of Davis County's salt works was the creation in 1887 of the Inland Salt Company, owned by the Church of Jesus Christ of Latter-day Saints. This south shore company was soon producing 40,000 tons of salt annually, nearly half of Utah's salt. Adams and Keisel Salt Company ranked second, with 15,000 tons; and Deseret Salt was fourth of the territory's seven operations, with 9,500 tons.[102]

In 1891 a Kansas company bought Inland Salt Company. With its proceeds from the sale, the LDS church organized a competing firm, the Inter-Mountain Salt Company, and built Saltair Resort and the Saltair railway. The two salt companies merged in 1898, with the Mormon church maintaining a controlling interest. The new Inland Crystal Salt Company monopolized Utah's salt industry and remained profitable by creating an artificial scarcity of refined salt.[103]

To eliminate competition in Davis County, Inland signed a five-year lease with Deseret Salt Company in 1898 and the following year bought out both Adams and Keisel and Crystal Salt. When Inland more than tripled salt prices to ten dollars a ton, Davis County pioneer saltmaker George Payne reacted by forming a partnership with Ed Bill and James Chesney. For a few years beginning in 1900, they produced and sold salt in Syracuse at $2.50 a ton, mostly to help local farmers, but no doubt also with an eye on profits. Similarly, in Farmington, John O. Johnston, James H. Tippets, and Charles Backman bought back the Deseret Salt lease and formed their own Utah Salt Company to create a competitive market in south Davis County.[104]

The small, local producers struggled to survive. Morton Salt entered the Utah market in 1918 as a competitor of Inland Crystal Salt Company. Within a decade, Inland was operating as a Morton subsidiary. As was true of other important Utah industries at the turn of the century, outside financiers played an important role in the local salt-production market. Profits rather than the economic well-being of local residents governed corporate actions. Davis County's home-owned salt industry melted away as part of the transition to a commercial economy.[105]

ENDNOTES

1. Quoted in Annie Call Carr, ed., *East of Antelope Island: History of the First Fifty Years of Davis County,* 71.

2. Leonard J. Arrington, *Great Basin Kingdom: An Economic History of the Latter-day Saints, 1830–1900,* 341–44, 348–49.

3. Ibid., 345; William Robb Purrington, "The History of South Davis County from 1847 to 1870," 74.

4. Clayton Holt, ed., *The Community of Syracuse, 1820 to 1995,* 59; Carol Ivins Collett, *Kaysville—Our Town: A History,* 29; Mary Ellen Smoot and Marilyn Sheriff, *The City In-Between: History of Centerville, Utah,* 34; Carr, *East of Antelope Island,* 71.

5. Kate B. Carter, comp., *Heart Throbs of the West,* 11:53–54; Hubert Howe Bancroft, *History of Utah, 1540–1887,* 726; Chris Rigby Arrington, "The Finest of Fabrics: Mormon Women and the Silk Industry in Early Utah," *Utah Historical Quarterly* 46 (Fall 1978): 378–79.

6. Arrington, *Great Basin Kingdom,* 227–28, 254.

7. Margaret Steed Hess, *My Farmington: A History of Farmington, Utah, 1847–1976,* 343.

8. Joseph L. Robinson, Autobiography and Journal, April 1876.

9. Chris Arrington, "The Finest of Fabrics," 382–83, 387–88; Carr, *East of Antelope Island,* 396–97, 283, 90, 244; Hess, *My Farmington,* 343.

10. Farmington Ward, Teachers Quorum Minutes, 23 January, 13 February 1876, 31 March 1878, 12 June 1881; Collett, *Kaysville—Our Town,* 85–86.

11. Carter, *Heart Throbs,* 11:54, 78–79; Robinson, Autobiography and Journal, 26–28 May, 16–17 June 1877; John Taylor, discourse, Kaysville, 2 March 1879, *Journal of Discourses,* 26 vols. (Liverpool and London: Latter-day Saints' Book Depot, 1855–1886), 20:169.

12. *Deseret News,* 13, 20 April 1877; Carter, *Heart Throbs,* 11:57; Carr, *East of Antelope Island,* 283; Hess, *My Farmington,* 343.

13. Hess, *My Farmington,* 344, says this dress preceded Clark's.

14. Collett, *Kaysville—Our Town,* 31; Carr, *East of Antelope Island,* 397; "John H. and Ada Arvilla Burk Earl," typescript, in private possession; Carter, *Heart Throbs,* 11:78–82, 312. Chris Arrington, "The Finest of Fabrics," 388–89, found reports of only four silk dresses made in the terri-

tory, three of them in Davis County. The information presented above suggests a much greater production.

15. Chris Arrington, "The Finest of Fabrics," 391; Carr, *East of Antelope Island,* 396; *Davis County Clipper,* 25 January 1894.

16. Chris Arrington, "The Finest of Fabrics," 393–96; *Davis County Clipper,* 4 August 1896, 8 April, 16 December 1898.

17. Charles L. Schmalz, "The Failure of Utah's First Sugar Factory," *Utah Historical Quarterly* 56 (Winter 1988): 36–47, 52.

18. *Deseret News* (weekly), 11 November, 20 May 1868.

19. Farmington Ward, Teachers Minutes, 13 April 1879; *Deseret Evening News,* 18 September 1880; *Davis County Clipper,* 2 April 1897; Fred G. Taylor, *A Saga of Sugar* (Salt Lake City: Utah-Idaho Sugar Co., 1944), 62–64.

20. Leonard J. Arrington, *Beet Sugar in the West: A History of the Utah-Idaho Sugar Company, 1891–1966.* (Seattle and London: University of Washington Press, 1966), 6–7; Taylor, *A Saga of Sugar,* 64–69, 73–84.

21. Leonard J. Arrington, "The Sugar Industry in Utah," in Allan Kent Powell, ed., *Utah History Encyclopedia,* 534–35; Kent Day, "The Layton Sugar Company," in Dan Carlsruh and Eve Carlsruh, eds., *Layton, Utah: Historic Viewpoints,* 264.

22. Holt, *The Community of Syracuse,* 102–3; Day, "Layton Sugar Company," 266–67.

23. Day, "Layton Sugar Company," 269, 273; Holt, *Community of Syracuse,* 103; Lee D. Bell, *South Weber: The Autobiography of One Utah Community,* 162.

24. Day, "Layton Sugar Company," 273–81.

25. Glen M. Leonard, "A History of Farmington, Utah, to 1890," 107–8; Holt, *Community of Syracuse,* 96–97.

26. Holt, *Community of Syracuse,* 97–98.

27. *Utah Gazetteer and Directory, 1888* (Salt Lake City: Lorenzo Stenhouse, 1888), 36, 44, 64–65, 81–85; *Utah Gazetteer, 1892–93* (Salt Lake City: Stenhouse and Co., 1892), 44, 51, 69, 90, 93; *Utah State Gazetteer and Business Directory, 1900* (Salt Lake City: R. L. Polk & Co., 1900), 66, 78, 80, 98, 122, 126; *Utah State Gazetteer and Business Directory, 1918–1919* (Salt Lake City: R. L. Polk & Co., 1918), 27–28, 41, 43, 59, 84–85, 87–88, 128, 328; Arlene H. Eakle, Adelia Baird, and Georgia Weber, *Woods Cross: Patterns and Profiles of a City,* 46; Holt, *Community of Syracuse,* 135–36.

28. *Davis County Clipper,* 19 March 1892; *Weekly Reflex* (Kaysville), 1 May 1913, 6.

29. For examples see *Davis County Clipper,* 8 June, 27 July 1893; *Deseret Evening News,* 31 October 1894.

30. L. R. Humpherys and A. C. Matheson, eds., *Utah—Resources and Activities: Supplement to the Utah State Courses of Study for Elementary and Secondary Schools* (Salt Lake City: Utah Department of Public Instruction, 1933), 428; F. Ross Peterson, *A History of Cache County* (Salt Lake City: Utah State Historical Society and Cache County Council, 1997), 228–29.

31. Alley S. Rose, Journal, entries each August or September from 1905 to 1910, LDS Church Archives; Joel E. Ricks, *The Utah State Agricultural College: A History of Fifty Years, 1888–1938* (Salt Lake City: Deseret News Press, 1938), 85; John A. Widtsoe, *The Principles of Irrigation Practice* (New York: Macmillan, 1914), 470.

32. Collett, *Kaysville—Our Town,* 44; Humpherys and Matheson, *Utah—Resources and Activities,* 281; Ricks, *Utah State Agricultural College,* 85

33. Holt, *Community of Syracuse,* 96–97; Humpherys and Matheson, *Utah—Resources and Activities,* 251, 277, 279–83.

34. Humpherys and Matheson, *Utah—Resources and Activities,* 277–83; *Utah Gazetteer, 1892–93,* 13

35. Carr, *East of Antelope Island,* 367, Leland H. Creer, *The Founding of an Empire: The Exploration and Colonization of Utah, 1776–1856* (Salt Lake City: Bookcraft, 1947), 340.

36. Leslie T. Foy, *The City Bountiful: Utah's Second Settlement, from Pioneers to Present,* 92; Smoot and Sheriff, *City In-Between,* 31, Hess, *My Farmington,* 337; Leonard, "A History of Farmington," 107; Bell, *South Weber,* 177; Carr, *East of Antelope Island,* 368, 425–26.

37. Holt, *Community of Syracuse,* 96–97.

38. Foy, *City Bountiful,* 92; Bureau of the Census, "Census Schedules for Davis County," (Seventh Census, 1850). Mower is not listed in the 1852 ward report and may have moved elsewhere by then.

39. Smoot and Sheriff, *City In-Between,* 31. The 1850 census lists William as a farmer and his older brother Osmyn as a blacksmith. Both men pursued both occupations in Utah.

40. *Deseret News,* 6 July 1850; Joseph Cain and Arieh C. Brower, *Mormon Way-bill to the Gold Mines* (Great Salt Lake City: published for the authors, 1851); Collett, *Kaysville—Our Town,* 10, 32. Burton was not listed in the 1850 census but is found in the 1852 bishop's report.

41. Carr, *East of Antelope Island,* 385–88; Foy, *City Bountiful,* 92–93; Hess, *My Farmington,* 334; Farmington Ward, Teachers Minutes, 13 May, 29 July, 5 August 1866.

42. Carr, *East of Antelope Island,* 385–87; Holt, *Community of Syracuse,* 142–43.

43. Inez Barker, comp., *John Weinel, Miller: Early Pioneer Builder and Operator of the First Flour Mill in Kaysville, Utah* (Kaysville: Daughters of Utah Pioneers, 1983), 38.

44. Ibid., 27, 41–45.

45. Foy, *City Bountiful,* 87; *Utah Gazetteer, 1888,* 36, 44; *Utah Gazetteer, 1892–1893,* 51, 69; *Utah State Gazetteer,* 1900, 98; Hess, *My Farmington,* 341.

46. Oma E. Wilcox and E. Harris Adams, "Layton Businesses," in Carlsruh and Carlsruh, *Layton, Utah,* 291–92.

47. Ibid.; Collett, *Kaysville—Our Town,* 112; Richard C. Roberts and Richard W. Sadler, *A History of Weber County,* 240.

48. Humpherys and Matheson, *Utah—Resources and Activities,* 33–35; Carr, *East of Antelope Island,* 162–63; *Deseret News* (weekly), 20 May 1868.

49. Eakle, Baird, and Weber, *Woods Cross,* 9–10, 46; Carr, *East of Antelope Island,* 162–63; J. R. Moss, "History of the Deseret Live Stock Company (M.A. thesis, University of Utah, 1965), 8–10.

50. Carr, *East of Antelope Island,* 128; Stanford J. Layton, "Agriculture in Layton," in Carlsruh and Carlsruh, *Layton, Utah,* 255–56.

51. *Utah State Gazetteer, 1918–1919,* 128; Roberts and Sadler, *History of Weber County,* 240.

52. LaRue Hugoe and Edith Deppe, *West Bountiful: A Pictorial History, 1848–1988,* 451; Moss, "Deseret Live Stock Company," 17–24, 49–50, 73; Humpherys and Matheson, *Utah—Resources and Activities,* 77–78.

53. Allen Roberts, "History of Antelope Island in the Great Salt Lake" (Salt Lake City, 1981), 25–27, 37–48, 56–57, 62; Holt, *Community of Syracuse,* 68–70, 73–86.

54. Humpherys and Matheson, *Utah—Resources and Activities,* 266–67, 284.

55. Layton, "Agriculture in Layton," 257.

56. Holt, *Community of Syracuse,* 92, 94–95.

57. Carr, *East of Antelope Island,* 163–64; Eakle, Baird, and Weber, *Woods Cross,* 9, 46.

58. Layton, "Agriculture in Layton," 257; Bell, *South Weber,* 186; Carr, *East of Antelope Island,* 173; *Utah Gazetteer, 1892–93,* 92; *Utah State Gazetteer, 1900,* 66, 78, 80, 98, 122, 126; *Utah State Gazetteer, 1918–19,* 59, 88.

59. Carr, *East of Antelope Island,* 421; Hess, *My Farmington,* 336.

60. Layton, "Agriculture in Layton," 257; Bell, *South Weber,* 102, 190; Hugoe and Deppe, *West Bountiful,* 233.

61. Foy, *City Bountiful,* 144; Layton, "Agriculture in Layton," 253.

62. Foy, *City Bountiful,* 93–94; Humpherys and Matheson, *Utah—Resources and Activities,* 42.

63. Foy, *City Bountiful,* 94, 144, 187.

64. Ibid., 186–88; Hugoe and Deppe, *West Bountiful,* 239.

65. Foy, *City Bountiful,* 185–86; Carr, *East of Antelope Island,* 414–15; Hugoe and Deppe, *West Bountiful,* 448–50; Wilcox and Adams, "Layton Businesses," 295; Don Strack, "Utah's Canning Industry," in Powell, *Utah History Encyclopedia,* 67–68.

66. Strack, "Utah's Canning Industry," 67–69; Holt, *Community of Syracuse,* 98–99.

67. Holt, *Community of Syracuse,* 99–100; Collett, *Kaysville—Our Town,* 112–13.

68. Hugoe and Deppe, *Woods Cross,* 448–50; Roberts and Sadler, *History of Weber County,* 238–39.

69. Holt, *Community of Syracuse,* 105, 100; Layton, "Agriculture in Layton," 253–55; Hugoe and Deppe, *Woods Cross,* 239–43.

70. Carr, *East of Antelope Island,* 136; Foy, *City Bountiful,* 91. Joseph Robinson mentions trading for coal in his Autobiography and Journal, 14, 19 September 1887. The advertisements are in Robert W. Sloan, ed., *Utah Gazetteer and Directory* (Salt Lake City: Sloan & Dunbar, 1884), 330.

71. Robinson, Autobiography and Journal, 8 April 1859; 14, 19 September 1887; Holt, *Community of Syracuse,* 91–94.

72. Collett, *Kaysville—Our Town,* 45; Carr, *East of Antelope Island,* 368; A. Garn Butcher, *Who Put the Fruit in Fruit Heights?* ([Kaysville and Fruit Heights]: Kaysville-Fruit Heights Centennial Committee, 1996), 1–3.

73. Bell, *South Weber,* 184–85; Carr, *East of Antelope Island,* 378; *Davis County Clipper,* 4 April, 4 July 1895.

74. Butcher, *Fruit Heights,* 4–5; Foy, *City Bountiful,* 91; Carr, *East of Antelope Island,* 368–69.

75. Collett, *Kaysville—Our Town,* 45; Carr, *East of Antelope Island,* 71; *Davis County Clipper,* 4 April 1895; Smoot and Sheriff, *City In-Between,* 34, 115; *Utah State Gazetteer, 1918–1919,* 28, 41, 59.

76. Hess, *My Farmington,* 338; *Davis County Clipper,* 7 March 1969.

77. Collett, *Kaysville—Our Town,* 45.

78. Carr, *East of Antelope Island,* 82–83.

79. Holt, *Community of Syracuse,* 47.

80. Family sources say the peach was propagated first in Fruit Heights by William Butcher or Grandison Raymond, Jr., and then promoted by Gleason (Butcher, *Fruit Heights,* 3–5).

81. *Reflex,* 27 November 1913, 5 February 1914.

82. Quoted in Carr, *East of Antelope Island,* 378

83. Collett, *Kaysville—Our Town,* 35; Smoot and Sheriff, *City In-Between,* 38.

84. Farmington Ward, Teachers Minutes, 7 March 1880; Journal History, 28 May 1878, 6, from *Deseret News,* 12 June 1878.

85. *Utah State Gazetteer, 1900,* 66, 98, 126; *Utah State Gazetteer, 1918–19,* 59, 88.

86. Humpherys and Matheson, *Utah—Resources and Activities,* 98–99.

87. Richard W. Sadler and Richard C. Roberts, *The Weber River Basin: Grass Roots Democracy and Water Development,* 104–7; Edward B. Clark, *Autobiography of Edward B. Clark,* 23–24; Collett, *Kaysville—Our Town,* 44.

88. Davis County, Court Minutes, 6, 14 March, 3 April 1876, Book B, 134–35, 141–44; Farmington Ward, Teachers Minutes, 7, 11 March 1877, 16 May 1880, 28 May 1882, 18 March 1883; *Davis County Clipper,* 26 August 1898.

89. Sadler and Roberts, *Weber River Basin,* 104–7; *Davis County Clipper,* 3 August 1893.

90. Sadler and Roberts, *Weber River Basin,* 54–55, 60–62, 253–55; *Davis County Clipper,* 24 April 1896; *Reflex,* 22 May 1913, 2.

91. Sadler and Roberts, *Weber River Basin,* 107–13.

92. Ibid., 59, 62, 66; *Deseret News,* 12 June 1864.

93. Sadler and Roberts, *Weber River Basin,* 62–66, 117–21; Holt, *Community of Syracuse,* 106–9.

94. Hess, *My Farmington,* 342–43.

95. Ibid.; Carr, *East of Antelope Island,* 186; Foy, *City Bountiful,* 154, 182.

96. Holt, *Community of Syracuse,* 86–87.

97. Smoot and Sheriff, *City In-Between,* 38–39; Bell, *South Weber,* 120; Foy, *City Bountiful,* 159.

98. Bell, *South Weber,* 101; John L. Clark and Norman Helgren, "History and Technology of Salt Production from Great Salt Lake," in J. Wallace Gwynn, ed., *Great Salt Lake: A Scientific, Historical, and Economic Overview,* Utah Geological and Mineral Survey Bulletin 116 (Salt Lake City: Utah Geological and Mineral Survey, 1980), 204.

99. Clark and Helgren, "Salt Production," 204–5; Carr, *East of Antelope Island,* 427.

100. Holt, *Community of Syracuse,* 55; Hess, *My Farmington,* 343; Carr, *East of Antelope Island,* 90, 99.

101. Holt, *Community of Syracuse,* 56, 59.

102. Clark and Helgren, "Salt Production," 205–6; Holt, *Community of Syracuse,* 56–57. These production figures are for 1890.

103. Arrington, *Great Basin Kingdom,* 392–93.

104. Clark and Helgren, "Salt Production," 205–7; Holt, *Community of Syracuse,* 56–59; *Davis County Clipper,* 22 April, 17 June 1898.

105. Clark and Helgren, "Salt Production," 207.

CHAPTER 8

A NEW ERA OF PROGRESS

Commercial agriculture, with its supporting industries, provided a stable economic base for Davis County throughout the first half of the twentieth century. But the expansion into new forms of agriculture and related businesses around the time of Utah's statehood in 1896 spurred other transformations in economic life. Taken together, these changes marked the transition to a world where private enterprise rather than cooperative economics governed the economic life of the region.

In the absence of Mormon church direction, the LDS businessmen of the Progressive Era formed their own informal networks and formal organizations to discuss common interests. In some towns, business owners formed a Commercial Club, the forerunner of the modern chamber of commerce. These groups hoped to improve their communities by promoting business growth through the sale of local products and services. Organizations began appearing around 1913 and remained active until the 1920s.[1] Local newspapers echoed their voice of optimism that Davis County would soon become a commercial Mecca. The editor of Kaysville's *Reflex* observed in 1914 that visionary businessmen could plainly "see the future of Davis County as one continuous city from Salt Lake to Ogden."[2] To them, it was a pleasant prospect.

Many of the signs of a newfound prosperity became evident by the end of the nineteenth century. Local brick plants and lumberyards supported the construction of a new generation of handsome brick homes on county farms and in towns. These Victorian showplaces and their adjacent carriage houses represented the entrepreneurial success of commercial agriculture and expanding commerce.[3]

Another sign of private enterprise was the appearance of business districts in Davis County's towns. These commercial zones began to replace the meetinghouse, the school, and the cooperative store as the centers of activity in towns. In many of the county's older settlements, the center of trade extended a block or two along Main Street, not far from the meetinghouse. In the newer homestead towns, a commercial core formed around an established gathering point such as a school or business, an old stage stop, or a railroad depot. In every community, it was private enterprise that created these new commercial centers.[4]

The Growth of Private Enterprise

The transition of Utah's local economy to a national model encouraged local entrepreneurs to pursue new private business opportunities. Feeling a release from the constraints of cooperative economics, Davis County merchants opened stores and specialty businesses to compete in the marketplace. Prosperous businessmen joined with commercial farmers to found banks. Local newspapers touted community interests. Professional services became increasingly available, and new technologies introduced other businesses. Telephone service, interurban railways, electricity, and automobiles changed the way people lived. All of these business, manufacturing, service, and technological developments convinced the people of Davis County that they truly had entered a new era of progress.

Modern Merchandizing. With the end of LDS church regulation of the economy, local cooperative mercantile stores became private businesses, most of them with the same management as before. Owners felt free to buy and sell their stock in the company without considering church counsel, and the co-ops became more interested in profits. The stores were not long without competition. During the decades of the 1880s and 1890s, new mercantiles appeared in almost every town. A second transition took place in the late 1920s and 1930s. At that time, many of the small hometown stores disappeared. In their place came self-service markets and regional mercantile affiliates with names such as Golden Rule Stores, Associated Grocers, and O. P. Skaggs.

North Davis County's commercial expansion served a growing population in the area. The mercantile business in Syracuse was launched in 1888 by a Salt Lake City investor who saw the need for a general store. Local residents soon owned the store, and by 1901 seven partners were operating it as the Syracuse Mercantile Company. The company's building housed Syracuse's grocery stores under various owners for most of the twentieth century. In nearby Clearfield, Richard Hamblin opened a mercantile around the turn of the century to serve that region. By 1918 Albert T. Smith was managing Consolidated Stores Company in Clearfield. He advertised a broad line of "general merchandise, dry goods, notions, hardware, groceries, grain and produce and agricultural implements." In South Weber, George W. and Adella P. Kendell operated a well-stocked, one-room mercantile west of Kingston Fort.[5]

In Layton, where no cooperative store had existed, Burton, Herrick & White opened for business in 1879. Two other general mercantile stores appeared in 1882 on opposite corners of Main and Gentile Streets. One was Farmer's Union, the other Barton and Company, which was soon purchased by George W. Adams and Sons. Layton's new merchants competed for local patrons who had previously looked to Kaysville for trade goods. In addition, they reached out to new settlers on the Sandridge and in West Layton.[6]

Competition to the north of Kaysville did not prevent the development of a thriving Main Street business district in the region's parent community. The privatized Kaysville Cooperative Mercantile faced three competitors. One of them was E. A. Williams, who pulled out of the co-op to reestablish his independent store; but that closed around 1898. The others were Hyrum Stewart and Heber J. Sheffield. After the last of these stores closed during the Great Depression, the

The typical Davis County mercantile offered a wide range of products, from dry goods to groceries, flour, and coal. L. H. Oviatt & Co., on Farmington's Main Street, had added gasoline (far left) to its products by 1912, when this photograph was taken. (Utah State Historical Society)

co-op survived for a time as an affiliate of the Golden Rule chain and later under the name of its owner, Joseph J. "Junior" Bowman.[7]

In the central and south Davis County communities of Farmington, Centerville, and Bountiful, the story followed a similar pattern. The cooperative stores survived under private ownership for many years, with new mercantiles competing for customers. Fred Coombs became sole owner of the Farmington co-op in 1881. Within a decade, J. D. Wood had his own mercantile, and a group of investors were operating the Farmington Commercial and Manufacturing Company. L. H. Oviatt launched a fourth store a few years later, but by 1936 the town's grocery business had been consolidated under one owner, Milt Hess. His successors, DeVaughn Jones and Ward Warnock, built the Farmington A.G. Market in 1956 and the building housed a series of short-lived ventures during the next forty years.[8]

Centerville's privatized cooperative, under a number of managers over the years, competed for customers with postmistress Mary M. Brandon and George W. Cleveland. These merchants operated their own mercantiles over a thirty-year period. Other general stores served residents for shorter lengths of time during this period.[9]

The Bountiful Cooperative Mercantile Institution found its initial competitors in mercantiles owned by Richard Duerden and John S. Thurgood. Over the following twenty years, four or five general stores were always in business in the town to serve local needs. Among the merchants were James Burns, William O. Lee, Mary Manger, W. Walter Barlow, and George Briggs. In West Bountiful, the Deseret Live Stock Company (DLS) opened a general mercantile in 1891 to serve the needs of stockholders and the general public. The DLS "merc" stayed in business for forty years.[10]

During the horse-and-buggy days, many of Davis County's rural residents could buy from itinerant salesmen who would stop by every three or four months peddling their wares. Some of these peddlers purchased gasoline-powered trucks to continue their services of bringing dry goods, spices, liniments, or other products to the customer's doorstep.[11]

A new form of general store appeared in Davis County near the end of World War I. The most widely known of these carried the Golden Rule name and represented the customer-service principles espoused by Wyoming founder James Cash Penney. By 1918, outlets formed in partnership with Penney were open in Bountiful, Farmington, Kaysville, Layton, and Clearfield. The Golden Rule stores specialized in dry goods and a full selection of clothing. In contrast, the earlier mercantiles carried a wider range of products that might include dry goods, groceries, drugs, small hardware items, glassware, grain, flour, farm produce, butter and eggs, coal, and lumber. Penney's stores in Bountiful and Layton were the only ones to survive the Depression. The operator of the Farmington and Kaysville outlets, Joseph J. Bowman, had included groceries in his stores and continued in business as a grocer under his own name. Another name in the regional grocery business was O. P. Skaggs, who franchised short-lived stores in Layton and Bountiful in the mid-1920s.[12]

As the mercantiles in the larger communities of Davis County

Specialization changed the look of business districts in the county. The influence of outside franchises is evident on Layton's Main Street in the locally owned Rexall Drug store, the Sanitarium Market, and (far right) the Morrison Merrill & Co. lumber yard. (Utah State Historical Society)

specialized in dry goods, grocery stores besides those noted above appeared. Stephens Brothers of Layton offered a typical range of products. A listing in 1918 included "Fresh meats and Provisions, Fruits and Produce, Poultry, Eggs and Butter, Fish and Game in Season." A competitor, Arthur H. Ellis, advertised "Staple and Fancy Groceries, Fruits and Produce and General Merchandize."[13]

In addition to the mercantile and grocery stores, most communities in Davis County were served during the first decades of the century by meat markets. Many meat dealers made weekly deliveries to the homes of customers in horse-drawn wagons or, later, in motorized vans. Many of the meat markets closed during the 1930s. Factors influencing these closures were the onset of the Depression, the hiring of butchers to work within grocery stores, and the creation of Cudahy Packing Company in North Salt Lake.[14]

Other Businesses and Banks. Until near the end of the century, a few sawmills still operated in Davis County, including that of William Beasley and the mills of Sheffield & Blamires of Kaysville, William Whipple of Farmington, and Robert Moss and John Lewis of Bountiful. These mills sold to both wholesale and retail customers. Some of the mercantiles of Davis County offered small stocks of lumber and operated coal yards to meet the needs of customers.[15]

The larger communities in the county were able to sustain specialized building supply dealers. The earliest of these was the Bountiful Lumber and Building Association, organized in 1892 by local contractors Levi S. Heywood and Heber A. Holbrook in association with William Loder and brothers Robert, Hugh, John, and Joseph Moss, who operated a steam-driven sawmill at the head of Bear River. The company opened a branch yard in Syracuse in 1900, but sold it three years later to Syracuse Mercantile. L. S. Heywood and Sons launched their own business in Layton in 1904. Jed Stringham joined the Bountiful firm in 1905 as manager, and eventually his family gained controlling interest. The company occupied a new brick building on Main Street in 1919 under the name Bountiful Lumber and Hardware. Conditions during an economic downturn forced the company into receivership in 1925. It was quickly reopened by Thomas L. Fisher, whose family was still operating the company at the dawn of the twenty-first century as the longest continuously operating retail store in Davis County.[16]

Other major companies opened lumber stores in Davis County before 1918. The Utah and Oregon Lumber Company served the Clearfield area. Morrison, Merrill and Company, with roots in Woods Cross, opened dealerships in both Layton and Bountiful. This firm became Tri-State Lumber in 1938 and Boise Cascade much later. These companies hired local agents to manage their stores.[17]

The era of specialization spawned a great variety of other commercial ventures in the business districts of the county. Among the businesses with the greatest lasting power were the furniture stores established in Bountiful, Kaysville, and Layton. In earlier decades, residents had depended upon local cabinetmakers or bought from furniture makers and import dealers in Salt Lake and Ogden. The twentieth century furniture stores of Davis County competed with the big-city businesses by importing furniture to supplement locally made items. Increasing prosperity brought on by the commercialization of agriculture created a customer base to sustain the new stores. Customers wanted the most fashionable contemporary items to furnish their new brick homes.[18]

John Barton operated one of the earliest furniture stores in the county. He was doing business as a sole proprietor in Kaysville before 1884. His inventory included fine Chippendale style furniture and Wilton rugs. During this time, Edward Thomas served south Davis County customers from a store on Bountiful's Main Street. Cabinetmaker Anson Call was a partner with Thomas for a time. Thomas sold his store in 1904. Barton and his son, Clifton, remained in business until at least 1918.[19]

The consortium of buyers who bought out Edward Thomas in Bountiful launched what would become the dominant furniture business in the county for a half-century. The partners in the new Holbrook-Smedley Furniture Company included Mark C. Holbrook, Ira C. Holbrook, and Frank Smedley. A few years later, Mark Holbrook formed the Bountiful Furniture Store. In 1914 he moved into the Old Opera House and, in partnership with G. E. Briggs and Chester M. Call, formed the Davis County Furniture Company. Two years later, the firm opened a branch on Layton's Main Street. A consolidation of the Davis County Furniture and Holbrook-Smedley companies in the early 1920s resulted in Union Furniture Company.[20]

Among the products made locally at these furniture stores were caskets. It was only a short step to the related service of undertaker. Until professional undertakers were available, women selected by the local LDS Relief Society laid out the dead, made their burial clothing, and lined the caskets built by local craftsmen. Cabinetmaker John Barton served the north end of the county as both casketmaker and undertaker. Edward Thomas began offering homemade redwood caskets in 1893. Holbrook-Smedley partner Ira Holbrook was Bountiful's first undertaker. The Bountiful Furniture Store hired George Graham as mortician. After the consolidation, he became manager and undertaker for Layton's Union Furniture. The two sides of the Bountiful business were separated in 1935 to create the Bountiful Union Mortuary in 1935, with Mark Holbrook's son

Farmers State Bank of Woods Cross moved out of the Deseret Livestock building into its own quarters in 1928. Just beyond the railroad crossing in this 1934 photo is the Wasatch Oil Company, which dominated the gasoline distribution business in Davis County for many years. (Utah State Historical Society)

Merrill as funeral director. Union Mortuary later opened a facility in Clearfield to serve that part of the county.[21]

Banking services became available in Salt Lake City beginning with the founding of four banks in 1864 by midwestern merchant-freighters. Another sixty banks were created before 1890—half of them in the capital city, a dozen in Ogden, and the rest in other areas—but none in Davis County. Only a few of these early banks survived to establish a permanent banking presence in Utah.[22]

Perhaps it was because of the distance from existing banking services that Davis County's first banks were founded midway between Salt Lake City and Ogden. Barnes Bank was organized in Kaysville in January 1891; it was followed a year later by Davis County Bank in Farmington. These two locally owned banks were capitalized at $25,000 each with funds drawn heavily from prosperous farmers and businessmen. John R. Barnes and others organized the Barnes Banking Company with Barnes as president and Will Barnes as cashier. The bank operated at first in a small annex to the co-op. In 1910 the bank, the cooperative, and the post office moved into a new yellow-brick business building designed by William Allen and known as the Barnes Block.[23] The first president of the bank in Farmington was Ezra T. Clark. His son Amasa L. Clark worked as cashier, and L. S. Hills served as vice-president. Davis County Bank operated out of a room in the Farmington Commercial and Manufacturing Co. store for thirty-eight years before erecting its own building across Main Street. Deposits were protected in a two-ton steel safe.[24]

During their first years, the banks in Farmington and Kaysville successfully reached out to serve patrons in neighboring communities. It was more than a decade before the next banks were organized in Davis County, then three more appeared in succession to serve residents a distance from the county's geographic center: the First National Bank of Layton (1905), Bountiful State Bank (1906), and Farmers State Bank, located in West Bountiful (1909). A group of Layton agriculturists and businessmen organized the Layton bank, with Ogden banker James Pingree as president, Ephraim P. Ellison and Rufus Adams as vice-presidents, and James E. and Laurence E. Ellison as cashiers. The bank operated from an office at 50 West Gentile Street until 1981, then moved into the renovated Farmers Union building.[25]

The first two banks in the southern part of the county sought residents in their own communities as clients. Soon after its founding, Bountiful State Bank established permanent quarters on Main Street. The bank's main clientele resided in Bountiful and Centerville. James E. Eldredge was president, N. T. Porter vice-president, and Charles R. Mabey cashier. The farmers, businessmen, and ranchers who invested $20,000 to start the Farmers State Bank defined their core service area as West Bountiful and South Bountiful but also attracted clients from as far north as Farmington and south into Salt Lake City. They elected William Moss as the first chairman of the board and Joel R. Parrish as cashier. Offices were in the Deseret Livestock Company building until 1928, when the bank built its own building nearby. In 1951 the bank moved to a new building at 530 West 500 South.[26]

Prior to World War I, Union State Bank was capitalized in Bountiful with $50,000 in stock. Henry H. Blood served as president, Herman Bamberger as vice-president, and Stephen H. Lynn as cashier. Key officers of the new Clearfield State Bank included E. P. Ellison and George E. Holt, with W. W. Steed, Jr., as cashier.[27]

Bricks, Building Materials, and Other Businesses. Many of the new merchants in Davis County sold their wares in handsome buildings made of locally manufactured bricks. The county's brickmaking industry, established in the 1870s, thrived during the building boom. Commercial brick plants were concentrated in two areas in the county—Kaysville and North Salt Lake. Other building materials were available at local lumber and hardware stores.

In Kaysville, Thomas and Samuel Brough pioneered brickmaking northeast of town in 1868. Samuel Ward established an enduring operation in 1875. For almost forty years Ward's kilns produced a molded, reddish brick that was widely used in the area. A competitor, Kaysville Brick and Tile, was organized in 1890. Amos Bishop later purchased the company and operated it for several years. Around 1908, Salt Lake industrialist Simon Bamberger established the Kaysville Brick Company. This firm quickly became one of the town's largest industries. During busy summer months one hundred men were involved in producing the wire-cut bricks from an imported light yellow clay. These bricks were used in the local elementary school, bank buildings, and the Kaysville LDS Tabernacle. Except for Kaysville Brick, which was served by the Bamberger Railroad, the town's brickmakers lacked a convenient rail connection and could not easily compete beyond the limited local market.[28]

In south Davis County, brickyards thrived in an area southwest of Bountiful known for its quality clay. In pioneer times five adobe yards in the greater Bountiful area furnished material for sun-dried adobe bricks. Fired bricks were produced as early as 1849. The Bountiful cooperative operated two of the late-nineteenth-century brickyards. Most of the commercial brickmakers succeeded by locating along the railroad lines in what is now North Salt Lake. The descendants of Ira S. Hatch owned or operated six of these companies. Eastern capital helped launch some of the plants. Over time, area brick firms included the Viglini Brickyard, Howard & Leddingham Brickyard, Empire Brick Company, F. F. Brickyard, Fryers Brickyard, Enterprise Brickyard, Hatch Brick Company, Simpkins Brickyard, the Improved Brick Company, and Leddingham Brickyard. The larger companies produced upwards of 30,000 bricks daily.[29]

The county's brickmakers served many local clients, and the south Davis yards shipped large quantities of brick by railroad to Salt Lake County. When the construction boom slowed during the Depression, the county's brick plants closed. From then until the end of World War II, many new homeowners built smaller, less expensive, frame homes. By 1930, eight large commercial plants, most of them in Salt Lake City, Ogden, and Provo, provided the brick for Utah's residential and commercial needs and exported bricks and tiles to surrounding states. However, many of the homes, churches, and business structures built with Davis County bricks during the Progressive Era remain in use as evidence of a once-thriving local industry.[30]

Much of the construction of houses, barns, and commercial buildings was accomplished at the turn of the century by hired tradesmen. In most Davis County communities, residents could find carpenters, cabinetmakers, plasterers, and painters. Stonemasons and brickmasons were available in the county as well, along with tinsmiths and sheet-metal workers. A few contractors were available to manage commercial building projects. William Allen was the county's only registered architect. Allen left his mark not just on many homes in various Davis County communities but on a number of fine business, religious, civic, and school buildings. Most were constructed using local brick and reflected architectural styles of the time.[31]

A number of the traditional trades were in transition during the era of commercialization. A watchmaker in Davis County in the early 1900s, for example, was more apt to repair and sell watches made elsewhere than to make them locally. Shoemakers, however, were actively plying their trade in every town in the county well into the 1920s. Tailors, milliners, knitters, and a stocking maker advertised their services in gazetteers of the period, but their skills were being challenged by imported goods offered at the new clothing stores. The industrialized eastern United States could mass produce and ship to Utah most clothing and many other products more cheaply than they could be made by hand in Davis County homes and shops. Besides, with the increasing availability of cash, many residents preferred to buy stylish imported goods.[32]

Professional Services. The new era of progress also challenged other practices common among families living a rural, agrarian lifestyle. Health care for many generations had depended upon home remedies, herbal medicines, and Thompsonian doctors. By the time of World War I, the medical field was become more professionalized, with standardized education defined by the American Medical Association. Doctors, dentists, and druggists were establishing themselves outside the major urban centers.

During this time, citizens of almost every Davis County town gained access to a resident physician. Unlike their predecessors, who often practiced medicine part-time, the new doctors were better educated and kept regular office hours besides making home calls. They opened small hospitals in Layton and Kaysville for short-term specialized care. The first of the university-trained physicians began arriving in Davis County in the 1890s. By 1910, licensed physicians were available in nearly every community. Most of these doctors remained until retirement. Among them were Walter Whitlock and A. Z. Tanner in Layton; William T. Ingram, Sumner Gleason (who also practiced dentistry), and G. D. Rutledge in Kaysville; Clarence Gardner in Farmington; J. E. Young in Centerville and Bountiful; and Byron L. Kesler (a dentist before he became a doctor) and John C. Stocks in Bountiful.[33]

A number of these physicians were active in civic life or contributed in the emerging public-health field. Doctors Kesler and Stocks served mayoral terms in Bountiful; Dr. Gardner served in the ambulance corps during World War I; Dr. Gleason became Davis County's first school doctor in 1920, launching baby clinics and sponsoring preschool immunizations. Dr. D. Keith Barnes, one of the few native sons to practice in the county, left his private practice after ten years to become director of the newly formed Davis County Public Health Department in 1937. Most of the doctors served on city health boards.

The county's first professional dentists, unlike most physicians, tended to be natives of the county. Those practicing in 1918 included Silas S. Burnham and Ernest W. Smedley in Bountiful, Charles H. Bird in Farmington, and Walter E. Whittaker in Kaysville.[34]

Traditionally, women gathered and prepared medicinal herbs for their families. New "patent" medicines were widely promoted in the nineteenth century. Both these new bottled medicines and traditional folk remedies could be purchased at local mercantiles. As these general stores were replaced by more specialized dry goods and grocery outlets early in the twentieth century, the marketing of drugs also became specialized. Most physicians compounded the drugs they administered, but an increase of mass-produced drugs in the United States between the Civil War and World War I led to the founding of drug stores. Pharmacists dispensed commercially made drugs and formulated others prescribed by doctors.

John V. Long may have been the first druggist in Davis County; he was doing business in Kaysville before the turn of the century. Another early dispensary was the Prescription Drugstore, set up by Dr. Byron Kesler and his brother Murray and later renamed Bountiful Drug Store. Farmington blacksmith Walter Rampton opened a drug and sundries store in 1907. Three years later, he built a fine brick building with oak interiors. He partnered with his son Walter, a trained pharmacist, who managed the operation. A. E. Williams carried a line of drugs in his mercantile in Kaysville until Robert Birkin opened a competitive drug store. The *Utah State Gazetteer* in 1918 listed Frank E. Gibbs as operator of the Kaysville Pharmacy. Robert Birkin was managing the Layton Drug Company, and C. H. Hesser was dispensing medicines at Bountiful Drug. Most of these outlets sold products other than drugs, and they attracted a young clientele with their ice cream and soda fountains.[35]

Other specialized services could be found in the county, including laundries, photo galleries, and barbers. The laundry of Hop Gee served Kaysville residents, while Ray and W. L. Riley operated their Davis County Laundry in Bountiful. Pioneer photographers were Reuben Kirkham, a Bountiful settler of 1864, and Stephen Hales, who set up his Centerville gallery in 1882. Alma Hardy and Oscar Lewis established photography studios around the turn of the century in

Bountiful and Kaysville, respectively. James Proudfoot opened Kaysville's first barber shop around 1885. Barbers appeared in a half-dozen other communities within the next decade or so. By 1945, beauticians were functioning in the larger towns.[36]

New Technologies

An industrialized America and the growth of private enterprise in Utah went hand-in-hand with the emergence of new technological developments that impacted life in Davis County. Some of them, such as telephones, community newspapers, and electricity, first served the needs of businessmen. Interurban trains, automobiles, and farm machinery reached broader clienteles. All of these developments of the 1880s to 1930s expanded horizons for residents of Davis County. The new forms of communication and transportation made the resources of Salt Lake City and Ogden even more available to county residents. Life improved with electricity.

Telephones and Newspapers. The two most important turn-of-the-century developments in communication in Davis County were the telephone and local newspapers. The first telephones arrived in Utah in 1880, just five years after Alexander Graham Bell invented the device. As with all new technological advancements, no one could anticipate how well telephones would be accepted or how widely used they would become. At first, phone service was an alternative to the telegraph or mail for placing orders or conducting business. Local exchanges appeared first in Ogden and Salt Lake City. In 1883 Rocky Mountain Bell Telephone Company, organized to provide long-distance service in four states, connected the two Utah exchanges with a line through Davis County. The first Davis County subscribers on this intercity line were businessmen Richard Duerden in Bountiful, Fred Coombs in Farmington, and John R. Barnes in Kaysville. The courthouse in Farmington installed a line in 1896 in the recorder's office. Subscribers paid $100 per year for the service.[37]

Eventually a demand for service away from the Main Street line developed. In 1903 Rocky Mountain Bell secured franchises to expand service along selected streets in Kaysville and Bountiful. The Kaysville exchange opened in August with twenty-seven subscribers; the Bountiful exchange began service in November to twelve customers. Other families soon signed on for party-line service at $1.50 per month, plus a fifteen-cent charge for out-of-town calls. The number of customers quickly grew to several hundred for each exchange, and service expanded into neighboring towns. The first party line reached lower Syracuse by way of Hooper in 1903 to serve Walker Brothers' mercantile. In 1906 Rocky Mountain Bell installed public telephones in the county for non-subscribers.[38]

When Rocky Mountain Bell raised its monthly rates to two dollars, a competitor entered the market and forced the price down again. Davis County Independent Telephone Company put up lines on city power poles in 1909 and opened exchanges in Clearfield, Layton, Kaysville, Farmington, and Bountiful. This awkward competitive system required subscribers to connect to both services in order to reach all patrons. Rocky Mountain Bell pulled ahead, and in 1911 the Independent company went into receivership. That same year, Mountain States Telephone and Telegraph Company took over Rocky Mountain Bell and bought out the Independent franchise. Mountain States Telephone kept open the exchanges in Bountiful, Farmington, and Kaysville (which served all of north Davis County). The final step in establishing a stable telephone service was the addition of transcontinental service, available after a line was connected near Wendover in 1914.[39]

Local newspapers created a greater sense of community and touted local accomplishments. In six of Davis County's communities during the 1890s, publishers and editors seeking advertisers and subscribers founded local newspapers. It was a time of rapid expansion in the local newspaper industry, but many weeklies lacked a sound economic base and lasted but a short time. All of the county's papers were politically neutral at a time when many of the state's newspapers lined up with a political party. Short-lived papers in south Davis County included Centerville's *Call,* founded in 1897 by publisher Melvie Smith and editor E.S. Carroll. It closed the following year. Nor did the *Watchman* of Woods Cross survive its first year. Samantha Sessions edited the paper, which was published in Salt Lake City. More successful was Farmington's *Davis County Argus.* The eight-page paper was launched in 1903 by D. P. Felt and F. Vernon Felt. It served more than 700 readers until at least 1911, and possibly through 1916.[40]

In Bountiful, the county's first and longest lasting newspaper appeared in February 1891 as an expanded advertising flyer issued monthly by merchant Lamoni Call on a small press in the basement of his watch repair and jewelry shop. It became a regular Friday newspaper a year later, with John Stahle, Jr., as editor. Call named the paper the *Little Clipper* after a Clipper ship model that he owned. John Held, a Salt Lake City artist later nationally known for his flapper girl illustrations, created the woodcut for the *Clipper*'s masthead. The paper adopted its present name—the *Davis County Clipper*—in April 1892 and secured correspondents from communities as far north as Farmington to increase neighborhood news coverage and report on county courthouse business. Subscriptions were $1.25 per year. A few years later, the partners divided the business and its equipment. Call took the job printing function, while Stahle became sole owner and editor of the newspaper. Call's son-in-law, Willard G. Carr, continued the printing business as Carr Printing Company, while Stahle's family was still publishing the paper more than a century after its founding.[41]

Publishers believed that Kaysville had a potential market like that of Bountiful. Kaysville's *Eagle*, an eight-page weekly founded by William E. and Eva B. Smith in February 1893, closed after a year when they moved to American Fork.[42] John V. Young and James McLaren followed in May 1896 with the *Kaysville Post*. That paper carried one page of local news for residents of Kaysville and Farmington, plus three more pages printed in Salt Lake City. It went out of business in 1898.[43] Possibly as early as 1904 LeRoy Shelby and John S. White were publishing the *Weekly Reflex* at the *Davis County Argus* office in Farmington. Benjamin F. Cummings managed and edited the *Reflex* under a lease for one year.[44]

The *Reflex* survived because of financing provided by six local investors who purchased the newspaper in 1912 to preserve it as a local voice when its founders moved on. The investors were Henry H. Blood, John G.M. Barnes, Heber J. Sheffield, John R. Gailey, Marchtin Kessler, and the Stewart–Burton Company. Colorado publishers William P. Epperson and his son Clyde moved to Kaysville, became stockholders, and leased and operated the paper. Within a year, they doubled its business. They attracted 1,200 subscribers with expanded news coverage of schools, government, and local sports and an unprecedented use of photographs. The paper was soon advertising itself as "the largest country paper published in the state of Utah."[45]

In common with most local papers, the company also ran a letterpress job printing operation beginning in 1916 when the operations moved to a new building and the firm was reorganized as Inland Printing Company. The *Reflex* served the Kaysville-Farmington community with a strong local focus. Following the senior Epperson's death in 1930, his family continued the business. In January 1965 the paper and its job printing operation were acquired by the Clipper Publishing Company. Though produced at the new owner's Bountiful offset presses, the *Weekly Reflex* continued to provide its 1,800 subscribers with a focus on north Davis County news and advertising until it ceased publication in 1987.[46]

The north Davis area had its own newspaper for a time. Hector C. Evans began the *Weekly News-Express* in 1926 to serve residents of Layton, Kaysville, Clearfield, and Syracuse. He printed the paper in his job printing plant in Ogden. In November 1933, John Stahle, Jr., purchased the paper, moved production to Bountiful, and published it as the *Layton News-Journal* until it merged with the *Reflex* in 1970.[47]

The local papers of Davis County prided themselves on their attention to local news and interests. Salt Lake City's newspapers had provided some local reporting, much of it Latter-day Saint church news. They named subscription/distribution agents in most towns and around 1900 began same-day carrier service in Davis County.[48] A regional news approach worked adequately for the nineteenth century, but in the era of commercialization, businesses wanted targeted advertising and subscribers welcomed more neighborhood news. Local boosters wanted to build a sense of civic pride around a public community rather than a religious one. The county weeklies provided that needed local identity. The Salt Lake City and Ogden dailies increased their local coverage late in the twentieth century to attract readers and advertisers to their regional editions. But the local papers continued with their news and advertising specialties, and the *Clipper*

Electricity furnished by the Utah Power and Light Company allowed this Davis County farmer to pump water from an irrigation pond onto his fields in 1913. (Utah State Historical Society)

included among its subscribers many who had left the county during the agricultural expansion but wanted news from "home."

Electrification. Thomas Edison's invention of the electric light bulb in 1879 introduced a practical use for electricity that ushered in a new age. By 1881, local generating plants were operating in Ogden and Salt Lake City. Utah's capital city became the fourth American city to set up lighting under a central power station. Local power plants appeared elsewhere using coal or water to generate a somewhat unreliable direct current. New technological developments and the development of alternating current increased the use of electricity. This led to cooperation among small companies and, in the 1890s, to the first consolidations.[49]

In Davis County, J. E. Willey and N. T. Porter received a charter in 1905 to build a generating plant to provide electricity to Bountiful homeowners. Two years later, seven other investors founded the Bountiful Light and Power Company to distribute electricity in

Bountiful and south Centerville. This company purchased electricity from the Utah Light and Railway Company, which had a line running through Davis County connecting its Ogden and Salt Lake operations. Businessmen in Farmington organized Davis County Light and Power Company in 1908 and built a power plant in Farmington Canyon to serve central Davis County. It also sold power to Farmington City, which organized its own municipal distribution company, and to Home Telephone and Electric Company, organized by local investors in 1908 to serve north Davis County.[50]

The consolidation effort entered a new phase with the creation of Utah Power and Light Company (UP&L) in September 1912. It acquired numerous power plants and distribution systems, including those of Davis County Light and Power, Home Telephone and Electric, and the Salt Lake and Ogden Railway. In 1915 it added Utah Light and Railway to its holdings; the following year, the Farmington distribution system was added. Utah Power upgraded existing generating plants, developed new generating capacity on the Bear River, and connected its local components into a single network. Power lines reached the Syracuse area in 1913 and South Weber four years later. By 1922 UP&L was serving more than two hundred towns in four states. Desiring to preserve local control when Utah Power obtained controlling interest in Bountiful Light and Power, Bountiful City built its own municipal generating plant in 1934 to serve patrons within city limits. The city distributed electricity over lines purchased from Bountiful Light and Power. The private company then sold the rest of its property to Utah Power.[51]

When electricity reached into the average home, lifestyles changed dramatically. Exposed wiring for hanging light globes ran along walls through ceramic holders. Kitchen appliances multiplied through an aggressive sales campaign originating with the power company. Refrigerators, electric stoves, irrigation pumps, toasters, irons, and washing machines began to find their way into Davis County homes.[52]

One of the most useful new appliances was the electric refrigerator. For more than a half century, Davis County residents had depended on ice to keep their food cool. Each winter, workers had harvested two or three crops of large blocks from mill ponds and other pools. The cubes varied in size from one to four feet. Harvesters stored the chunks in sawdust or straw inside an ice house, granary, or cool cellar for summer use. Like many other pioneer efforts, the production and distribution of ice had been commercialized by the 1890s. Owners of gristmills, mercantiles, creameries, and resorts were among those who stockpiled ice and then delivered it to customers until their supplies dwindled, usually in August. Meat shops and ice cream stores were among the commercial customers. Homeowners also gradually replaced their burlap-covered coolers with ice boxes. Electric refrigerators changed all this and soon eliminated local ice businesses.[53]

The availability of electrical appliances created new enterprises in Davis County. Some national manufacturers looked to direct sales marketing; others franchised local dealers or power companies to set up display rooms. R. C. Willey of Syracuse began going door to door selling electric refrigerators and ranges to supplement his income as a power company employee. He secured his inventory from Graybar Electric, an appliances distributor. From this beginning in 1932, Willey's sideline soon became a full-time job. After eighteen years, Willey built a small store in Syracuse in order to keep his business license, but continued his door-to-door contacting. Family members expanded the operation after his death in 1954. With outlets all along the Wasatch Front by the 1990s, R. C. Willey and Sons had become the largest furnishings retailer in the West.[54]

As previously noted, refrigerated railcars supported an expansion of Davis County's livestock industry. In the 1940s cold-storage plants in Layton, Kaysville, and Bountiful served patrons who brought in slaughtered farm animals or the harvest from the annual deer hunt. On-site butchers cut, wrapped, labeled, and froze the meat for patrons. When home freezers became available after World War II, the need for commercial cold storage diminished and these facilities closed.[55]

The Interurbans. The creation of viable electric plants spawned a new generation of railcars in American cities to replace mule-drawn trolleys. Electrified trolleys began operation in Salt Lake City in the fall of 1889. For Davis County, this beginning led to a half-century of short-distance passenger and light freight service by what came to be called the Bamberger Electric. Simon Bamberger, a Salt Lake City restaurant and mine owner, launched his Salt Lake to Ogden service in 1892. At first, the trolley was pulled by a small, steam-powered engine known as a "dummy" because it was enclosed with a wooden body to look like a passenger car. The "Dummy Line" reached as far as Beck's Hot Springs, near the county boundary, and was called the Great Salt Lake and Hot Springs Railroad. The following year, Bamberger extended the line along Bountiful's 200 West Street to serve a resort named Eden Park. By 1894, the cars were carrying passengers to Centerville, and the following spring to Farmington's State Street, where connecting passengers could take the stagecoach for Kaysville. Then, financial problems stopped expansion.[56]

From the first, the railroad had supplemented its income by carrying light freight. In addition, it had added a special caboose in 1895 to transport milk and butter for Davis County farmers. But the company's primary business was passengers. The initial success of the routes to the Hot Springs resort and Eden Park prompted Bamberger to create a pleasure park in Farmington to ensure a higher passenger load for his railroad. He moved buildings from the old Lake Park Resort on the shores of the Great Salt Lake west of Farmington to a new location right on the path of his trolley line. Opened in 1896, the Lagoon Resort could be entered only on Bamberger's trolley. The company was reorganized as the Salt Lake and Ogden Railway Company. Trains left Salt Lake City every two hours from 7:00 A.M. to 9:00 P.M. A round-trip Lagoon fare was sixty cents.[57]

Profits from the new resort helped fund a steady expansion of the railroad northward. Bamberger continued his policy of buying the land for his right-of-way and maintaining a maximum grade level of 1.1 percent. Service reached Kaysville in 1903, Layton the next year, and Clearfield and Sunset the year after that. Tracks reached Ogden in 1908, following a court battle with established railroad companies that opposed Bamberger's franchise request. The thirty-six-mile line was electrified two years after that and renamed the Bamberger Electric Railroad. To keep costs down, the company generated its own electricity with a steam-powered plant at Lagoon. Substations in Ogden, Clearfield, Farmington, and North Salt Lake converted the high-voltage power to 750-volt alternating current. The electrified

Simon Bamberger's Salt Lake and Ogden Railway extended service into Ogden in 1908. A year later, this Shipler photo documented one of the passenger trains at the Bountiful station. (Utah State Historical Society)

line increased service with ten high-speed trolley cars. The interurban trolleys left Salt Lake and Ogden "on the hour every hour" for a forty-five-minute ride through Davis County. During rush hours, the trains ran every half-hour, with as many as eighteen trains a day. Double tracks were completed in 1913 from Kaysville to Salt Lake City to serve what a local paper called "The Little Kingdom of Davis."[58]

Bamberger's original dream had included an extension from downtown Ogden through Weber Canyon to Coalville. That plan was dropped for lack of financing, and the company concentrated on its Salt Lake–Ogden service. The bright orange Bamberger railcars served Lagoon patrons, students heading for the Davis County Central High School in Kaysville, shoppers, and commuters, with more than a dozen designated stops and small depots in each city. A devastating fire in 1918 destroyed the Ogden car barn and ten cars, challenging the company's ability to survive. To preserve profits,

Bamberger secured a franchise through Union Pacific to haul fruit and vegetables from the county's productive orchards and market gardens.[59]

The increase of private automobiles, fluctuating national economic conditions, and a world war all had their impact on Davis County's interurban. In 1926, the year of Simon Bamberger's death, the company organized the Bamberger Transportation Company and put buses on the highways in an attempt to retain some of its passenger traffic. Some local communities initially opposed this move, feeling that the trolley and trains provided adequate service and that busses would only add to road traffic and endanger lives. They finally accepted the transition and urged the Public Utilities Commission to accept the Bamberger application over those of two other companies.[60] Eventually, only the bus service would survive.

The Depression cut Bamberger's trolley business to a single railcar daily in 1933 and forced the company into receivership. A reorganization six years later retained Julian M. Bamberger as president. Five high-speed coaches, each seating fifty-four passengers and operated by a single conductor, attracted new passengers. World War II increased the freight business. Railway passenger service peaked in 1945, then rapidly declined. In 1952 a fire destroyed the company's North Salt Lake maintenance shop. The company increased bus service and cut back on trains. A second fire, in the Ogden substation, forced the end of passenger rail service. The last car drove north through the county on 6 September 1952. A few months later, Bamberger Transportation sold its bus line to Lake Shore Motor Coach Company.[61]

The Bamberger Railroad continued to haul light freight until December 1958. Its major clients during World War II were Hill Field, the Naval Supply Depot, and the Ogden Arsenal. That need declined rapidly after the war, with trucks and the interstate railroads filling the need. The Bamberger Railroad was the last interurban rail service in America to close. The line's founder was memorialized in 1963, when a bronze bust of Simon Bamberger was placed in the gardens at Lagoon.[62]

Supplementing Bamberger's service in south Davis County was a competitive trolley along a more eastern route. The Oregon Short

Line (later part of the Union Pacific) formed the Utah Light and Railway Company to provide local electric service and operate a trolley line. The "Electric Trolley" served Bountiful, and commenced service to Centerville in December 1913. The trolley continued until Bamberger's buses appeared on the route thirteen years later.[63]

None of the trolley lines passed through northwestern Davis County. Bamberger had considered routing his line through Syracuse and Hooper in 1910 but decided that business would be greater on the direct route from Layton to Ogden. In 1914 Utah Light and Railway Company explored the viability of extending its line from Centerville on a route through west Layton, Syracuse, and West Point to Hooper, then northward through Roy to Ogden. The new competition was expected to force lower rates on Bamberger's line. However, a limited rural population along the proposed route north of Kaysville and existing freight lines killed the idea.[64]

Automobiles and Highways. Ultimately, electric trolley service through Davis County bowed to the gasoline engine. Bus lines on greatly improved roads served as public transportation, while private automobiles eventually threatened even that service. The first automobile appeared in Utah in 1899; and Eli Olds introduced the mass production of cars in the United States two years later. In 1908 the American automobile industry began targeting a general market that reached into Davis County. In that year, Henry Ford introduced the first Model T and William C. Durant bought out Buick, Cadillac, Oakland, Oldsmobile, and other makers to form General Motors.[65]

The first purchasers of gasoline-powered motor vehicles in Davis County were market gardeners, merchants, and doctors. Produce growers, such as Andrew Sjoblom, who purchased a truck in 1910 to haul his fruit and vegetables to the Salt Lake market, found business reasons for buying. Physicians purchased cars to visit patients, but found a horse and buggy more reliable on muddy roads during wet and wintry seasons.[66] Others who could afford motorized transportation for business travel and pleasure rides were successful businessmen and farmers. By 1915, when the first automobile registration law passed in Utah, auto purchases had begun to climb in Davis County. The number of locally owned cars continued to rise until the onset of the Depression, then stabilized until the end of World War

II. Studebaker, Paige, Franklin, Case, Ford, Dodge, Pierce Arrow, Hupmobile, Buick, Oldsmobile, and Chevrolet were among the makes seen in Davis County before 1920.[67]

The shift from horsepower to the internal combustion engine marked the end of livery businesses and the beginning of automobile dealerships, repair shops, and service stations. The need to buy gasoline for motorized vehicles created a new industry that emerged gradually. By 1913 an "oil wagon" was delivering gasoline to stores in Davis County weekly, and the Continental Oil Company had gasoline for sale at some of the Oregon and Short Line railroad depots. Repair shops began appearing at this time—some of them in renovated livery stables—to meet the specialized needs of motorized vehicles.[68] As demand for gasoline increased, retailers added underground storage tanks served by hand-cranked pumps in front of their stores. Electric pumps soon followed. By the early 1920s, selling gasoline was no longer a sideline—full-service garages existed in many parts of the county, offering gasoline, auto parts, and repairs. The number of service stations increased rapidly during the 1930s to serve a growing clientele. Conoco, Shell, and Sinclair were familiar company names. Wholesale distributors, such as Wasatch Oil, supplied local stations with oil products.[69]

Car buyers could look to Salt Lake City or Ogden for dealers selling motorized vehicles, but local agents soon appeared in Davis County. The Studebaker Wagon Company set up an outlet for wagons and carriages in Layton in 1896, and the firm began selling motorized carriages after moving into expanded quarters on Layton's Main Street in 1910. Another early car dealer was Lucius Laudie, who moved his Layton Auto Company into a new showroom in 1916. In Bountiful, descendants of one of the town's early blacksmiths became involved in automobile sales. While Fred Rampton remained at the forge, Lewis S. and James H. Rampton joined with William C. Hardy to found Rampton Auto Company. Several other implement and wagon companies served the county during the early decades of the twentieth century; however, their numbers decreased with the advent of motorized machinery and the appearance of tractors and other farm machinery. Dealers specializing in the newly popular automobile prevailed. Because new cars were not manufactured during the latter part of World War II, local dealerships closed at the time or traded only in used cars. A new generation of automobile dealers appeared in the 1940s.[70]

Automobiles needed better roads than horses, wagons, and carriages. As a result, a highway improvement campaign spread throughout the nation and impacted Davis County. With the arrival of the railroads in 1869–70, the construction and maintenance of wagon roads between cities in Utah had shifted to county courts (county commissioners after statehood). Designating major public roads and maintaining them with property and poll taxes was a local responsibility. Cities took care of streets under a similar arrangement. Funding subsidies from territorial and state governments were sparse,[71] thus limiting progress toward better roads.

Impetus for improving roads came through lobbying by automobile clubs and citizens who met in "good roads" meetings. This was a national movement that included the creation of the Lincoln Highway, an east-west route that crossed through Salt Lake City on a route from New York City to San Francisco. The first road improvement meeting in Utah was held at Farmington in July 1908. Commercial interests in the two adjacent counties were especially anxious to create better roads between them. A *Deseret News* report noted, "Beautiful, bumpy boulevards are what stretch from Salt Lake to Lagoon via Davis County, and from Ogden to Lagoon via Weber and Davis counties, according to the testimony of a great force of good roads enthusiasts who yesterday launched a good roads boom at the Davis county resort. Good roads in Utah from now on are to be demanded with a vigor heretofore little known."[72] After hearing a pledge from Governor John Cutler to promote passage of a law creating a uniform state road program, the one hundred delegates organized a three-county road commission to improve the main roads through Davis County. As a result of this and other cries for improvement, the 1909 legislature created the Utah State Road Commission. The commission was charged with designating and administering a state highway system.[73]

In 1911 the road commission sent its state road convict gang into Davis County to improve the designated state road, Highway 1. A prominent Ogden resident that year had described the route as

The concrete road built through Davis County can be seen running along the middle of a wide right-of-way in this August 1920 view of Kaysville's Main Street. (Utah State Historical Society)

"rougher than a newly made road through a growth of heavy sage-bush" and virtually impassable in wet weather. Deciding against macadamizing the Salt Lake-Ogden road in favor of packed earth, the commission had the workers install a sprinkling system along the main road with stand pipes at designated intervals. "The sprinkling wagon, the road grader, and the split-log drag became the order of the day on this important road," according to highway historian Ezra Knowlton.[74]

Two years later, the State Road Commission provided convict labor and the Davis County Commission passed a road tax levy to buy materials for the first concrete paved roads in the county (and the second in Utah). The convicts set up camp and work began at the south county boundary. The four-mile section built in 1913–14 extended northward to the south limits of Bountiful City. A segment laid in 1915 began just north of Clearfield and reached into north Layton. After three years, Davis County claimed over ten miles of paving—nearly one-third of all concrete roads in Utah. The new highway was a two-lane road measuring eighteen feet wide. Work moved ahead slowly during the next two years, extending the road north through Bountiful. The pioneering project served as a test of the appropriateness of concrete highways in Utah.[75]

During this time, the shift from horse-drawn to motorized vehicles was well underway, as evidenced by a survey of traffic at North Salt Lake. On 23 April 1915, the census station counted 276 wagons, 43 carriages, and 87 saddle horses traversing the all-weather highway, compared with 287 automobiles, 74 motorcycles, and 11 trucks.[76] After Governor Simon Bamberger took office in January 1917, the legislature authorized bonding for state roads. This shifted some of the tax burden from counties, which were still required to buy the rights-of-way. The road commission ended sprinkling of state roads and authorized more paving. Commissioners in Davis County agreed in 1918 to levy heavy taxes to pave the remaining fifteen miles of dirt road through Layton, Kaysville, Farmington, and Centerville and a short section from Clearfield to the Weber County line. Reinforced concrete was installed along all of this central section except through Centerville, where a hard oil surface failed within three years and was eventually replaced with concrete.[77]

In August 1920 the mayors and many residents of the seven cities along the route joined in a automobile parade that converged on Lagoon to celebrate completion of the "Million Dollar Highway." Governor Bamberger and former Governor Spry addressed the celebrants from the tri-county area at a gathering sponsored by the Kaysville Commercial Club. The paved road was applauded for its usefulness for commercial traffic. "It is the longest stretch of hard surfaced country road in the vast region which lies between the Missouri River and California," the *Weekly Reflex* reported.[78] The newspaper lauded the accomplishment as a step toward realizing the day "when Davis County would be a continuous city from Salt Lake City to Ogden." "It no doubt means the most to the interior portions of the county," the *Davis County Clipper* said, "as it has practically brought them as near to the big cities on either end as the nearby settlements were."[79] A road previously impassable during wet weather now served farmers throughout the county sending produce to market. Local governments were urged to hard-surface major connecting routes and oil other roads. Farmers in East Layton organized their own road improvement association in order to gravel local roads.[80]

Increased traffic on the completed road led to accidents involving vehicles and some pedestrians.[81] Even before the new ribbon of concrete passed through Davis County, city councils worried about the safety of their citizens. In every town, councilors set speed limits for motor vehicles and bicycles—another popular means of transportation at the time. Typical laws limited automobiles to thirty miles per hour on the paved state road, fifteen on county roads, ten on city streets, and four miles per hour in business districts. Bicycles could not exceed eight miles per hour. Enforcing these regulations was a constant challenge for city marshals. City and county officials also had to deal with billboards (which they banned from city streets), street lighting, traffic signs, and the impact of heavy truck traffic and roving cattle on oiled roads.[82] The state legislature passed a uniform code for vehicles and pedestrians in 1921 that set speed limits and made age sixteen the minimum age for drivers on public highways. Licensing of drivers was introduced in 1933. Utah adopted the U.S. numbering system for national highways and created its own state numbering system in 1927.[83]

Highway construction provided work for some local laborers hired by contractors, since using convict labor was only one option available. The state launched a period of gravel road construction in 1924 that created many new jobs over a six-year period. These roads cost one-sixth that of a concrete surface and could be built faster, but they required more careful maintenance. Oil-mix roads came to Utah in the late 1920s. In the late 1940s, a two-lane paved highway west of Bountiful, Centerville, and Farmington was widened to four lanes to eliminate the "Death Strip" highway created in 1935. Designated U.S. Highway 91, it connected in north Farmington with the existing state highway and the Mountain Road (U.S. 89).[84]

The improvement of the main arteries led to increased commercial traffic, which sustained a steady hospitality industry. The small inns and hotels in Davis County served a new traveling business clientele along with a few tourists and some unmarried boarders. As always, the hotels were located along the main-traveled roads of the

Among the locally owned cafes that served motorists in Davis County was Tommy's Place at the North Farmington Junction of Highway 89 and Farmington's Main Street. (Harry Thompson Collection, Utah State Historical Society)

county. A number of the newer hotels occupied the upper rooms of business buildings.[85] Hotel-keeping in Davis County was an enterprise that often involved couples. In the first decades of the twentieth century, women were just as likely as their husbands to be listed as the proprietor. Women looked after the front desk, food services, and housekeeping; their husbands often managed the adjacent livery and boarding stable. By the 1920s, local residents were patronized hotel dining rooms as part of a new interest in "eating out." Near the close of the Second World War, motels began to appear in the county—catering to the automobile tourist.[86]

The new age of automobiles also inspired entrepreneurs to start restaurants and cafes apart from hotels. In the largest towns, a number of lunch-stand cafes targeted local workers. Locally owned and operated, the cafes changed owners rapidly in the early years, but a few of them became familiar landmarks and popular gathering places in their communities. Typical of restaurant offerings was that of William Johnson of Kaysville, whose 1918 directory listing advertised: "Short Orders and Regular Dinners, Catering to Auto Parties, First Class Service."[87]

Commercialization and Community

The new era of progress had an impact in areas of life other than the work-a-day world, including that of leisure time. For generations, rural Americans had enjoyed community-centered recreation. Utah's founders continued the simple pastimes of their youth and handed them on to their children. New commercialized forms of recreation emerged at the end of the nineteenth century. Many of these leisure-time activities reflected patterns created by urban lifestyles—living in apartments, eating in restaurants, and working in offices, with hours that left evenings free for socializing. Among the options appearing in Davis County and adjacent cities were private halls, cafes, saloons, pool halls, bowling alleys, roller skating rinks, movie theaters, and pleasure resorts. These and other activities were made more accessible by trolleys, automobiles, and improved highways. A new generation that had not known the hardships of pioneering basked in an era of relative prosperity and increased leisure time. They worked hard and they played hard.[88]

Recreation and Resorts. Before halls were built especially for recreational activities, the people of Davis County met in larger homes or in the community building that doubled as a school and meetinghouse. Summertime gatherings, especially those for the July holidays, often took place in a shaded grove. For Layton and Kaysville residents it was Webster's Grove. Haight's Grove attracted people from Kaysville and Farmington. By the 1870s most communities had access to a multipurpose cultural hall that was used by organized groups and for dances, dinners, and socials.[89]

During the thirty-year period beginning in the mid-1880s, a new generation of halls was built that replaced the older recreation halls while hosting similar activities. People went there for dances, dinners, and music concerts, such as those of the newly organized brass bands. Local and traveling theatre groups performed in them, as did traveling vaudeville acts. In most communities the hall was known as

The Centerville Dramatic Club took its production of *A Noble Outcast* on the road in 1914. Following a showing in the West Bountiful Amusement Hall, the troupe entertained and were photographed in the Kaysville Opera House. (Intellectual Reserve, Inc., courtesy LDS Church Archives)

the Opera House. A hall manager or sponsoring groups collected admission to offset expenses. Some places were operated commercially and were known by their owner's name; others were built by local Latter-day Saint wards or were funded through the time-honored process of selling shares to stockholders.[90]

New recreational interests during this period included both playing and observing organized sports and competitive games of skill. Baseball became popular in the 1880s as a community sport. Intercity leagues under the sponsorship of local merchants vied for championships, and playing fields could be found in every community. Bicycle racing emerged around 1900 and survived as a sport for a shorter time. A track at Beck's Hot Springs and an annual race from Salt Lake to Lagoon attracted dozens of participants and hundreds of spectators. Basketball began as a neighborhood pastime and emerged as a team sport after local halls suited to the sport became available. Wrestling matches attracted competitors from neighboring towns. Roller skating rinks, pool halls, and bowling alleys were built during

Spencer Adams, third from left, was second baseman for the Layton Baseball Club when they were Wasatch League Champions in 1920. Adams became the first Utahn to play major league baseball and played with the championship Washington Senators (1925) and New York Yankees (1926). (Roselyn Slade)

the early part of the century to house these and other specialized recreational activities.[91]

The first movie theaters appeared around 1910, and Bountiful and Layton led the way in this new kind of entertainment. Lamoni Call of Bountiful offered an early experience with motion pictures in 1909 with a hand-cranked projector. Electric projectors were introduced in Bountiful in 1916 by a Mr. Gabbott and a few years later by Jed Stringham. Layton's first theater, the La'Tonia Picture Show House opened in 1914; it was renamed the Roxy Theater in 1936. A second facility, Latona Motion Picture Theater, opened in 1917. All of these halls offered silent movies, with live musical accompaniment. The "talkies" appeared in the 1920s. Some Latter-day Saint wards offered weekly movies in the ward amusement hall. This sponsorship also allowed the church to exercise some control over the kinds of movies available to the public.[92]

The commercial resorts developed along the shores of the Great Salt Lake attracted the greatest general interest in the new age of enterprise. Of those opened between 1870 and the late 1890s, more than half were in Davis County. These popular resorts offered swimming, dancing, dining, boating, and other entertainment. All of them depended on rail service to bring passengers to their doors. In fact, the railroad companies were often major investors in the resorts. The lake was ideal for development; its waters were expanding and deepening to a degree unprecedented since the Mormon settlers began recording its fluctuating size and depth.

The Great Salt Lake had attracted swimmers and boaters before the establishment of commercial resorts. The resorts simply made it easier for visitors by providing boats, changing rooms, food services, and other recreational activities—all for a small fee. The first to open were Lake Side in south Farmington and Lake Point (also known as Steamboat Landing) on the south shore. John W. Young operated the pleasure grounds near Farmington, and in 1872 made it the home port for the converted freight steamboat *City of Corinne.* Moonlight excursions on the triple-decker stern-wheeler took pleasure seekers to Jeter Clinton's Lake Point and back for twenty-five cents. Church groups, families, and youth found Lake Side an attractive site for socials, reunions, and outings. It had convenient access from the Utah Central Railroad.

When a rail line reached the south shore in 1875, Lake Point added a hotel and other facilities and replaced Davis County's recreational center as the most popular site for Salt Lake area pleasure seekers. The steamboat was renamed the *General Garfield,* and the south shore became its home port. As summer visitors increased, new competitors appeared. Black Rock Beach opened in 1876 at a south shore location that had been used for bathing since Brigham Young visited it in 1847. Three years later, Ephraim Garn and George O. Chase developed a small bathing resort called Lake Shore north and west of Centerville. Patrons used the Utah Central to get there.[93]

To investors it seemed an ideal time in the ancient lake's history to build shoreline resorts. The lake reached its highest historic level in the mid-1870s, a record 4,211 feet above sea level. However, it was about to enter a ninety-year downward cycle that would soon leave the resorts stranded in the mud. Optimistic businessmen could not foresee the lake's future, and during a temporary rise in the lake level

A spur of the Denver and Rio Grande Railway brought patrons to the popular Lake Park Bathing Resort west of Farmington. The resort's open-air pavilion (later moved to Lagoon) offered band concerts and dancing. (Utah State Historical Society)

in the late 1880s, they ventured forth with new resorts that offered more comfortable facilities.[94]

The first of the new offerings was Lake Park, which opened in July 1886 in west Farmington on a 215-acre tract of lakeshore property. During its second year of operation, the resort attracted more than 50,000 visitors. Patrons paid a fifty-cent train fare to reach the facility on a spur built by the Denver and Rio Grande Railroad. Lake Park offered bathhouses, picnic kiosks, a shooting gallery, band concerts, race track, and an open-air pavilion for dancing—all for a fifty-cent admission. Special holiday activities, footraces, a restaurant, rental cottages, rowboats, and island cruises attracted thousands, including school and church groups. The resort became the most popular of its time.[95]

In 1886, the same year that Lake Park opened, the Utah and Nevada Railroad built a huge pavilion and added other improvements at the Garfield Beach resort. Lake Park attracted 60,000 visitors in 1887, but Garfield Beach had deeper swimming water than the shallow, muddy-bottomed beaches west of Farmington. When Daniel

Patrons enjoyed fine beaches at the Syracuse Bathing Resort and a picnic grove shaded by tall poplars among other offerings at the popular Great Salt Lake resort. (Utah State Historical Society)

C. Adams and Fred J. Keisel opened the Syracuse Lakeshore bathing resort in 1887, patrons discovered one of the lake's finest beaches, with a mud-free swimming area. The new Syracuse resort soon had a hundred bathhouses, freshwater showers from a deep artesian well, a horse-drawn merry-go-round, a restaurant, boating, and special concerts. Crowds gathered for baseball games and bicycle races, while a transplanted grove of poplars and willow-covered boweries attracted picnickers.[96]

With the successes at Garfield and Syracuse, Farmington's Lake Park responded with plans to build an on-shore saltwater bathing pool. But the Great Salt Lake was receding rapidly. Because the lake's bottom is essentially flat, the retreating water soon forced all of the resorts to close. In twenty years since its high point, the lake had dropped ten feet; it would drop another five feet before beginning a ten-foot rise over the twenty-year period beginning in 1905. Lake Park struggled until 1893 to survive. The Syracuse resort, served by a spur of the Union Pacific Railroad, closed its bathing facility in 1892, but for about ten years it continued its dances and picnic facility. Adams allowed the community to use the pavilion for holiday celebrations. The shady grove sheltered an annual conference for the six north Davis LDS wards.[97]

When Saltair opened in 1893 on the south shore with its grand pavilion built out over the lake on pilings, only the nearby Garfield Resort remained, and it burned in 1904. Saltair became the longest-lived of the pleasure resorts. Even though the Syracuse resort offered some recreational opportunities until 1906, Davis County's church groups chose Saltair for many of their outings. The resort's owners, the Church of Jesus Christ of Latter-day Saints, promised a morally safe environment at the "Coney Island of the West."[98]

Lagoon Resort. The death of Lake Park led to the immediate birth of a freshwater pleasure park in central Davis County. Simon Bamberger, one of Lake Park's investors, opened Lagoon Resort in wet pasture land against Farmington's west edge in 1896. By draining the swamp, harvesting the frogs—selling many of them as a delicacy in Montana mining camps—and scraping out a large four-foot-deep boating pond, Bamberger created an immediate attraction. He brought in boats from Lake Park and expanded the pond over several years until it covered more than eight acres.[99] A natural spring supplied the water. Using ten teams, workmen hauled in a partially dismantled dancing and concert pavilion and placed it on a new stone foundation. They also moved and reassembled the Lake Park restaurant and erected a bowery.[100] Bamberger extended his railroad line into the new park and opened Lagoon on Sunday, 12 July 1896, two months behind schedule. In subsequent years, Memorial Day marked the official commencement of the season.[101]

Bamberger had developed the Eden Park pleasure garden along the line of his steam rail line in Bountiful in 1894. The three-acre park along Barton Creek offered shaded picnic tables, a dance pavilion, bowery, ball field, and refreshments. The resort closed when Bamberger shifted his resources to develop and promote Lagoon. The Eden Park pavilion was hauled to the Hot Springs Resort, owned by Bamberger's friend John Beck.[102]

Lagoon quickly captured the market vacated by Davis County's lake resorts. Under the management of Lewis Bamberger, the resort attracted hundreds of visitors from Salt Lake City and, later, from Ogden, with inexpensive rail transportation and a variety of entertainment. Groups of all kinds rode the Dummy Line to Lagoon for scheduled outings. Two thousand patrons, most of them from Salt Lake City, crowded the resort on the first Pioneer Day holiday. A year later, nearly 7,000 people bought twenty-five-cent train tickets on Independence Day.[103]

Lagoon offered dancing, band concerts, boating, swimming, bicycle racing, and picnicking—the staple of the lake resorts. And Lagoon emphasized its parklike character with dozens of transplanted shade trees and shrubs, garden arbors, flowers, and walking paths. But the Farmington resort quickly built upon that beginning. Officials contracted with concessionaires for special entertainments and later introduced rides that led gradually to the creation of a modern amusement park. Added attractions included a fun house, merry-go-round, balloon ascensions, reenactments of the sinking of the Battleship *Maine,* high divers, a shooting gallery, waterchutes, and a miniature steam engine railroad ride. The county's first "moving" pictures were shown at Lagoon in 1896 on an instrument called the Edison vitascope.[104] The following year, a German-made "orchestrian," a twelve-foot-high, electrically powered musical instrument, replaced live bands for dancing. Lagoon contract workers also began collecting wild deer, elk, bears, and birds for a menagerie.[105]

Before long, Lagoon's dance pavilion became a roller skating rink. Competitive baseball games were introduced early in the century. By mid-century the resort's freshwater swimming pool was one of its primary attractions. Advertisements declared, "Swim in Water Fit to Drink." A wooden roller coaster became another popular drawing card at the fifty-acre resort. Other action rides followed over the years,[106] and a Pioneer Village added a historic component.

Values and Leisure Time. In many instances, the offerings of Davis County's privately operated recreation halls and commercial resorts raised questions in the minds of the moral guardians of the county's religiously based communities. As might be expected, the competing values introduced by secular recreational opportunities created tensions. Resort owners listened to concerns, and local governments constrained the activities complained about through police patrols and by licensing concessionaires. The result was a balance

Moonlight dancing at Lagoon Resort's new dance pavilion, seen here in May 1905, attracted large crowds and raised complaints from an LDS church watchdog committee. (Utah State Historical Society)

between personal values on the one hand and individual and commercial freedoms on the other.

A commonly voiced concern was that certain activities would adversely affect the moral character of the youth. Religious leaders in Davis County cautioned against drunkenness, profanity, rowdyness, and immoral behavior. Mormon bishops and their counselors discouraged swimming parties that involved both young men and young women. They also disapproved of skinny-dipping by young men, whether at the lake or in the local canyon streams.[107]

The concerns of church officials were magnified when dancing, boating, and other recreational activities were offered outside church or parental supervision. "Have nothing to do with it," one leader cautioned when the steamboat *City of Corinne* docked at Lake Side. Similar counsel advised youth to stay away from Lake Park and Lagoon.[108] In response to central church direction, local retrenchment committees were organized to exert pressure on resorts. Lagoon manager Andy Christensen responded to specific displeasures when one of these committees took its complaints to the city. Christensen agreed to halt moonlight dancing and to prevent dancing on Sunday to the music of an electric organ.[109]

Swimming at the resorts prompted regular complaints. Speakers at a Mormon stake conference in 1896 condemned scantily clad bathers. In 1920 a citizens group in Farmington lobbied the city to prevent a "Ladies Bathing Review" at Lagoon. That summer, another group asked the city council to build dressing rooms at the abandoned Lake Shore resort. Pleased with the idea of a community bathing beach isolated from the influences of commercial operations, the council purchased building materials and volunteers built the private cubicles.[110]

The consumption of alcohol troubled many citizens. Even though Lagoon's founder suggested "that no saloon will be run in connection with the resort," liquor had been sold at Lake Park under a county license.[111] It was not long before a concessionaire at Lagoon was selling beer without a permit. When discovered by a Farmington City officer, the bartenders "moved all their goods over the line into the county and took out a county license." The *Davis County Clipper* explained: "The west line of the city runs through the centre of the barroom." Thereafter, bartenders dutifully applied each year for city licenses. Councilmen limited the number of bars and prevented sales to minors through monitoring by city police officers whose salaries were paid for by the resort.[112]

Because most of the objectionable activities were not prohibited by law, Farmington's government used its licensing power to limit access. Concessionaires were required to keep youth away from Lagoon activities such as boxing exhibitions, lotteries, and horse races.[113] Gambling at the race track became a public issue of special concern in Davis County. The race track, built in 1911 on forty acres at the north end of the park, extended beyond city boundaries, raising the question of city versus county jurisdiction. The matter was solved when Lagoon owners threw their support behind a city proposal to annex the county land.[114]

Racing attracted a large following, and horses from many parts of the world participated. Stables were located on two sides of the

Fans await a racing event at Lagoon's muddy track in October 1914. (Utah State Historical Society)

track, and a large grandstand held hundreds of spectators. Racing was good for local businessmen. The season was concentrated in a three-week period in the summer and was sometimes repeated in the fall. Supporters rented local cottages and filled hotel rooms.[115] Racing at Lagoon ended abruptly after two years through legislative action. Representative Charles R. Mabey, a Republican banker from Bountiful and a later governor, introduced the controversial bill at the request of Davis County citizens concerned about the influence on young people of open betting at the race track. A statewide letter-writing campaign helped shore up support for the action.[116]

With the track closed, horse owners shipped their animals to Couer d'Alene, Idaho, for racing there. Local farmers bought many of the animal sheds for use in their pastures and barnyards. In November 1919 a wind flattened many of the remaining sheds and stripped the grandstand, causing $20,000 damage. Racing was revived at Lagoon around 1925 for a short time on a parimutuel betting system. That ended when Democrat Henry H. Blood, a Kaysville businessman and LDS stake president, became governor in 1933. He sought and approved another legislative restriction on the sport.[117]

Utahns had allowed most commercial recreational activities, but gambling was one of those excluded from the list of permitted pastimes. Other recreational activities at the commercial resorts, halls, and movie houses continued. They became the legacy of a new era of cultural opportunities, tolerated but not always trusted.

ENDNOTES

1. Margaret Steed Hess, *My Farmington: A History of Farmington, Utah, 1847–1976,* 401; [Clayton Holt, ed.], *The Community of Syracuse, 1820 to 1995: Our Heritage, Centennial Edition* (Syracuse: Syracuse Historical Commission, 1994), 136; John S. White, *Farmington, The Rose City* (Farmington: Farmington Commercial Club, [1913]).

2. *Weekly Reflex,* 26 February 1914, 5. The prospect of a border–to–border city was remembered as a prophecy of Brigham Young (see *Reflex,* 12 August 1920); interview with Harris Adams, May 1999.

3. Peter L. Goss, "William Allen, Architect–Builder, and His Contribution to the Built Environment of Davis County," *Utah Historical Quarterly* 54 (Winter 1986): 52–73; Glen M. Leonard, "William Allen's Clients: A Socio–Economic Inquiry," *Utah Historical Quarterly* 54 (Winter 1986): 74–87. See also LaRue Hugoe and Edith Deppe, *West Bountiful: A Pictorial History, 1848–1988,* 56, 58, 70.

4. For examples see Leslie T Foy, *The City Bountiful: Utah's Second Settlement, from Pioneers to Present,* 175; Arlene H. Eakle, Adelia Baird, and Georgia Weber, *Woods Cross: Patterns and Profiles of a City* (Woods Cross: Woods Cross City Council, 1976), 20–22; Hugoe and Deppe, *West Bountiful,* 437–38; Carol Ivins Collett, *Kaysville—Our Town: A History,* 121–22; Oma E. Wilcox and E. Harris Adams, "Layton Businesses," in Dan Carlsruh and Eve Carlsruh, eds., *Layton, Utah: Historic Viewpoints,* 285, 287, 319.

5. Holt, *The Community of Syracuse,* 120–21, 136–37, 365; *Utah State Gazetteer and Business Directory, 1918–19* (Salt Lake City: R.L. Polk & Co., 1918), 43; Lee D. Bell, *South Weber: The Autobiography of One Utah Community,* 395–96.

6. Wilcox and Adams, "Layton Businesses," 288–90.

7. Collett, *Kaysville: Our Town,* 94, 121–22, 113–14; Annie Call Carr, ed, *East of Antelope Island: History of the First Fifty Years of Davis County,* 395.

8. Hess, *My Farmington,* 304–9.

9. *Utah Gazetteer and Directory, 1888* (Salt Lake City: Lorenzo Stenhouse, 1888), 44; *Utah Gazetteer, 1892–93* (Salt Lake City: Stenhouse and Co., 1892), 51; *Utah State Gazetteer and Business Directory, 1900* (Salt Lake City: R.L. Polk & Co., 1900, 78; and *Utah State Gazetteer, 1918–19,* 41.

10. *Utah Gazetteer and Directory, 1884,* (Salt Lake City: Sloan & Dunbar, 1884), 303; *Utah Gazetteer, 1888,* 35–36; *Utah Gazetteer, 1892–93,* 43–44; *Utah State Gazetteer, 1900,* 66–67; *Utah State Gazetteer, 1918–19,* 27–28; Hugoe and Deppe, *West Bountiful,* 453–59.

11. Bell, *South Weber,* 391–93.

12. *Utah Gazetteer, 1888,* 44, 64, 81, 83–85; *Utah State Gazetteer, 1918,* 28, 59, 84, 88; Collett, *Kaysville: Our Town,* 94; Wilcox and Adams, "Layton Businesses," 311.

13. *Utah State Gazetteer, 1918–19,* 88.

14. Wilcox and Adams, "Layton Businesses," 291, 298; *Utah Gazetteer, 1892–93,* 44, 51, 69, 90, 93; *Utah State Gazetteer, 1900,* 66, 98, 122, 126; *Utah State Gazetteer, 1918–19,* 28, 41, 43, 84, 88, 128, 328; Holt, *Community of Syracuse,* 137.

15. Hess, *My Farmington,* 341; *Utah Gazetteer, 1884,* 303, 305, 307; *Utah Gazetteer, 1888,* 36, 64, 81; *Utah Gazetteer, 1892–93,* 44–45, 69–70; *Utah State Gazetteer, 1900,* 98, 122, 126; Wilcox and Adams, "Layton Businesses," 301.

16. *Davis County Clipper,* 21 August 1991, 44–45; Carr, *East of Antelope Island,* 408–9; Foy, *City Bountiful,* 176–77; Holt, *Community of Syracuse,* 121, 136; Wilcox and Adams, "Layton Businesses," 295.

17. *Utah State Gazetteer, 1918–19,* 28, 43, 88; Eakle, Baird, and Weber, *Woods Cross,* 55; Wilcox and Adams, "Layton Businesses," 306.

18. Foy, *City Bountiful,* 85–86; Collett, *Kaysville: Our Town,* 122.

19. Collett, *Kaysville: Our Town,* 122; Foy, *City Bountiful,* 179; *Utah Gazetteer, 1884,* 307; *Utah State Gazetteer, 1918–19,* 84, 88.

20. Foy, *City Bountiful,* 179–80; *Utah State Gazetteer, 1918–19,* 27; Wilcox and Adams, "Layton Businesses," 304–5. Foy dates the furniture consolidation at 1923; Wilcox and Adams say 1921.

21. Collett, *Kaysville: Our Town,* 49–50; Foy, *City Bountiful,* 179–80; *Utah Gazetteer, 1884,* 307; *Utah State Gazetteer, 1918–19,* 88; Wilcox and Adams, "Layton Businesses," 304–5.

22. Ronald Stucki, *Commercial Banking in Utah, 1847–1966* (Salt Lake City: Bureau of Economic and Business Research, 1967), 43–46, 141–43.

23. Collett, *Kaysville: Our Town,* 63, 94, 111–12; Journal History of the Church of Jesus Christ of Latter–day Saints, 13 October 1896, 9.

24. Hess, *My Farmington,* 319; *Davis County Clipper,* 27 May, 10 June 1892.

25. Wilcox and Adams, "Layton Businesses," 296–97.

26. Foy, *City Bountiful,* 182–83; Hugoe and Deppe, *West Bountiful,* 459–60.

27. *Utah State Gazetteer, 1918–19,* 28, 43.

28. Carr, *East of Antelope Island,* 388–89; Collett, *Kaysville: Our Town,* 37–38; Bell, *South Weber,* 279; *Utah Gazetteer, 1888,* 81.

29. Foy, *City Bountiful,* 89, 182; Carr, *East of Antelope Island,* 403; Eakle, Baird, and Weber, *Woods Cross,* 9.

30. Foy, *City Bountiful,* 89, 182; L. R. Humpherys and A. C. Matheson, eds., *Utah—Resources and Activities* (Salt Lake City: Utah Department of Public Instruction, 1933), 360–61.

31. Selected tradesmen are listed in the entries for Davis County cities in state gazetteers cited above; Hess, *My Farmington,* 334–35; Goss, "William Allen, Architect–Builder," 54–60.

32. In addition to entries in state gazetteers, see Carr, *East of Antelope Island,* 424; Hess, *My Farmington,* 327, 345; Collett, *Kaysville: Our Town,* 32–33.

33. Wilcox and Adams, "Layton Businesses," 298; Collett, *Kaysville: Our Town,* 125–28; Foy, *City Bountiful,* 184–85; *Utah Gazetteer, 1892–93,* 69; *Utah State Gazetteer, 1900,* 122; *Utah State Gazetteer, 1918–19,* 27–28, 41, 59, 84, 88.

34. See note 33.

35. *Utah State Gazetteer, 1900,* 122; Foy, *City Bountiful,* 184; Hess, *My Farmington,* 310; Collett, *Kaysville: Our Town,* 95; *Utah State Gazetteer, 1918–19,* 27, 59, 84, 88.

36. Carr, *East of Antelope Island,* 421–22; *Utah State Gazetteer, 1900,* 66–67, 98, 122; *Utah State Gazetteer, 1918–19,* 27–28, 59, 84–85, 88, 328; Collett, *Kaysville: Our Town,* 33–34; Wilcox and Adams, "Layton Businesses," 311, 317.

37. Allan Kent Powell, ed. *Utah History Encyclopedia,* 545–46; Collett, *Kaysville: Our Town,* 104, 106; Carr, *East of Antelope Island,* 412–13; Foy, *City Bountiful,* 147; *Davis County Clipper,* 10 January, 21 February 1896.

38. Collett, *Kaysville: Our Town,* 104, 106; Foy, *City Bountiful,* 159–60; Holt, *Community of Syracuse,* 138.

39. Collett, *Kaysville: Our Town,* 106–8; Foy, *City Bountiful,* 159–61.

40. J. Cecil Alter, *Early Utah Journalism* (Salt Lake City: Utah State Historical Society, 1938), 385, 390; William V. Sanders, "A History of the

Weekly Reflex, Kaysville, Utah" (M.A. thesis, Brigham Young University, 1966), 18–21.

41. Alter, *Early Utah Journalism,* 39–40; Foy, *City Bountiful,* 177; Carr, *East of Antelope Island,* 398–402; *Davis County Clipper,* 19 March, 17 June 1892.

42. Alter, *Early Utah Journalism,* 95–96; *Davis County Clipper,* 12 January, 16 February 1893, 25 April 1895; *Reflex,* 28 August 1913.

43. *Davis County Clipper,* 1 May 1896; Alter, *Early Utah Journalism,* 95.

44. Sanders, "History of the Weekly Reflex," 19–21; Alter, *Early Utah Journalism,* 95–96, 385. Alter gives a 1904 beginning date, Sanders 1911; however, other sources confirm that the *Reflex* was publishing at least by 1909 (see Farmington City Council, Minutes, 1:94, 10 November 1909, Farmington City Hall).

45. *Reflex,* 3 April 1913; 12 March 1914, 8 April 1915, 3 June 1915, 4.

46. Collett, *Kaysville: Our Town,* 122–24; Sanders, "History of the Weekly Reflex," 23–25, 39–43, 91.

47. Alter, *Early Utah Journalism,* 96; "Capsule History of Davis County Newspapers," *Historical Newsletter* (Kaysville-Layton Historical Society), Fall 1988.

48. *Deseret Evening News,* 18 September 1899.

49. Obed C. Haycock, "Electric Power Comes to Utah," *Utah Historical Quarterly* 45 (Spring 1977): 174, 183, 186–87; John S. McCormick, "The Beginning of Modern Electric Power Service in Utah, 1912–22," *Utah Historical Quarterly* 56 (Winter 1988): 6–7.

50. Foy, *City Bountiful,* 162, 229; Utah Power & Light Company, "History of Origin and Development," (11 May 1941), 244–48, 252–53, 276, and fold–out chart "Succession of Predecessor Companies," Utah State Historical Society.

51. McCormick, "Modern Electric Power Service," 8–9, 12; Utah Power & Light Company, "History of Origin and Development," 242–45, 248, 276; Holt, *Community of Syracuse,* 139, Bell, *South Weber,* 117–19; Foy, *City Bountiful,* 229.

52. McCormick, "Modern Electric Power Service," 12–20; Bell, *South Weber,* 118–19.

53. Carr, *East of Antelope Island,* 413; Bell, *South Weber,* 90; Foy, *City Bountiful,* 181–82, Smoot and Sheriff, *City In–Between: History of Centerville, Utah,* 58; Hess, *My Farmington,* 339, 379.

54. Holt, *Community of Syracuse,* 352–53.

55. Wilcox and Adams, "Layton Businesses," 314.

56. Clayton J. Holt, "The Bamberger Railroad," typescript, 1996, 1–2,

copy in possession of author; Carr, *East of Antelope Island,* 485; Foy, *City Bountiful,* 158.

57. *Davis County Clipper,* 23 May, 18 June 1895; 21 January 1898; Holt, "Bamberger Railroad," 2–3; Holt, *Community of Syracuse,* 140; Foy, *City Bountiful,* 158.

58. Holt, "Bamberger Railroad," 3–5; Collett, *Kaysville: Our Town,* 128, 130; *Reflex,* 31 July 1913.

59. Holt, "Bamberger Railroad," 2, 5–6; Collett, *Kaysville: Our Town,* 128, 130; Jack Goodman, "Light Rail a Rehash of Zippy Interurbans," *Salt Lake Tribune,* 24 December 1995, E2; *Reflex,* 25 December 1913.

60. Holt, "Bamberger Railroad," 6; Layton Town Board, Minutes, 13 April 1925, 25 January, 14 December 1926, Layton City Hall.

61. Holt, "Bamberger Railroad," 6–9; Collett, *Kaysville: Our Town,* 128, 130.

62. Holt, *Community of Syracuse,* 141.

63. Hugoe and Deppe, *West Bountiful,* 469–70; *Reflex,* 1 January 1914.

64. Holt, *Community of Syracuse,* 140–41; Holt, "Bamberger Railroad," 5; *Reflex,* 5 March 1914.

65. Kate B. Carter, ed., *Heart Throbs of the West,* 9:236.

66. Hess, *My Farmington,* 140; Foy, *City Bountiful,* 163; *Reflex,* 30 March 1922.

67. Smoot and Sheriff, *City In–Between,* 47; Holt, *Community of Syracuse,* 140, Bell, *South Weber,* 293; *Reflex,* 8, 22 May 1913, 24 June 1915.

68. *Reflex,* 12, 18 June 1913; Wilcox and Adams, "Layton Businesses," 301, 303–5.

69. Foy, *City Bountiful,* 169; Farmington City Council, Minutes, 11 March 1914, 3 January 1923; Hess, *My Farmington,* 332; Wilcox and Adams, "Layton Businesses," 305, 309, 312–14.

70. Wilcox and Adams, "Layton Businesses," 293, 295, 297, 301, 305, 308; *Utah State Gazetteer, 1918–19,* 28, 88.

71. Ezra C. Knowlton, *History of Highway Development in Utah* ([Salt Lake City]: State Road Commission, [1965?]), 78–80, 84–86, 92, 122–23.

72. Quoted in ibid., 126–27.

73. Ibid., 128–30, 136–37.

74. *Ogden Morning Examiner,* 28 July 1911; Knowlton, *History of Highway Development,* 153.

75. Knowlton, *History of Highway Development,* 157–58, 163; *Davis County Clipper,* 5 September 1913, 14 May, 4 June, 5 November, 1915, 13 August 1920; *Reflex,* 22 July, 18 November 1920.

76. Republished in *Deseret News,* 12 March 1983.

77. Knowlton, *History of Highway Development,* 157–59, 168–74, 176, 195; *Davis County Clipper,* 29 March 1918; *Reflex,* 19, 26 June 1919, 30 March 1922.

78. *Reflex,* 29 July, 5, 12, 19 August 1920.

79. *Reflex,* 12 August 1920; *Davis County Clipper,* 13 August 1920.

80. *Reflex,* 20 November 1919, 3 March 1921.

81. *Davis County Clipper,* 20 August 1920; *Reflex,* 13 January, 2 June 1921.

82. Foy, *City Bountiful,* 163; *Davis County Clipper,* 4 January 1894, 17 February 1922; *Reflex,* 1, 15 May, 3 July, 21 August 1913, 19 January 1922.

83. Knowlton, *History of Highway Development,* 220, 263, 273; *Weekly News Express* (Layton), 14 December 1933.

84. Knowlton, *History of Highway Development,* 220, 241–42, 270, 491; *Davis County Clipper,* 28 June 1935, 19, 26 December 1947, 15 October, 4 December 1948.

85. Carr, *East of Antelope Island,* 395; Hess, *My Farmington,* 313; Wilcox and Adams, "Layton Businesses," 292–94, 300.

86. Hess, *My Farmington,* 9, 313–14; *Utah Gazetteer, 1892–93,* 44–45, 69–70, 93; *Utah State Gazetteer, 1900,* 67, 98, 122; *Utah State Gazetteer,* 1918–19, 59, 128; Wilcox and Adams, "Layton Businesses," 300, 306, 315.

87. Bell, *South Weber,* 395; Adams and Wilcox, "Layton Businesses," 300, 303, 309, 311, 312, 317; *Utah State Gazetteer, 1918–19,* 84, 88.

88. For an overview of life at the turn of the century see Holt, *Community of Syracuse,* 127–35, 155. The 1920s are profiled in Collett, *Kaysville: Our Town,* 150–52.

89. Collett, *Kaysville: Our Town,* 21–24; Hess, *My Farmington,* 353; Tom Busselberg, "Social and Cultural Life," in Carlsruh and Carlsruh, *Layton, Utah: Historic Viewpoints,* 203

90. Bell, *South Weber,* 327–32; Collett, *Kaysville: Our Town,* 23, 137; Foy, *City Bountiful,* 178–19, 189, 194; Hess, *My Farmington,* 352, 256–57; Holt, *Community of Syracuse,* 123, 141; Hugoe and Deppe, *West Bountiful,* 215, 285; Smoot and Sheriff, *City In–Between,* 36–37, 52–55, 114, 116.

91. Busselberg, "Social and Cultural Life,"205, 214–15, 225–31; Foy, *City Bountiful,* 194–95; Hess, *My Farmington,* 353; Holt, *Community of Syracuse,* 122–23, 143; Hugoe and Deppe, *West Bountiful,* 494–95.

92. Foy, *City Bountiful,* 193; Wilcox and Adams, "Layton Businesses," 301, 305.

93. Dale L. Morgan, *The Great Salt Lake,* 353–56; Busselberg, "Social

and Cultural Life," 206–7; Holt, *Community of Syracuse,* 88–89; Smoot and Sheriff, *City In–Between,* 32.

94. Lake elevations are charted in J. Wallace Gwinn, ed., *Great Salt Lake: A Scientific, Historical, and Economic Overview* (Salt Lake City: Utah Geological and Mineral Survey, 1980), 262, 276.

95. Morgan, *Great Salt Lake,* 356–57; Nancy D. McCormick and John S. McCormick, *Saltair* (Salt Lake City: University of Utah Press, 1985), 8–14; *Davis County Clipper,* 10 June, 31 August 1892, 2 May 1895, 2 December 1898; Hess, *My Farmington,* 379; Busselberg, "Social and Cultural Life," 207–9.

96. Morgan, *Great Salt Lake,* 356–57; Carter, *Heart Throbs* (1944), 5:83–86; Holt, *Community of Syracuse,* 59–62; Carr, *East of Antelope Island,* 188; Busselberg, "Social and Cultural Life," 209–11; McCormick and McCormick, *Saltair,* 15–16.

97. Morgan, *Great Salt Lake,* 358; Holt, *Community of Syracuse,* 62–63, 123; Carr, *East of Antelope Island,* 189.

98. Morgan, *Great Salt Lake,* 358; *Davis County Clipper,* 7 August 1894, 15 August 1895.

99. *Davis County Clipper,* 14 November, 6 December 1895, 18 September 1896, 1 October 1897.

100. *Davis County Clipper,* 28 February, 8 May, 26 June, 10 July 1896.

101. *Davis County Clipper,* 22 May 1896, 28 May, 4 June 1897.

102. Foy, *City Bountiful,* 192; *Davis County Clipper,* 7 June 1894; 28 March 1895.

103. *Davis County Clipper,* 24 July, August 7, 1896, 9 July 1897.

104. *Davis County Clipper,* 10 April, 11 June, 23 October 1896, 4 June 1897, 22 April, 24 June, 5 August, 30 December 1898; *Reflex,* 29 May 1913, 8 July 1915; Charles Rendell Mabey, *Our Father's House: Joseph Thomas Mabey Family History* (Salt Lake City: Beverly Craftsmen, 1947), 210.

105. *Davis County Clipper,* 26 February, 26 March, 2 April 1897, 27 August, 22 October, 19 November, 1897, 28 January, 1898.

106. *Reflex,* 29 May, 13 August 1913; Work Projects Administration, *Utah: A Guide to the State* (New York: Hastings House, 1941), 283.

107. Farmington Ward, Teachers Quorum Minutes, 1 February 1880, 30 May, 13 June 1886, 19 October 1897.

108. Ibid., 31 August 1873, 8 September 1887. See also ibid., 5 September 1886, 20 June, 26 September 1897.

109. Thomas G. Alexander, "Between Revivalism and the Social Gospel: The Latter–day Saint Social Advisory Committee, 1916–1922," *BYU Studies* 23 (Winter 1983), 26; Farmington City Council, Minutes, 2 July 1919.

110. *Davis County Clipper,* 11 September 1896; Farmington City Council, Minutes, 9 August, 8 September 1920, 13 July, 3 August 1921.

111. *Davis County Clipper,* 10 April 1896, 20 July 1892.

112. *Davis County Clipper,* 17 July 1896; Farmington City Council, Minutes, 29 June 1912, 20 August 1913.

113. Farmington City Council, Minutes, 20 January 1908, 5 June 1918.

114. Ibid., April 17, 1912.

115. Hess, *My Farmington,* 381; Farmington City Council, Minutes, 26 June, 3 October 1912.

116. George Quincy Knowlton, *A History of Farmington, Utah,* 71; Mabey, *Our Father's House,* 288.

117. *Reflex,* 8, 22 May 1913; Hess, *My Farmington,* 381.

CHAPTER 9

CONFRONTING NEW WORLDS

The residents of Davis County approached the twentieth century with optimism. Times were good. A thriving commercial agriculture, supportive industries, and expanding commerce had brought prosperity to many of the county's farmers and ranchers. Businessmen were doing well in the commercial arena. The town boosters could imagine only more progress in a progressive age; no one could anticipate the new challenges that lay ahead. A major economic crisis sandwiched between two world wars plus the steady expansion of technology would change many lives and leave Davis County's citizens living in a different world. Before the end of the Second World War, the county would experience an infusion of new people and be introduced to civil service at military installations. None of this could have been anticipated; but all of it left an indelible mark on the communities of Davis County.

Foreign Wars and Home Improvements

The process of growing out of a governing system built around ecclesiastical leaders into one controlled more directly by the people was reflected in Davis County through both local and outside issues. One of the national issues was the Spanish-American War. During Utah's political struggle to achieve statehood, the national media had projected an image of a politically disloyal people in the territory. This image improved after 1896 because of the provisions separating church and state. When Congress declared war on Spain in 1898, Utahns received the opportunity to demonstrate their support for national policy. Some concerned citizens spoke against enlistment in the military, but the First Presidency of the LDS church formally encouraged loyalty to national policy. In a show of patriotism, Utahns exceeded the state's volunteer quota of 500 men with 660 enlistees. Davis County furnished around two dozen men, a few from each community. Nine Utahns died and thirteen were wounded while suppressing subsequent insurrection in the Philippines, none of them from Davis County. As a result of the war, besides gaining control over the Philippines and some Caribbean islands, the United States emerged as a world power. For Davis County's Latter-day Saints, basking in their place as part of the newest American state, the war had moved them one step closer to acceptance and understanding in the eyes of the nation.[1]

The war with the Spain was the first foreign war for the United States since its invasion of Mexico in 1846. Two major international conflicts lay ahead in the first half of the twentieth century. Utahns responded to both as did other Americans. The United States under President Woodrow Wilson had remained neutral in a European war that began in 1914; but on 6 April 1917 Wilson responded to the sinking of several American supply ships by entering the war to "keep the world safe for democracy." Davis County residents responded to Utah's Council of Defense by loaning money through Liberty Loan drives, growing and saving food as part of the Victory Garden movement, and supporting the Red Cross in activities such as making bandages. About half of the Utahns in the armed forces enlisted as volunteers, the rest were drafted.

In the Davis County draft lottery, the first name drawn was that of J. Leo Ware of Layton. He served as a clerk in France and saw some combat. In August 1917 a regiment of light artillery under Col. Richard W. Young was organized from the Utah National Guard.

Designated the 145th Artillery Regiment at their Camp Kearney, California, training site, the Utah troops served a depot function and provided replacements to front-line units. Although the regiment itself finally was ordered to France, it arrived just before the 11 November 1918 armistice and did not see action. The personal sacrifice of Utahns in the armed forces was notable—of nearly 25,000 who served from the state, some 300 died of disease and another 147 lost their lives on the battlefields of eastern France. Davis County's contribution was 474 enrolled in the army, thirty-one in the navy, and fifteen in the marines.[2]

The war's end brought celebrations in the streets and a parade that moved from Ogden into north Davis County. Local groups of the American Legion were organized in Bountiful, Layton, and other communities to help find jobs for returning servicemen, raise funds for a veterans' hospital in Salt Lake City, and remember the dead in Memorial Day programs. A decade later, the Davis County Commission set aside a room in the courthouse as an American Legion Hall, where the war veterans could be honored.[3]

During the war, the farms of Davis County flourished. While small family farms of twenty to eighty acres remained the norm, many larger farms had been created through homesteading, buying, and trading. Ezra T. Clark, one of Davis County's largest landowners, accumulated 700 acres before his death in 1901. His methods, according to a daughter, included resourcefulness, independent effort (he stayed out of the united orders), good business judgment, frugality, and avoidance of debt. His acquisitive watchword: "Keep what you have and get all you can."[4]

Clark was not the county's only acquisitive farmer. By 1917, thirteen Davis County men owned more than 400 acres of farmland. The value of this land was enhanced because of commercial agriculture. For example, eighty-three landowners held acreages valued at more than $10,000. Thirteen farmers on this list, most of them residents of Layton, reported assessed values above $20,000. More typical forty-acre spreads in Davis County were appraised for around $1,000.[5]

Even the most prosperous Utah farmers faced challenges during the postwar years when a national depression hit agriculture especially hard. Income in the 1920s declined noticeably from fruits and field crops such as grain and sugar beets. These were staples for commercial farmers in Davis County. On the positive side, the cost of seed, fertilizer, and machinery remained steady. While farmers worked to rise above some decline in income, Utah businessmen involved in commerce, manufacturing, construction, and transportation did well during the economic downtime.[6]

Political Issues and Government Services. For a time after the end of World War I, Utahns returned to the Republican party. In 1920 the state's voters helped elect the GOP presidential ticket—Warren G. Harding, an Ohio senator, and his running mate Calvin Coolidge, a Massachusetts governor. Bountiful businessman and former mayor Charles R. Mabey, a Davis County Republican, defeated Provo businessman Thomas N. Taylor to become Utah's fifth governor. Congressman Milton H. Welling, a Democrat born in Farmington, gave up his U.S. House seat in 1920 to run against Republican Senator Reed Smoot, who won reelection.[7]

Most residents of Davis County supported Utah's legislature in 1917 when it curbed the manufacture and sale of alcoholic beverages. Three years later they applauded passage of the Eighteenth Amendment to the Constitution establishing national Prohibition. Residents hoped these efforts would curb drunkenness and improve community morals. Consumption declined, but clandestine stills, including some in Davis County, continued to produce hard liquor. Speakeasies distributed huge quantities of locally made and imported spirits, malt liquors, wine, and mash. Bootlegging was difficult to stop. It continued even when federal officials seized more than 400 distilleries in Utah over a seven-year period. In an attempt to tighten control, the Bountiful city council adopted its own ordinance in December 1928 eliminating the sale of wine and tonics.[8]

In 1933 Congress invited the states to consider ending Prohibition by repealing the Eighteenth Amendment. In Utah, it was the chambers of commerce, Democratic officials, and the *Salt Lake Tribune* that encouraged repeal. Leaders of the LDS church celebrated the centennial of the church's Word of Wisdom—which advocates abstinence from alcoholic beverages—and preached against the return of saloons and "Demon Rum." Others supporting Prohibition were Utah's Methodist, Baptist, Presbyterian, and Seventh-day

Among the road improvements in Davis County was the Ogden–Salt Lake Cut-off, seen here reaching northward toward the viewer from Lagoon in the 1940s. (Utah State Historical Society)

Adventist churches. Mormon leaders were disappointed when, by a 5–3 ratio, Utah became the thirty-sixth (and deciding) state to ratify the proposed Twenty-first Amendment. By a similar majority, citizens repealed the state's prohibition law. Davis County joined with sixteen other counties, thirteen of them totally rural, in opposing repeal. All other Wasatch Front counties from Juab to Weber revealed their urban character by favoring the end of the "noble experiment."[9]

While national issues caught the attention of everyone in the county, local governments quietly went about their task of providing services to citizens. Services in the cities that had been incorporated in the 1890s increased steadily in the early decades of the new century. Bountiful, Farmington, and Kaysville gave special attention to the paving of city streets and development of city water systems. Graded or gravel-surfaced roads were the most common county and city streets well into the twentieth century; yet the effort to pave streets to meet the demands of local citizens and to match the quality of state roads moved forward steadily. Paving of city streets in Bountiful began in 1918, with the first curbing the following year. In contrast, because of its much later incorporation as a town, Syracuse laid its first paving in the 1930s. Other cities moved forward according to citizen interest and willingness to be taxed for the modernizing benefits.[10]

By 1940 fully two-thirds of the roads built by the state in Davis County had some kind of paved surface, compared with only one-third of municipal streets, and just over one-tenth of county roads. Twelve years later, 93 percent of state roads, 61 percent of city streets, and 24 percent of county roads in Davis County were paved. These figures were well above state averages, but they tell only part of the story. Between January 1940 and July 1952, no new state roads were built in Davis County, and the county itself added only ten miles of roadways, bringing its total to 172 miles. During these years, municipal streets increased by nearly half, from 106 miles to 147 miles. Clearly, the towns and cities were taking on added responsibilities by opening new streets and moving toward higher quality surfaces to serve the increased motor traffic.[11]

Culinary water was another convenience provided during the early decades of the century by municipal governments. Officials in Bountiful and Farmington tried unsuccessfully in 1898 to provide the service but were rebuffed by those who controlled water rights—the local irrigation companies. Bountiful City responded by authorizing the Stone Creek and Barton Creek irrigation companies to serve their own stockholders. Farmington councilmen initiated a proposal but then tabled it for further study.[12]

It was not many years later that Bountiful, Farmington, and Kaysville—the county's three incorporated cities—succeeded in installing culinary water systems to replace private wells and ditches. Bountiful resolved the question of water rights by developing an independent source from underground water. The city built a reservoir with money loaned by Bountiful State Bank and began offering culinary water service in 1906. Citizens in Farmington voted 100–8 to bond for a city waterworks that same year, and officials purchased water shares from the North Cottonwood Irrigation Company. Two years later, Kaysville decided to allow private enterprise to provide the service. The city council granted Heber Steiner the franchise to build and operate a piped culinary and irrigation system for city residents.[13]

Because the existence of some form of legal entity was necessary to fund and manage a water system, thirteen new towns were created in Davis County to accomplish that objective and to offer other municipal services. Centerville led out in this movement to incorporate in 1915. Layton followed five years later, after several failed efforts by its Commercial Club. Nine other communities gained permission from the county commission to become incorporated towns during the late 1930s. These included Woods Cross, Syracuse, West Point, and Sunset in 1935; Clinton and East Layton in 1936; Laytona in 1937; South Weber in 1938; and Fruit Heights in 1939. The final incorporations were North Salt Lake, in 1947, and West Bountiful, two years later. Most of these new towns became third-class cities between 1950 and 1970, as the populations increased to the required number of residents.[14]

For most of the new communities, the incorporation petition was essentially a manifestation of interest in installing piped culinary water. This was true for Centerville, which was incorporated to qualify for a $15,000 waterworks bond. Voters gave near-unanimous support for the funding proposal. The city acquired water from Deuel Creek Irrigation Company and built a reservoir to ensure steady service. The Syracuse town board secured water from a deep well near the cemetery, but the system served only residents above Bluff Road. The waterworks improvements were supported by a grant from the Public Works Administration (PWA), as were projects undertaken by Woods Cross and Sunset.[15] When the Works Progress Administration (WPA), another Depression-era federal agency, offered loans to build community water systems, a handful of residents living outside Layton's town boundaries organized the Town of East Layton in 1936. The following year, they bonded for a water system and received matching funds from the WPA, which appointed a local supervisor to oversee construction. Before long, cast-iron pipes carried water to the homes of most of the town's 160 residents. The same process was followed in creating the Town of Laytona in 1937 to provide a water system for thirty-seven households. For twenty years, the Laytona Town Board managed the water system without providing any other municipal services; it then merged with Layton City. Residents of West Point followed a similar WPA track in providing culinary water to their newly incorporated town.[16]

The political process for approving a municipal water system did not always follow immediately after incorporation. The interest in West Bountiful was present with incorporation, but it was seven years, in 1957, before residents voted 131–61 to approve a $296,000 bond. The funds were used to purchase the Weber Basin Reservoir Company, which had been providing water to about one-third of West Bountiful homes; most other residents had relied on private wells.[17]

Prior to the incorporation of city governments, community cemeteries had been established in the older towns, often under the auspices of local Mormon wards. One of the last of these was the cemetery created to serve residents of the Syracuse-Clearfield area in 1896 so that families would not need to bury their dead in the Kaysville-Layton cemetery or take them to Bountiful. During the 1920s and 1930s, incorporated cities accepted responsibility for maintaining and expanding local cemeteries. Fees charged for burial lots and interments supported maintenance costs; but maintenance was not always ideal. Centerville City acted to improve its cemetery in 1933 after Mormon leader J. Golden Kimball eulogized his associate B. H. Roberts, a Davis County resident, with the words, "This is a good man we are laying away and what a hell of a place to lay him."[18]

Centralizing Education. The secularization of Utah society that accelerated with statehood led to a movement to consolidate local school districts in Utah. The territorial law that created free public schools in 1890 had permitted the formation of consolidated districts within large cities and in counties. Objectives were to improve the quality of instruction, replace one-room schools with graded classes, and increase attendance. In Davis County, the movement eventually resulted in new community elementary schools, the establishment of a countywide school district in 1911, and the creation of a central high school three years later. The change was not easy, given the long tradition of local control. It first was necessary to abolish the nineteen separate district school boards that the county court had set up to oversee the local ungraded schools. With the creation of the Davis School District, the county school board's responsibilities expanded from advisory to administrative. The new district board and staff not only set standards and curriculum but took on the tasks of providing facilities and hiring teachers and principals. In the 1930s the district added school-lunch and transportation programs.

Implementing the consolidation law meant closing the district schools and combining classes in the center of town in an elementary school built to accomodate eight grades. In some areas this transition went in stages because of limited funding and small enrollment. The first local districts in Davis County to respond were those at the ends of the county. A one-room school named the Syracuse Central School was built in 1900 to serve students in a consolidation of Districts 13 and 14. Two additional rooms were soon needed; then in 1906 a separate Clearfield Elementary School was built to serve an expanding population. Syracuse Elementary eventually grew to the standard eight-room school.

Voters in the Layton area struggled with the issues of funding and district boundaries, but decided in 1901 to build a three-room school. It was expanded to eight rooms in 1915 and absorbed the last of the area's one-room schools seven years later. Additional elementary schools in the Layton area were not needed until 1942. In the Bountiful area, local districts were combined in two fully graded schools in 1907, Stoker School in Bountiful and West Bountiful Elementary.[19]

A new state law in 1905 authorizing local tax support for public schools and allowing countywide consolidation prompted creation of the Davis County School District in the summer of 1911. District leaders combined the remaining local school districts and brought all county schools under centralized management. An eight-room elementary school in Farmington was completed that year atop a hill overlooking the center of town. Because of its limited population, South Weber built a brick building with two classrooms in 1913; instructors taught students from four grades in each room. In 1917–18, handsome two-story brick schools, all of a similar pattern, were built in three other communities to serve grades one through eight. These elementary schools were in south Bountiful (to serve the Woods Cross-North Salt Lake area), Centerville, and Kaysville. With the completion of these schools, and new elementaries in Woods Cross and Clearfield in the early 1930s, the county had fully moved into the era of the graded school for children.[20]

One of the first of the new eight-room consolidated elementary schools built in the county was this one, completed in 1911 atop a rocky prominence in Farmington. (Charles G. Miller)

Consolidation also raised the question of establishing schools for grades nine through twelve. The idea of establishing public high schools in Utah emerged in the 1890s, and by 1905 thirty-three were in operation, most of them offering fewer than four years of study. They provided an alternative to secondary education then being offered by various churches. A 1911 state law encouraged the creation of a single county high school. Four years later, the legislature mandated consolidation of high schools within counties (and large cities) and created an elected board of five members to oversee the elementary and secondary schools within each district.[21]

It was within this context that public high schools appeared in Davis County. The county school board granted permission in 1909 to create North Davis High School in Syracuse to serve that region. A high school had been functioning in Bountiful since 1906, when the state legislature authorized funding for secondary education. Bountiful voters authorized a new building in 1910. Davis County school officials thus generated a protracted discussion when they

Vocational training in carpentry skills was offered in the manual training room at North Davis High School, seen here in a 1917 photograph. (*The Community of Syracuse*)

tried to apply the optional provisions of the 1911 law. Citizens at both ends of the county resisted construction of a geographically centralized high school. They expressed concern about transportation and lamented the loss of local control over education. Eventually district leaders worked out an agreement that allowed Davis County Central High School in Kaysville to be built. Mormon leaders closed the church's Davis Academy in Kaysville, and the nine-room high school opened in 1914 near the county's geographic center. It graduated thirty students from its senior class the following year. Students in the northwest region of the county continued to attend the two-year North High School until 1925.[22] Meanwhile, the new building in Bountiful became South Davis Junior High School (renamed Bountiful Junior High in 1959) to serve students in grades nine and ten. The idea of a junior high school was new at that time and underwent a number of adjustments during the 1920s and 1930s.

Combining neighborhood schools into citywide elementaries and countywide high schools created a transportation need. Horse-drawn school wagons originally transported the most distant students to school and home each day. Those living close to schools found their own way. Many older students reached Davis High aboard the Bamberger railroad, while others arrived in private buses. The school district launched its own bus system in 1929 to serve students at all grade levels living more than 2.5 miles from a school. Busing students was at that time a purely local option, and Davis was one of the last districts to assume that responsibility.[23]

Depression and War, 1930–1945

The political transitions that saw towns increase their services and consolidate schools were important parts of Davis County's experience. Of greater impact on more lives were the events associated with the Great Depression and World War II, which would leave major legacies on the economic and social landscape.

The Great Depression. When the stock market crashed in October 1929, many Utahns shared the pervading national optimism. Prior economic downturns had been short-lived. Most people expected this one to work itself back to normal in a traditional way. Instead, however, conditions worsened. Unemployment in Utah increased to nearly 36 percent by late 1932, and the market for agricultural goods declined. Farm income statewide dropped by more than half. Complicating the challenges for farmers was a devastating drought in 1934, the worst in Utah's recorded history. It limited harvests from field crops and dried up reservoirs. Banks began to foreclose on mortgages. Local governments seized homes and farms for unpaid taxes. All of these conditions impacted the citizens of Davis County in one way or another.[24]

Utah's state leaders took some actions to help relieve the problems. Governor George Dern implemented a program to help the unemployed by accelerating new road construction projects and by encouraging businessmen to shorten the work week and hire more employees. In order to broaden the state's tax base and shift the burden from farmers, Utahns approved constitutional amendments to enact corporate and personal income taxes. Subsequent laws in 1931 most heavily impacted businesses and individuals with higher incomes. To help people find jobs, the LDS church set up local employment bureaus and also provided clothing, food, and commodities for the needy. Other churches also joined with community agencies and the Red Cross in the cooperative relief effort.[25]

Federal relief funds began to flow in mid-1932, after Herbert Hoover signed the Emergency Relief and Reconstruction Act. The election of that year put Franklin D. Roosevelt into the White House. Kaysville businessman Henry H. Blood, who was serving as chair of the Utah State Road Commission and as president of the North Davis LDS Stake, won office as Utah governor. Because the state had received property taxes from only half the usual number of landowners in 1932, it was near bankruptcy. Blood, a Democrat, and a supportive legislature were able only to offer modest help to Utah's unemployed. They did build trust in stable banks, liquidated those unable to remain in business, and worked with the public works projects launched under Roosevelt's New Deal set of programs. The governor also lobbied successfully in Washington for additional funds for public works projects, including buildings, reclamation projects, and highways.

Davis County benefited from these efforts, with watershed restoration work by the Civilian Conservation Corps (CCC), crop support payments through the Agricultural Adjustment Acts, private loans from the Farm Credit Administration and Home Owners Loan Corporation, and building projects under the Public Works Administration and Works Progress Administration. This infusion of work opportunities for 30,000 Utahns pushed unemployment in Utah steadily downward. It dropped below 10 percent in 1935, then leveled off until 1941, when wartime jobs punched it down to less than 3 percent. Residents appreciated the government helping hand that eased the personal burdens of lives lived frugally.[26]

Debris Floods and Conservation. Another kind of burden was more selective in its devastating effect in Davis County. During three summers in the first decades of the twentieth century, several canyons in the Kaysville-Centerville area disgorged huge quantities of mud and rocks in flash floods that spilled out into the settlements below. The debris floods caused an estimated $1 million in damage in 1940 prices. Within minutes the floods swamped buildings, covered highways, disrupted railroads, toppled electrical power poles, clogged water systems, and destroyed croplands in central Davis County. The

Centerville residents stretch their arms to indicate the size of a two-hundred-ton boulder dropped at the mouth of Parrish Creek in the 1930 flood. (Utah State Historical Society)

first of these rainstorm floods happened on Haight (Bair Canyon), Kays, and Holmes Creeks east of Kaysville in August 1912. The Kays Creek debris flood left an alluvial fan of mud and rocks ten feet deep and 300 feet wide where it emerged from the canyon.

More serious damage was caused by the floods of 14 August 1923 that issued from Farmington, Steed, and Ford (Ricks) Creek drainages. Four Boy Scouts and a honeymooning Ogden couple camping in Farmington Canyon were killed in the fast-moving flood. Damage in the south Farmington and north Centerville area was extensive, with mud up to thirteen feet deep inundating homes and cars. The last of the major floods hit during the summer of 1930 from Kaysville through Centerville, involving Kays, Davis, Ricks, Barnard, and Parrish Creeks. Debris floods of 10 July, 11–12 August, and 4 September caused extensive property damage in Farmington and Centerville. Mud, rocks, and hundred-ton boulders covered farms, orchards, and residential property. The Centerville Elementary School was surrounded by the slimy swath from Parrish Canyon.[27]

The first systematic search for the causes of the destructive floods and ways to prevent them began immediately after the 1923 problem. Similar flooding had occurred in other areas along the Wasatch

Front, from Cache Valley to Sanpete County, and some preventative measures were taken in the early 1920s using dikes. Luther M. Winson, an irrigation engineer employed by the state, supervised this early work and organized similar efforts at Willard and Farmington in 1924. With funding from local water users, the Utah Highway Commission, county commissioners, and railroad companies, diversion dams and catchment basins were built to control the flow of the mountain streams above the impacted towns. Meanwhile, J. H. Paul of the University of Utah and F. S. Baker of the U.S. Forest Service published a report in 1925 pinpointing fires and overgrazing as the basic causes of the debris floods in Willard and Farmington. They recommended revegetation of the damaged watersheds and county regulation of the land. It would be another five years, and another damaging flood season, however, before their recommendations would lead to action.[28]

The devastation of the 1930 floods prompted Governor George H. Dern to appoint an eighteen-member flood commission to study the causes and propose ways of preventing further flooding. An independent survey conducted by the Intermountain Forest and Range Experiment Station at Ogden agreed with the committee's findings. Torrential rainfall, or cloudbursts, had provided ample water for the floods, but the underlying cause was overgrazed mountain watersheds. In Davis County—the focus of both studies—investigators confirmed that the watershed feeding into Steed, Davis, Ford, and Parrish Creeks had been denuded, mostly by sheep. As much as one-fourth of the upper watershed zone of each offending creek was nearly barren of vegetation, leaving it unable to absorb the water from summer thunderstorms. Nearby canyons that had not been overgrazed or scorched by fire produced no damaging runoff. "The flood commission's study made it very clear," Bernard DeVoto reported, "that not nature, but the inhabitants of Davis County were responsible."[29]

The governor's committee looked for solutions. One recommendation was that the federal government purchase the private grazing lands and manage them. Both study groups suggested that the land be restored and revegetated. These proposals changed the approach to flood control. The state legislature asked the Utah State Land

The unique terraced trench system built by Civilian Conservation Corps men on the Davis County watershed (seen here) had application in many other western American locations. (Utah State Historical Society)

Board to conduct further studies and create a plan of action. The first investigations confirmed earlier findings of the need to restore vegetation to the overgrazed watersheds. A long-range mountain slope study launched by the U.S. Forest Service continued for years after the floods. The agency set up a Davis County Experimental Watershed area in the affected areas east of Centerville and Farmington. Investigators measured erosion to understand the impact of barren watersheds on sediment and stream flow. One seventeen-year study begun in 1930 found that the amount of sediment moving down Parrish Creek was more than 2,500 times that of a nearby watershed that had not been overgrazed.[30]

Efforts to prevent further flooding on the damaged watershed included both preventive and corrective measures. In the region above Centerville, the city purchased some of the damaged drainage for public management and reseeding, and the remaining private owners agreed to adopt conservative grazing practices. Over time, the plant cover was restored and the soil stabilized. During subsequent summer cloudbursts, no flooding occurred. Restoration costs for 1,300 acres of Davis County watershed totaled an estimated

$300,000.[31] In 1933 the U.S. Forest Service pioneered the building of contour trenches. The ditches were nine feet wide and spaced up to twenty feet apart, and they effectively controlled both melting snow and torrential rains on the damaged watersheds. Over a period of six years, workers scraped more than 700 miles of these trenches into Wasatch mountainsides using horse-drawn plows, tractors, bulldozers, and hand labor. The Davis County trial project worked so well that trenching was used on more than eighty other projects in the Forest Service's Intermountain Region to restore 30,000 acres of watershed land. Range research also resulted in improved methods for managing grazing, improving natural forage, understanding runoff from rainfall and snowmelt, and measuring other factors impacting soil erosion and floods.[32]

Unemployed young men who had enrolled in the Civilian Conservation Corps helped build the mountainside trenches and replant barren slopes in the damaged Davis County watershed. They worked out of a base camp called Lake View Camp that was established in 1933 in north Farmington. Another reclamation camp operated from the entrance of Mueller Park in Bountiful. These conservation camps were two of 116 set up at various times in Utah by the Federal Emergency Relief Agency to protect and enhance the national forests and to prevent soil erosion on public lands. Unemployed local tradesmen were hired to supervise the eighteen-to-twenty-five-year-old youth enrollees.

The Davis County flood-control project had been launched by county officials with funds from the Reconstruction Finance Corporation, a federal agency. Also joining in the effort were the Army Corps of Engineers and the U.S. Forest Service, the technical supervisors. The cooperating agencies cut a new road into Farmington Canyon, blasting out switchbacks with dynamite, and connected it around the mountain to Bountiful. This roughly graded road gave the "CCC boys" quicker access to the area. In the mountains, workers created a huge network of erosion-control terraces under the guidance of Dr. Reed W. Bailey of the Intermountain Forest and Range Experiment Station. When the initial ninety miles of compartmentalized trenches proved successful in preventing erosion and floods, the men carved out additional terraces totaling

Workmen from the Lake View Camp constructed roads into Farmington Canyon and several flood control barriers to control stream flow coming out of the major canyons. (Utah State Historical Society)

another 600 miles. At the mouth of the flooded canyons, the CCC men built catch basins to control silt, earthen dikes, rock retaining walls, and rock foundations for bridges where the impacted creeks crossed the main road in Fruit Heights, Farmington, and Centerville. At Farmington Bay Wildlife Refuge, crews built dikes and nesting islands for birds.[33]

Involvement in the CCC program had a personal impact on the men who improved Davis County's physical environment. The young men, 80 percent of them from outside the state, were fed, clothed, and housed at government expense. They kept only five dollars of their thirty-dollar monthly salary; the rest was sent home to aid their families, who were on government relief. Many of the young men learned skills useful later in the private sector. At the Lakeview Camp in Farmington, the men raised vegetables and tended pigs and cows on an adjacent ten-acre farm. Some of the CCC enrollees stayed behind after their eighteen-month stint in the corps. They had made friendships in local communities, met local young women during outings at Lagoon Resort and elsewhere, married, and became Davis County residents.[34]

The Second World War. Americans had been preparing for war before the Japanese attack on Pearl Harbor on 7 December 1941. They did so by supporting the Allies through what President Franklin D. Roosevelt called an "arsenal of democracy." These preparations readied the United States for an unwanted but inevitable involvement against the Axis forces. Congress reacted immediately to the loss of life in Hawaii by bringing the nation into the conflict. Roosevelt's approval of the war declaration rapidly lifted Davis County and most of the country out of the Depression and into a period of patriotic service and support that prepared the way for an era of growth and prosperity.

Davis County contributed its share of men and women to the Allied fighting forces through enlistments and military drafts. Of the 62,107 Utahns serving in 1945 in the U.S. Army, Navy, Marine Corps, and Coast Guard, 1,450 were killed in action and another thousand died from other causes. Each Davis County community sent off sons and daughters to the war, honored those who returned, and memorialized those who died. Fifty-two women were among those who served in World War II from the county. Fatalities from Davis County included forty-one members of the army and sixteen from the navy.[35] Latter-day Saint meetinghouses installed plaques in their foyers listing ward members who served, with a small star beside the name of each person who paid the ultimate sacrifice.

On the home front, Davis County residents lent their patriotic support to the war effort through a variety of programs. Many residents became full- or part-time workers at military installations in the north Davis and south Weber area. The county's agricultural production was at the forefront of the patriotic endeavor. George E. Dibble, chairman of the county defense board, challenged area farmers to increase food production. "In behalf of national defense," he said, "we call upon every farmer in the county to do his best to bring his production into line with the county quotas on food output. It is as much our duty to comply with this request of our government as it is the duty of a draftee to report to his training station."[36] The canning crops increased in the county the following year, but the loss of farmland to the Naval Supply Depot at Clearfield kept production below hoped-for expectations.[37]

Virtually every citizen, not just Davis County's farmers, was involved in federal programs created to produce goods, manage shortages, and raise funds for the war. The OPA label of the Office of Price Administration became familiar to every county resident through the agency's programs of rationing scarce items and setting price controls. Between 1942 and 1945, local rationing boards set up by the OPA reviewed requests for automobiles, tires, stoves, and typewriters. Such items were nearly impossible to get because manufacturing plants focussed on making weapons, tanks, military vehicles, and warships. After nylon replaced silk in parachutes, women could not buy nylon stockings. Also scarce were gasoline, fuel oil, kerosene, shoes, sugar, coffee, butter, canned fruits and vegetables, and beef steak. Many products could be acquired only with rationing coupons. Red coupons authorized the purchase of meat, fish, and dairy products; blue coupons were used for canned goods.

In a show of patriotism, Davis County residents accepted the inconveniences of rationing, reused everything possible, stepped up home gardening and home canning, and generally avoided buying black market items. Even though most residents already kept backyard gardens, during World War II the fruit and vegetables raised and stored became part of the "Victory Garden" strategy. To support the war effort, people responded to government quotas for scrap iron and steel and turned in used rubber, rags, and kitchen fat (used to make glycerine for black powder). Schools, churches, newspapers, and businesses promoted the sale of savings bonds to help fund the war. Schoolchildren bought stamps for a book that could be redeemed for a ten-dollar or twenty-five-dollar U.S. Savings Bond when full. In these and other ways, the residents of Davis County lent their support to Allied forces fighting in the devastating European and Pacific theaters of the war.[38]

The war was brought close to home in another way. Several thousand German and Italian prisoners of war were interned in fenced stockades at thirteen base and branch camps in Utah during the war. All of the prisoners received good food, health care, recreation, and humane treatment as guaranteed by the 1929 Geneva Convention.

Rarely mistreated, they did sometimes feel that the American guards reflected a negative attitude, a situation no doubt exaggerated by wartime tensions. One of the base camps was at the Naval Supply Depot in Clearfield, home to 500 German prisoners between April 1945 and the end of the war. The men lived in twenty-two barracks built on what had been local farmland. Catholic and Lutheran services were held in the camp each Sunday. On other days, the men raised crops on a farm in Syracuse and performed other labor both inside and outside the camp when local workers were not available. A second base camp in Davis County, located at Hill Field, was known as Camp Hill Field or the Ogden Air Technical Service Counsel. It housed mostly Italian POWs. They were offered high school education programs and, because all were Catholics, attended religious services conducted by Monsignor Alfredo F. Giovanoni from St. Mary's of the Wasatch in Salt Lake City. When Italy capitulated, the Italian prisoners were allowed to work on local farms and in defense industries if they renounced Mussolini's regime and signed a parole agreement.[39]

Military Installations. World War II brought four new military support installations to Utah and an expansion of the Ogden Arsenal, which had been operating since 1921. All of these facilities except the Tooele Army Depot directly impacted residents of Davis County. The Ogden Arsenal at Sunset, the Ogden Air Materiel Command area at Hill Field, and the U.S. Naval Supply Depot at Clearfield occupied land in Davis County. The Utah General Depot near Ogden was located in nearby Weber County. All of these facilities served as supply depots, and some of them provided maintenance and repair services. The military support zone in the Clearfield-Ogden area resulted in new jobs and increased populations during the war and a lasting impact on the economy and social makeup of the area.[40]

The first of the depots established in Davis County was set up after the close of World War I. Investigators chose the Ogden area when they sought out inland sites that were close to railroads and highways. Opened in 1921, the Ogden Arsenal stored 15 percent of the unused and obsolete ammunition left over from the war. The munitions were housed in large hollow tile magazines built on a 1,200-acre site east of Sunset, property formerly used as family farms.

Over time, the facility languished. The Ogden Chamber of Commerce petitioned federal authorities in 1935 to reactivate the neglected depot to help relieve the impact of the Depression. The Works Progress Administration spent several million dollars building a new ammunition loading plant that employed a hundred workers beginning in 1938. During World War II, the Ogden Arsenal loaded small-caliber artillery shells and bombs and shipped all types of ordnance items plus vehicles, small arms, and artillery to various ports in the western United States. As the facility was expanded to accommodate its new wartime mission, employment mushroomed by 1943 to 6,000 civilians. With the close of the war, employment dropped to fewer than 1,500, but it doubled during the Korean conflict. It then dropped to 500 before the depot was closed in August 1954. At that time, the depot's inventory was shipped to Tooele Ordnance Depot and the land became Hill Air Force Base's West Area. In 1960 the Air Materiel Command gave Hill the worldwide responsibility for U.S. Air Force ammunition. When the assembly and storage of Minuteman missiles was assigned to Hill, it was the old Arsenal site that housed that program.[41]

Hill Air Force Base (HAFB), originally known as Hill Field, was the site for the Ogden Air Depot, whose name underwent several changes until it became the Ogden Air Materiel Area. The depot's original mission was to repair and maintain aircraft and provide supply services for the Army Air Corps. Launched in 1938 as a WPA project on a hilltop section of Davis County dry-farm land, by 1943 Hill Field was the largest employer in Utah. In addition to 6,000 military personnel on duty during World War II, the base hired 15,000 civilians, many of them from north Davis County, and put several thousand prisoners of war to work.[42]

Like the Arsenal, the Ogden Air Depot at Hill Field was established through the encouragement of the Ogden Chamber of Commerce in an attempt to boost the local economy. The site was selected in 1935 and the first facility built by the WPA four years later. The chamber of commerce donated some of the land to make the project possible. Hill Field was named after Major Ployer P. Hill, who was killed in 1935 while testing a Boeing XB-17 "Flying Fortress" bomber at Wright Field in Dayton, Ohio. During World War II, the

By early 1944, the runways, aircraft operations hangars, shops, officers' quarters, and Hillcrest Villa—civilian dormitories for single men and women (lower left, near the South Gate)—were among the facilities completed at Hill Field. (Utah State Historical Society)

depot's mission included repair of various aircraft and engines, parachutes, bombsights, and radios. As a supply depot, the installation shipped parts and equipment for airplanes.

After the war, Hill Field became a storage facility for surplus materiel, including the B-29 Superfortress. It was during the late 1940s that the depot was renamed the Ogden Air Materiel Area (OOAMA) and Hill Field became Hill Air Force Base. The Korean conflict saved the base from closing in 1950 and prompted construction of a modern runway. Civilian employment jumped again to more than 12,000. During the 1950s, as part of a specialization plan adopted by the U.S. Air Force, the base was given responsibility for specific airplanes. Among them were the F-89, F-84, and F-101 jet fighters. As the base's maintenance work increased, its depot function was dispersed. By 1958 more than half of OOAMA's supply work had been given to local contractors, who shipped goods directly to West

Coast ports. Even with this dispersal, the base retained a steady civilian employment of nearly 12,000 men and women during the 1950s and 1960s; another 3,000 military personnel also worked at the base.[43]

Hill Air Force Base took on a new profile when Utah became a major player in the missile industry. The base continued its specialized work with airmunitions and explosives and its aircraft maintenance work while adding responsibilities for a variety of experimental missiles, including the Genie rocket and Bomark ground-to-air interceptor. In 1959 the Minuteman missile became a mainstay. This three-stage, solid-propellant missile was assembled at Hill Air Force Base by the Boeing Company using components made in Utah by Thiokol Chemical Corporation, Hercules Powder Company, and other firms. Boeing leased the government-owned plant. Hill provided logistical support, maintenance, and repair for the missile system. By 1970 Hill Air Force Base was a well-established presence in Davis County and the state's largest employer, with a payroll of more than $100,000 million.[44]

Though not as large nor as lasting in their impact, two other depots contributed to the transformation of northern Davis County from an agricultural economy to one with a strong federal presence. During World War II, the U.S. Navy set up three inland supply depots to buy and ship equipment and supplies and handle the movement of personnel. The U.S. Naval Supply Depot at Clearfield managed this task for three West Coast ports serving the Pacific Fleet. In addition to managing an inventory of about 500,000 items, the depot distributed automotive and other materiel for selected activities in three naval districts stretching from North Dakota to Texas. Navy scouts chose the Clearfield site over Farmington because of its potential for expansion. When farm families opposed the loss of 1,600 acres of choice sugar beet and vegetable cropland, local government, business, and church leaders suggested other sites, including one near Woods Cross. The Clearfield site received strong support from the Ogden Chamber of Commerce, however. When the Navy stood by its original decision, Utah officials convinced the Clearfield farmers to sell for the economic good of the entire area.

The $37 million depot opened in 1943 with warehouses spanning nearly 8 million square feet, plus a similar amount of open stor-

Among the equipment and supplies transhipped by the Naval Supply Depot at Clearfield to West Coast ports were these buoys made in Minneapolis. (Utah State Historical Society)

age space. The depot soon counted nearly 8,000 civilian employees and an inventory valued at three times all the property of Utah. At its peak in 1944, the depot received 2.5 million tons of materiel in nearly 31,000 boxcars and shipped half that amount in an around-the-clock operation. Workers dispatched items such as clothing, general supplies, spare parts, hospital units, and electronics.[45]

As World War II drew to a close, employment at the Naval Supply Depot was scaled back gradually. Closure was rumored in the late 1940s, but the base remained open. During the postwar years, the Clearfield depot warehoused and surplused unused materiel. In April 1946 the prisoner of war camp was disbanded and the men were returned to their homelands. The depot's civilian force remained stable until after the Korean War, then slid downward from around 3,000 to 1,300 as local workers left to take jobs in private businesses. All but the disposal operations were phased-out during this period.

When the depot closed in 1962, its remaining $430 million inventory was transferred to the Defense Depot Ogden and the Tooele Army Depot. Most of the remaining 435 employees found work at other Utah military installations.[46]

After the base's closure, the depot buildings were put to other uses. The dissemination of hydrographic charts for the Pacific Area remained at Clearfield under the Navy Oceanographic Distribution Office. Added was a supply distribution facility operated by the General Services Administration to serve six western states. Of special significance to Davis County's economy was the sale of nearly two-thirds of the depot's land for use as an industrial park—the Freeport Center. The Clearfield Job Corps, operated by Thiokol Corporation under a contract with the Department of Labor, occupied another seventy acres in 1966. Facilities were built to house and train more than a thousand youths annually to prepare them for jobs or military service. Many of the 350 Job Corps staff members became residents of the north Davis area.[47]

The fourth area military facility, the Utah General Depot, was built in 1941 to serve the U.S. Army. Later known as Defense Depot Ogden, the repository warehoused quartermaster supplies and shipped them to the war zones through ports on the West Coast. The site, known locally as "Second Street," was located on nearly 1,700 acres of prime farmland near Marriott, northwest of Ogden. The facility was built with a small subsidy from the Ogden Chamber of Commerce and was expanded during World War II to accomodate an expanded mission. At its peak, the facility employed 4,000 civilians and 5,000 prisoners of war and was the largest wartime quartermaster depot in the country.

The depot's eight original warehouses increased to twenty-eight during the war, with a total of 5 million square feet of enclosed space. Shipping 200 boxcars a day during the war, the storehouse handled more supplies than the other three northern Utah depots combined. After the war, the depot housed returned materiel for storage and disposal. It served during the Korean conflict, then reduced its employment to around 3,000. During the 1950s, the depot became host to other government facilities, including some functions of the Ogden Arsenal and a service center of the Internal Revenue Service. With 6 million square feet of covered storage space available by the late 1960s, "Second Street" remained one of the largest supply depots in the nation and an important factor in the Weber-Davis economy.[48]

The economic impact of wartime spending created a new prosperity unknown in Davis County since before the Great Depression. The most obvious boost was the creation of thousands of new jobs at the depots and thousands more in temporary construction work to meet the need for facilities, housing, and schools. Sunset, Clearfield, and Layton became "bedroom communities" to the military depots. In addition, the government and its employees purchased goods and services locally. Some farmland was sacrificed for military installations and housing in the northern region and for oil refineries along the county's southwest border; even so, price supports and the demand for farm products increased agricultural income. Government controls and quotas were a continuation of the Depression-era programs of the Agricultural Adjustment Administration. During the war, the AAA's Davis County office—renamed the Davis County Defense Board—set higher crop production goals in the federal "Food for Victory" drive. Local farmers generally approved of these actions because of the positive impact on profits.[49]

Recruiting thousands of workers for the Davis-Weber depots was a challenging task, as there often was a need for additional help. Many of the resident civilian employees of the two-county region liked the security of government employment. Farming became a part-time occupation for many; for others a defense job was viewed as overtime work to supplement farm income. Most employees saw the work as a patriotic duty. Enlistment in the military had diminished the pool of available white men, so recruiters encouraged nonwhites and women to apply. The limited number of nonwhite residents in Utah led to recruiting outside the state. The Naval Supply Depot, for example, brought in more than 2,400 African Americans from the South. The depot also employed Native Americans recruited from New Mexico and Arizona as part of the federal *bracero* project. Japanese Americans who had been interned during the war hired on as well. Students commuted to the federal workplaces from as far away as Logan. Retired persons and people with physical handicaps also

Mardell Burnett, seen with fellow supervisor Ervin G. Heslop in the parachute repair shop at Hill Field, was one of many women who found work at military installations in the Davis-Weber area. (Utah State Historical Society)

joined the work force. Nonwhite residents found that work was readily available not just in the defense installations but on the railroads and farms as well. Many of the new arrivals worked a combination of these jobs.[50]

During World War II, many Utah women joined the civilian forces at defense plants and military installations. They worked as drivers, guards, ammunition inspectors, safety specialists, machinists, and in other traditionally male jobs. For most women, this was their first job outside the home. They went to work in slacks, a new phenomenon for American women. Other women volunteered in hospitals, helped the Red Cross or USO, or cared for children whose mothers were working. Utah's newspapers joined the plea for women workers, reminding them that it was their patriotic duty to apply for the positions at the military depots. Women responded in such great numbers that by 1944 they constituted 37 percent of the Utah labor force, double the percentage of four years earlier. Even with this government work for men and women, agriculture remained a dominant way of life in the Davis region and women retained primary responsibility for housework and the care of young children. On-site nurseries offered help at many government facilities.[51]

While the defense jobs attracted thousands of local and transplanted workers, many positions at the military installations remained unfilled. Davis County farms experienced a similar labor shortage, caused largely by the loss of farm workers to high-paying defense jobs. To compensate for the loss, government agencies increased wartime food production quotas on the farms and helped recruit farm laborers. In 1942, for example, sixty-six Japanese Americans from a relocation camp in Arizona helped with the tomato and beet harvest in Davis County. Two years later, the county commissioners rented land in Laytona and set up a farm labor camp for around 200 Mexican nationals. Some POWs from the Italian and German camps in Ogden also augmented farm labor.[52]

Temporary workers moving in from other locations created an unprecedented demand for housing in the Davis-Weber region. Because living quarter were scarce, some local residents took in single workers as boarders. Apartments were developed hastily in basements or spare rooms, and even in chicken coops. To prevent profiteering in what was a nationwide housing shortage, Congress froze rents in July 1942. New accommodations were rushed to completion to fill the local need. In the Layton area, private landowners developed the Hill Villa, Skyline, and Ellison subdivisions. When these failed to meet the need, the government shipped in 300 trailer homes to create the twenty-acre Layton Trailer Park on Easy Street (Hill Field Road, on land later developed as the Layton Hills Mall). Prefabricated Quonset huts were built at the Naval Supply Depot as dormitories for single men. New government villages appeared almost overnight to house families who could not find housing—200 units at Anchorage in the Clearfield area; 400 at Verdeland Park, just east of downtown Layton; a similar number at Arsenal Villa in Sunset; and 600 multiplex apartments at Sahara Village near Hill Field's south gate. Some of the government housing was built over the protests of local home builders and property owners, but more than half of all new housing was privately built. Most of that was financed through loans from the Federal Housing Administration. To compensate for gasoline and automobile shortages, buses were provided to transport personnel to work from the satellite communities.[53]

Typical of the temporary government homes were the 600 four-plex units built by the Federal Public Housing Authority at Sahara Village, a symmetrical assemblage near the south gate of Hill Field. For about thirty-four dollars a month, a renter got an apartment with a concrete floor in a painted cinderblock building. Each unit came with a coal heater, gas stove, gas water heater, and electric refrigerator, along with a table, four chairs, and single beds. Utilities and maintenance were provided at no extra cost. Serving the community of 1,800 residents were a grocery store, meat market, drug store, barber shop, beauty shop, tailor shop, weekly newspaper (the *Sahara Star*), and post office. Religious services, a children's nursery, dances, and other recreational activities were available in a recreation hall within the village's administration building. "Utah's Fastest Growing Community," as it was called, was created in the pattern of the company towns seen previously in Utah only in mining areas. Similar support services were available at the other government housing parks built to sustain the war effort.[54]

Wartime military installations created a need for new schools. In the early 1940s the Davis School District built the Sahara Village, Verdeland Park, and Hilltop elementary schools in the Layton area and Wasatch Elementary in Clearfield. In 1939 the district had opened North Davis Junior High School in Clearfield and added a southwest classroom wing to Davis High School to serve increased enrollments.[55]

The Home Front in Transition

The precedent-setting recruitment of women into the work force proved to be temporary for many of these workers. As employment was scaled back, a good number of the women workers once again became full-time homemakers. They did so with the encouragement of civic and church leaders, who sustained a widely held belief that most jobs should be reserved for returning war veterans. Most women agreed that they had done men's work only as a patriotic obligation and preferred to return to the home. Those who remained in government jobs often did so at reduced pay in comparison to that received by men. Many of them were shunted to "pink collar" work such as secretaries and clerks. A number of the women who left military jobs did so to get married or follow their husbands, and those who remained at work were usually older.[56]

During the war, the percentage of Utah women in the labor force jumped from 17.6 percent in 1940 to a wartime high of 36.8 percent in 1944. It slid to 24.3 percent in 1950, then began a steady climb. By 1960 the rate was 32.4 percent; a decade later it had reached 41.5 percent; and in 1980 there were 49.6 percent of the state's women working outside the home. Ten years later, the rate had increased to 61 percent, with Davis County's participation two percentage points below the state's. Women in the labor force discovered an increasingly greater social tolerance, and job opportunities became increasingly available. Two incomes were needed by many families to keep up with inflation and economic necessity. The trend in Utah, including Davis County, echoed the national experience.[57]

A study of women leaders in Davis County at mid-century found them goal-oriented, well-educated, and satisfied with life and with their families and social involvements, work, and income. These community leaders had found ways to contribute both professionally and through community service. According to this 1959 study, women dominated the administrative staff of the county library system; however, in the county school system no women were serving in administration, on the board, or as school principals. Women were found only as nurses, case workers, or clerks in the county health and public welfare organizations. "Women have fitted their time into the cultural molds which the prevailing system of values prescribes," the study concluded. "Well over half of their public [volunteer] effort is given to religious activities."[58]

The cutback in employment at the area's military facilities after the world war left vacancies in many of the housing units built by the government as temporary quarters. Federal agencies dismantled the Layton Trailer Park on Hill Field Road in 1945, and many renters in the government housing villages purchased permanent homes in new subdivisions. The deterioration of the homes in Verdeland Park and

Sahara Village created a special problem for Layton. The Davis County Commission, the Layton Town Board, and a local housing advisory committee discussed various options, including one that would have designated Sahara Village as a segregated community for African Americans and Hispanics. The cinderblock four-plex rental units at Sahara Village eventually were demolished, and many former residents lived for a time at Verdeland Park.[59]

When the federal government offered to sell the eighty-five-acre Verdeland Park residential area for $600,000, Layton accepted the opportunity. With an agreement to buy the park over a ten-year period, in 1957 Layton City became a landlord. But city officials found it difficult to collect rent on the deteriorating houses. Built of plywood walls and hardwood floors, the twenty-five-year-old duplex units were judged not worth the expense of upgrading. Therefore, the city paid off its government mortgage and in 1964 offered the homes for sale at an average of $260 each. Buyers agreed not to relocate the houses in Layton. The Davis School District purchased twenty-eight acres of the cleared land for a new high school. Over the next twenty years, Layton City developed a large park on the remaining forty-five acres and used an abandoned administrative building as a city office. Later, the city built a municipal building and museum at the site. Some of the original trees planted by Verdeland Park's first residents are the only reminder of the wartime housing development.[60]

Social and Cultural Transformations. The Depression and subsequent world war set in motion significant lifestyle transformations of Davis County residents. Before the war, with people concentrating mostly on economic survival, traditional ways prevailed. During the international conflict, hundreds of citizens fought on the battlefront and thousands more went to work at defense installations. These disruptions exposed people to life outside Utah and altered perspectives at home. During the war, the state's birth rate dropped and divorces became more common. When the veterans came home, Utah's birth rate followed the national trend upward, but at a pace about 25 percent higher than the U.S. average. Even though the Utah divorce rate declined after the war, it remained above the national average. The state's ethnic makeup became more diverse, a changed noted in Davis County mostly in the northern communities.[61]

Peoples with racial, cultural, and religious backgrounds different from those of Davis County's dominant Latter-day Saint majority were drawn to the region mostly because of economic factors. The cultural roots of most Mormons were firmly planted in British and Scandinavian countries. The new families represented other geographical backgrounds. Most of the Asian, African American, Latin American, and southern European immigrants who arrived in Davis County seeking jobs brought other religious and cultural traditions with them. Their presence created a more cosmopolitan community, but, until the broadening of tolerance in the 1960s, all of the new residents faced challenges or prejudices because of their ethnic backgrounds.[62] Even relocated Utah Mormons sometimes found themselves classified by Davis County's old-timers as outsiders. "Protect us from the transients among us," an established farmer prayed from the pulpit of a north Davis LDS meetinghouse in 1944. A transplanted Latter-day Saint mechanic from Park City who was renting a local farmhome while working at the naval base understood the appeal to apply to himself. As soon as housing became available, he moved his family.[63]

Most of the immigrants to northern Davis County overcame such personal affronts and settled in to become permanent residents and contributing citizens. Most of the African Americans who took civilian jobs at the military posts lived in Weber County. In 1942 Ralph Price breached the color barrier to become the first twentieth-century black to settle in Davis County. He was followed by the Leander Henry and James Spinks families. Price was an Army sergeant who oversaw a 250-man construction crew at Hill Field. After his discharge, Price brought his wife, Ruby, and their children to Layton, where they purchased a home. Ruby Price worked at Hill Field and at the Arsenal, where she was a supervisor. After two years' persistence, she received a teaching position in the Davis School District in 1950, becoming the first black teacher in Utah. She taught for twenty-five years and was an active political and religious leader. The African American families who chose to live in Davis County found it difficult to find real estate agents willing to help them buy a home. Sometimes the only way to avoid this prejudice was to work through an Ogden company using multiple-listings.[64]

Japanese immigrants in northwestern Davis County preserved a sense of community in this building, where they educated their own children and attended church. (*The Community of Syracuse*)

Only a few of the immigrants were able to establish their own businesses in Davis County during the middle decades of the century. One of those who did was Greek immigrant Peter Photinakas, who operated a produce stand on the corner of U.S. Highway 91 and Antelope Drive during the late 1930s. John and Katherine Alex opened the Hill Villa Market in 1947 and operated it for nearly twenty years. Besides groceries, they sold fresh produce from their small farm. In Syracuse, Roy Miya opened a garage in 1949 and operated it for thirty-six years. Excellent mechanics, he and his brother Kazuo worked on the Job Corps fleet.[65]

A number of Japanese and Greek immigrants got their first jobs working on Oregon Short Line Railroad maintenance crews, but eventually they joined others who found more satisfying lives as farmworkers. Many fieldhands also found supplementary work at the Layton Sugar Factory. A university student, one K. Ono, whose father was a sharecropper, supervised the workers' camp at the factory. The "K. Ono Camp," as it was known by the workers, became a clearinghouse for new Japanese immigrants seeking work.[66]

Agricultural jobs were easily obtained on the farms of north Davis County. Large landholders hired Filipino, Japanese, Greek, and

Hispanic workers to do the intensive hand work on their sugar beet and vegetable crops. A number of the farmers contracted with immigrants to operate large parcels as sharecroppers. In turn, many of these sharecroppers hired other immigrants as fieldworkers. As early as 1915, at least two dozen Greek families were working farms in the Layton area. Other immigrants found opportunities in nearby communities. When they heard of wartime labor shortages in Davis County's Garden Belt, other Hispanic farmhands relocated from Colorado or New Mexico, where the Depression had deprived them of work. Many of them lived in a worker's camp for Mexican nationals east of the Hill Field Road on Antelope Drive and were transported to their jobs by local farmers.[67]

Over time, increasing numbers of Davis County's sharecroppers desired to own the farms they operated for others. At first, many of the Greek and Japanese sharecroppers did not try to buy land, because their dream was to develop resources to return to their homelands. In 1937–38, Ysaburo Yamane, a Japanese man with American citizenship, was among the first of the ethnic immigrants to buy land in Davis County. A Layton bank agreed to finance his purchase only when the seller, a Mormon farmer, told the banker, "If you aren't going to help this fellow, I am going to take him to a different bank."[68] Other Japanese sharecroppers were not as lucky; in part because of the distrust created by the war, their attempts to become landowners in the Layton area during the 1940s were rebuffed. Even with U.S. citizenship, Japanese families faced obstacles. Wakichi Imada gave up after twelve years as a sharecropper and moved to West Jordan, where local prejudices did not stand in the way of farm ownership. Experienced Hispanic sharecropper Ralph Lopez bought his own farm in the early 1940s and specialized in chili peppers and tomatoes at his Rancho Lopez.[69]

The new wave of nonwhite residents of Davis County did what they could to lessen the social stigma and prejudices they faced. Many first-generation settlers struggled because of language barriers, but their children eventually became proficient in English. Even so, at school the children found themselves shunned or embarrassed by their differences. Mexican-American students felt the brunt of student intolerance. They quickly learned who were their friends and

Greek immigrant farmers Bill and Pete Manis, standing in front of their West Gentile home in 1930, were among those who established farms in northwestern Davis County. (*Layton, Utah: Historic Viewpoints*)

who to avoid. When other youths called them names, they defended their personal dignity with their fists. Such reactions sometimes got the Hispanic youths in trouble with school officials, who were themselves not always sensitive to the need for understanding and accommodation. When ethnic youth were not allowed to join a Little League Baseball program, their spokesmen appealed to the local Community Action Policy Board and then organized two award-winning teams of black, white, and Hispanic youth living in the Anchorage housing unit.[70]

One way some ethnic people found to make assimilation easier was to adjust their names. Greek immigrants typically shortened their surnames to help the English-speaking residents better accept them; for example, Theodorogianos became Thiros and Alexopolos was shortened to Alex. Japanese immigrant men adopted American nicknames (such as Isamu "Harry" Satomura) for the same reason.[71]

Most of the ethnic families retained old-world customs and organized their own social groups to help them manage the transition to life in America. George Nabor started the Filipino Association, which attracted farm families as far away as Brigham City for an annual pork barbecue. The Filipino, Japanese, and Greek communities celebrated their own traditional holidays to keep alive the spirit of their ancestral homes. Before World War II closed it, the "K. Ono Camp" at the Layton Sugar Factory was a gathering place for Japanese bazaars and other get-togethers. Greek residents of Davis County looked to Salt Lake City's Greek Orthodox Church for marriages and other religious rites.[72] Latinos worked together to form the Spanish Speaking Organization for Community Integrity and Opportunity (SOCIO) in the late 1960s to promote Latino culture and equality in housing.[73]

A number of the new residents bridged the gap between cultures and pioneered in areas previously restricted to white citizens. Their example helped open opportunities to others who had been denied their rights as citizens. When the Layton Town Board refused to grant Clarence K. Okuda a business license, he opened his Chop Suey Parlor without one. The city threatened to close the parlor, but Okuda obtained a restraining order and was eventually granted his permit. When Okuda moved to California in 1947, Toko Kuroiwa bought the restaurant and renamed it the Layton Noodle Parlor. The Kuroiwa family operated the popular eating place until the mid-1980s. One successful Latino businessman was Charles Rodardi, Sr., who became lessee of Layton Cold Storage Company after working for a time as a meat cutter with owner B. M. Anderson.[74]

A number of north Davis Hispanics softened area prejudice through their involvement in government and civil rights projects. Erastus Trujillo worked with a civilian contractor who built the government housing at Verdeland Park; he then became maintenance superintendent for that development and for Sahara Village and the Layton Trailer Park. Even though most of the government workers lived in housing apart from the established community, their interactions with established residents increased over time. Some new tenants noticed preferential treatment being given to the area old-timers at Layton businesses. Housing-project managers worked with local communities to resolve issues of water rights and police protection. After the war, returning veterans occupied some of the units, local residents rented others. In time, friendships developed that help erase the barriers between people of different backgrounds.[75] When a chapter of the American G.I. Forum was organized in Ogden in 1954, Joe Trujillo formed a Davis County group in Layton, and he later became

The swimming pool at Lagoon had not been opened to African Americans when this photograph was taken during the July Fourth holiday in 1931. (Utah State Historical Society)

chairman of the state organization. The Forum helped Spanish-speaking veterans obtain schooling and jobs. The organization, founded in Texas in 1947, also helped workers obtain improved living conditions at migrant camps and fair pay for their factory and farm work. Sam Trujillo broke the ethnic barrier and became the first Latino to serve on the Layton City Council.[76]

Through persistence and courage, Davis County's new generation of ethnic pioneers found acceptance and opportunity to become an integral and contributing part of the community—which, in turn, was enriched and broadened by diversity. By 1990 the ethnic component in Davis County remained a distinct but important minority, accounting for 7.3 percent of the total population. The largest ethnic group in the county was Hispanic, at 3.9 percent. In comparison, Salt Lake and Weber Counties registered 10.2 and 10.4 percent minorities in the census count, the state as a whole had 11 percent, and the United States 27 percent. Because of their minority status, the ethnic residents needed and appreciated the help of a number of progressive citizens of Davis County who helped to break the color barriers in various public venues. One of these was Lagoon owner Robert E. Freed, who opened the resort's ballroom and swimming pool to African Americans in the late 1940s and who integrated the company's Rainbow Rendezvous ballroom in Salt Lake City. Other businessmen followed, and Ogden City subsequently ended its longstanding discriminatory policies at the city swimming pool. Greater acceptance, tolerance, and understanding were the products of the melding of peoples with differences into a multifaceted community sharing a broadened social perspective.[77]

Looking back over the first half of the twentieth century must have given many residents of Davis County a sense of relief. They had been part of traumatic national and global events that reshaped the world and left their mark along the Wasatch Front. By the end of World War II, the sense of identity of Davis County citizens had matured as they faced and overcame difficult economic, political, and social challenges. Many residents emerged from the process with a new way of looking at themselves. The population was more diverse and society had become more complex. Many political practices, economic activities, and social relationships had changed. Utah's coming of age as a state had marked the beginning of shifting political patterns; but, more importantly, a state that had shunned a federal presence was now heavily dependent upon military contracts and jobs. New political party affiliations had created divisions within communities as well as political bridges between towns. In addition, as informal communities within the county grew and more of them were incorporated as towns, a civic identity began to replace that of the Mormon ward. Reinforcing that new way of looking at community was the arrival of people of different ethnic and religious backgrounds. Their contributions toward creating a more cosmopolitan population were more evident in the north but still influenced the county as a whole.

Taken together, the political and cultural changes of the early decades of the twentieth century created a new social overlay that reinforced the idea that Davis County consisted of many parts. Those components included religious and political affiliations, place of residence, occupation, and ethnic background. The county had moved from its nineteenth-century rooting in Mormon culture and had begun the gradual process toward a multifaceted redefinition. It was becoming a county made up of people who saw themselves as members of several communities at once. Not only were they members of their religious community, their neighborhood, and their family—typical patterns of identification in the nineteenth century—but they had a heightened sense of being part of an incorporated town, social or civic clubs, an ethnic group, an employment circle, and a county. Most residents lived comfortably in their multifaceted world. Many of them placed one segment ahead of another to give their lives an ordered sense of their own worldview. But the world in 1950 was a great deal different than the world had been one hundred years earlier, and changes would continue beyond the century's midpoint as other generations faced their own experiences with fresh ways of meeting and solving challenges.

ENDNOTES

1. D. Michael Quinn, "The Mormon Church and the Spanish–American War: An End to Selective Pacifism," *Pacific Historical Review* 43 (August 1974): 342–66; Carol Ivins Collett, *Kaysville—Our Town: A History,* 119–20; Annie Call Carr, ed., *East of Antelope Island: History of the First Fifty Years of Davis County,* 500; Margaret Steed Hess, *My Farmington: A History of Farmington, Utah, 1847–1976,* 396.

2. Thomas Alexander, *Utah, The Right Place: The Official Centennial History,* 276–79; "Layton Man First WWI Draftee in County," *Davis County Clipper,* 19 November 1996; Richard C. Roberts, "The Utah National Guard in the Great War, 1917–18," *Utah Historical Quarterly* 58 (Fall 1990): 314–15, 318, 325–29, 333; memorial plaque, Davis County Courthouse, Farmington.

3. Hess, *My Farmington,* 395; Leslie T. Foy, *The City Bountiful: Utah's Second Settlement from Pioneers to Present,* 274; Tom Busselberg, "Social and Cultural Life," in Dan Carlsruh and Eve Carlsruh, eds., *Layton, Utah: Historic Viewpoints,* 218.

4. Annie Clark Tanner, *A Biography of Ezra Thompson Clark* (Salt Lake City: Tanner Trust Fund, University of Utah Library, 1975), 45–53.

5. Author's analysis of census data in *Utah State Gazetteer, 1918–1919* (Salt Lake City: R.L. Polk, 1918), 392–405.

6. Alexander, *Utah, The Right Place,* 279, 296, 302, 310.

7. Ibid., 296–97.

8. Richard D. Poll, Thomas G. Alexander, Eugene E. Campbell, David E. Miller, eds., *Utah's History*, 478–79; Foy, *City Bountiful*, 220.

9. John Kearnes, "Utah, Sexton of Prohibition," *Utah Historical Quarterly* 47 (Winter 1979): 5–21; Poll et al., *Utah's History*, 491.

10. Foy, *City Bountiful*, 310; [Clayton Holt, ed.], *The Community of Syracuse, 1820 to 1995: Our Heritage, Centennial Edition*, 139.

11. Utah State Road Commission, "Mileage of Roads by Surface Type and Administrative System," 1940, typescript, Utah State Archives; Department of Engineering, *Twenty–second Biennial Report of the State Road Commission, 1951–1952*," 144–46, Utah State Archives.

12. Foy, *City Bountiful*, 156–59; *Davis County Clipper*, 24 June, 28 October 1898.

13. Foy, *City Bountiful*, 156–63; Farmington City Council, Minutes, 2 April, 7 May, 18 June 1906; Collett, *Kaysville—Our Town*, 134.

14. Janice P. Dawson, "The Incorporation and Growth of Layton," in Carlsruh and Carlsruh, *Layton, Utah*, 339–41; Collett, *Kaysville—Our Town*, 159–61, 164–65.

15. Mary Ellen Smoot and Marilyn Sheriff, *The City In–Between: History of Centerville, Utah*, 174–76; Holt, *Community of Syracuse*, 311–12, 321–22; *Davis County Clipper*, 17 July 1958.

16. Dawson, "East Layton," 349–51; Doneta McGonigle Gatherum, "Laytona," in Carlsruh and Carlsruh, *Layton, Utah*, 355–57; *Davis County Clipper*, 17 July 1958.

17. LaRue Hugoe and Edith Deppe, *West Bountiful: A Pictorial History, 1848–1988*, 345, 348–51, 353–56.

18. Holt, *Community of Syracuse*, 124; Hess, *My Farmington*, 14; Foy, *City Bountiful*, 219, 230; Lee D. Bell, *South Weber: The Autobiography of One Utah Community*, 427–33; Smoot and Sheriff, *City In–Between*, 120.

19. Holt, *Community of Syracuse*, 114–16, 387; Doneta McGonigle Gatherum, "Layton Elementary: The Beginning of Graded Schools and Consolidation," in Carlsruh and Carlsruh, *Layton, Utah*, 141–47; Foy, *City Bountiful*, 83, 203–5; Hugoe and Deppe, *West Bountiful*, 98–99.

20. Hess, *My Farmington*, 351; Bell, *South Weber*, 213; Smoot and Sheriff, *City In–Between*, 74–76; Collett, *Kaysville—Our Town*, 62, 117; Arlene H. Eakle, Adelia Baird, and Georgia Weber, *Woods Cross: Patterns and Profiles of a City*, 45; Holt, *Community of Syracuse*, 144–45.

21. L. R. Humpherys, ed., *Utah—Resources and Activities* (Salt Lake City: Utah Department of Public Instruction, 1933), 221–22.

22. Holt, *Community of Syracuse*, 146–47; Collett, *Kaysville—Our*

Town, 139; Gatherum, "Layton Elementary," 147; "*Deseret News,* 19 October 1963.

23. Foy, *City Bountiful,* 206–9; Hugoe and Deppe, *West Bountiful,* 139; Humpherys, *Utah—Resources and Activities,* 231.

24. Alexander, *Utah, The Right Place,* 311; Leonard J. Arrington, "Utah's Great Drought of 1934," *Utah Historical Quarterly* 54 (Summer 1986): 245–64.

25. Alexander, *Utah, The Right Place,* 313–15.

26. Ibid., 316–20, 323. For additional information see Wayne K. Hinton, "The Economics of Ambivalence: Utah's Depression Experience," *Utah Historical Quarterly* 54 (Summer 1986): 268–85, and R. Thomas Quinn, "Out of the Depression's Depths: Henry H. Blood's First Year as Governor," *Utah Historical Quarterly* 54 (Summer 1986): 216–39.

27. A. Russell Croft and Reed W. Bailey, *Mountain Water* (Ogden: U.S. Department of Agriculture, 1964), 45; A. Russell Croft, *Rainstorm Debris Floods: A Problem in Public Welfare* (Tucson: University of Arizona, 1967), 3, 15; Andrew M. Honker, "'Been Grazed Almost to Extinction': The Environment, Human Action, and Utah Flooding, 1900–1940," *Utah Historical Quarterly* 67 (Winter 1999): 36–37, 40–41.

28. Honker, "Utah Flooding," 35–39; Joshua H. Paul and F.S. Baker, "The Floods of 1923 in Northern Utah," *Bulletin of the University of Utah* 15, no. 3 (March 1925): 3–20.

29. Croft and Bailey, *Mountain Water,* 46; Honker, "Utah Flooding," 42–44; Bernard DeVoto, "Restoration in the Wasatch," *The American Scholar* (Autumn 1949): 428.

30. Honker, "Utah Flooding," 42–45; Croft and Bailey, *Mountain Water,* 25, 32–34; Croft, *Rainstorm Debris Floods,* 24–25.

31. Croft and Bailey, *Mountain Water,* 46; Croft, *Rainstorm Debris Floods,* 28.

32. Croft and Bailey, *Mountain Water,* 30–31, 55–57.

33. Kenneth W. Baldridge, "Reclamation Work of the Civilian Conservation Corps, 1933–1942," *Utah Historical Quarterly* 39 (Summer 1971): 265–70; *Deseret News,* 15 April 1990; Beth R. Olsen, "Utah's CCCs: The Conservators' Medium for Young Men, Nature, Economy, and Freedom," *Utah Historical Quarterly* 62 (Summer 1994): 262–63; Hugoe and Deppe, *West Bountiful,* 268–69; *Weekly Reflex,* 19 September 1940.

34. Twila Van Leer, "CCC Camp Changed Utah—and Lives of Workers," *Deseret News,* 8 August 1995; Olsen, "Utah's CCCs," 264–65; Gingery, "Watershed Terraces."

35. Poll et al., *Utah's History,* 509. List of women provided by Utah

State Historical Society; those who died are listed in a 1996 Centennial Legacy memorial at the Davis County Courthouse.

36. *Weekly Reflex,* 16 October 1941.

37. See *County Agent Annual Report, 1942* (Farmington, Utah: Davis County Extension Service, 1943).

38. Jessie L. Embry, "Fighting the Good Fight: The Utah Home Front during World War II," *Utah Historical Quarterly* 63 (Summer 1995): 242–65; Holt, *Community of Syracuse,* 338–39.

39. Holt, *Community of Syracuse,* 337–38; Ralph A. Busco and Douglas D. Alder, "German and Italian Prisoners of War in Utah and Idaho," *Utah Historical Quarterly* 39 (Winter 1971): 57 n., 62–69.

40. Antonette Chambers Noble, "Utah's Defense Industries and Workers in World War II," *Utah Historical Quarterly* 59 (Fall 1991): 367–69.

41. Thomas G. Alexander, "Ogden's 'Arsenal of Democracy,' 1920–1955," *Utah Historical Quarterly* 33 (Summer 1965): 237–47.

42. Noble, "Utah's Defense Industries," 368; Christensen, "Impact of World War II," 500; Collett, *Kaysville—Our Town,* 165–68.

43. Leonard J. Arrington, Thomas G. Alexander, and Eugene A. Erb, Jr., "Utah's Biggest Business: Ogden Air Materiel Area at Hill Air Force Base, 1938–1965," *Utah Historical Quarterly* 33 (Winter 1965): 9–21.

44. Ibid., 22–31; Leonard J. Arrington and John G. Perry," Utah's Spectacular Missile Industry: Its History and Impact," *Utah Historical Quarterly* 30 (Winter 1962): 9–11, 35–36.

45. Kent Day, "The Impact of Hill Air Force Base," in Carlruh and Carlruh, *Layton, Utah,* 399; Leonard J. Arrington and Archer L. Durham, "Anchors Aweigh in Utah: The U.S. Naval Supply Depot at Clearfield, 1942–1962," *Utah Historical Quarterly* 31 (Spring 1963): 109–17.

46. Arrington and Durham, "Anchors Aweigh," 118–23.

47. Ibid., 115–26; Collett, *Kaysville—Our Town,* 170–71.

48. Leonard J. Arrington and Thomas G. Alexander, "Supply Hub of the West: Defense Depot Ogden, 1941–1964," *Utah Historical Quarterly* 32 (Spring 1964): 99–121; Noble, "Utah's Defense Industries," 367–68.

49. Christensen, "The Impact of World War II," 498–504; *Reflex,* 12 February 1942.

50. Noble, "Utah's Defense Industries," 371–74; Holt, *Community of Syracuse,* 335–38; Arrington and Alexander, "Supply Hub of the West," 104–5; Arrington and Durham, "Anchors Aweigh," 113–15; Joel Passey, "Ethnic Groups," in Carlsruh and Carlsruh, *Layton, Utah,* 364–65, 371, 378.

51. Holt, *Community of Syracuse,* 335–38; Arrington and Alexander,

"Supply Hub of the West," 104–5; Noble, "Utah's Rosies: Women in the Utah War Industries during World War II," *Utah Historical Quarterly* 59 (Spring 1991): 126–30.

52. *County Agent Annual Report, 1942.* See also reports for 1944, 1945, and 1946.

53. Holt, *Community of Syracuse,* 335–36; Day, "Impact of Hill Air Force Base," 400; Ross Poore and Stephen Ronnenkamp, "Government Housing Projects," in Carlruh and Carlruh, *Layton, Utah,* 407–9; Noble, "Utah's Defense Industries," 374–75; Arrington, Alexander, and Erb, "Utah's Biggest Business," 14, 19.

54. Poore and Ronnenkamp, "Government Housing Projects," 407–9, 411–13.

55. *Davis County: Land of Peace, Beauty, and a Quality Life* (Davis School District, 1994), 11, 33; Gatherum, "Layton Elementary," 147.

56. Noble, "Utah's Rosies," 130–38, 142–45.

57. Ibid., 139–41; Kimberley A. Bartel, *Davis County: A Demographic and Economic Profile* (Salt Lake City: Utah Department of Employment Security, 1996), 26.

58. Carmen Daines Fredrickson, *The Impact of Women Leaders of Davis County on a Changing Order,* Agricultural Experiment Station Bulletin 406 (Logan: Utah State University, 1959), 4–10, 17–18, 21–25.

59. Day, "Impact of Hill Air Force Base," 402, 404; Poore and Ronnenkamp, "Government Housing Projects," 412, 416.

60. Day, "Impact of Hill Air Force Base," 402, 404; Poore and Ronnenkamp, "Government Housing Projects," 412, 417–19; *Deseret News,* 26 January 1965, 8A.

61. Christensen, "Impact of World War II," 508–9, 512.

62. Passey, "Ethnic Groups," 363–93.

63. The story was shared with the author during an informal conversation in the late 1960s.

64. Passey, "Ethnic Groups," 386–90.

65. Ibid., 379; Holt, *Community of Syracuse,* 357.

66. Passey, "Ethnic Groups," 363–65.

67. Ibid., 365, 370–71, 380–81.

68. Ibid., 366, 372.

69. Ibid., 366, 382.

70. Ibid., 368, 376–77, 383–85.

71. Ibid. 369.

72. Ibid., 364–65, 368–77.

73. Alexander, *Utah, The Right Place,* 391.

74. Passey, "Ethnic Groups," 367–68, 382.

75. Ibid., 382–83; Day, "Impact of Hill Air Force Base," 402.

76. Passey, "Ethnic Groups," 384–85.

77. Alexander, *Utah, The Right Place,* 390; Bartel, *Davis County: A Demographic and Economic Profile,* 10–11; Day, "Impact of Hill Air Force Base," 402; Poore and Ronnenkamp, "Government Housing Projects," 412, 418–19.

CHAPTER 10

PLANNING FOR THE FUTURE

Davis County's history in the twentieth century was clearly part of a larger story. In all corners of the American West, the Second World War left its impact. Defense industries and military installations created an economy increasingly dependent on the federal government. After the war, politicians worked to keep the jobs for their hometown voters. At the same time, businessmen sought to diversify the economy in the federally impacted areas. The New Deal's "alphabet agencies" changed the way local governments worked. A pent-up demand for consumer goods fueled an economic boom, and increasing prosperity and population growth sustained it. Sprawling suburban developments in the Los Angeles area spawned a new limited-access local highway system. It was much imitated in western and southwestern metropolises and elsewhere. In many respects, it was the western urban revolution that set the pattern for a new American way of life.

The West also gained new political clout. Hollywood rolled out a glitzy pop culture. California ranch homes and backyard pools became the standard for leisure living. In these and other ways, western ways began to dominate American lifestyles in the late twentieth century. Although influenced by national events—such as the civil rights movement, a restructured national economy, the international energy crisis, and foreign wars—the West (and Davis County as one component of the West) developed its own identity. That identity was centered around the rapid growth of metropolitan areas and defined by suburbs and freeways.[1]

Creating Suburbia on the Land In-between

Without question, one of the major stories in Davis County's late twentieth-century history was that of growth. The county experienced a phenomenal burst of population in the years during and after the Second World War. The increase continued through the remainder of the century, and with it came ribbons of asphalt, dozens of new schools and churches, a flowering of local businesses, and a landscape blanketed with homes. The migration of new workers to the county's defense depots started the upward swing of population. Then war veterans returned home to marry and establish families. Soon a new generation of postwar babies contributed to the county's growth. Davis County's population grew from 11,450 in 1920 to 15,784 in 1940. Then, in the next ten years, it doubled to 30,867. The county doubled in size again to 64,750 residents by 1960. At that point, given the large population base and the increasingly limited amount of buildable land, it would seem unlikely that the county would ever again see another doubling in a single decade. Statisticians ranked Davis County's explosive swelling during the 1950s as the second-fastest growth rate for any county in the nation.[2]

Beginning in 1960 the county added more than 40,000 people each ten years, with the larger numbers in the earlier decades. These numerically similar increases meant that the growth rate, or percentage of increase, was slowing, as was true in other counties along the Wasatch Front as their land was gradually built upon. Nevertheless, 40,000 new people every decade made a significant difference in Davis County. Sustained growth was made possible due to people moving into the county as well as a high birth rate. During the 1960s, for example, there was a net in-migration of 15,855 people, who purchased the new housing available in the county's suburban develop-

In 1931, one thousand people lived in a still rural Kaysville. The community doubled in population during the next twenty years, and by 1990 counted nearly fifteen thousand residents. (Utah State Historical Society)

ments. Natural increase during this same decade (births minus deaths) accounted for the remaining 18,413 new residents.[3] Davis County's population grew to 99,028 in 1970, to 146,540 in the 1980 census, and to 187,941 by 1990. At that time, state planners projected 229,264 people in the county by the year 2000, a number that was reached by the beginning of 1999. New estimates anticipated around 235,000 residents by the dawn of the new millennium. With only 149 acres of habitable land, the state's smallest county faced build-out with a projected population of 382,000 about the year 2030—that is, if the 2 percent annual growth rate of the 1990s continues.[4]

If viewed from the perspective of someone living in the county at mid-century, the growth has been almost unimaginable. From 1900, with a base population of some 8,000 people, it had taken forty years to achieve a net increase of 7,000. Then, beginning in 1950, the county added more than the entire population of that year in each succeeding decade. In the 1980 census, Davis County had 2,000 more people than its neighboring county to the north, and the difference has widened since then. Since 1980, Davis has been ranked third in population among Utah's counties—after Salt Lake and Utah.

Because in land area Davis is Utah's smallest county, it is not surprising that in population density it has ranked second behind Salt

Lake County since 1960. Davis County's population density grew from 242 people per square mile in 1960 to 333 ten years later. During that same time, Salt Lake County's density moved from 501 to 600 per square mile. By 1995, Davis County had become as densely populated as Salt Lake County was in 1970; Salt Lake was nearing 1,000 per square mile.[5]

The county's growth moved it from a rural to a suburban designation, or, as defined by federal measurements, into the realm of the urban. The 1920 census revealed the beginnings of an urban metropolitan area along the Wasatch Front in Utah, Salt Lake, Davis, and Weber Counties. In Davis County at that time no towns had the minimum population of 2,500 people needed to qualify as urban; the largest cities in 1920 were Bountiful, with 2,063 people, Farmington with 1,170, Layton with 1,150, and Kaysville with 809. Bountiful crossed the line to become an urban city in the next census, Layton and Clearfield during the wartime boom of the 1940s, and Sunset and Kaysville in the early 1950s. Centerville followed in the early 1960s and Woods Cross later in that decade. Farmington qualified in 1970, followed within a few years by Syracuse and North Salt Lake. Clinton, Fruit Heights, and West Bountiful also became urban during that decade. The last of Davis County's cities to reach urban status were West Point, during the early 1980s, and South Weber, later in that decade.

The growth in individual towns and cities was influenced by economic incentives that fed the growth. In south Davis County, growth during the 1950s and 1960s followed a suburbanizing pattern. The greater Bountiful area reflected the expansion of Salt Lake City northward. Orchards disappeared and subdivisions blossomed as new suburban bedroom communities for workers in Salt Lake. Northern Davis County included some suburban growth because of its proximity to Ogden. More important was the presence of the defense installations. These government employers and buyers of goods and services caused phenomenal growth along the transportation corridor defined by U.S. Highway 91 and the Union Pacific Railroad line.[6] It was military-oriented employment that pushed Layton's population during the 1940s from 646 to 3,456, and in the next decade to 9,027. Unprecedented growth in the 1980s made

From a population of thirty-four hundred in 1940, when a *Salt Lake Tribune* photographer made this picture, Bountiful doubled in the next ten years, then nearly tripled by 1960 as subdivisions expanded the city's boundaries south and east toward the mountains. (Utah State Historical Society)

Layton the county's fastest-growing and largest city, with 41,784 people. Bountiful had peaked in the late 1970s and counted 36,659 in 1990. Other cities exceeding 10,000 people in the 1990 census were Clearfield, 21,435; Kaysville, 13,961; and Centerville, 11,500. Farmington counted 9,028 in 1990 and Clinton 7,945. Most of the other cities had populations ranging between 4,000 and 5,500.

The conversion of farmland into homesites did not win universal acceptance in Davis County. Governor George D. Clyde echoed the sentiment of those who favored a retention of the county's agrarian base. During remarks at a dedicatory program for an addition to the county courthouse in 1958, the governor cautioned farmers not to sell their rich black soil to developers. "The day will come," he said, when we will regret having covered our valuable, productive farm lands with concrete. The homes should be built along the mountain terraces where land is unproductive agriculturally, but the view as home sites is excellent."[7] Most of the early subdivisions did hug the foothills, for that is where land was available for purchase. The Bountiful area saw such expansion replace the productive orchard land. In later decades, the rich loam of the lowland farms from North Salt Lake and Woods Cross to Clinton and West Point felt the encroachment of suburbia.

Planning for Growth. The process of change did not go without notice in Davis County. Community leaders and the people they served cared about the county's future and the impact of expanding populations. "Urban growth is a challenge," the Board of County Commissioners noted in 1966: "A challenge that directly concerns the people."[8] To prepare for the future, the commissioners organized citizen planning councils to study various issues and to prepare plans for the two halves of the county. The South Davis plan was completed in June 1966 under the chairmanship of Ezra T. Clark and Harold J. Tippetts. A North Davis plan followed two years later, under the guidance of Stanley H. Stringham and C. G. "Bud" Tice. In the interest of unity, the second report was expanded at the request of the county commissioners to create an overall master plan for the entire county. The countywide summary was drawn from individual plans created by each city as guidelines for managing future growth.[9]

These plans were the product of a cooperative effort of county planners, economic analysts at the University of Utah, and seven citizen committees from each city. Each citizen group focussed on specific aspects of the physical development of the area, such as land use, traffic patterns, and public facilities. In all of the reports, countywide planning and coordination was strongly recommended.[10]

The issues defined by the study committees became a focus not just for the 1970s but for the 1980s and 1990s as well. In other words, the challenges of growth identified in those reports continued to be important as the years rolled on. The citizen groups urged planners to lessen the impact of urban sprawl on agricultural land and preserve the county's rural flavor. Even so, they recognized that first the southern farms and eventually the entire county might someday succumb to urbanization. They hoped at best that planning would prevent a fragmented, leap-frog approach to expansion resulting in landlocked farm parcels. The study committees recommended clustering subdivisions around a neighborhood center consisting of a school, playground, and city park. They urged multiple uses for school buildings. Other recommendations included establishing recreational trails and scenic roads, including one through Farmington Canyon to Morgan County. The committees hoped to consolidate the buying power of Davis County residents and end the haphazard spread of commercial development. Rather than more strip developments, they recommended strengthened downtown business areas or establishing new clustered shopping centers. The study groups liked the taxes and jobs generated by industries but were concerned over the related pollution, waste disposal, and other environmental and zoning matters. The need for the careful study and coordination of transportation needs was obvious. Among the long-range proposals were a border-to-border West Davis expressway and a boulevard to run along the east bench from Ensign Peak to East Layton. Of immediate need, the report said, were more east-west and intercity connecting roads.[11]

These studies of the late 1960s and a subsequent evaluation of the work gave county officials by 1970 a comprehensive view of where most residents wanted it to go over the next twenty years. Implementation was left to those in municipal offices with zoning and permit-granting authority. "Actual happenings will probably fall somewhere in between recommended development and current land uses," the county plan acknowledged.[12] Much that was viewed as favorable was accomplished. Some recommendations failed under the pressures of growth. Many hopes remained unfulfilled thirty years later. Most of the issues remained of concern to citizens trying to prepare Davis County for continued growth in a new century.

Urban and Suburban Models. By 1960 Davis County had qualified under federal guidelines as an urban county. Ten years earlier, the census had identified 46 percent of the county's total population as urban and 54 percent as rural. The 1960 census certified that the county had changed radically in ten years. By that year, 80 percent of residents, or nearly 52,000 people, lived in areas of the county defined as urban.[13]

Urbanization generally signalled a shift toward a different approach to life than that found in rural agricultural regions, and greater diversity among the population. Among the factors evident in Davis County's gradual move toward urbanization during the 1950s were increased numbers of women working outside the home and a greater variety of religious denominations and special-interest groups. Urban areas not only had more businesses but many specialized services and stores. Better libraries, more living conveniences, and expanded educational offerings were other characteristics of urban areas. Each of Davis County's cities organized a planning commission to consider ways to deal with the suburbs sprouting in the areas surrounding the town centers. Newcomers brought fresh ideas into each community, but the established residents often opposed their views. In all of these categories, Davis County qualified as an urban area moving away from its rural past.[14]

A survey of county residents in the mid-1950s found them divided but generally satisfied with the changes that had taken place. Not surprisingly, the strongest negative reactions were expressed by older residents living in Layton and Clearfield, two of the areas hardest hit by the intrusion of the defense installations onto fertile farms. Residents of south and central county communities enjoyed the economic benefits of expansion without carrying the obligation of accommodating so many new people. Their satisfaction with the changes was higher.[15]

Because Davis County's growth was part of a much larger pattern along Utah's Wasatch Front, statisticians in the U.S. Census Bureau proposed to attach the county to an adjacent metropolitan area for planning and statistical purposes. This recommendation in October 1963 brought mixed reactions from county residents and from neighboring counties. For a number of years the chambers of commerce in Salt Lake and Weber Counties had used half of Davis County in describing their own metropolitan areas. But the definition was informal and did not meet federal standards. Census Bureau officials agreed that commuting patterns in the three-county area supported the idea of attaching the county to both neighbors. Since regulations did not allow a county to be divided for statistical purposes, officials had to make a choice. Their studies identified 4,600 workers from Davis County commuting to Salt Lake County for work and 1,800 Salt Lakers commuting north into Davis County. At

The "Lots for Sale" sign on this field along the route of the Bamberger Electric in 1939 was an early sign of the potential for suburban growth in the Bountiful area. (Utah State Historical Society)

the north end, 5,700 Weber County residents worked in Davis County and 1,700 from Davis drove to Weber County for employment. On a close call, the bureau decided that "Davis County has a stronger, and possibly a more permanent type of economic relationship with Salt Lake County than it has with Weber County." Members of the Salt Lake Chamber of Commerce were pleased, those in Ogden expressed disappointment.[16]

The Davis County Commission immediately asked for a reconsideration, proposing creation of a new single-county metropolitan area for Davis County. But, without a city of 50,000 people and a population of at least 150,000, the county did not qualify. Davis County's 80,000 people became part of the Salt Lake metropolitan area for reporting purposes, business planning, and market analysis. With the decision made, Commissioner Wayne M. Winegar saw one benefit. The county had been somewhat divided, he said, by economic and cultural attractions that pulled people in north Davis County toward Ogden and those in the south into Salt Lake City.

Including the entire county in the Salt Lake district would "help pull Davis County together," he believed.[17]

In succeeding years, county officials encouraged this one-county notion. They combined a number of north and south committees during the late 1960s and encouraged independent organizations and groups to do the same. Despite these hopes, however, Davis County continued to exist in many minds as a county divided at the Farmington-Kaysville line. Planners often looked at the two halves in their studies. The U.S. Bureau of the Census had the greatest impact because of its statistical reports, but federal highway programs created separate study programs, and Mountain States Telephone Company and some other businesses looked at the county as two separate economic entities. Because of natural population splits, many churches found it convenient to divide jurisdictions at a midpoint north or south of Kaysville.[18]

The boundaries of Utah's metropolitan areas changed from time to time to serve various economic or political interests. When the question was revisited in 1969, Davis County was once again assigned to the Salt Lake area. This time, county commissioners encouraged the affiliation, preferring it to having the county split in half. Some officials expected the county to qualify for its own metropolitan area by 1980. As the *Davis County Clipper* put it in 1969, "Davis County was never destined to be a part and parcel of some outside metropolitan area, but eventually a metropolitan area all its own." The county reached the necessary total population figure in 1990; however, at that time Layton was still 10,000 people short of meeting the large-city requirement. The question remained open for reconsideration after another federal census.[19]

In the late nineteenth century, being part of an urban, metropolitan area in America meant that people lived in compact areas and depended upon public transportation. That supposition influenced all American cities and their suburbs, including Salt Lake City and its environs. Under the urban model, city trolley lines and interurban lines such as the Bamberger Railroad were developed. Davis County was part of that turn-of-the-century experiment in public transportation. But the automobile quickly ended much of that urban dream. Davis County's electric trains were among the nation's last to cease running; they stopped during the postwar boom when motor vehicles became widely available. "The old order changes, yielding place to the new," a *Deseret News* editorial declared on the day of the last Bamberger freight run to Ogden. The line's usefulness, the paper said, "was before the whole country took to private cars."[20] Automobiles required improved roads and highways to connect country residences with the city workplace and department stores. The suburban model prevailed. California freeways rather than New York busses became the pattern followed in Utah's metropolis. Western ranch houses, not eastern apartments, became the symbol of the good life in Davis County.[21]

Eventually, again following California's lead, the Wasatch Front moved from suburbia to post-suburban metropolises, where residents from Provo to Ogden both lived and worked in their "bedroom" suburbs. In Davis County, the process differed in the two ends of the county. The southern section began with small towns and cities that added their own suburbs but depended upon the large city for economic vitality. Clustered shopping centers worked, but attempts to establish a new postsuburban city center did not. In contrast, northern Davis County developed jobs inside county boundaries because of Hill Air Force Base and other federal entities. This encouraged the development of a vibrant regional economic center around the Layton Hills Mall. All of north Davis County to some extent then became a suburb to this new economic core. In Salt Lake County, similar developments occurred in Sandy and West Valley City. By 1990, Utah had a larger percentage of its population living in large cities than did the state of New York. California led the nation with 92.6 percent urban dwellers, followed by New Jersey and three western states; Utah was sixth with 87.0 percent.[22]

Suburbia and the Freeway. Construction of north-south Interstate 15 through Davis County in the 1960s made the suburban development model a reality and eventually led to the rapid growth of Layton as a new commercial hub. By shortening travel time to Salt Lake City, the new freeway encouraged subdivisions in the middle of the county. The communities along the freeway's route rightly envisioned a new incentive for growth. Interstate 15 made the greatest difference in the Centerville, Farmington, and Kaysville areas, which had lagged behind other parts of the county because of their distance from both Ogden and Salt Lake City. Also, as in the Syracuse region, a stable agricultural population existed in the central core. Small subdivisions began appearing in these central cities about the time the interstate began reaching into the county from the south. Suburban sprawl brought the first, small subdivision to Syracuse in that same decade.[23]

The national highway system was launched during the Eisenhower administration by the Federal Interstate Highway Act of 1956, which also expanded federal subsidies for major state highways. Washington paid 95 percent of the costs, making construction of the Davis County section not a matter of "if," but "when." The Davis County Planning Commission recommended a route that closely followed U.S. Highway 91, although in Bountiful and Layton it bypassed the established highway in order to avoid displacing businesses.[24] North of Layton, the proposed route followed the abandoned Bamberger Railroad line. The Ogden Chamber of Commerce preferred the Mountain Road (U.S. Highway 89) north of Farmington. The state hired a San Francisco engineering firm to study the options. The company found the lower route a shorter distance to military job centers and less costly to build than a route through the mouth of Weber Canyon. Because Congress had designated the national system as both an interstate and a defense highway, the more direct route through Davis County was approved.[25]

A new Beck Street overpass at the county line was built in two parallel segments in 1955–58 as part of Highway 89/91 and was later widened and integrated into the interstate system. Similarly, portions of the interstate between Bountiful and Layton were upgrades of an existing "super highway" that the state had built as a four-lane divided highway in the early 1950s.[26]

Because of the urgency of providing for increased traffic between Salt Lake City and Ogden, the Utah State Road Commission chose a six-mile section in south Davis County to be Utah's first highway built to interstate standards. In a ceremony in North Salt Lake in January 1958, Governor George D. Clyde launched the project by driving a bulldozer into Amasa Howard's ninety-year-old dairy barn to clear a route for the new $7.3-million segment. Utah's first section of

In July 1959 construction was well underway on the Pages's Lane overpass in Centerville, the northern limit of the first segment of the Interstate Highway built in Davis County. (Utah State Historical Society)

six-lane divided interstate highway reached north to Pages Lane and was completed in 1962.[27] The original plan did not include an interchange between Bountiful and Lagoon. Through the efforts of Centerville City officials, however, one was added at Parrish Lane to serve local residents. Hearings on the 6.4-mile segment between Pages Lane and Lagoon were held beginning in 1963, but plans were not ready for bidding for another six years. Northbound lanes on that $10.1-million section opened late in 1971 and the southbound side opened the following year.[28]

Meanwhile, the northern sections of Interstate 15 were being built from the Weber County line south to Layton. Widening and resurfacing the existing section of Highway 91 from Layton to Lagoon was accomplished in 1977 as a $9.9 million project. With the route finished through Davis County, motorists could travel on an uninterrupted interstate from northern Juab County to northern Box

Elder County.[29] Long freeway stretches in other parts of the state would not see completion until the early 1990s.

Meeting transportation needs remained one of the pressing concerns for Davis County citizens as the twenty-first century approached. Fearing a gridlock situation because of increased traffic on the arterial routes, highway officials and local governments explored options for increasing highway capacity and improving mass-transit options.[30] Countywide planning for major transportation routes had begun with the growth surge in the 1950s. To prevent a choking of existing arterial routes and to create a scenic drive, in 1951 the county planning commission proposed a new foothills highway through the county along Highway 89 from Weber Canyon to Fruit Heights, and then along the old Lake Bonneville terrace to Bountiful, with links to Highway 91 and around Ensign Peak to the state capitol. Salt Lake County planners extended the route along the old Lake Bonneville terrace to connect with Salt Lake City's Wasatch Boulevard and then plotted a route all the way into Utah County. At first called Wasatch Drive, the proposed route eventually came to be known as Bonneville Drive.[31] The concept of a valley-rim route was included in Davis County master plans of the 1960s and 1980, along with a proposed lowlands highway along the shore of the Great Salt Lake. Opposition from Salt Lake County eventually stymied efforts to realize a multicounty Bonneville Drive. The shoreline route took on the name of Salt Lake County's West Valley Highway and became a much-discussed topic in the 1990s as population growth in north Davis County surged.[32]

The shoreline route was named the West Davis Highway by county planners and then renamed the Legacy Parkway by Governor Michael Leavitt, who included it as part of a proposed 120-mile route extending from Brigham City to Nephi. Beginning in the early 1990s, Representative Marda Dillree, a Republican from Farmington, became a regular voice in the Utah Legislature in favor of the western route and an active proponent seeking solutions for the Highway 89 issues. As chair of the Transportation and Environmental Quality Appropriations Subcommittee in the mid-1990s, she urged legislative action to provide funding to solve the problems. Representative Don Bush (R-Clearfield) headed the House Transportation

Committee, another key position of help to Davis County.[33] Local officials worked through the Davis Council of Governments to draw attention to the needs. Republican Congressman James V. Hansen, a Farmington resident, added his support to the effort to unclog a congested I-15 in central Davis County. That bottleneck, he said, should be the state's top highway priority.[34]

Location and wetlands issues stalled the West Davis Highway. Centerville and Farmington residents were most concerned about its placement. Because the first stage of construction would end in Farmington, the road needed a junction with I-15 and Highway 89 near Lagoon. That intersection would displace a new city road shop and dominate the landscape just outside Farmington's historic downtown district. Centerville planners wanted to push the highway west against the lake, but conservationists preferred a more easterly route to limit encroachment on wildlife preserves and federally protected wetlands. As the south-end debate ended in a temporary deadlock, city officials in Syracuse and West Point acted to divert developers and protect a hundred-foot swath for a transportation corridor adjacent to Bluff Road for a future extension of the highway.[35]

While debates continued over the West Davis Highway, planners moved forward to resolve traffic congestion problems along the thirteen-mile stretch of U.S. Highway 89 from the north Farmington junction to south Ogden. Residents in Kaysville and Fruit Heights pushed the issue to the forefront when they approached planners in the early 1990s seeking help in improving the safety of the route. Options included adding traffic lights, expanding bus service, and creating a limited-access freeway. As an interim solution, state highway officials installed three traffic signals at the busiest intersections in 1992 and at others in subsequent years. A new interchange at the Hill Field Road (Utah Highway 193) was approved as well.[36] Davis County residents were divided in their options about how to resolve the problem, or uncertain even if there was a traffic problem on the Mountain Road. A poll in 1995 found that a majority of those contacted didn't like the idea of traffic signals or turning the route into an expressway.[37]

After additional study and discussion over a five-year period, the Utah Department of Transportation proposed a long-term solution.

Officials announced that the busy road would be transformed into a six-lane expressway with a narrow median between the north and south lanes. A series of nine interchanges, several overpasses, and new frontage roads would give local motorists access while limiting cross-traffic to prevent collisions with through traffic. The upgrade would eliminate 136 homes and twenty-two businesses over the course of the ten-year project. The first of the interchanges, already under construction at the Hill Field Road (U-193), was completed in early 1996.[38] Planning began immediately afterward for a second interchange at the Cherry Hill Resort exit (U-273) in Fruit Heights. Work began in the spring of 1999 on that project.

An aging Interstate 15 also needed attention during the 1990s. A number of rehabilitation projects replaced and patched deteriorating concrete and replaced some asphalt shoulders along the entire span of the thirty-year-old route.[39] Motorists grumbled over the delays and wondered what they had gained when the repair crews left and the freeway still lacked the additional lanes many of them thought it needed. The idea of adding one lane in each direction received strong support from Davis County citizens—80 percent of respondents in a *Deseret News* poll in 1995 liked the idea. Cities in all parts of the county encouraged action on the plan through the Davis County Council of Governments and the Wasatch Regional Council.[40]

Highway planners had designated start-up funds for the West Valley Highway as a higher priority, citizens were told. However, when progress on the controversial western route stalled, Governor Leavitt made the addition of two lanes on the I-15 stretch from 2600 South in Bountiful to 200 North in Kaysville first on the transportation agenda. Part of the $260 million tagged by the Utah Transportation Commission for the West Davis Highway between Salt Lake City and Farmington was diverted to widening Interstate 15. The freeway from the I-215 merge to the south county line had already been expanded. Also, meters installed in 1996 at three on-ramps in Bountiful and Centerville helped regulate merging traffic during the morning rush hour.[41]

"Widening I-15 in Davis County will not replace the need to build the Legacy Parkway," a *Deseret News* editorial noted, "it just buys the state some time." Highway officials estimated that a widened interstate would handle increased traffic until about 2004. Freeway traffic in south Davis County had climbed by one-third in the four years between 1994 and 1998. The traffic flow of more than 115,000 cars a day was expected to continue growing by at least 8 percent a year. Planning would continue on the four-lane Legacy route and possible light rail and commuter rail systems. The $50 million interim solution was slated for a summer 1999 construction start.[42] Some Layton officials urged the Utah Department of Transportation (UDOT) to continue the widening project northward, but the suggestion was rejected. The decision to go ahead with a short-term solution postponed for five years the full reconstruction of I-15 in Davis County; UDOT moved its start date for that project to 2008.[43]

Subdividing Benchlands and Farmlands. Many people chose to live in Davis County because of its traditional, rural flavor; yet their presence contributed to the decline of open space. They sought out benchland homesites to get away from the traffic and commercial hubbub of city centers. More exclusive neighborhoods at higher elevations provided the additional aesthetic benefit of views overlooking the valley and the Great Salt Lake. The lowlands typically became lower-priced housing developments; but all of the new subdivisions altered the dwelling patterns that had prevailed in Davis County's first cities with their surrounding farmlands.

The original city plats of Davis County had imitated the orderly four-square communities so popular in nineteenth-century America. Bountiful, Centerville, Farmington, and Kaysville had that look. Although the intent was that farmers live in the city, many of them built homes on their farms, creating a mixed pattern of settlement. The homesteaded areas outside the platted cities followed this rural pattern. Until the end of World War II, the county remained agricultural. The earliest recorded subdivision, platted in 1889, was Sulphur Springs. Nothing came of this paper town situated along the Jordan River pasturelands on Cudahy Lane in North Salt Lake.[44]

Many of the early subdivisions imitated traditional right-angle street patterns, but wandering streets gradually became the preferred model. The curved roadways both discouraged through traffic—often with cul-de-sac dead-ends—and ensured more privacy for residents. The arrival of interurbans and the subsequent age of the

An aerial view in February 1959 reveals the beginnings of subdivision development to the east and south of the original four-square platted city of Bountiful. (Utah State Historical Society)

automobile created a heightened interest in suburban living. Numerous subdivisions appeared on the gently sloping land lying along the roads leading southwest from Bountiful to the Hot Springs. They carried names such as Carlton Place, St. Joseph, Stockdale, Bonneville, Enterprise, Cleverly, Odell, and Val Verda.[45] One that retained its identity was Val Verda, immediately south of Bountiful. When the arch that had marked the development's entry for more than sixty years fell down in 1977, residents rebuilt it. They fought off incorporation with Bountiful for decades, until proponents in 1996 finally convinced a two-thirds majority to sign the annexation petition.[46]

The surge in home building throughout Davis County supported an active construction industry. Hundreds of new homes were built in the county every year. The pace remained relatively level during the 1950s and 1960s, then tripled and even quadrupled in some cities in the 1970s. Home building dropped significantly during the economic slowdown of the early 1980s; this was followed by an upswing and another slump. It was possible to say in 1990 that most of the homes existing in the county had been built since 1970. Nearly a thousand new permits were issued in the county in 1990. During the next few years, the annual count was double that figure, but as the decade ended planners anticipated a slowdown in home construction.[47]

The number of new dwelling units for the population would even have been higher had Davis County's family structure been more like the nation's. Households with married couples in 1990 made up 77 percent of the county's population, compared with 66 percent for Utah and 56 percent for the nation. Each home in Davis County averaged 3.45 people, compared with 3.15 in Utah and an average of 2.63 in the nation. The suburban living standard for Davis County in 1990 was a single family home with from two to four bedrooms and an attached garage. Nearly half of the families owned two cars, and another one-fourth had three or more vehicles.[48] The rate of home ownership in Davis County was one of the highest in the United States. According to the U.S. Census Bureau, 76 percent of homes in the Salt Lake-Ogden metropolitan area were owned by their inhabitants. The national average was ten percentage points lower.[49]

While most residents of Davis County lived in traditional families, 12 percent of families were headed by a female, and another 10 percent of adults lived alone. Many of these citizens lived in manufactured housing or in apartments. Young couples and low-income families also chose apartments to live in. City planners created special zones for multi-unit dwelling places. Typically they were located as a buffer between single-family housing and commercial zones. The numbers available varied greatly from one city to another because of local markets or preferences.[50] In North Salt Lake, for example, half of all housing in 1995 was multifamily. Clearfield, Layton, and unincorporated areas had permitted 30 percent in that category; Bountiful and Woods Cross were at 22 percent. At the bottom of the list were South Weber and West Point, with 2 percent, followed by Clinton (4 percent), Farmington, and Syracuse (both at 8 percent). Overall, the ratio in Davis County was 22 percent, compared with 31 percent in Salt Lake County. A shortage of apartments in Davis

County in 1995 became a glut four years later when new construction outpaced needs.[51]

Communities struggled with proposals from developers to build more multi-unit buildings or to develop mobile home parks for manufactured homes. Owners of single-family homes sometimes opposed such units because of concerns over traffic congestion. In response, proponents of multi-unit construction raised questions of property rights and discrimination against low-income families. Most cities sought to balance local apartments and starter homes on small lots with upscale subdivisions. In the 1990s every growing city faced issues of rapid new expansion. At the end of the decade, Syracuse found itself one-quarter full, with room for another 35,000 people, while Clinton anticipated it could triple in size and, with space for another 20,000, reach build-out by the year 2030.[52] Clearfield was engaged in discussions on whether the city should move away from policies allowing low-income housing in order to achieve a greater balance.[53] Layton's city council was willing to approve additional multifamily units to meet a pressing local need.[54] Farmington residents, on the other hand, opposed the introduction of multi-unit housing in a city with very few apartments.[55]

To help cities work together on these and other common growth-related issues, county planners created the Davis County Planning Coordination Committee as a clearing house for information on growth, open space and parks, apartment locations, affordable housing, street alignments, and land use. It was the third county land-use coordinating group created in the state.[56]

In every community in Davis County, as agricultural property disappeared under houses and black-top, residents began seeking ways to preserve open space. Those accustomed to rural life wondered if farming was not preferable to any suburban development.[57] For those who accepted as inevitable the move towards suburbanization, a mixed-use option combining single-family and twin-home units with professional offices and a neighborhood park won acceptance. Other cities proposed open space ordinances that would require homes to be built on small lots clustered around park-like open areas. When a developer proposed an open-space project in Farmington, residents were divided: some preferred large lots and city parks for the city's west side; others believed that shared open space in a tightly clustered subdivision was the only way to provide needed housing for the future. City officials moved ahead in drafting a conservation ordinance that would penalize developers by requiring many fewer lots in developments without open space. "Farmington is no longer a rural area," one developer noted in proposing clustered urban townhouses with garages hidden in a back alley.[58]

Even with support for clustered homes coming from Salt Lake City's *Deseret News* and various regional planning groups, including Envision Utah, decisions such as these would not be any easier. For communities to change their thinking from the rural and suburban housing models to an urban pattern would mark the beginning of another transition in the way Davis County's people would live on the land. "It takes thick skin to change the pattern of urban sprawl," a *Salt Lake Tribune* reporter noted. "There is no guarantee Utahns will want to buy into experimental neighborhoods that shun the traditional suburban home on a half-acre lot." Cities such as Farmington, Clinton, and Kaysville moved ahead with the concept, however, and listened to proposals for clustered homesites.[59]

An incentive for local communities to take control of their future was passage by the 1999 Utah Legislature of the Quality Growth Act. Sponsored by Layton representative and House Majority Leader Kevin Garn, the measure had the support of several Davis County mayors and county officials. "It is born of the ethic of preservation and planning," Governor Michael Leavitt said of the bill as he signed it into law. "We will not subsidize urban sprawl, but care for future generations."[60]

New Schools for New Students. As the county's population increased during the 1950s and 1960s, so too did the number of schools. The district enrolled more than 2,000 new students each year during much of this period. Enrollment at the end of 1963 was 16,000 students in elementary classes and another 10,000 in secondary grades. By 1970 the Davis School District counted 33,990 students, making it second only to Granite School District. Twenty years later, enrollment reached 54,558 in the Davis district. Granite and Jordan districts were larger by 20,000 and 10,000 students, respectively.[61] These figures reflected the fact that all along the Wasatch

Front, Utah's population was young and comprised of families larger than average in America. In 1970 only 6 percent of Davis County's residents were age sixty-five or older; 9 percent of Utahns and 13 percent of Americans were senior citizens. In contrast, the 1990 census found 40 percent of the population age seventeen or under. Demographers noted, however, that since 1970 the percentage of older citizens had been growing and the younger age group shrinking.[62]

To accomodate expanding enrollments under tight budgets, the Davis district built many new schools, usually in phases. In some years a third of the construction budget was dedicated to adding classrooms to existing schools, including some built before 1950. Each step forward required community approval of bonding issues to fund the required expansion.[63]

Once the younger students reached their teens, Davis County saw the beginning of a new trend in high schools. The last countywide class graduated from Davis High in 1956. The following year, Bountiful High became a four-year school, and for the first time the district had two high school graduating classes. Postwar expansion in north Davis County soon led to the construction of four more high schools. The new facilities were Clearfield High School in 1959, followed by Viewmont (in north Bountiful) in 1964, Layton two years later, and Woods Cross in 1972.[64] The Woods Cross school introduced a layout not previously used in the area. The brightly colored school featured movable wall partitions in two large eight-room classroom pods and in the multipurpose gymnasium, the cafeteria, the homemaking suite, and an interior open court.[65] Because of expansion projects at four of the high schools during the late 1960s, it would be twenty years before another new high school would be needed in the county. The new school was called Northridge High School and opened in 1992 in Layton. Anticipating further growth, the district purchased land in 1990 for a future Syracuse High School.[66]

The first new junior high schools in nearly fifteen years were Central Davis Junior High, built in Layton in 1955, and South Davis Junior High, opened five years later in Bountiful. The 1960s saw construction of five additional facilities: Kaysville Junior High in 1961, Centerville and Sunset in 1965, and Millcreek (Bountiful) and North

Layton in 1967–68.[67] The school-age population continued to grow during the 1970s and succeeding decades. The district built its next six junior highs to redistribute the load on existing schools. The new facilities were Farmington and Syracuse in the mid-1980s, followed by Fairfield, Mueller Park, and North Layton schools.

At the elementary school level, construction surged, with fourteen new elementary schools built in the 1950s and nine more in the next decade. Because growth got a head start in the southern communities, thirteen of the twenty-three new schools were built in the region from Centerville south. That ratio was reversed in later decades.[68] The pace of new construction was moderated somewhat by the use of portable classrooms and year-round schools, but these strategies did not eliminate the eventual need for new buildings. The Davis School District built seven new elementary schools in the 1970s. With twelve additional buildings added during the 1980s, construction moved at a faster pace than it had since the frenetic 1950s. In 1984 the Provo School District opened the first year-round school in Utah; Davis District adopted the program four years later and soon had a number schools participating in this cost-saving program. Even with this economizing, another eight elementaries were built in the 1990s. With each new school came boundary adjustments—a painful situation for students, but a fact of life for a growing county.[69]

During the 1970s, the district introduced the first of its specialized schools, all of them with countywide clienteles. The Monte Vista School, located in Farmington, was created to offer special-education classes for elementary students; it later added regular classes. Specialized programs for high-school-age students were established in an educational complex built behind Davis High in Kaysville. The Davis Area Vocational Center, established in 1978 (renamed the Davis Applied Technology Center in 1990), offered courses in technical fields. Mountain High School oriented its services to students needing help in adjusting socially. A Young Parents Program is also offered at this education complex. The district also sponsors the Farmington Bay Youth Center in Farmington and the Pioneer Adult Rehabilitation Center in Clearfield.

With the growing load of managing expanding numbers of schools and assisting teachers, the Davis School District built its first

This 1963 photograph of the Naval Supply Depot marks the beginning of the site's use as the Clearfield Freeport Center, a manufacturing and warehouse park offering special state and federal tax exemptions. Early occupants included Westinghouse, Fram Utility Trailer, Hercules, and Thiokol. (Utah State Historical Society)

administration building at a cost of nearly $700,000. Located north of the courthouse, the four-story building was at the time the tallest building in Farmington and possibly in the county. School officials moved out of the courthouse to the new quarters in mid-1969.[70]

As social patterns changed, the county's schools faced the challenge of adjusting to meet new needs. A policy created to discourage early marriages raised challenges that sent the case all the way to the Utah Supreme Court. A newly married senior at Davis High School challenged the policy that prohibited married students from holding student offices or participating in extracurricular activities. The policy also kept pregnant students out of the classroom. The lawsuit, supported by the American Civil Liberties Union, allowed the courts to review an earlier ruling by the state attorney general's office. The ruling declared similar policies in other districts unconstitutional.

Second District Judge Thornley K. Swan supported the Davis School District, as did the Utah State Supreme Court, creating a benchmark for all Utah schools. The district did not ignore the special needs of married or pregnant students: among the district programs created to help these students were the Mountain High School and Young Parents Program in Kaysville.[71]

The returning veterans from America's mid-century wars found opportunities for college training under government-funded schooling made available by the GI Bill of Rights. This incentive, and an expansion of the college-age population along Utah's Wasatch Front, pushed university and college enrollments up at steadily increasing rates through the early 1960s. This was a turnaround from the war years, when Selective Service siphoned off so many young men that enrollments fell nearly 70 percent.[72] With post-high school numbers approaching 44,000 students at Utah's nine institutions of higher education, legislators considered a proposal to establish a college in Davis County. "We need, and can support a community college," said Utah Senate President Haven J. Barlow, a Layton Republican. At that time, the University of Utah served 12,000 daytime students; Weber State College's enrollment stood at almost 4,000, with nearly a third of the students from Davis County. Barlow was joined in the proposal by Senator Ezra T. Clark, a Republican from Bountiful. They viewed the possibilities optimistically and gained the support of local government, civic, and church leaders. They noted that Davis County was the fastest-growing county in the state and, of the larger counties, the only one without a college or university. The proposal did not win legislative approval, however; still, county planners placed the dream of at least one community college, or a combination college and vocational school, in the county's 1970 master plan.[73]

Another try for a community college surfaced in the 1990s. For a number of years the county had hosted university classes to fill local requests, demonstrating a need for a closer-to-home campus. The University of Utah had established off-campus classes in Bountiful and also offered courses leading to master's degrees in selected fields at its center at Hill Air Force Base.[74] But the U of U was not the only school interested in expanding into Davis County. Weber State University began offering courses in the 1970s at Hill Air Force Base.

It gradually expanded its enrollment to nearly 7,000 students annually, with classes at its Davis Center in Layton, the Davis Applied Technology Center in Kaysville, and at six public high schools. When Weber State decided in the 1990s to build a branch facility in the county, Farmington and Layton both proposed sites for the campus. Property one mile west of the south gate of Hill Air Force Base was selected, and the university acquired 104 acres for its future campus.[75]

Libraries, Histories, and Museums. Public libraries in Davis County had their roots in a system of ward libraries set up in LDS meetinghouses and similar collections in local schools. Books for teens dominated the small church collections, usually housed in a cupboard in the meetinghouse and promoted by the Young Men's and Young Women's Mutual Improvement Associations. Sunday Schools also took an interest in the circulating libraries. Beginning in 1899, each public school established its own "unit library" under the guidance of the Davis School District. Layton's ward library opened its books to the general public in 1900, in what was described as Utah's first free circulating library. The experiment lasted only a few months, apparently dying for lack of interest. Some high schools in the county provided public access to their collections, but the difficult times brought on by depressions and wars delayed creation of a public library system.[76]

The Davis County Library was organized in 1946 when the county commission appointed five men to the governing board and gave them two charges: develop a countywide free public library system and serve secondary school libraries. The director and staff, all women, were headquartered at Davis High School and furnished books for five secondary schools. Within a few years, the library board established branch public libraries in Bountiful, Clearfield, Farmington, and Verdeland Park. Services were expanded in the 1960s with a bookmobile that visited more remote neighborhoods in the county. In the fall of 1963, the staff moved into a new Davis County Library Processing Center just east of the courthouse. The $200,000 facility was built as a joint project of the county and the Davis School District. Books for both the county library system and the school district were processed at the center, which also had a main-floor public library, including a special section for children.

Civil Defense headquarters occupied part of the basement. The school and public library programs went their separate ways in 1977, after thirty years as a consolidated system. After that time, the schools got their library books through the Utah State Library processing service, and the county library system specialized in the public library function, serving readers of all ages.[77]

As patronage increased, the county library board built new facilities for the South Branch in Bountiful in the late 1960s and the North Branch in Clearfield in 1977. Despite local protests, the county's Layton branch, which had operated since 1960 in the old city hall, was closed and its 5,000-book collection moved to Clearfield when that branch opened. A new Central Branch Library in Layton was completed in 1988. The next step for expanding service was announced by the Davis County Library Board in the spring of 1999. Plans called for new branches near the Syracuse City Hall and at Parrish Lane in Centerville as well as anticipated additions to the library buildings in Layton and Bountiful.[78]

That announcement may reopen a longstanding question in Kaysville, where an independent library exists under city sponsorship. The Kaysville Library grew from humble beginnings in a renovated blacksmith shop before finding a home and sponsor in the Kaysville City Building. At various times, most recently in the mid-1990s, city officials have explored the possibility of Kaysville's library joining the county system, with its more extensive holdings. Each time, however, local convenience has been given higher priority: fears that the county might close the Kaysville facility, requiring patrons to travel to Layton or Farmington, kept Kaysville with its library.[79]

The normally placid work of administering a library erupted into controversy in 1979 when County Commissioner Morris F. Swapp, a member of the Davis County Library Board, removed a contested adult novel from the shelves. He did so after library director Jeanne Layton and two six-member review committees had decided the book should remain despite patron complaints that it was obscene. At issue were questions about book selection, access to adult books, and censorship. The matter was complicated when two new members of the library board supportive of Swapp's position were appointed during the controversy. An ad hoc group called the Library

The proliferation of ranch homes in Davis County subdivisions eventually gave the older Victorian homes a special appeal. One of the more elaborate of these historic places is the Kaysville home of Governor Henry H. Blood, built about 1896. (Utah State Historical Society)

Coalition rallied behind Jeanne Layton. The coalition challenged the board appointments as unrepresentative of a diverse county population. The group especially opposed the selection of a member of Citizens for True Freedom, an ultraconservative group. In a 3–2 vote, the library board fired Layton in September, listing a half-dozen reasons, including insubordination. Layton took the issue to federal court, claiming that Swapp had exceeded his legal authority. Before the court could rule, the county merit board decided that Layton was covered by the merit system and reinstated her. Layton went back to work, but with new limits placed on her authority by the library board, including a mandate to involve more outside voices in the book-selection process.[80]

As an adjunct to learning, museums have played a supporting role in Davis County. The Daughters of Utah Pioneers (DUP) organization was the first in the county to preserve artifacts. Many of these found their way into the central collection displayed in Salt Lake City's Pioneer Memorial Museum. A number of local DUP camps kept their treasures at home. Preserved in pioneer log homes, the clothing, photographs, and household furnishings of the pioneer period offered glimpses of an earlier generation. The various DUP groups in the county also compiled some of the first town histories and wrote biographical sketches of early settlers. A compilation of these writings was published in 1948 for the settlement centennial. Titled *East of Antelope Island: History of the First Fifty Years of Davis County,* the book remains a valuable reference on the county's beginnings.

The U.S. bicentennial in 1976 sparked a nationwide interest in history that translated into hundreds of new histories and museums being created. In Davis County during the mid-1970s, the first book-length histories of Bountiful, Centerville, Farmington, and Kaysville appeared. These histories of the county's first settlements were followed in subsequent years with books on other communities, most of them appearing around 1990. An active Kaysville-Layton Historical Society published a collection of historical essays in *Layton, Utah: Historic Viewpoints* in 1985 and also issued a number of topical studies in pamphlet form. Davis County families remembered ancestral contributions to the county's early history by publishing dozens of biographical and family history collections. These form another resource for historical reading and research.

Layton City, the youngest of the older cities, created the first town history museum. Centerville's historical society furnished a historic home to preserve artifacts collected for that purpose. Other communities began discussion of options for town history museums. The display of the work of local artists found sponsors in two communities. Kaysville patrons of the arts organized a Community Art League and sponsored a gallery featuring the work of LeConte Stewart, a Kaysville resident celebrated as Utah's dean of landscape artists.[81] Bountiful accepted the support of the University of Utah to launch what became the locally supported Bountiful/Davis Art Center. The gallery expanded its program under a new director in the 1990s and moved into the renovated Public Safety Building in the city government complex in 1998, where its cycle of exhibits spotlights county artists and encourages student talent.[82]

The Geography of Religion. Employees attracted to Davis County because of jobs at the military installations brought with them religious backgrounds not well served by existing area churches. Their arrival lessened the dominance of the Church of Jesus Christ of Latter-day Saints and introduced the first meaningful diversity to the county's religious makeup. Most of that variety existed in the northern communities. Because of the new immigration, Latter-day Saint membership in the county between 1940 and 1950 dropped from 80 percent of the total population to 72 percent. At the same time, membership in other denominations grew from 20 percent to 28 percent.

In raw numbers, however, LDS membership increased considerably. The number of wards increased during the 1940s from nineteen to twenty-nine, and church officials created a third stake. A half-century later, dozens of new LDS meetinghouses were to be seen, each serving two or three wards. A 1999 roster listed 114 wards in the four southernmost cities; another 99 wards in the central region reaching from Centerville to Kaysville; 76 wards in Layton; and 64 others in the other six northern communities. These 353 wards were clustered into forty-nine administrative units known as stakes, each of them encompassing six to nine wards.

A highlight for south Davis Latter-day Saints was the dedication on 8 January 1994 of a temple on a foothill site overlooking Bountiful. LDS President Howard W. Hunter offered the dedicatory prayer. Twenty-seven other sessions over the next six days allowed thousands of people to attend the sacred event. Tens of thousands more walked through the temple during a public open house. The temple's service district included members from Kaysville south to the county line. Latter-day Saints in north Davis remained in the Ogden LDS Temple district.

As school districts in Utah were setting up public high schools early in the century, the LDS church tested a weekday religious education program to compensate for the loss of spiritual instruction in the church schools. Seven years later, in 1919, an LDS seminary began adjacent to Davis High School. Named in honor of John R. Barnes, who helped the North Davis and South Davis Stakes fund the new yellow-brick building, the seminary offered released-time classes for Latter-day Saint high school students.[83] The church's program expanded with the addition of each new high school in the county, and later seminaries were added to serve ninth-grade students attending junior high schools.

Religious influence in the public schools became a sensitive issue during the last decades of the twentieth century. The church-state issue in Davis County was, in effect, a local manifestation of a nationwide dialogue over the boundaries of religion in public education.[84] Along the Wasatch Front, concerns were raised about the use of religious music in school choral presentations and the offering of prayers in graduation programs. The Davis School District recognized the sensitive nature of these issues in a cosmopolitan population. Consequently, officials invited representatives from the PTA, Davis Education Association, an atheist group, and leaders of eleven religious faiths to examine the question and prepare written guidelines for teachers and students. In January 1997 the Davis Board of Education became the first in Utah to adopt a comprehensive policy addressing religion. "The Davis District is plowing new ground," Superintendent Darrell White told a reporter. "We are out on the frontier." The policy was designed to protect First Amendment rights of free religious expression and to prohibit coercion and harassment in the schools. Among other things, the groundbreaking guidelines permitted private student religious expressions and the wearing of religious clothing and jewelry by students and volunteering clergy and missionaries. Choral teachers were allowed to include selected sacred music in the curriculum, and students could choose to lead a moment of silence at graduation ceremonies. Classroom discussions had to relate to academic subjects and avoid proselytizing.[85]

In 1940 most non-Mormon area residents looked outside the county for religious services. For many years, the Bountiful Community Church, established in 1882, had been the only non-Mormon church in Davis County. Its membership doubled during the 1940s. During that decade, new churches appeared in other areas of the county—most in the northern region. In Clearfield, a community church organized in 1945 grew quickly to 235 members. Two other Protestant groups lacked buildings but had their own ministers. One was the Community Church in Verdeland Park, and the other was the First Southern Baptist Church in Clearfield. All of these churches catered to the new influx of people attracted by the wartime defense depots.[86]

The few Catholics in pre-war Davis County were affiliated with the St. Joseph Parrish in Ogden or looked to the Salt Lake Cathedral of the Madeleine. Most were migrant workers who lived in the county only during the summers. The arrival of defense industry employees created a new but also somewhat transient membership. Beginning in 1941, a Paulist mission established itself in Bountiful. The priests offered services in rented spaces in Bountiful for families living as far north as Kaysville. In the northern communities, they met for a time with members in a portable trailer, but membership grew rapidly. Permanent facilities were erected in 1942 for the Saint Rose of Lima Catholic Church in Layton. By 1950 the church listed 800 members. Bountiful's congregation at that time was around eighty parishoners and grew slowly. Saint Olaf's Catholic Church opened on Orchard Drive in 1959. A school for elementary students was added the following year.[87]

The Protestant faiths with the largest followings in Davis County have been the Baptists and Lutherans. The county's nine Baptist churches are found in the larger cities at both ends of the county, where they serve thriving congregations. The Grace Baptist Church and First Southern Baptist Church were the earliest, organized in the early 1960s in the Bountiful area.[88] Some Baptist churches in the county serve ethnic congregations. The True Vine Baptist Church was organized in Layton in 1978 for African Americans, although its congregation also includes many Hispanic and some Caucasian members.[89] A more recent group, the Layton Bilingual Baptist Church, offers services in Spanish and English. Also in Layton are the Mountain View Baptist Church and the Layton Hills Baptist Church. The Korean Baptist Church is based in Clearfield, as is the Salt Valley Landmark Mission Baptist Church. Two Baptist churches in nearby Roy also attract followers from Davis County.

For forty years, the Cross of Christ Lutheran Church in Bountiful served as a gathering point for Lutherans of various traditions in the south and central regions of Davis County. The church was formally organized in 1958 as an affiliate of the Lutheran Church—Missouri Synod. A second Lutheran congregation in Davis County, the Grace Lutheran Church, planted itself in Centerville and attracted a following as far north as Layton.[90] The newer Light of the Valley Lutheran

Church in Layton serves members of the evangelical tradition in northern Davis County.

The 1960s and 1970s brought a number of additional Christian churches to Davis County to minister to relatively small congregations. By the 1990s the religious landscape reflected a well-established religious diversity in Davis County. Southern Davis County congregations included the Abundant Life Assembly of God Church in North Salt Lake, Jehovah's Witnesses in Bountiful, the Episcopal Church of the Resurrection in Centerville, the Kaysville Bible Church, Kaysville Church of Christ, Kaysville Assembly of God Church, Westminster Presbyterian Church in Fruit Heights, and Pilgrim's Christian Fellowship in Bountiful. In Clearfield were found the Wasatch Church of Christ, Saint Peter's Episcopal Church, AMIGO International Assembly of God Church, and the Clearfield Community Church. Layton churches include the Church of the Nazarene, Cavalry Chapel Christian Fellowship, First Assembly of God Church, Jehovah's Witnesses, Jesus' People Ministries Church, and the Liberty Christian Church.

The growing number of Davis County Asian residents brought new religious organizations outside the Christian religion to the county. The first Japanese Buddhist church was built in Syracuse in 1925 to serve farm workers and sharecroppers who had been gathering in the area since 1917. It was merged with the Ogden Buddhist Church in 1979. Late in the century, the Wat Dhmmagunaram Thai Buddhist Temple was established to serve eighty families in the Layton area.[91] As the twentieth century drew to a close, the Bahai faith was functioning in Clearfield, Layton, Bountiful, and Farmington.

Economic Growth in a Suburban County

During the first decades after World War II, Utah's economy expanded on a solid base that had been strengthened by wartime spending. Residents of Davis County enjoyed a new era of prosperity that created a standard of living and personal incomes much higher than in the Depression and war years. Much of this growth related to the continuing presence of defense installations and related businesses. Commercial agriculture's role steadily declined during the second half of the century, while local businesses thrived and a strong service sector emerged as a major economic contributor.[92]

Davis County's location between an economically healthy Salt Lake County and a promotion-conscious Weber County had at least two impacts. First, its location reinforced Davis County's role as a suburban, bedroom community. Second, its proximity to the two urban centers created opportunities for businesses that could benefit from being close to the larger centers. Prosperity sustained a growth economy and prodded consumers to spend. The U&I beet-processing factory in Layton churned out sugar to meet the surging postwar demand. Cudahy packaged beef to satisfy a generation that had endured years on limited meat rations. The Woods Cross cannery found in the county's expanding population new mouths ready to taste Davis County's high-quality fruits and vegetables.

Between 1950 and 1963, more than 80 percent of the non-farm jobs created in Utah were located in the five Wasatch Front counties, where defense-related jobs had burgeoned during the war. In the late 1960s, nearly half of Utah's direct defense employment was concentrated in the Ogden metropolitan area (Weber and north Davis counties). Around 25 percent was located in the Salt Lake metropolitan area (Salt Lake and south Davis Counties), while the remaining jobs were about equally divided between Tooele and Box Elder Counties. Per capita income in Utah, only 80 percent of the national average in 1940, exceeded that average a few years later. The war had revitalized a dormant economy and gave the state a head start on a postwar era of prosperity. Davis County benefited significantly because of the defense installations. Salt Lake and Box Elder Counties had larger numbers of workers in defense-related private industries, but the Weber–north Davis area consistently led in government employment.

The later decades of the century saw these trends continue. Hill Air Force Base remained Davis County's largest employer. Agricultural employment declined. Manufacturing remained small but stable. Retail trade expanded rapidly to serve a population that seemed intent on fostering rapid growth. New jobs were created in the service sector. As the century ended, Davis County was part of a healthy Utah economy centered on the Wasatch Front. By one economist's measurement, the Salt Lake–Davis–Weber metropolitan area

Employment related to defense installations and industries remained a strong influence in Davis County. The radomes atop Francis Peak above Kaysville were operated by the 229th Radar Squadron at Hill Air Force Base. (Utah State Historical Society)

ranked sixth highest among 313 regions evaluated over a quarter-century. County planners echoed glowing state forecasts that the economy would remain healthy. Local chambers of commerce and businessmen anticipated a steady future of profits and jobs, with only a slight moderating after nearly a decade of rapid growth.[93]

At the end of the Second World War, the dominant influence in Davis County's economy was the defense depots. Fifty years later, this influence continued. In addition, Davis County increasingly had become part of a thriving national and state economy. County residents found themselves working for and buying merchandise from branches of national stores. Large clothing, hardware, computer, and department stores invaded suburban markets wherever they found a new regional mall. Similarly, fast-food and restaurant franchises planted themselves in these same commercial gathering places and clustered around freeway off-ramps.

County planners in 1970 anticipated that most shopping needs in the county would be met through a combination of local stores and the larger shopping centers in Salt Lake and Ogden. "One large Regional Shopping Center might be able to survive now in Davis County," it was concluded, "and possibly another by 1990."[94] These forecasts anticipated malls at interstate interchanges in Layton and Farmington.

Davis County's first enclosed mall was the Five Points Mall, built in the late 1950s on a sixteen-acre site on the outskirts of Bountiful. Unlike the later and larger regional malls, Five Points brought together mostly local specialty stores. The clustered businesses did well for many years. Eventually, competition from national stores in the Wasatch Front's growing number of regional malls eroded the mall's customer base. In 1998, with half of its retail space vacant, the aging mall was purchased by a Las Vegas firm. The new owners promised physical upgrades, aggressive marketing, a grocery store, a possible theater, plus the addition of a sports mall to serve Bountiful's aging population.[95]

The anticipated regional mall in Layton, built by an out-of-state developer, was opened in 1980. The 700,000-square-foot complex imitated the successful formula of the major Salt Lake County malls. Layton Hills Mall was anchored by ZCMI and Mervyn's department stores, and later added a J. C. Penney store. It took some time for Layton Hills to build a clientele that could ensure profits for its approximately ninety retailers. During the recession of the mid-1980s, business growth at the mall stalled. Concerned that Davis County could support at most one regional mall, developers who had taken options on land near Farmington's Burke Lane off-ramp released those options. Layton Hills Mall and the surrounding clusters of movie houses, restaurants, and national retail outlets benefited from the burgeoning population growth in Layton and surrounding areas. By 1998 Layton City was listing the mall as the its largest property taxpayer, with a valuation of $38 million. Sales taxes furnished additional income to the city.[96]

During the last decades of the twentieth century, businessmen in the county's largest cities developed successful new commercial centers outside the traditional downtown Main Street shopping areas.

Commuters and shoppers driving Highway 91 through Bountiful in the 1950s were attracted by Slim Olson's competitive prices and rapid service at the "World's Largest Station." (Utah State Historical Society)

These developments challenged old buying patterns by introducing nationally known anchor stores along with regional supermarkets with grocery, drug, and banking services. Typically these clusters appeared near freeway interchanges to make them accessible to customers outside the host city. One projected commercial center on the Bountiful-Centerville boundary failed to expand beyond its first tenant, J.C. Penney, because it lacked such access.

In the south county area, where undeveloped land rapidly was becoming scarce, commercial clusters appeared just outside Bountiful City's western boundary in Woods Cross. The Gateway Crossing development near the 500 South interchange attracted such national retailers as T.J. Maxx, Barnes and Noble, and ShopKo,in addition to a theater, bank, and restaurant. Bountiful City itself had no remaining options. Planners estimated in 1998 that with more than 95 percent of the city's land under development for commercial and residential use, the remaining vacant land would be gone by 2005.[97] Centerville still had large stretches of open land available near its Parrish Lane interchange. One site attracted national marketers including Home Depot, Target, and Land Rover to form a new Centerville Market Place. New fast-food restaurants joined others already in the area and other franchised national stores were expected to fill remaining space. When the Centerville Redevelopment Agency decided in 1998 to open a twelve-acre city-owned ballpark for development as a $20 million commercial center, some residents challenged the decision. Development prevailed on that site after officials promised new neighborhood parks in the city's four quadrants.[98]

The three central Davis communities found themselves well served by major shopping centers at both ends of the county and beyond. Land-poor Farmington rejected options to follow the Bountiful-Woods Cross model of tucking commercial development along collector roads leading to I-15. Instead, officials allowed a commercial center to develop two miles north of the downtown area at the intersection of U.S. Highway 89 and Shepard Lane. Accessible from Kaysville and Centerville, the development offered a K-Mart, Smith's Food and Drug, small businesses, and professional offices.[99] Kaysville's business and civic leaders chose to support a healthy Main Street commercial zone that had a stable customer base. The city deferred to the Layton regional mall and concentrated on improving its 200 North and Main Street offerings to appeal to the local market.

The new cities in north Davis County likewise had little choice but to follow this local option. Sunset had no land left for major development, and, except for Clearfield, the other cities lacked direct freeway access. All of these communities boosted their sales-tax revenues and served local shoppers by encouraging neighborhood developments. The major coup for most of them was to entice a major grocery store into the area. Syracuse residents were delighted in 1997 when Smith's Food and Drug selected a site west of the Freeport Center, and Clearfield residents welcomed Winegar's Supermarket to a plot designated years earlier for commercial development.[100]

An indicator of Davis County's urbanization was the increased number and variety of businesses that developed in the county in the 1940s, 1950s, and beyond. Besides the military installations established in the northern part of the county during the 1940s, the southwestern lowlands welcomed the oil refining industry, which also was a product of wartime needs. Phillips Petroleum, Standard Oil of California, and Western States Oil Company set up refineries during the 1940s. The number of businesses in the county jumped from fewer than 200 in 1940 to nearly 500 ten years later. Most of these represented an expansion in the number of businesses offering products and services already available in the county. Exceptions were the automobile stores, repair shops, and service stations. By 1970 there were 800 businesses operating in the county.[101] A quarter-century later, businesses would number more than 10,000.

One way to profile these businesses is by measuring jobs created in various non-farm industries. The nature of employment in Davis County changed significantly between 1975 and 1995. According to a report from the Utah Department of Employment Security:

> In 1975, more than half of the positions in Davis County were in government. By 1995, the percentage dropped to 25 percent. The percentage of trade jobs jumped from 15.8 percent in 1975 to 26 percent in 1995 and the percentage of service positions increased from 8 percent in 1975 to almost 20 percent in 1995. . . . The construction industry increased its share of jobs in Davis County from 5.0 percent of total employment in 1975 to 7.0 percent in 1995. Finance/Insurance/Real Estate also has shown a noticeable increase in its portion of jobs in the county, growing from 1.5 percent in 1975 to 4.0 percent in 1995. Transportation/Communications/Utilities/Manufacturing has remained virtually unchanged [at 3.2 percent].[102]

It is apparent from this report that the dramatic drop in government employment has been replaced by an equally notable increase in jobs in the trade (mostly retail) and service sectors. New housing accounted for an important part of the new jobs in construction and real estate.

The shift toward private-sector employment resulted in part from a decline in defense spending, but Davis County was less impacted by this general trend than were most other such areas in Utah because of the continued presence of Hill Air Force Base. With around 20,000 employees in 1990, the base remained the largest employer in Utah. Because of missile construction and maintenance, federal defense employment in Utah has not decreased to the post–World War II levels nor to the 18,000-level after the Korean War. Federal outlays in Davis County in 1980 totaled $512 million, with 80 percent of this for defense, and the second largest amount ($39 million) for health and human services. Only Salt Lake County received more federal money in Utah. Weber County's share was 20 percent less than Davis County's.[103]

In the civilian arena, service industries in Davis County were numerous and varied. An increased reliance on trained professionals for personal services spawned a burgeoning increase in such businesses. These ranged from attorneys to wedding-reception centers, and included various types of health, business and financial, automotive repair, legal, social, and educational services. Hotels, motion picture theaters, amusements, and museums were other categories counted among the service industry by statisticians.[104]

During the final decade of the century a mixed-use concept of business parks appeared in some of Davis County's urban centers, introducing a new way to locate businesses. Popular with residential neighbors and adaptable to parcels of varied sizes, the business parks brought jobs and services to cities seeking opportunities for residents and tax dollars to pay for city services. They won higher acceptance among citizens than earlier efforts to attract heavy industry to the west Davis borderlands. North Salt Lake welcomed business parks as alternatives to the city's trucking companies, oil refineries, and distribution centers. The potential of a West Davis Highway through the commercial zone complicated planning, but competitive land prices and proximity to transportation hubs and Salt Lake City attracted many businesses to the new industrial and business parks.[105]

Centerville and Kaysville also created business parks west of I-15 in areas deemed unsuited to residential development. Beginning in the 1960s, Centerville encouraged industrial development in the area but attracted very little interest. In 1996 the city rezoned 300 acres as a business park and left a smaller parcel near Syro Steel for future heavy industry. Kaysville City created its 200 North business park in 1993. When only four businesses had located on the site in as many years, the city increased its promotional efforts.[106]

Among the businesses that flourished in Davis County were several that expanded to markets beyond the county. The furniture store started in Syracuse by Rufus C. Willey was noted in an earlier chapter. As an indication of its size as an interstate merchandizer, an 860,000-square-foot warehouse built in Salt Lake County in 1997 ranked as the largest in the United States. Kaysville's Clover Club Foods was another early enterprise that quickly expanded its market to a multi-state area. It then was acquired for a time by Borden's Foods before returning to local ownership. The home-grown Smith's Food and Drug expanded from the Wasatch Front into five other states and built up a chain of 152 stores (forty-one of them in Utah). Smith's was bought out in 1998 by Portland-based Fred Meyer. Soon after this merger, even larger Kroger Company acquired Fred Meyer, and with it Smith's.[107] Davis County's first high-tech giant was Iomega Corporation, a maker of computer-storage peripherals. The firm's local manufacturing plant was located in the Freeport Center. It has other locations in the United States and Asia to manufacture and market its products.

One of Davis County's healthiest industries in the years since the 1950s was building construction. Fueled by growth, it became an important economic influence in modern Davis County. Dormancy of the local construction industry during World War II was caused in part by the Great Depression and by wartime building restrictions. In the 1930s, no money was available for new construction. During the war, building materials were funneled toward the war effort. Existing businesses did very well because of exploding populations in the north end of the county, but new buildings had to await the end of the war.

Both business buildings and new homes were possible during the prosperous 1950s and 1960s. When temporary government housing was dismantled, federal employees sought new housing. Local developers opened subdivisions to meet that need and expanded businesses to serve the growing population. The pace of building during those decades was rather steady, closely following trends for the expanding Wasatch Front. Growth in both housing and business construction surged during the early 1970s, slowed later in the decade, and picked up again after the recession of the early 1980s. The pace during the 1990s almost matched the peak period of housing construction in the 1970s, when 17,113 new homes were built.[108] As building tracts in the greater Bountiful area became harder to find, suburbanization moved to the hillsides and spread northward into Centerville and Farmington. Expansion in north Davis moved westward from the transportation corridor into the flatland farm fields and eastward into the foothills along the Mountain Road.

As previously noted, the expansion of homes and businesses in Davis County was at the expense of the agricultural land that had led Davis County to be known as the "Garden Spot of Utah." Market gardens had furnished garden produce and fruit that was marketed in nearby urban areas. Sugar beets, vegetables, and orchard crops kept processing plants and canneries in business. Dairy and livestock operations also contributed to commercial agricultural in Davis County. But local agriculture could not thrive under the increasing pressures of urbanization.[109]

When corporate agriculture turned to larger producers for fruits and vegetables, Davis County's canneries closed, and with them went most local commercial gardeners and many of the orchardists. Those who remained sold mostly to the fresh-produce market. Family farms became prime candidates for development when the last generation that tilled the soil died off, their children already employed in other kinds of work. Meat-packing plants closed because larger and newer facilities served the bigger producers. Davis County, once one of Utah's leading beef producers, became a minor player as cattlemen moved their operations elsewhere. Suburban dwellers and Herefords were not always compatible neighbors, and the problems that developed usually prompted the ranchers to leave.[110]

The highways that developed to facilitate travel opened a new avenue for employment to Davis County residents. Along with a heavy load of commercial and recreational traffic, the roads served a steady clientele of suburban commuters. In the 1960s, more workers from Salt Lake and Weber Counties commuted to jobs in Davis County than did Davis workers to those counties. A large share came from Weber County to the defense installations in north Davis. Over the next twenty years, the attraction of suburban living in Davis County and the increase of high-paying jobs in Salt Lake County reversed the pattern. In 1990 nearly 37,000 Davis County residents commuted elsewhere to work, while only 22,000 workers commuted into Davis County. Those who both lived and worked in the county numbered around 44,000.

Another study in 1980 looked at where workers lived and

Clearfield's Main Street (lower left) merges with northbound Highway 91 (State Street) in 1940. Within a few years these roads were serving Weber County workers commuting to Hill Air Force Base and the Naval Supply Depot. (Utah State Historical Society)

worked. The study found that 95 percent of Salt Lake County workers and 90 percent of Utah County's work force were employed within their county of residence. Defense jobs in Davis County attracted 19 percent of Weber County's workers, while 72 percent found jobs in their home county and another 5 percent traveled to Salt Lake. Residents of Davis County were attracted to employment opportunities in both directions: 56 percent of the county's workers worked within the county, 31 percent commuted to Salt Lake County, and 12 percent went to Weber County. These figures emphasize the importance of transportation to Davis County and why most residents supported the improvement of existing highways and construction of the West Davis Highway.[111]

The decision to leave Davis County for employment paid financial dividends for most workers. Outbound commuters earned an average of $6,000 a year more for comparable work than in-county workers. Davis County's suburban status within a major metropolitan area created a level of prosperity greater would have been possible had it maintained an agricultural economy. Overall per-capita earnings in Davis County ranked fourth in the state in 1996, after Summit, Salt Lake, and Weber Counties. The county had maintained similar rankings consistently during the previous quarter-century.[112] Three Davis County cities—Fruit Heights, Farmington, and Centerville—ranked among the top ten Utah cities in a 1992 list of the largest median household incomes. Not surprisingly, Davis County claimed the smallest percentage of poor in the state, and five of its cities were in the bottom ten in the poverty ranking.[113]

Issues in County Government

One of the distinctive features in Davis County politics has been the tradition of nominating and electing county commission candidates as representatives of three specific regions. The first members appointed in 1852 to what was known as the county court fit this prescription only generally. Probate Judge Joseph Holbrook, who chaired the first court, lived in Bountiful. His associates were selectmen Truman Leonard of Farmington and Daniel Carter of Bountiful. The idea of three districts for the south, central, and north regions was formalized when, during their first term in office, these men created three voting precincts. The North Canyon Precinct served the Bountiful area, the Farmington Precinct included Centerville, Farmington, and what later became Fruit Heights, and the North Precinct represented Kaysville and the largely unsettled region north to the county boundary. At statehood, the precinct system was officially abolished, but its practice continued as an unwritten "gentlemen's agreement." The political parties nominated candidates for specific regions, even though voters were technically electing them "at large." As the northern towns grew in size, the central "district" was defined as Farmington, Kaysville, and Layton, with the other two districts lying north and south of that cluster.[114]

From time to time, candidates have challenged this unwritten understanding; however, its supporters have successfully defended the practice by arguing that local citizens want to be represented by someone who knows them and understands local needs. For example, in 1965, the county Republican central committee was faced with recommending candidates to fill a Republican vacancy on the commission. The two sitting county commissioners, Glen W. Flint of Clinton and Stanley M. Smoot of Centerville, both Republicans, defended the tradition as necessary to prevent residents of the county from being "taxed without representation." The central committee considered sixteen applicants for the job, all but one of them from the central area. The vacated slot had been held by Wayne M. Winegar of Layton. A Clearfield candidate challenged the geographical practice, then withdrew his candidacy when the commission appointed him to chair a committee to study the traditional gentlemen's agreement. With the question tabled, the party selected six candidates from the central region. Three of them were Kaysville residents, the others were from Farmington, west Layton, and east Layton. Smoot and Flint picked Richard S. Evans, a west Layton farmer.[115]

Because the agreement is not a written rule, Wendell N. Zaugg, a Clearfield Republican, was able to win a two-year seat on the commission in 1976 even though the north end was already represented by Glen W. Flint of West Point. Two years later, Zaugg was challenged in a rare primary contest for a four-year commission seat. Centerville Republican Ernest Eberhard, Jr., restored the commission's geographical balance and went on to win in November over his Democratic opponent. More recently, north-end commissioner Gayle Stevenson was challenged in 1992 and again in 1996 by Bountiful candidates who ignored the gentlemen's agreement but failed to convince voters to support them. Political observers did not agree on whether the electoral tradition would survive its next challenge.[116]

The first twenty years after the end of the Second World War marked a dramatic increase in the number and kinds of services provided by state and local governments. At the same time, there was a proliferation of services offered by special agencies, some of them completely independent of traditional government entities. The *Census of Governments* in 1967 listed sixteen municipalities in Davis County, plus the county government, the school board, and ten special districts. All but one of these agencies had taxing authority.[117]

Many of the new functions of county government were added in

The Davis County Memorial Courthouse was built in 1931–32 as an expansion and major renovation of the 1890 building. Two major additions since then have expanded the building southward to create office space for new county agencies. (Utah State Historical Society)

the 1960s and 1970s because of financial incentives established by the federal government over the previous years. Davis County was part of a broader movement and followed only slightly behind the national trend in creating new service functions. To the traditional elected offices of commissioner, sheriff, assessor, attorney, clerk, and judge were added numerous agencies offering health and social services. All of these fell under the general oversight of the county commissioners, and some of them were attached to existing agencies with similar responsibilities. Among the new agencies were Job Services, Vocational Rehabilitation Services, Employment and Training, Human Services (a state agency), Housing Authority, and the Council on Aging. The county also presently oversees senior citizen centers in Bountiful, Clearfield, and Kaysville. The professionalization of county administration added the departments of administrative services, data processing, purchasing, human resources, and personnel. In addition, the county provided economic development, animal control, building inspection, and public works services. Not to be outdone by competing development agencies in the Ogden and Salt Lake metropolitan areas, the Davis County Economic Development Office netted 18 percent of the new companies with fifty or more employees coming into Utah during the early 1990s. The task was accomplished with the help of federal community-development block grants.[118]

The Public Works/Flood Control Department was a carryover from the Civilian Conservation Corps work of the 1930s. It expanded during the 1970s to coordinate local flood-prevention efforts. The agency played a key role after the devastating floods of 1983 in securing funding through a bond issue to build catch basins and culverts. More recently, the office has consulted on wetlands issues.[119]

Prior to 1970, community needs had brought about a limited expansion of the role of county government. Among the early county agencies were the offices of Public Health and Public Welfare. Davis County created the first countywide health department in the state of Utah in 1923. A local physician traditionally serves as director, with a sanitation officer and public health nurses assisting. School programs and basic guidance for the needy are the core of the departments' offerings.[120] The county welfare agency, organized in 1936, assigns case workers to help families provide for their basic needs.

Planning was one of the most far-reaching of the early departments. Coordinated planning began in 1918 when a county Farm Bureau was organized. W. D. Criddle was its first president. The group considered the common needs of the agricultural community and worked with government to solve related problems. In succeeding years other interest groups emerged, until it became necessary to create a single umbrella organization. Thus, in 1936, the Davis County Planning Commission came into being. A year later, a county commissioner became chair of this sixty-four-member group and it was renamed the Davis County Planning Board. Its interests initially remained strongly agricultural, with projects such as flood control and noxious weed eradication. The board offered guidelines for improving home health practices, family finances, and vocational training. Small subcommittees handled these and other projects, including crop and dairy herd improvement and accident prevention.

Every county agency and major interest group in the county was represented on this comprehensive coordinating council.

The focus of planning in Davis County changed radically because of the influx of new people and defense industries during World War II. By 1946 the Davis County Planning and Zoning Commission's work included preparation of a master road plan, consideration of recreational areas, use of public lands, population studies, and a subdivision study. These were the major topics considered by planning commissions of the last half of the twentieth century. The large group that had coordinated agricultural efforts no longer met the needs of a county moving toward urbanization, and it was time for a new format.[121]

In response to rapid growth, the county organized a seven-member planning commission in 1948, with Keith Barnes as chair. Around this same time, all towns and cities in Davis County except Fruit Heights and West Point organized local planning commissions. The cities developed local master plans and regularly updated them as circumstances changed. Planners at all levels were involved in zoning issues, including the projected location of roads and streets. They reviewed subdivision plans, ensured compliance with building codes, and issued building permits. From the outset, almost one-fourth of the local planning commissioners were women. At the county level, however, men dominated the work for some time.[122]

In succeeding years, the Davis County Planning Commission adapted to changing circumstances. It became involved in promoting economic development in an effort to create a more diversified economy less dependent on Hill Air Force Base. As subdivisions expanded onto the foothills in the 1970s, the commission created a Hillside Development Control Model that was subsequently adopted by most other Utah counties. The office hired professionally trained planners in the 1980s and offered their services to the cities. Tourism and the county fair were added to the planning commission's portfolio in the 1990s.[123]

In the late 1960s, the county became part of a regional planning effort. In response to federal encouragement and with two-thirds of its operating budget funded by Congress, Davis, Weber, and Salt Lake Counties recognized the need for a forum to discuss shared problems of urbanization. They organized the Wasatch Front Regional Council in March 1969 and were joined by Morgan and Tooele Counties three years later. Issues of regional concern were fed to the council by a county Council of Government (COG) in each participating county. The membership of each local COG included elected officials from city and county governments and sometimes from the school districts. Air pollution, transportation, water supply, housing, recreational open space, the Great Salt Lake, and land-use topics were among those discussed by the regional council through standing committees in five critical areas of interest. In the sense that the council established guiding principles and goals for the region, it functioned as a multicounty planning body.[124]

For many years, cities in Davis County had been providing parks for their citizens. The county developed its first public park in the early 1960s, with the featured attraction an eighteen-hole golf course. To make it more accessible to all residents, the 213-acre Davis County Memorial Park was located at the county's midpoint, on the Mountain Road near Fruit Heights. The idea of a single park won out over an alternative option—separate parks in the two ends of the county, as planners decided that too many issues already divided the county. The park's first phase, a picnic area, opened during the summer of 1963. A playground and day-camp facilities were available for use the following year along with the first nine holes of the golf course. The park facilities subsequently included a golf clubhouse, tennis courts, ball diamonds, and an amphitheater.[125]

The development of a county fair got off to a slow start in Davis County. The Davis County Fair Association sponsored its first exhibition in 1906 at Lagoon, but it was not until 1924 that another county fair was held. In the interim, residents showed their produce and livestock at the state fair or at multicounty fairs. The fair subsequently became a regular offering in a location at Davis High School. Initial planning for the Davis Memorial Park anticipated relocation of the county fair to the park. When those plans proved unworkable, the Davis County Commission signed an eight-year contract to use the old racetrack at Lagoon. Lagoon and the county built new bleachers for the rodeo, the resort got an exclusive option for rides and concessions, and in 1966 the Davis County Fair found a temporary home

The burial of Enoch Barton in 1918. (*The Community of Syracuse*)

there, with displays continuing at the high school. In the late 1990s, the county developed its own fairgrounds near the new Justice Center in west Farmington, centered around an arena for rodeos.[126]

Trails to the Future

The year after Utahns celebrated the centennial of statehood, the people of Davis County observed another anniversary. In the fall of 1847, Perrigrine Sessions and a few companions had herded some livestock from the pioneer encampment at City Creek north past the hot springs. They wintered the stock on the lush grasses along the lakeshore and became the first Mormon settlers in future Davis County. The 150th anniversary of that event was noted mostly in the Bountiful area, where Sessions is revered as the founding father. In 1997 Farmington noted the sesquicentennial of the arrival of herder Hector C. Haight as well. Other anniversaries were noted by Centerville and Kaysville the following year.

For residents with ancestral roots planted deep in the soils of these old communities, the anniversaries were meaningful. In some ways, the celebrations marked the end of another generation. The first Mormon settlers were being buried in the decade that Utah achieved statehood. The entrepreneurs of the new era of progress were disappearing when Utahns celebrated the hundredth anniversary of Brigham Young's arrival. The generation that came of age during the Depression and Second World War was filling the obituary columns at Utah's statehood centennial in 1996. The rural Utah they had known was gone; and the suburban communities of their children were now transitioning into a carpet of homes and businesses. Brigham Young's anticipation of wall-to-wall cities for Davis County was coming to pass.

German-born emigrant Heinrich Lienhard had not imagined such a populated place as he rode his horse along the bottomlands near Farmington Bay on a hot August day in 1846. Following a well-traveled route used by generations of Native Americans, Lienhard was part of a wagon company headed to California. Impressed by the scenic beauty of the landscape, certain that the rich, black soil would produce a munificent harvest, and lifted in spirits by the warm sunny air and shimmering lake, Lienhard was charmed. "The whole day long I felt like singing and whistling," he reflected in his report of the journey; "had there been a single family of white men to be found living here, I believe that I would have remained. Oh, how unfortunate that this beautiful country was uninhabited!"[127]

Lienhard might have started the settlement process himself had his traveling companions agreed; however, California seemed more enticing to the group, with its promise of certain prosperity. Some 150 years later, this beautiful country was densely inhabited, even, according to some, overpopulated. The "splendid plane" of rich soil that Lienhard had observed stretching downward from the mountain to the lake no longer offered the potential of becoming a productive garden spot. Instead, it served as a platform for homes and churches, schools, businesses, and connecting streets and highways.

Mormon settlement of Davis County began the summer after Lienhard's party passed through the region with his wagon party. Over the century and a half since then, public discourse has moved from the pioneers' eagerness over agricultural opportunities to lively discussions about rationing space and providing for the needs of yet another generation. The issues imbedded in these continuing discussions include population growth and associated housing and transportation needs; economic development and the creation of work opportunities for the county's varied population; and a desire to preserve the quality of life that has attracted and retained a people who like living in the friendly communities of Davis County. Conscious of their heritage and optimistic about their ability to achieve their goals, Davis County's citizens have set out on a familiar venture, following well-understood ways while charting new paths as they plan for the future.

ENDNOTES

1. Richard White, *"It's Your Misfortune and None of My Own": A New History of the American West* (Norman: University of Oklahoma Press, 1991), 514, 538–39, 542. Also see Gerald D. Nash, *The American West in the Twentieth Century: A Short History of an Urban Oasis* (New Jersey: Prentice–Hall, 1973).

2. Population figures used in this chapter are from Allan Kent Powell, ed., *Utah History Encyclopedia,* 432–38. Demographic analysis is based on these figures or drawn from other sources cited below. A useful analytic overview is Kimberley A. Bartel, *Davis County: A Demographic and Economic Profile* (Salt Lake City: Utah Department of Employment Security, 1996), cited below as *Davis County Profile.* Much of the information in this publication is updated regularly on the department's web page, <http://udesb.state.ut.us/lmi>. The growth claim is from the *Salt Lake Tribune,* 1 December 1963.

3. *Davis County Clipper,* 6 August 1977.

4. *Deseret News,* Davis Edition, 23 February 1997, B1; *Metropolitan Utah Demographic Atlas 1991–1992: Salt Lake City, Ogden, Provo, Orem, and Surrounding Areas* (Salt Lake City: Economic Development Corporation, 1991), "Population—Demographics."

5. *Davis County Profile,* 7–10.

6. Kent Day, "The Impact of Hill Air Force Base," in Dan Carlsruh and Eve Carlsruh, eds., *Layton, Utah: Historic Viewpoints,* 395; James L. Clayton, "An Unhallowed Gathering: The Impact of Defense Spending on Utah's Population Growth, 1940–1964," *Utah Historical Quarterly* 34 (Summer 1966): 240–41.

7. *Weekly Reflex,* 19 June 1958.

8. Commissioners Glen W. Flint, Stanley M. Smoot, and Richard S. Evans to South Davis County Citizens, July 22, 1966, letter in preface to *South Davis County Today and Tomorrow: A Final Report of the Davis County Citizen Planning County . . . for the South Davis County Master Plan* (Salt Lake City: Bureau of Economic and Business Research, 1966), vi.

9. *Davis County Master Plan: A Guide for Growth, 1970 to 1990, for the County and Its 16 Incorporated Cities and Towns,* prepared by C. Clay Allred & Associates and the Davis County Planning Office (n.p.: n.p, 1970), VIII-1–2.

10. *South Davis County Today and Tomorrow,* passim; *Deseret News,* 24 April, 11 June 1968, 20 April 1971; *Davis County Clipper,* 14 June 1968; *Davis County Master Plan* (1970), I-12–14, II-1.

11. See previous note.

12. *Davis County Master Plan* (1970), facing page IV-1.

13. See U.S. Bureau of the Census, *Census of Population,* 1960, Report for Utah.

14. *The Impact of Urbanization in Davis County, Utah,* Bulletin 369 (Logan: Utah State Agricultural College, Agricultural Experiment Station, 1954), 4–5.

15. Ibid., 20–21.

16. *Deseret News,* 8 October 1963.

17. *Deseret News,* 9, 11, 18 October 1963.

18. *Davis County Master Plan* (1970), ix.

19. *Davis County Clipper,* 12 April 1968, 25 April 1969.

20. *Deseret News,* 31 December 1958, A8.

21. For the western pattern, see White, *A New History of the American West,* 542.

22. White, *A New History of the American West,* 548; *Deseret News,* 18 December 1991, A1.

23. *Deseret News,* 19 June 1964; [Clayton Holt], *The Community of Syracuse, 1820 to 1995: Our Heritage,* 344.

24. *Davis County Clipper,* 11 April 1952; *Deseret News,* 25 September 1957, B10.

25. *Deseret News,* 20 January 1958, A8, 15 August 1958, B12.

26. *Deseret News,* 27 May 1958, 21 May 1964; *Salt Lake Tribune,* 6 July 1958, C11.

27. *Deseret News,* 5 September 1957, A7, 16 January 1958, A1, 27 May 1958; *Salt Lake Tribune,* 17 January 1958.

28. *Deseret News,* 7, 10 February, 1 August 1963, B1, *Davis County Clipper,* 17 January 1969; *Salt Lake Tribune,* 24 May 1971, 24.

29. *Davis County Clipper,* 4 February 1977.

30. *Deseret News,* 22 April 1991, A1.

31. *Salt Lake Tribune,* 12 March 1951, 25 March 1953.

32. *Deseret News,* 26 January 1977, E3.

33. *Davis County Clipper,* 27 December 1996, A2.

34. *Deseret News,* 20 January 1994, B1, 24 August 1995, B2.

35. *Deseret News,* 22 August 1997.

36. *Deseret News,* 10 May 1991, B8, 26 September 1991, B1, 26 February 1992, B1.

37. *Deseret News,* 17 January 1995.

38. *Deseret News,* 7 December 1995, B1, B8, 8 July 1996, B1; *Davis County Clipper,* 12 December 1995; *Ogden Standard–Examiner,* 17 December 1996.

39. *Deseret News,* 3 March 1992, B1.

40. *Deseret News,* 17 January 1998, B1, 7 February 1995.

41. *Davis County Clipper,* 1 December 1998; *Deseret News,* 23 September 1996, B1.

42. *Deseret News,* 22 October 1998, B1, 14 July 1998, A8, 2 December 1998, A12; *Salt Lake Tribune,* 25 April 1999, C9.

43. *Deseret News,* 1 July, 22 October 1998.

44. *Davis County Master Plan,* I-10.

45. Arlene H. Eakle, Adelia Baird, and Georgia Weber, *Woods Cross: Patterns and Profiles of a City,* map on page 3.

46. *Deseret News,* 6 May 1977, A21, 29 May 1996, B1, 12 November 1996, B1, 14 November 1996, B4.

47. James A. Wood, "Construction Cycles in Utah," *Utah Economic and Business Review* 55 (November–December 1995), 2; *Davis County Profile,* 11–12; *Davis County Clipper,* 24 March 1998, A3.

48. *Davis County Profile,* 11–12.

49. *Deseret News,* 3 March 1997, B5.

50. *Davis County Profile,* 12.

51. *Salt Lake Tribune,* 16 April 1995, B1; *Deseret News,* 24 May 1999.

52. *Deseret News,* 10 March 1999, B3, 30 January 1998, B6.

53. *Deseret News,* 2 September 1997, 20 October 1998.

54. *Deseret News,* 22 April 1995.

55. *Davis County Clipper,* 25 July 1995; *Deseret News,* 14 August 1997.

56. *Davis County Clipper,* 27 March 1998, A3.

57. Holt, *Community of Syracuse,* 344.

58. *Deseret News,* 19 June 1998; 8, 20 March 1999; *Davis County Clipper,* 19 March 1999, A5; *Salt Lake Tribune,* 1 September 1998, A1, A6.

59. *Deseret News,* 4 September 1998, 29 January 1999; *Salt Lake Tribune,* 11 September 1998, A1.

60. *Davis County Clipper,* 12 March 1999.

61. *Deseret News,* 18 November 1963, 8A, 17 September 1970, A16; "School Enrollment Projections in Utah 1991–2000," *Research Briefs,* No. 90–20 (Salt Lake City: Utah Foundation, 1990).

62. *Davis County Profile,* 11.

63. For examples of district construction budgets see *Deseret News,* 30 April 1957, 24 September 1958, 6A, 6 February 1963, 10A, 2 July 1963, 18A; *Salt Lake Tribune,* 1 December 1963.

64. Leslie T. Foy, *The City Bountiful: Utah's Second Settlement, from Pioneers to Present,* 209; Holt, *Community of Syracuse,* 394; LaRue Hugoe and Edith Deppe, *West Bountiful: A Pictorial History, 1848–1988,* 140.

65. Eakle, Baird, and Weber, *Woods Cross,* 51–52; *Deseret News,* 18 July 1972.

66. *Deseret News,* 9 June 1969, 20A; Holt, *Community of Syracuse,* 392.

67. *Davis County: Land of Peace, Beauty, and a Quality Life* (Farmington: Davis School District, 1994), 7, 11, 33, 47, 59; Hugoe and Deppe, *West Bountiful,* 139–40; Carol Ivins Collett, *Kaysville—Our Town,* 62.

68. The schools are listed in town profiles in *Davis County: Land of Peace.*

69. "Year Round Schools in Utah," *Research Report,* No. 459 (Salt Lake City: Utah Foundation, 1985); *Deseret News,* 12 September 1996, B1.

70. *Deseret News,* 4 October 1968, D4, 9 June 1969, A20.

71. *Deseret News,* 8 January, 27 March (editorial), 2, 10 April, 25 May 1963; *Salt Lake Tribune,* 9 January, 5 March, 2 April 1963.

72. John E. Christensen, "The Impact of World War II," in Richard Poll et al., *Utah's History,* 512.

73. *Deseret News,* 11 November 1963, B1, 9 January 1969, C6; *Davis County Clipper,* 22 February 1969; *Davis County Master Plan* (1970), II-1.

74. *Deseret News,* 4 April 1979, D1.

75. *Deseret News,* 5 August 1998.

76. *Deseret News,* 21 January 1992, A10.

77. Carmen Daines Fredrickson, *The Impact of Women Leaders of Davis County on a Changing Order* (Logan: Utah State University Agricultural Experiment Station, 1959), 24; *Deseret News,* 16 June 1962, 11 July 1977; *Salt Lake Tribune,* 28 July 1963, B7.

78. *Deseret News,* 21 January 1992; 29 April 1999, B1.

79. Collett, *Kaysville—Our Town,* 186; *Deseret News,* 21 January 1992, 8 November 1996.

80. *Deseret News,* 24 September, 25 October 1979, 14 January 1980; *Davis County Clipper,* 10, 24 October 1979.

81. Collett, *Kaysville—Our Town,* 186; *Deseret News,* 6 November 1964, A12.

82. *Deseret News,* 7 April 1997, B3; *Davis County Clipper,* 19 November 1996, A3, 11 April 1997, A1.

83. Collett, *Kaysville—Our Town,* 146–47.

84. *Davis County Clipper,* 22 November 1996.

85. *Deseret News,* 22 January 1997, B3; *Davis County Clipper,* 22 November 1996.

86. *Impact of Urbanization,* 13; Foy, *City Bountiful,* 270.

87. Doneta McGonigle Gatherum, "Saint Rose of Lima Catholic Church," in Carlsruh and Carlsruh, *Layton, Utah,* 197–200; Foy, *City Bountiful,* 270.

88. Foy, *City Bountiful,* 271–72; *Deseret News,* 6 May 1995.

89. *Davis County Clipper,* 24 March 1995; *Deseret News,* 1 April 1995, D1.

90. *Deseret News,* 6 May 1995; *Davis County Clipper,* 15 April 1997, 4 September 1998; Foy, *City Bountiful,* 270–71.

91. *Davis County Clipper,* 31 December 1996, C6; *Deseret News,* 21 June 1992, A1.

92. Collett, *Kaysville—Our Town,* 171.

93. *Deseret News,* 26 March 1997, A3; *Davis County Clipper,* 12 November 1998.

94. *Davis County Master Plan* (1970) III-9.

95. *Davis County Clipper,* 29 December 1998, 12 March 1999; *Deseret News,* 12 August 1998.

96. *Deseret News,* 3 January 1997, B4, 1 January 1998.

97. *Davis County Clipper,* 11 August 1992, B1, 17 November 1998.

98. *Deseret News,* 7 August 1997, 11 May 1998, B1, 2 February 1999, B1, 20 April 1999, B1; *Davis County Clipper,* 19 January, 2 February 1999.

99. *Deseret News,* 14 January 1997, B1.

100. *Deseret News,* 29 January 1997.

101. *Impact of Urbanization,* 13; *Davis County Master Plan,* II-6.

102. *Davis County Profile,* 21.

103. Jan Crispin–Little and James A. Wood, "Utah's Adjustment to Declining Defense Budgets," *Utah Economic and Business Review* 50 (November–December 1990): 1–11; "Federal Expenditures in Utah, 1980," *Research Briefs,* 81–9 (Salt Lake City: Utah Foundation, 1981).

104. *Davis County Profile,* 20.

105. *Deseret News,* 17 July 1996, B7, 29 January 1998, A17, 24 March 1999, B3.

106. *Deseret News,* 7 October 1996.

107. *Deseret News,* 29 July 1997, 19 October 1998, A1.

108. Day, "The Impact of Hill Air Force Base," 401–2; Wood, "Construction Cycles in Utah," 1–10.

109. *Davis County Master Plan*, II-4.

110. *Deseret News,* 1 July 1997, B9.

111. *Davis County Profile,* 56; "Employment and Income—Labor Force Participation," in *Metropolitan Utah Demographic Atlas, 1991–1992.*

112. *Davis County Profile,* 56; "Personal Income in Utah Counties, 1996," *Utah Economic and Business Review* 58 (March–April 1998): 2; "Personal Income in Utah Counties, 1979," *Utah Economic and Business Review* 41 (April–May 1981): 3; "Personal Income in Utah, 1975," *Research Briefs,* No. 76–9 (Salt Lake City: Utah Foundation, 1976).

113. *Deseret News,* 11 July 1992, B3.

114. Davis County, County Court Minutes, 14 June 1852; *Davis County Argus* (Farmington), 29 November 1904; *Davis County Clipper,* 23 November 1900.

115. *Deseret News,* 11 December 1964, B1; 15 December 1964, A14; 19 December 1964, B5; 4 January 1965, B2; 6 January 1965, A8; 15 January 1965, B1.

116. *Deseret News,* 12 October 1998.

117. *Davis County Master Plan* (1970), I-1.

118. *Deseret News,* 2 May 1991.

119. Sid Smith, County Director of Public Works, interview with Cory W. Leonard, 18 August 1993, Kaysville, Utah.

120. Fredrickson, *Impact of Women Leaders,* 22.

121. Information provided to the author by Wilf Sommerkorn, Acting Director of the Davis County Planning Commission, from the commission minute books.

122. Fredrickson, *Impact of Women Leaders,* 23.

123. Wilf Sommerkorn, interview with Cory W. Leonard, 21 May 1993, Davis County Courthouse, Farmington.

124. *Wasatch Front Regional Council, Utah, First Annual Report,* (n.p., 1972), 1–7.

125. *Davis County Clipper,* 25–29 November 1968; *Deseret News,* 19 July 1963, 10A.

126. *Davis County Clipper,* 13 August 1996; *Reflex,* 18 March, 20 May 1965; *Deseret News,* 19 September 1964, 18 March, 7 April, 18, 21 May 1965.

127. J. Roderic Korns and Dale L. Morgan, eds., *West from Fort Bridger: The Pioneering of the Immigrant Trails Across Utah, 1846–1850,* 2nd. ed., revised and updated by Will Bagley and Harold Schindler (Logan: Utah State University Press, 1994), 144.

Selected Bibliography

Alexander, Thomas G. *Utah, The Right Place: The Official Centennial History.* Salt Lake City: Gibbs Smith, Publisher, 1995.

Allred, R. Clay, and Associates, and Davis County Planning Office. *Davis County Master Plan: A Guide for Growth, 1970 to 1990, for the County and Its 16 Incorporated Cities and Towns.* Ogden: R. Clay Allred and Associates, 1970.

Anderson, C. LeRoy. *For Christ Will Come Tomorrow: The Saga of the Morrisites.* Logan: Utah State University Press, 1981.

Arrington, Leonard J. *Beet Sugar in the West: A History of the Utah-Idaho Sugar Company, 1891–1966.* (Seattle: University of Washington Press, 1966.

———. *Great Basin Kingdom: An Economic History of the Latter-day Saints, 1830–1900.* Cambridge, MA: Harvard University Press, 1958.

———. "Utah and the Depression of the 1890s." *Utah Historical Quarterly* 24 (January 1961): 3–18.

Arrington, Leonard J., and Archer L. Durham. "The U.S. Naval Supply Depot at Clearfield, 1942–1962." *Utah Historical Quarterly* 31 (Spring 1963): 109–26.

Arrington, Leonard J., and Thomas G. Alexander. "Supply Hub of the West:

Defense Depot Ogden, 1941–1964." *Utah Historical Quarterly* 32 (Spring 1964): 99–121.

Barber, James V. "The History of Highways in Utah from 1847 to 1860." M.A. thesis, University of Utah, 1949.

Barker, Inez Foy. *History of Fruit Heights, Utah (Kaysville Mountain Road) 1850–1975, with Brief Update to 1986.* Kaysville: Author, 1986.

Barker, Inez, comp. *John Weinel, Miller: Early Pioneer Builder and Operator of the First Flour Mill in Kaysville, Utah.* Kaysville: Daughters of Utah Pioneers, 1983.

Bartel, Kimberley. *Davis County: A Demographic and Economic Profile.* Salt Lake City: Utah Department of Employment Security, 1996.

Bell, Lee D. *South Weber: The Autobiography of One Utah Community.* South Weber: [South Weber Town Council], 1990.

Bennion, Lowell "Ben." "The Incidence of Mormon Polygamy in 1880: 'Dixie' versus Davis Stake." *Journal of Mormon History* 11 (1984): 27–42.

Black, Theral R. *Impact of Urbanization in Davis County.* Bulletin 369. Logan: Utah State Agricultural College, Agricultural Experiment Station, 1954.

Blood, Henry H. "Early Settlement of Kaysville." *Utah Historical Quarterly* 2 (January 1929): 14–18.

Butcher, A. Garn. *Who Put the Fruit in Fruit Heights?* [Kaysville and Fruit Heights]: Kaysville-Fruit Heights Centennial Committee, 1996.

Bybee, Cora Bodily. *History of Syracuse, 1877–1965.* Springville, UT: Art City Publishing Company, 1965.

Carlsruh, Dan, and Eve Carlsruh, eds. *Layton, Utah: Historic Viewpoints.* [Layton]: Kaysville-Layton Historical Society, 1985.

Carr, Annie Call, ed. *East of Antelope Island: History of the First Fifty Years of Davis County.* 1948; 2nd ed., [Bountiful]: Daughters of Utah Pioneers, 1961.

Collett, Carol Ivins. *Kaysville—Our Town: A History.* Kaysville: Kaysville City, 1976.

Croft, A. Russell. *Rainstorm Debris Floods: A Problem in Public Welfare.* Tucson: University of Arizona, Agricultural Experiment Station, 1967.

Croft, A. Russell, and Reed W. Bailey. *Mountain Water.* Ogden: U.S. Forest Service, Intermountain Region, 1964.

Davis County. Citizen Planning Council. *South Davis County: Today and Tomorrow.* Salt Lake City: University of Utah, Bureau of Economic and Business Research, 1966.

Davis County Court. Minutes. Davis County Clerk's Office.

Dibble, G. Ralph, Carmen Dibble, and Stanley S. Cunningham, eds. *West Layton/Layton 2nd Wards, 1895–1995.* Layton: Layton 2nd Ward, 1995.

DeVoto, Bernard A. "The Lesson of Davis County." *Reader's Digest* (December 1949): 89–92.

Eakle, Arlene H., Adelia Baird, and Georgia Weber. *Woods Cross: Patterns and Profiles of a City.* Woods Cross: Woods Cross City Council, 1976.

Embry, Jessie L. "Fighting the Good Fight: The Utah Home Front during World War II." *Utah Historical Quarterly* 63 (Summer 1995): 241–67.

Fleming, L.A., and A.R. Standing, "The Road to 'Fortune': The Salt Lake Cutoff," *Utah Historical Quarterly* 33 (Summer 1965): 248–71.

Foy, Leslie T. *The City Bountiful: Utah's Second Settlement, from Pioneers to Present.* Bountiful: Horizon Publishers, 1975.

———. "Davis County History of Education." Draft of manuscript, n.d., possession of Leslie T. Foy.

Gatherum, Doneta M., and Kent C. Day, comps. *Kaysville and Layton General Stores.* Kaysville and Layton: Kaysville-Layton Historical Society, 1987.

Gabbott, Mabel Jones, comp. *A Tabernacle in the Land Bountiful.* [Bountiful: Bountiful Area Centennial Committee, 1992].

Goss, Peter L. "William Allen, Architect-Builder, and His Contribution to the Built Environment of Davis County." *Utah Historical Quarterly* 54 (Winter 1986): 52–73.

Gwinn, J. Wallace, ed. *Great Salt Lake: A Scientific, Historical, and Economic Overview.* Salt Lake City: Utah Geological and Mineral Survey, Bulletin 116, June 1980.

Harvey, Alpheus, and Ivy B. Harvey. *Kaysville 1847 . . . : Map of the Early Settlers of the Kaysville, Mountain Road, and South Layton Area.* Kaysville and Fruit Heights: Kaysville-Fruit Heights Utah Centennial Committee, 1995.

Hess, Margaret Steed. *My Farmington: A History of Farmington, Utah, 1847–1976.* Compiled and edited by Irene B. Olsen and Mable R. Ferguson. [Farmington]: Daughters of Utah Pioneers, 1976.

[Holt, Clayton, ed.]. *The Community of Syracuse, 1820 to 1995: Our Heritage, Centennial Edition.* Syracuse: Syracuse Historical Commission, 1994.

Howard, G.M. "Men, Motives, and Misunderstandings: A New Look at the Morrisite War of 1862," *Utah Historical Quarterly* 44 (Spring 1976): 112–32.

Hough, C. Merrill. "Two School Systems in Conflict: 1867–1890." *Utah Historical Quarterly* 28 (April 1960): 113–28.

Hugoe, LaRue, and Edith Deppe. *West Bountiful: A Pictorial History, 1848–1988.* [West Bountiful]: West Bountiful City, 1989.

Humpherys, L.R., and A.C. Matheson, eds. *Utah—Resources and Activities: Supplement to the Utah State Courses of Study for Elementary and Secondary Schools.* Salt Lake City: Utah Department of Public Instruction, 1933.

Journal History of The Church of Jesus Christ of Latter-day Saints." Scrapbook compilation, photocopy and microfilm, LDS Church Historical Department Library.

Kaysville-Layton Historical Society. *The Establishment of Davis High School: A 75th Anniversary History.* Kaysville and Layton: Kaysville-Layton Historical Society and the Heritage Museum of Layton, 1989.

Knowlton, George Quincy. *A History of Farmington, Utah.* Compiled and edited by Jannetta K. Robinson. [Farmington]: Robinson, 1965.

Korns, J. Roderick, and Dale L. Morgan, eds. *West from Fort Bridger: The Pioneering of Immigrant Trails across Utah, 1846–1850.* Revised and updated by Will Bagley and Harold Schindler. 1961; rev. ed., Logan: Utah State University Press, 1994.

Leonard, Glen M. "A History of Farmington, Utah, to 1890." M.A. thesis, University of Utah, 1966.

———. "William Allen's Clients: A Socio-Economic Inquiry." *Utah Historical Quarterly* 54 (Winter 1986): 74–87.

Morgan, Dale L. *The Great Salt Lake.* New York: Bobbs-Merrill, 1947.

Olsen, Beth R. "Utah's CCCs: The Conservators' Medium for Young Men, Nature, Economy, and Freedom." *Utah Historical Quarterly* 62 (Summer 1994): 261–74.

Paul, J.H., and F.S. Baker. *The Floods of 1923 in Northern Utah. Bulletin* 15, no. 3 (University of Utah; March 1925).

Poll, Richard D., Thomas G. Alexander, Eugene E. Campbell, David E. Miller, eds. *Utah's History.* Provo: Brigham Young University Press, 1978.

Powell, Allan Kent, ed. *Utah History Encyclopedia.* Salt Lake City: University of Utah Press, 1994.

Purrington, William Robb. "The History of South Davis County from 1847 to 1870." M.S. thesis, University of Utah, 1959.

Rice, Helen. *History of Ogden Air Materiel Area, 1934–1960 [plus] Chronologies: 1934–71.* N.p: Author: [1971?].

Roberts, Allen. *History of Antelope Island in the Great Salt Lake.* Salt Lake City: Wallace N. Cooper II and Associates, 1981.

Sadler, Richard W., and Richard C. Roberts. *The Weber River Basin: Grass Roots Democracy and Water Development.* Logan: Utah State University Press, 1993.

Smith, David F. *My Native Village: A Brief History of Centerville, Utah.* [Centerville: Privately Published, 1943].

Smoot, Mary Ellen, and Marilyn Sheriff. *The City In-Between: History of Centerville, Utah, including Biographies and Autobiographies of Some of its Original Settlers.* Centerville: Authors, 1975.

Steed, John W. "The Wall Around Farmington." *Utah Historical Quarterly* 4 (October 1931): 109.

Taylor, Fred G. *A Saga of Sugar.* Salt Lake City: Utah-Idaho Sugar Co., 1944.

Torrential Floods in Northern Utah, 1930. Utah State Agricultural College, Agricultural Experiment Station, Circular 92, 1931.

U.S. Air Force Logistics Command. *History of Hill Air Force Base.* Revised edition. [n.p.]: U.S. Air Force, 1988.

Van Alfen, Peter. "Sail and Steam: Great Salt Lake's Boats and Boatbuilders, 1847–1901," *Utah Historical Quarterly* 63 (Summer 1995): 194–221.

Vorhees, Tamara Lasson. *Val Verda, 1848–1976.* [Bountiful: Val Verda Ninth Ward Relief Society], 1976.

Westenskow, Clifford. "The Economic Development of Davis County, Utah [1847–1940]." M.S. thesis, Brigham Young University, 1946.

Index